The Throughput Accounting Series for Knowledge-Work Vol. 1

Seeing Money Clearly

Using Throughput Accounting to Understand and Manage Knowledge-Work

Daniel Doiron, CPA

Foreword by Jim Benson

TABLE OF CONTENTS

SEEING MONEY CLEARLY
Using Throughput Accounting to Manage and Understand Knowledge-Work

Published by Agile Agonist Press, Montréal, PQ

agileagonist.com

Book cover by Mihail Barakoski and Kavi Phimmasone

ISBN (Book) – 978-1-7781232-0-7

ISBN (eBook) – 978-1-7781232-1-4

First Edition – published on 2023-02-01, revised 2023-04-29

ABOUT THE AUTHOR

Daniel has been involved in IT his entire career in a wide range of roles and responsibilities, primarily in client-facing consulting projects covering government, banking, insurance, and telecom industries to name a few.

Daniel's involvement with Agile started with Scrum in 2005 and more recently with Kanban and Management 3.0.

He is proficient and has working expertise in Finance/Accounting/Managerial control (MBA-CPA-CMA), Agility, Project Management, Kanban coupled with decades in IT (Bachelor studies & career). He loves systems and enjoys measuring improvement while embracing teamwork that actually works!

This book is the second book dealing with Knowledge-Work following 'Tame Your Work Flow: How Dr Goldratt of the GOAL would apply the Theory of Constraints to rethink knowledge-Work Management' published in 2020

DEDICATION

A ma femme, Elisabeth

A Magali, ma fille

From the 1997 Amazon Letter to Shareholders, Jeff Bezos candidly wrote:

> "When forced to choose between optimizing the appearance of our GAAP accounting and maximizing the present value of future cash flows, we'll take the cash flows"

PROLOGUE

Getting the first line out of this Prologue is difficult as my aim is to have you think differently and lose your reflexes and cognitive biases that are the fabric of society. There are many 'ways' to deprogram yourself as an individual - as the unit of measure of this book is not at the team level – and I can think of three off the top of my head:

- The most cumbersome and lengthy being to ride the learning curve with the support of training and the experience gained thru the passage of time.
- Another, quicker but less sticky way is to run a good quality simulation. Within a day or two, you get the feel of what could work without having to experience it.
- A third way is to read books. A good friend of mine once told me that were you to read 10 books on a topic, you become a world expert compared to the masses. He was right.

Depending on context, I have a favorite for each of the alternatives prescribed above. In the real world, when the pressure at work can be sliced, you can run but you can't hide. In the long haul, one thing never changes: repetition is the mother of all skills and good technique is simply invisible but needed just as much as talent. (Raw talent seldom comes at birth even for the greatest)

At this point, I need to carry my message – in an evocator manner – through the lens of high caliber athletes. They do not get at the top - at least most of them – without a lot of repetition. The more you have performed a certain skill or pattern, the less you need to think about it to the point were your training takes over your instincts and have you act in an inconsistent manner at first glance:

- To kneel down before an opponent and take a standing eight count as a boxer to stay in the bout;
- Tap out in numerous combat sports to stop the pain when all your brain wants to do is scream;
- Peculiar to NFL football, and late in the game, the offence team on the field must opt to not score and the defensive team will not prevent you from scoring. Every time this gambit is offered, players on the field experience a brain meltdown and are totally confused. I have included what are considered the best videos on the topic in the References section along with the statistical reasoning behind the approach under the NFL tag at the end.

The above examples show how the brain can be molded to support operational survival in professional sports. These skills are aligned to keep victory in sight at execution time for professional athletes.

Knowledge Workers need the same reflexes and training to know when to engage, or not, with new work. In that regard, subordinating to the constraint is the toughest mental challenge to tame overproduction.

To that end, we can thank great thinkers for designing stratagems that are sending counterintuitive signals to halt work, on one hand, and to hurry to wrap things up, on the other.

While Ford and TPS – Toyota Production System - dealt with the physical world and assembly lines, Dr Goldratt's applications tackled that and Knowledge-Work at par as well.

The above situation shows how systems, some of which designed to trap common cause, can support management by exception and send signals that the workers will comprehend to enable them to mint money!

Overproduction is the road to oblivion since the beginning of commerce. Financial and Cost Accounting have taught us well and given us the ill practice to trade cash – the company's most valuable asset – for idle inventory in the want of paper profits. The economic version of the businessman Faustian bargain no less.

It is now time for you to develop into a top tier Knowledge Worker – no matter where you stand in the hierarchy. Making money is never addressed because no one knows how to make it repeatedly and in a predictable manner. It is also a team sport, and thus very agile.

At times, you may be wondering why causality will be addressed repeatedly in a book dealing with Throughput Accounting. Decision making and causality are joined at the hip in Throughput Accounting! With Throughput Accounting, the decisions you make will have an economic impact almost immediately if you follow the rules. The relatively short timespan between the enactment of your decisions and the results is the stamp of Throughput Accounting's causality and inherent simplicity.

A word about the foreword from Mr Jim Benson

In the next page, you will read Jim Benson's foreword to the book. I did not expect such a generous outcome from the creator of Personal Kanban. Getting a foreword is always a long process as my job was done as an author, the content was pretty much in an end state. All you have to do is ... wait.

When you talk operational excellence – as is the case in this book – you can rest assured that the best content comes out of the Shingo Institute. Jim Benson's 'Personal Kanban: Mapping Work, Navigating Life', won a Shingo Research and Publication award.

'Quite the honor', Mr. Benson told me! I concur.

An interesting outcome I did not envisage was on the urge for all CPAs to comprehend my book as it deals with invisible work whereas accountants dominate in the tangible world. I did target agilists and Knowledge Workers. I must admit that calling the CPAs by name did not cross my mind. This is taken care of in Mr. Benson's foreword. The CPA profession has enormous clout to change the way we think and go about management.

FOREWORD BY JIM BENSON

Well, you wore out your welcome with random precision
Rode on the steel breeze
Come on, you raver, you seer of visions
Come on, you painter, you piper, you prisoner, and shine
~ Pink Floyd

There is incredible strength in numbers. Integers are reassuring. They have instant meaning, allow rapid scrutiny and, when they turn red, invite focused attention.

As with any strength, that which is a powerful tool can often become a weapon, knowingly or unknowingly applied to the skulls of detractors, proponents, or the not-so-occasional innocent bystander.

Welcome to the world of accounting, a wholly necessary field of endeavor without which all business would rapidly die in a mess of confusion and ignorance, yet also a field which historically over-applies precision so precisely that all, including the initiated, lose sight of the actual meaning of the numbers.

In this book, Dan covers territory I am very familiar with. Not accounting, but coming passionately from the inside of a craft and pointing out long-held, but counterproductive models and offering solutions, extensions, or even evolutions. In this book, he grounds his models of throughput accounting firmly in existing accounting traditions by defining what he calls **Flawed Mental Models** that are nothing more than the existing status-quo of cost accounting.

For example, he shows that the over-exposure of certain metrics favored by accounting models over the last 100 years are aging out in a world where learning and rapidly changing outweighs the simple reduction of cost per unit. There are real, scientific measures, however, for value and profit generation that transcend cost per unit metrics, that lend themselves to operating a prudent, professional, and purposeful endeavor.

Make no mistake, the status quo is evolving. Not being replaced. This is important, as the companies you are a part of are moving toward Lean, Agile, or other more advanced ways of working, accounting must move with them. Not simply because they are bandwagons to jump on, but because if the CAs and CPAs of the world don't evolve with the company, both the company and accounting will fail.

Lagging companies will not have accounting that matches the reality of current operations.

There are no survivors in that scenario.

So, how do you as a CA or CPA evolve when there are industry standards, legal requirements, and heaping helpings of professional bias? It seems like an unclimbable hill, an uncrossable river.
Rest assured you are not alone, everyone in your company is fighting a century of sluggish planning, management, and execution.

Luckily, everyone is also working diligently to find ways to not go bankrupt in a fickle knowledge economy that can rapidly shift its expectations of your teams and your company multiple times a day. This is what the market demands, which means we all must shift our focus to elegantly respond.

This means, my friendly bookkeeper turned change-agent, that you need to think deeply about how your company really operates. *Where do bottlenecks lie? How might the unhindered flow of work become more important than costs per unit? How might the accounting department, out of nowhere, become the standard bearer for efficient and enjoyable work?*

And, most importantly, *how can that happen while maintaining the expectations of regulators, investors, boards of directors, and the others you deal with on a daily basis?*

As your company searches for ways to create collaborative cultures, to see work as it happens, to solve problems as they arise and not after they fester, you must be at the forefront of figuring out the value actually generated by these actions and how to fine-tune them to create more value. This means you will be the main proponent of and translator between the methods your company is employing to stay alive and the information required to keep it legal.

That is truly exciting.

Jim Benson
Co-Author of Personal Kanban & The Collaboration Equation
Co-Founder of Modus Institute
Winner of the Shingo Research Award
Seattle December 2022

ACKNOWLEDGEMENTS

Martin Nantel for insisting that I write this book.

I would like to thank the following thought leaders for answering me over the years when I had questions pertaining to Throughput Accounting, ToC and/or their books:

> Eli Schragenheim, Ravi Gilani, Etienne du Plooy, Dr Kelvyn Youngman, Bob Sproull, Dr John Ricketts, Donald Reinertsen, Dr Lisa Lang

I am in debt with the Québec CPA Order for the rigorous, long and generous process they guided me through to become a training partner and to include Throughput Accounting in their Professional Development Program for the 2021-2022 and 2022-2023 year. It is a rare feat as I am the only one to give face to face (not pre recorded) classes on the topic in the world. You are invited to come and learn more about the subject by visiting my website and register for one of my trainings.

To Donald Reinertsen and Etienne du Plooy for getting the title of my book on the right track.

To Donald Reinertsen and Joseph Pelrine for reading the book and providing valuable insights.

To Etienne du Plooy for providing me for the correct 'right word' so many times and making a difference in sharpness of many of my arguments.

To Joseph Pelrine for bringing some key insights

And a special and heartfelt thank you to Dr John Ricketts for taking the time to review the entire book and provide comments. His contribution to the penultimate chapter is beyond value as it allows the reader to take notes on the thought leaderships of both Donald Reinertsen and Dr John Ricketts himself. Two giants. The contrasts are for the sole pleasure of learning and growing.

To Ravi Ginali and Etienne du Plooy for helping me get from here to there with the 'Flows and Pools of Money' diagram. This integration work needed to be done and now I understand why it required so much time: because it takes a long time to reconcile all of the dense existing versions!

To Bob Sproull – the ultimate kind man of ToC – for mapping the DBR buffer components to the CCPM Buffer. It inspired me late in the writing of the book to create a new staggering management by exception signal with the color blue!

CHAPTER 1 – FLAWED MENTAL MODELS

"It ain't what you don't know that gets you into trouble. It's what you know for sure that just ain't so."– Mark Twain

Introduction:

Throughput Accounting is a topic that is addressed in the Theory of Constraints' Handbook and has a chapter – number thirteen as it were - written by Professor Charlene Spoede Budd. Throughput Accounting does not have a Handbook per se. This book deals with Throughput Accounting for Knowledge-Work[1] and has a few twists that distinguishes it from 'brick and mortar' Throughput Accounting.

At this point, I would like to align the pendulum with modern thinking, trace a new perimeter and draw a few lines in the sand regarding Throughput Accounting. We will start here, forge ahead in untamed territory and possibly remove a few things that have lost their seats in Knowledge-Work.

Throughput Accounting is a lot of things[2]:

- an accounting system,
- a financial application,
- an improvement initiative – POOGI – **P**rocess of **O**n-**G**oing **I**mprovements and,
- most importantly, the decision-making arm of Dr Eli Goldratt's Theory of Constraints.

Deep understanding of the 5 Focusing Steps is essential in being successful with Throughput Accounting. The Game - Herbie Walk - in Appendix at the end of the book can bring some fun into experimenting with the concepts at your place of work!

There is this peculiar attribute to Throughput Accounting being the decision-making arm of the Theory of Constraints. This attribute is causality. Causality operates on the favorite axis of Dr Eli Goldratt: the time dimension. Were you to take a decision today with the model, you would have no doubts that the results are directly triggered by operating on the three financial levers of (T) – Throughput, (I) – Investments or (OE) – Operating Expenses.

Throughput Accounting first saw the light of day around 1984.

In 2019, the biggest Financial Accounting body in the world, the AICPA, included the topic of Throughput Accounting in its syllabus[3].

---

[1] Knowledge Workers are defined as workers whose work is invisible and main capital is knowledge. The usual suspects are participants in the software industry, physicians, architects, scientists and dare I say accountants.

[2] I am leveraging William Hoefle's taxonomy from an interview with Philip Marris. The video can be found here: https://www.youtube.com/watch?v=QumnBvwf4Pk

[3] A long time ago, both Taiichi Ohno from Toyota and Dr Eli Goldratt did not mince words with traditional accounting. They did not want accountants around as they were deemed public enemy number one of productivity. That did not help adoption of Throughput Accounting within the traditional CPA profession.

Today, many flawed mental models - that are the fabric of society - find their roots in the very origins of accounting. Notwithstanding that, Financial Accounting drives the markets. It is meant for external reporting, while Management Accounting's focus is internal. The two are distinct and operate on separate bodies of knowledge and different paradigms. The line that separates these two sciences is blurred by the practice of absorption costing in Cost Accounting. More on this turn of events as we proceed.

Note: Data from Etienne Du Plooy from the book 'Throughput Accounting Techniques' – page 7

In the Accounting world, Financial Accounting is the 900 pounds gorilla. It is essential for markets to operate smoothly, for external stakeholders to have a comparable understanding of firms' performances over time as well as within and across industries and, finally, for the taxman to collect his dues. For these reasons, the CPA profession (or CA in certain countries) operates within a legal and regulated framework. Management Accounting is represented by other certifying bodies (CMA, CIMA, etc) who do not have the legal authority to audit Financial Statements, which is a task reserved for CPAs. Management Accounting is inclusive and will use any tools, processes or ways of working that can help decision-making such as all accounting flavors, Lean, Six Sigma, KPI, balanced scorecards, and the likes.

Throughput Accounting rightfully belongs under the large and welcoming umbrella of Management Accounting in order to align motivation, behavior and performance.

Financial Accounting brings neutrality to the table. It is essential for market efficiency. Throughput Accounting's sole purpose is to influence.

The discussion that follows is in accordance with thought leaders in the field of Throughput Accounting regarding decision-making. It often diverges from the perspective of traditional accounting, where cost information per product is of paramount importance. That same information is moot in Throughput Accounting when it comes to decision-making. Companies make profits, not products.

To that aim, this chapter will highlight eleven of the most common flawed mental models that impair our judgment. To fully explore and understand this subject, we will tackle all topics from the perspective of physical goods that we manufacture and sell. The nuances and subtleties will be easier to grasp as a result. Transposing those to the invisible world is simply a question of will[4].

Subsequent chapters will address novelties in Throughput Accounting applied to Knowledge-Work, which is invisible by nature.

As a reminder, a constraint is the bottleneck – possibly one out of many – that prevents an organisation from reaching its goal.

Flawed Mental Models

Flawed Mental Model One – Cost Accounting as part of Management Accounting

Cost Accounting is paradoxical. It is found in both Financial and Management Accounting. According to Steven M. Bragg[5], Cost Accounting is meant - and designed primarily - to support Financial Accounting reporting. For Debra Smith[6], Cost Accounting is a technical, hybrid process designed to satisfy generally accepted accounting principles (GAAP).

Cost Accounting[7] is, for all intents and purposes, Financial Accounting's best friend, as it feeds it the carrying cost of inventory - the 'Holy Grail'[8] of Financial Accounting - in order to assess profits.

The chaos that warranted the birth of formal and rigorous Financial Accounting Standards - circa 1916 in the US railroad industry and forcefully after the Great Depression - was in part due to the lack of guidelines or consistent approaches regarding unit costs to tally fair reported profits from revenues. Revenues are always easy to reconcile as they are contemporaneous to sales. The actual matching[9] of expenses to sales is much harder to assess as costs are unknown and unknowable[10] - and always will be - hence the need for Cost Accounting to support Financial Accounting!

---

[4] Functional areas like architecture, security, business analysis can all fall into local optima mode and over produce. This creates an excessive amount of inventory that will decay with the passage of time.

[5] Bragg, Steven M. 'Constraint Management: A Financial and Operational Guide'. Accounting Tools Series. 3rd edition

[6] Smith, Debra. 'The Measurement Nightmare'. Page IX

[7] A history of Financial Accounting with an interesting twist can be found in Appendix A

[8] Schragenheim, Eli and Camp, Henry and Surace, Rocco. 'Throughput Economics', Page 53

[9] US GAAP has let go of matching as a principle. Instead, it adopted allocation to replace it.

[10] Smith, Debra. 'The measurement nightmare'. Page 55

Cost Accounting does have practical uses for managerial purposes[11] – medium to long term capacity planning is one, followed closely by the very practical standard costing in some industries where repetition of tasks is predominant – but curiously enough, its most distinguishable 'absorption costing' functionality has found a niche in the field of Management Accounting despite its limited value for daily operational issues. Cost Accounting occupies more than 50% of the curriculum offered in Management Accounting[12].

Take the example of the 'cost per call' in a new call center. The landline requires a cash outlay at a CO$T[13] of $1,000 per month. In the first month, 100 calls are made. The COST per call is therefore $10. The ensuing month, 1000 calls are made. The COST per call has dropped to $1!

Is this knowledge actionable? Does this type of allocation have any managerial value for any type of decisions? The monthly charge will remain $1,000 per month no matter the number of calls.

We also often hear of the 'COST per meeting', where twenty people are found in a room for a day. Again, all the salaries are paid for along with the meeting room. No cash outlay actually occurs. The 'COST per meeting' fallacy belongs the same category as 'cost per number'.

All 'cost per number' metrics have no cash outlays and are irrelevant for operational and day-to-day decision-making. All projects that aim at improving or leveraging 'cost per number' statistics have 2 things in common they: 1) will require green money[14] and will not generate any profit and 2) those cost per number are arrived at by a cost allocation driver. In these scenarios, nothing will change the cash outlays that have been committed as those were never based on utilisation of some sort of capacity that you can chose to use or not. No matter what changes you make to the utilisation of such capacity, you will not change any economics.

Beware of those projects.

Note well that these 'cost per number' are of great significance, and essential in Financial Accounting and Cost Accounting. Yet, the notion of profit per product is irrelevant in decision-making as far as Throughput Accounting is concerned and therefore, so is the notion of cost per product!

---

[11] The use of 'standard costing' in numerous industries to charge clients for work – car repairs for example – has great managerial benefits

[12] Smith, Debra. 'The Measurement Nightmare'. Page 45

[13] The term 'CO$T' in this article implies a cash outlay. On the other hand, the term 'COST' simply depicts a Cost Accounting construct arrived at by allocating fixed costs to products or services. (Fixed costs that have already been paid for and do not infer a second cash outlay.)

[14] Green money and Brown money will occupy a full chapter. For now, suffice it to say that a new influx of fresh money is green money

‘Costs per numbers’ – notably cost per unit - are still used today for decision-making but as early as 1916, W. Hooper[15] from the Interstate Commerce Commission had this to say regarding cost allocation:

> *“There is no difference of opinion, however, as to the fact that no one basis for division or no general rule for a division of these expenses can be made which will conform to the facts, even approximately, under all conditions.[16]”*

In the brick-and-mortar economy of the physical flow of goods, Cost Accounting (read: absorption costing used for Financial Accounting) is fit for purpose and reflects reality for the carrying cost of products in only three scenarios[17], the first two occurring only rarely:

1) Actuals meet budget at end of period;
2) No change in inventory levels from one period to the next;
3) Companies that operate as distributors and mark up products for a profit.

Throughput Accounting is clear on the issue of fixed costs and Operating Expenses: they are predictable, do not change with sales or production, and therefore do not need to be allocated or ‘absorbed’ to products transiting in inventory to arrive at a ‘cost per unit’. All inventories in Throughput Accounting – raw materials, work in process and finished goods – are carried at purchase price or TVC (Totally Variable Costs[18], calculated as purchase price plus freight-in.)

Throughput Accounting is more concerned with the incremental impact (delta) of decisions upon the following variables in the precise order presented below:

Δ (T) Throughput = Sales minus TVC – Totally Variable Costs

Δ (I) Investments/Inventory = All the money in the system

Δ (OE) Operating Expenses = All period expenses, excluding TVC, required to turn Investment into Throughput

To get in harmony with Throughput Accounting, one would be advised to think like a financial analyst! Marginal, direct and variable costings have a lot in common with Throughput Accounting except for the flawed mental model regarding labor costs, which we will cover next.

---

[15] Hooper, W. The Accounting System Prescribed for Railroads by the Interstate Commerce Commission. The Annals of the American Academy of Political and Social Science. Vol. 63, National Industries and the Federal Government (Jan. 1916, pp 222-231).

[16] US GAAP abandoned the matching principle – which aimed at ‘tightly coupling’ unit costs with sales – for the cost allocation principle which simply states that cost could be allocated to units produced on any basis that made sense; all of which would be speculative under all conditions as W. Hooper would admit as early as 1916.

[17] Doiron, Daniel, CPA. Throughput Accounting class for CPA & CxO at https://agileagonist.com 2021.

[18] In Knowledge-Work, the concept of TVC (Totally Variable Costs) – meaning costs that vary with a correlation coefficient of 1:1 with sales – seldom applies.

Flawed Mental Model Two – Labor as Variable Cost

There are two tragedies in traditional accounting regarding the treatment of labor as a variable cost. One is human and the other financial. We need to thank Dr Goldratt on both counts for exposing and resolving those two flaws.

This first part is tragic, and demonstrates Dr Eli Goldratt's contributions towards building a more humane workplace with its handling of labor costs. In the early 1900s, workers were paid on a piece rate basis. If the chair you built was not acceptable, it was discarded and you were simply not paid.

In that context, labor is indeed a variable cost. Today, Knowledge Workers are paid no matter what. That goes for full time employees and consultants alike that are under contracts for general support, those hired

for staff augmentation more specifically. The proper accounting angle is therefore to consider labor as a fixed cost, such as capacity. Our modern treatment of labor is perfectly in line with the 1900s, and not the 2020s!

Today, in the Western world, this handling of labor costs as variable has dire consequences. Variable costs are always subjected to more managerial scrutiny than fixed costs. Idle machinery at night is totally acceptable even if the interests to pay it off continue to accrue when the plant is closed.

Capacity can therefore be idle, in a wait state, in a blocked state, etc., and no one would give it a second thought. Such is the nature of fixed costs. Knowledge-Workers often find themselves in an idle, wait, feedback delay or blocked state! Do you see the filiation and analogy between Knowledge-Work and capacity? ... Stunning.

But so much for the humane aspect. Let's address the second tragedy: the financial and cash flow incongruity insofar as project planning and control are concerned. No one likes to leave money on the table. But we do so all the time by ignoring projects that are profitable and replacing them with projects that are less attractive.

When we budget for a project, we must find the benefits (revenues) and match the proper costs in order to arrive at a profit to rank and prioritize our various undertakings.

Remember the cost per number fallacies we discussed earlier? The 'cost per project' is often time blurred by the human resource COST, not CO$T, that we associate to it. Throughput Accounting is concerned with the incremental impact, the marginal effect of decisions. No matter what you choose to do, or not to do, labor expenses are incompressible and therefore not pertinent to marginal decision-making.

Let's say that you have, on a permanent basis, ten full time employees and ten consultants each on a five-year contract. Employees all require cash outlays of $100,000 per year and each consultant, $200,000. Let it be understood that no matter what, three million dollars will be spent on labor. The notion of variable cost is moot in this scenario.

Including a single penny of this money to create a CO$T for a project will falsely raise the bar and serve no economic purpose. Heavy loaded labor projects will always face a higher bar when it should never be the case – except of course when consultants are hired specifically for one such project and will leave upon its completion!

The proper approach to measure absolute profitability is with incremental Net Profit. In Throughput Accounting it is appraised according to this formula:

$$\Delta \text{ Net Profit: NP} = \Delta \text{ (T) Throughput} - \Delta \text{ (OE) Operating Expense}$$

Using the work force actually in place will in no way increase Operating Expenses and treating it otherwise as a project cost is a mistake.

If you were to hire 2 consultants for a very specific project and would not be required for anything else, then this would fall into the category of TVC!

Given this knowledge, could you take a quick look at how you ranked, selected and discarded projects in the last 18 months? A lot of green money has been left on the table. Why? Already budgeted and planned monies for human resources costs are not marginal costs and in no way do they fit the delta rules of Throughput Accounting. There is a lot a low hanging fruit money to be pocketed at no extra efforts but to understand the marginal impact of our decisions.

Flawed Mental Model Three – Capacity as everything but a horizontal line!

One of my favorite managerial quotes is from Albert Allen Bartlett and has nothing to do with management.

"The greatest shortcoming of the human race is our *inability to understand the exponential function.*"

For accountants of all breeds, a simple flat horizontal line is not how capacity is envisioned. But, in reality, capacity is always a flat line. Yet accountants will go beyond and above the call of duty to shape this function into anything *but* a horizontal line. The obsession of Cost Accounting to change the behavior of fixed cost is the cause of flawed decision-making. Common sense dictates that once you have acquired something at a CO$T, you use it as you deem fit and necessary without hesitation. There is no subsequent CO$T to be had upon usage.

But not for capacity. Not for accountants. There has to be double counting. Cost Accounting must indeed assign an additional COST value upon usage of capacity that has already been paid for, raising the bar at each attempt you make to use existing capacity.

In Throughput Accounting, data relevancy is king and transactions cease to be a concern upon completion of the economic activity in the current period. For Cost Accounting – and Financial Accounting – data accuracy is mandatory and the historical details of a transaction can persist during and after the economic undertaking[19], as transactions have no predetermined cut-off requirements for post financial recording – read auditing.

To set the record straight, I like the following logic paraphrased from Reginald Thomas Lee Sr[20] regarding capacity:

- There *must* be a cash transaction;
- The CO$T is determined by how much you buy and the price you pay for the amount you bought;
- The COST is *independent* of how it is used, so never hesitate to benefit from the capacity that has already been paid for!

Let me explain using the following three illustrations where Cost Accounting always tries to change the behavior and shape of the capacity function. Throughput Accounting accepts the true nature of fixed costs, irrespective of sales, production, usage and other subterfuges.

Figure 1 below – The more we produce, the lower the unit COST. This totally ignores the fact that Operating Expenses are totally predictable and fixed per period. Producing more or producing less will not change that.

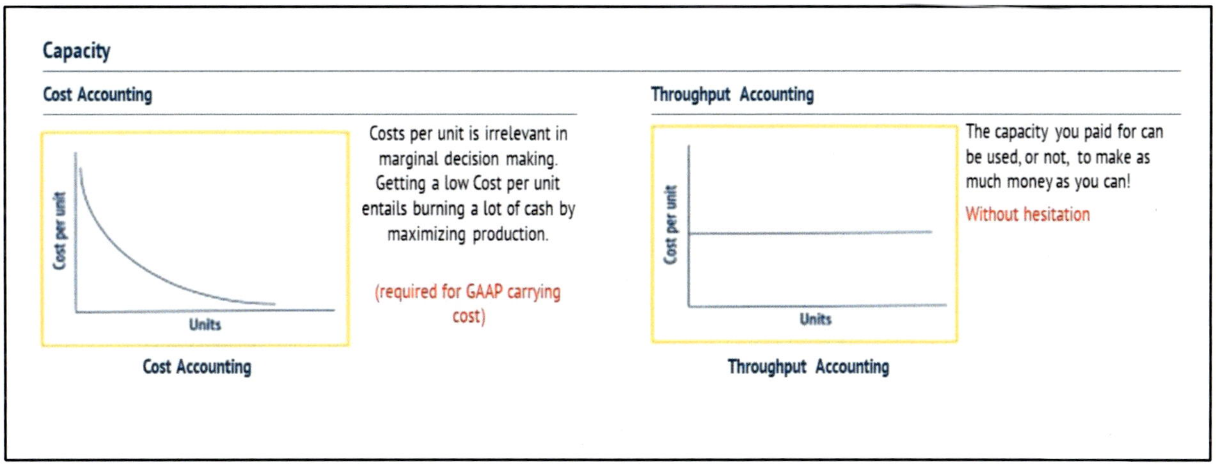

Figure 2 below – Each unit sold must 'carry' its fair share of fixed costs. If it fails to do so, it will simply not be produced and will not generate additional Throughput! This, despite the fact that fixed costs are predictable and seldom change in relation to sales volume or production!

[19] Du Plooy, Etienne. 'Throughput Accounting Techniques'. Page 63. The final results in terms of data accuracy are known once the Financial Statements have been audited. Long after the transactions have settled,

[20] From the book: 'Lies, Damned Lies, and Cost Accounting: How Capacity Management Enables Improved Cost and Cash Flow Management'.

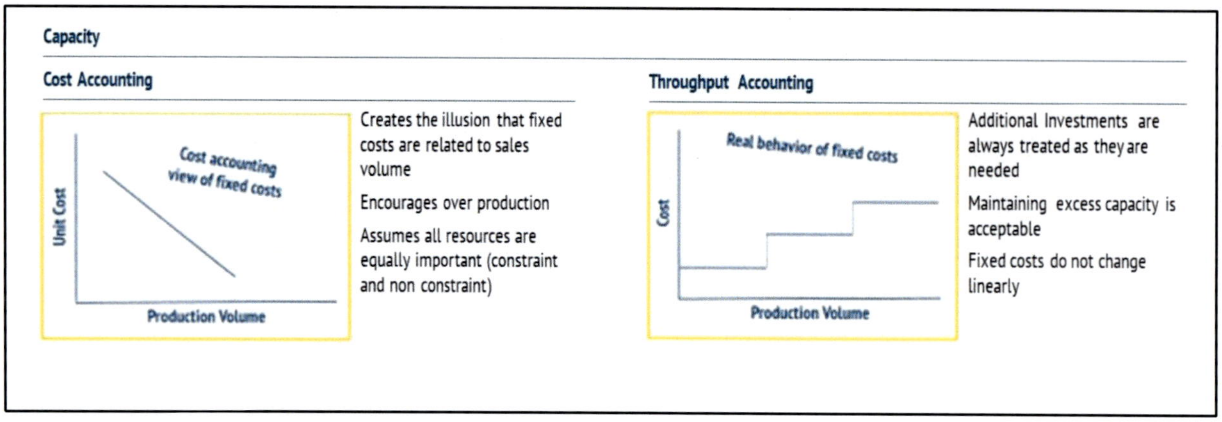

Figure 3 below – The more units produced, the more you need to pay for capacity. This COST illusion is in no way related to CO$T. There are no reasons why you should not use capacity that has already been paid for!

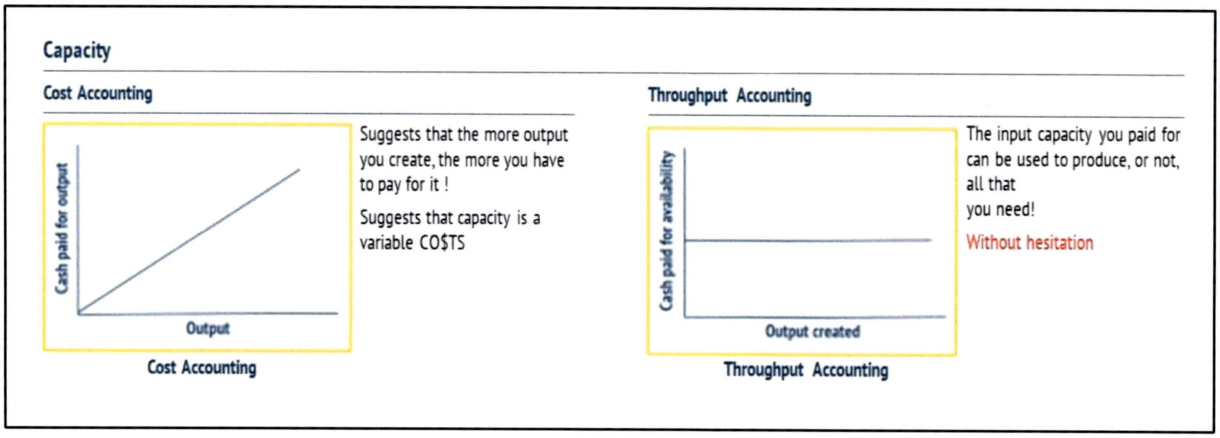

Figure 3 is indicative of what is called "semi-variable" costs. There are no such things in a Throughput Accounting world, where the costs and expenses paradigms are shared by either TVC or OE.

Flawed Mental Model Four – Use of Cost Allocation data as an aid for Financing of Assets and Market Price Determination

Figure 3 just above warrants further explanation by providing yet another illustration[21] just below.

---

[21] Inspired from Sproull, Robert and Nelson Bruce. 'Epiphanized'. Page 280 and Schragenheim, Eli and Camp, Henry and Surace, Rocco for T Generators

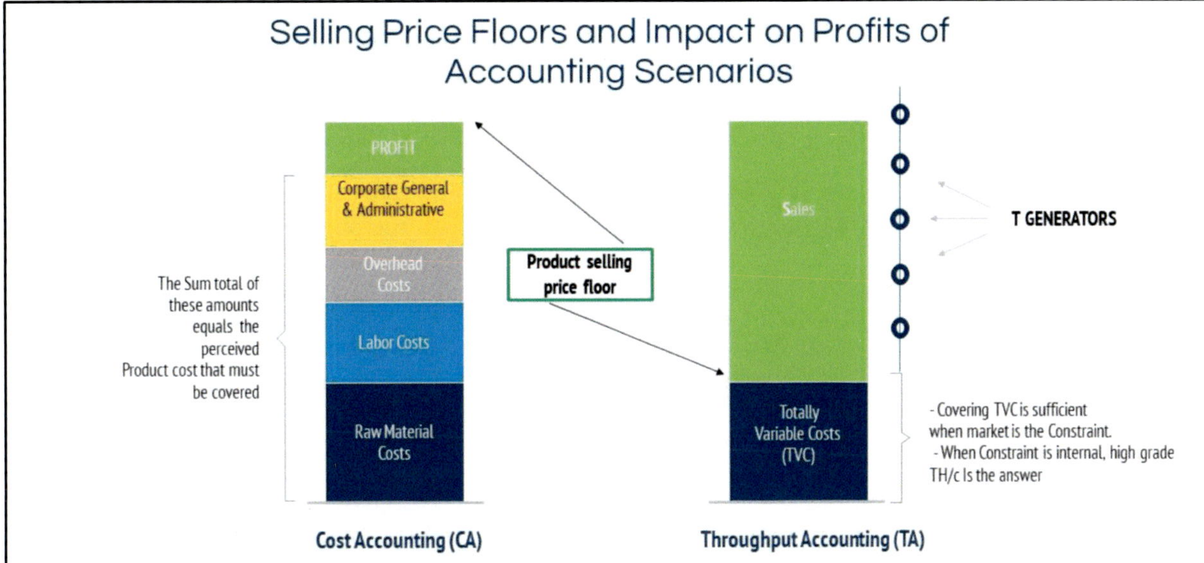

Note: Setting price at COST + MARGIN is the biggest mistake in pricing strategy as it limits overall profits. Capacity changes over time and keeping a COST + MARGIN target at 10% for example, limits growth when sales are exploding (You are stuck at a 10% spread margin!)

In Cost Accounting, the product selling floor appears at the top left corner of the above picture. The floor price is set on top and above of what is deemed to be an acceptable profit, after all the perceived significant costs have been covered. At budget time, after you have 'guessed' your sales volume for the year, all the costs are allocated according to some arbitrary drivers (hours worked, square footage, units of production, etc.) that will never reflect reality.

Once you have reached your sales volume for the year, the hurdle remains. You still need to pass the line drawn in the sand by the contribution margin required and cover all your share of fixed costs allocated to you at every single item sale. This model totally ignores the fact that capacity is malleable and changes during the course of the year. What needs to be covered is TVC and nothing else! Fixed costs are taken care of by OE – Operating Expenses.

And I will say this in point form as it warrants the prize of flawed mental model of this book and the ultimate homage to Lucas' critique[22]:

- The cost allocation model was created to 'trap' costs in inventory in order to 'guess' an acceptable product carrying unit cost to render possible the notion of profit per product for Financial Accounting. This cost allocation predicament is the foundation of Financial Accounting and the reason why it was created **and of paramount importance to provide coherence in the market place**.

- Cost allocation is an inventory and cost matter. It can never support a floor selling price as costs are not contemporaneous to sales, are **unknown and unknowable** by nature. One needs to take stock and stop using this to set the selling price of products on the market. This is not an accountant's job but a salesman!

[22] Lucas' critique will be covered later on in depth. It states that we often use proven models out of context in ill suited situations thinking they are proper.

- Accountants often – or should I say always – state that this model is necessary to guarantee that we pay for the (I) Investment and assets that produce these goods by making sure the selling price of such goods covers the costs. The discussion gets interesting in the classroom when I ask them if this would be needed if those assets were all paid for by cash? The answer to that is always slow coming, if at all. After a few seconds of consciousness building silence, I move on.

- Cost allocation of goods for inventory purposes is mandatory and independent of how the producing assets are financed. Financing of assets should be based on the proper mental model described just below:

    - Investment – or financing decision – must be supported by the TOE[23] spread, not by a cost allocation mechanism that is flawed by nature, even for costing and inventory purposes. A growth focus is required for financing assets, not a model based on costs. Profits drive growth, not a flawed cost baseline. Too often times, we look for external funding when the TOE spread is all about driving growth internally.

To raise the odds of making money, Throughput Accounting paves the way for T generators[24]. All selling prices above TVC can be molded to target markets, empowering Sales and Marketing in the process. In the Cost Accounting world, the product selling floor is off the mark, detached from reality and can really frustrate the Sales and Marketing departments!

Just to make sure we understand one another: a model fit for inventory costing is ill suited to support financing decisions or market pricing strategies. This is the gist of Lucas' critique in this specific case.

Sometimes, I cannot get thru the most 'loyalists' of accountants who have been raised this way. And I need to come up with the ultimate rebuttal technique described below:

There is nothing more powerful than using the lowest common denominator to convince everybody: US GAAP! The chapter and verses are with the matching, allocation, prudence and conservatism principles. Here it comes:

- Over the years, US GAAP has struggled to get to the perfect solution to align the cost of a product with the sale of that product as what is sold today may have been built months ago and its true cost simply eludes us. If only we could live from hand to mouth and sell as we produce. It will never be the case and those costs have to transit in inventory with each unit.

- At the beginning, the 'Matching' principle tried to promote that the costs of sales match the revenues at the time of sale. This was a noble principle that never actually stood the test of time. It was eventually debunked by US GAAP.

- Then, the 'Allocation' principle replaced the 'Matching' principle. It is more noble in the sense that it is attainable. The preciseness of which will always be unreachable for reasons covered earlier.

---

[23] An expression that I coined and that we will discuss at length later on. Assets and investments ought to be based and financed by the difference between T and OE. It has the benefit of motivating one to decouple T – Throughput from OE – Operating Expenses, which are by nature very predictable. The model we are demonizing is trying to leverage useless and unpredictable costs to the aim of supporting asset purchasing decisions.

[24] T Generators are the newest thing in Throughput Accounting and will be addressed later.

- The final argument is that Operating Expenses are predictable and knowable. And if we were to throw the book at Financial Accounting and ask them which of Throughput Accounting or Financial Accounting shows more 'prudence' or 'conservatism' toward the matching of revenues to expenses in their model, the answer would be Throughput Accounting as Operating Expenses are always clear, stable over time and in that sense, more contemporaneous to sales.

- There are no arguments as well when it comes to managerial duties. Financial Accounting's solar knife – cost allocation to support market prices or financing decisions – is no match with Throughput Accounting in a nuclear gun fight when it comes to 1) being in harmony with the pulse of the market, 2) showing our true internal capacity, 3) being able to match revenues and expenses at the time of sales at the period level and 4) decoupling (T) – Throughput from (OE) – Operational Expenses to support the growth of (I) – Investments thereby making cost allocation data totally moot to that end.[25]

There are no debates to be had either that cost allocation – as flawed as it is - is the only way to support a fair Financial Accounting profit rendition and that without proper and comparable Financial Accounting Statements within industries and across time, the markets would be in chaos and our economy in disarray.

Financial Accounting is the 900 pounds gorilla in the room, need I remind us? But it is orthogonal to Management Accounting, need I remind you!

Back to Lucas' critique. Cost allocation is at the core of Cost Accounting and is proper to ascertain the carrying cost per unit and serves at the pleasure of Financial Accounting. It is not to be used for any other purpose!

Flawed Mental Model Five – Capacity or Capacities?

Whether we like to admit it or not, we behave as if we manage in an unconstrained world, where all parts of a system carry equal weight. This is in harmony with Cost Accounting. Each one is responsible for optimizing its part and, as if by magic, the sum of all local optima will be carried forward on the bottom line.

The Theory of Constraints has a generous view on capacity and grants it three attributes: Productive capacity (to feed the constraint), Protective capacity (to protect the constraint from starving), and on top and above, the welcomed Excess capacity to provide slack and idleness and other significant managerial benefits. Lean and traditional accounting accept productive capacity at par but do not tolerate the existence of either Protective capacity or Excess capacity, as they are considered wasteful and must be eliminated. The mere presence of slack or observed idleness is chastised.

[25] Accountants' argument is to decouple profits from operating expenses. It is wrong. Sales must be decoupled from operating expenses, not profits!

Let's consider the below value stream from a cold, detached managerial angle. Each step of the value stream is associated with a geometric shape that depicts its capacity. The BUILD phase has the lowest capacity (where a ticket spends the most amount of time when compared with the other phases) and is the identified constraint.

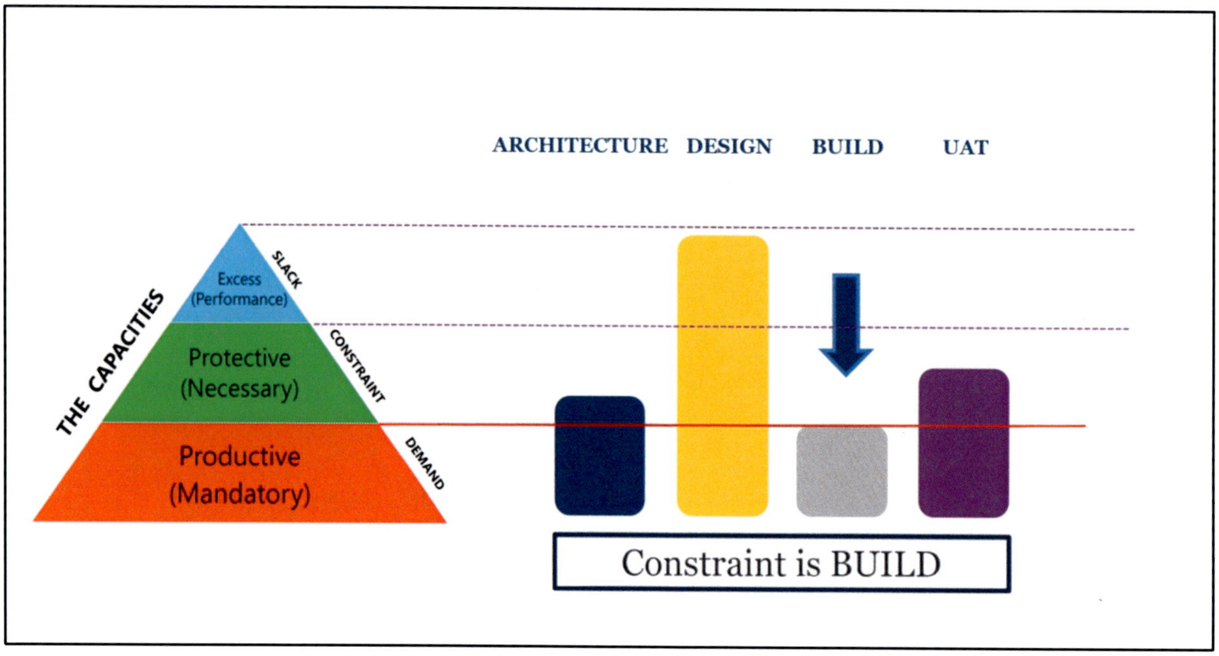

Traditional management would dictate that the entire value stream be managed and that all non-productive capacities be eliminated[26]. In that scenario, we would have not one but four constraints and live in an unpredictable, unstable, and costly environment.

Under the lens of the Theory of Constraints, we would be satisfied with simply keeping an eye on the BUILD phase as it dictates the Throughput of the system. All Throughput Accounting decisions should be geared in light of the 5 Focusing Steps.

The choice is clear: manage the entire system or focus on the one part that dictates Throughput. Operational excellence is greatly simplified when you have *unbalanced*[27] capacity and where the constraint governs the process.

Many Kanban schools of thought reckon that constraints in Knowledge-Work move all the time and that managing them is fruitless. Constraints in the physical world are visible and can be managed and kept in place at will by acting on the three levers of Throughput Accounting: (T) Throughput (sales), (I) Investments, and (OE) Operational Expenses in that order.

It is important to note that, in the following illustration, the traditional accounting lens is inverted. It puts emphasis first on reducing Operational Expenses, then shrinking Investments

[26] Balancing FLOW is not done by balancing CAPACITY! FLOW issues are self-revealing in a low WIP system!

[27] Ricketts, John A. 'Reaching the Goal'. IBM Press. Page 14

and lastly, augment sales to increase profits. This is the opposite of Throughput Accounting, where we argue that there is only so much cutting that you can do before making yourself obsolete!

Focus to Trigger Profits – Mental Model Adjustment

Cost Accounting Decision Filter	Throughput Accounting Decision Filter
Diminish Operating Expenses	Increase Throughput
Decrease Investments	Decrease Investments
Increase Revenues	Diminish Operating Expenses

The fact that work is invisible in Knowledge-Work is not an impediment to strategic Constraints management. Let me illustrate with this trivial example: if you wish UAT[28] to be the constraint, then just put one resource in this phase as opposed to dozens in each of the Architecture, Design and Build phases. I guarantee that the constraint will freeze and never leave UAT!

All that is required is that the non constraint phases have excess capacity above and beyond that of the constraint. Visible or invisible work is simply not an issue. We all have ways – especially in Kanban - of gathering metrics pertaining to capacity, queues and constraint awareness. These include Lead Time, WIP ageing, Backlog Size, Queue Size, Throughput, Flow Efficiency, Order to Cash cycle, Touch Time, Wait Time, etc.

Nevertheless, let us build a better case and see where pinning a constraint (or not) makes sense according to 1) (OE) Operating Expenses, 2) (I) Investments and 3) (T) Throughput. (The same rules apply for physical goods.)

First (OE) – Operating Expenses. Let's assume here, for the sake of argument, that it is fair to consider that Operating Expenses are directly linked to operating complexity. Usually, the further upstream we are in Knowledge-Work, the more we are wading through the 'fuzzy front-end'. We are talking here about requirements as expressed by the client and that the technical team must materialize. Of all places, this is not where one would like to see a constraint where capacity is kept to a minimum. On the contrary, whenever we are dealing with upstream complexity, capacity should be plentiful. Slack and idleness belong here and the Architecture and Design gates in our illustration deserve the protective and excess capacities reserved for them, even if this capacity must be harvested downstream from UAT!

Next, let us assume that (I) - Investments, meaning all the equipment and software for running our business, are prohibitive cost wise. It clearly impacts the BUILD phase in the earlier illustration. We all know that the non-constraint must have excess capacity. Thus, putting the

[28] UAT – User Acceptance Testing

constraint at the BUILD phase and keeping capacity to a minimum at that point makes sense. Doing otherwise would require to pack up the BUILD phase capacity with expensive investments so that it could support the constraint being elsewhere. Having slack at the most expensive spot is not indicated in any case. When you are indecisive about where you should put a constraint, think in terms of slack. You do not want slack at the constraint as it must be kept busy at all times!

Lastly, (T) - Throughput considerations as a constraint. The further you are downstream, the closer you are to the market and on the verge of cashing in. For example, Amazon with its 'one click' feature wants to

1) make life easy for you,
2) confirm the inventory availability of your cart,
3) bill you, and
4) ship ASAP.

All parts of the system are subordinated to the 'one click' constraint and they all have plenty of capacity across the value stream to get you out the door in no time! Amazon's 'one click' never waits for upstream resources.

The presence of a constraint has an impact on how we treat transaction and coordination costs. When we are away from the constraint, idle capacity is plentiful. At those locations, there is plenty of slack and transaction and coordination costs have no bearing on the Throughput of the system and should be used to increase capacity. Increasing capacity at the non constraints is totally in line with a form of exploitation of the constraint. By increasing capacity through existing operating expenses, a non-constraint can then be better equipped to 'sprint' should the system require it upstream. Alternatively, increased capacity downstream can improve lead time to achieve better due-date performance.

Coordination and transaction costs do, however, have an impact at the constraint. All activities matter at the constraint. Here, it is of paramount importance to guarantee that these activities impact Financial Throughput positively. A CO$T is either defined as 1) an incremental cash outflow – never the case with existing operating expenses that are used in transaction/coordination costs – or 2) a lost opportunity for *Throughput (incremental cash inflow)*[29], which is more likely here if the constraint is not optimized and kept busy at all times. Calling in your top architect or specialist for daily ritual meetings is an example where coordination and transaction costs are senseless and absurd were they to be located at the constraint.

Planning, scheduling, orchestrating, working in parallel, and handling big batches are significant transaction and coordination activities, which are essential to having the constraint run at full throttle. These activities are less of a concern at the non-constraint points since slack and idleness is in abundance, cherished and must be present. Think of the non-constraint points as 'walk-in' clinics.

Agile organisations wishing to adhere to the precept of 'maximising the amount of work not done', should minimise managerial oversight at the non-constraints.

---

[29] Smith, Debra. 'The Measurement Nightmare'. Page 92

Flawed Mental Model Six – Inventory as an asset or liability?

Financial Accounting treats Inventory as an asset. The more inventory, the shinier the Balance Sheet and the better looking your Income Statement will appear to the detriment of your Cash Flow position. Window dressing and the doctoring of Financial Statements are easily achieved by manipulating inventory levels[30].

Cost Accounting and Financial Accounting have these innate and perverse properties in the manufacturing[31] sector:

1. No matter what you do, notwithstanding the quality of your actions, if inventories rise then cost accounting will show higher profits as all things being equal you will debit an asset account (increasing inventory) instead of debiting an expense account (increasing profit)
2. No matter what you do, notwithstanding the quality of your decisions, if inventories shrink then cost accounting will report lower profits
3. Reducing batch size is a bad decision in all scenarios

The astute reader will quickly decipher the underlying motivations as to why top management might be tepid in their adoption of Throughput Accounting. The apprehended and immediate negative impacts of reduced inventory levels on the Income Statement is deemed a primary impediment in embracing Throughput Accounting. And this will happen regardless of the quality of your actions or decisions: when inventory decreases so will reported Income.

A second reason that scares management is thinking that 2 sets of books must be maintained. Rest assured as reconciliation of traditional accounting with Throughput Accounting is straightforward and should never be a concern not to use both models, which is the optimal scenario. The reconciliation level usually stops at the Income Statement to align behaviors, a tenet of management accounting that we could associate to social engineering. Why? Because at the operational level – and from the top of the organisation down – people understand that growth resides in the spread between (T) and (OE). Workers can then act in congruity.

A third reason, emotional in nature, lies in the fact that since companies have invested heavily in their Cost Accounting systems, it has value and can support daily decision-making. Why invest in yet another system? Throughput Accounting – to reconcile at the Income Statement – is child's play.

Stellar financial performance systems have one thing in common: their quest to minimize Inventory to enable flow. (In Agile parlance, we can equate Inventory to WIP, Work in Process. The lower the amount of WIP, the better the flow and performance of the system.)

---

[30] When goods go into inventory, one debits (increases) an asset account instead of an expense account, making the Income Statements look better. Continuously growing inventories over time will always delay the recognition of expenses on the Income Statement. The value of inventories always decay with the passage of time and 'garbage' on the Balance Sheet will eventually have to be written off and report a loss on the Income Statement!

[31] Does not apply to distributors as goods transiting in inventory are not subject to 'value added activities' that would alter the merchandise and thus require some sort of cost allocation.

Manufacturing pioneer Henry Ford built his high-performance system in part by minimising WIP to enable flow. His assembly lines featured homogeneous parts, very small workstations and restrained space between workstations to prevent inventory from piling up, and a simple automobile design with few features. We all remember Ford's famous quote regarding the T model: 'You can have any color you want as long as it is black'.

Ford was in an assembly line environment. He wanted to achieve flow and came to the following conclusions:

- Flow is observed when the inventory levels are low
- When there is an inventory pile up, flow is perturbed
- Therefore, do not make provision for storage space where inventory could grow!

In post-war Japan, where supplies were scarce, Taiichi Ohno – father of the Toyota Production System – demonstrated brilliance by adapting to the situation and embracing small batch sizes and frequent replenishments and faster setups as he observed that the short production runs where in fact slowed down by setup times. He pursued this approach after a memorable visit to a US supermarket where he witnessed the practice of filling shelves many times per day, if required, with just enough supplies. Inventory was never left in the aisle, which was one of Mr. Ohno primary concerns as he conceived TPS. High item variability was a factor that Ford didn't have to cope with despite both Ohno and Ford operating in an 'assembly' line environment. No one at the time would think that the assembly line was the optimal choice for making cars where the models were not standard. Toyota was beyond the 'any color you want as long as it is black' era. Letting go of the practice of long runs to reduce unit costs was contrary to common practice at the time and is a tribute to Ohno's vision[32].

As Ford limited workstation space to contain WIP accumulation and Ohno embraced small batch sizes, frequent replenishments, short production runs and faster and shorter setup times to tame inventory levels, along came Dr Eli Goldratt – developer of the Theory of Constraints - who decided to replenish on the time axis with his Drum-Buffer-Rope construct. As opposed to Just-In-Time, where inventory buffers are witnessed at every gate, Goldratt chose to place a physical Buffer at the constraint that would be an equivalent of the time it took to empty that buffer. The Rope function – a replenishment signal mechanism - made sure that materials upstream would find their way to the constraint in due time once a replenishment signal was triggered by the pace of the Drum – the beat of work performed at the constraint.

When JIT talks of the many adjacent processes, DBR was architected with time consumed at the constraint, upstream of the constraint and downstream of the constraint. Those are the equivalent to the JIT adjacent processes. Each 'JIT' individual process steps were not a concern in the total time it took to travel to and from the constraint!

While Ford and Ohno excelled in the physical and manufacturing world, Dr Eli Goldratt's applications covered many topics that resonate with Knowledge-Work, like his Marketing

[32] Saying that Taiichi Ohno solved the Inventory problem by fixing the Inventory problem is too often served as a bad cold side dish, especially when it is self evident that Post WW II Japan had no inventory problem to solve in the first place as supplies were scarce! His visit to a super market in America brought 2 things to light: small batches and frequent replenishments. What this entailed for reducing setup activities (which rose tensions with employees), miniaturisation of tools and parts are very well described in the article in References 'Standing on the shoulders of giants' by Dr Eli Goldratt.

application and CCPM for project management. He competed on time, while Ford tamed space and Ohno focussed on small batch size and frequent replenishments. All of this to enable flow, which is the conduit to stellar financial performance!

We could not leave this discussion on reducing Inventory (WIP) in Knowledge-Work without mentioning Little's Law and its impact on Agility, especially with Kanban where it is used in a *probabilistic* manner.

The Theory of Constraints is also a consumer of Little's Law and uses it in a *deterministic* fashion for operations management[33].

We will revisit Little's Law for Knowledge-Work and its impact on the 5 Focusing Steps in other chapters but not before making the following observations on the merits of reducing WIP in Knowledge-Work. The passage of time – which is in direct correlation with high WIP – renders impossible all planning and estimating efforts. It has a direct decay effect on all our deliverables that spend too much time awaiting treatment. The 'piling' up of deliverables at non constraints – architecture, design, written code, etc. – must be subordinated to the pace of the constraint if, for example, were it to be located at the UAT phase as per our illustration.

In Agile, the speed of feedback loops is key. The faster the answer, the more agile we become. Once, someone introduced me to this agile metric: *agility = 1/time it takes for you to get an answer*. It gets the message across. Low WIP enables this.

There are two ways to cut WIP for Knowledge-Work:

a) The **Lean** approach would dictate that someone in authority cuts the amount of WIP in the system, therefore creating a chain reaction. How? When WIP is reduced, cooperation is forced as there are more people than work items and as collaboration grows, so does WIP reduction. It is an example of a self-reinforcing feedback loop.

b) The other way to cut WIP lies in the **agile** approach which ignites the process in another way. It begets cooperation first, which reduces WIP, which begets more collaboration, and so on.

Those are the only 2 alternatives to cutting WIP: Lean or Agile.

In Knowledge-Work, new dimensions exist for minding Inventory levels. Another kind of Inventory that impacts (OE) – Operating Expenses must be kept in mind, and it has to do with the depth of your bench.

A good Business Analyst or Architect takes a long time to ramp up. It may take up to a year to appreciate their worth. When these resources are not in abundance with current demand for these skills, it is imperative to keep them on hand, as business domain knowledge is *slow* to amass.

On the other hand, a shortage of DBAs or SYSADMINS can easily be dampened with the ad hoc hiring of resources, as knowledge of the business domain is orthogonal to their performances. The quality of a DBA can be assessed at interview time with little risk. A good Business Analyst, on the other hand, will have to understand the business and take the time required to do so.

[33] Nothing to do with Operations Research!

Flawed Mental Model Seven – The Corbett Sanction

I cannot stress enough the link between the lack of protective capacity and skyrocketing WIP levels in a system. In his excellent book on Throughput Accounting, Thomas Corbett addresses protective capacity[34] – at times called sprint capacity or upstream capacity – and its impact at the constraint and then on WIP. Throughput Accounting is very much in tune with the 3 levels of capacities[35] as illustrated below. They impact the constraint, lead time and the level of inventory that the system must bear in order to support the constraint and maintain flow while limiting WIP.

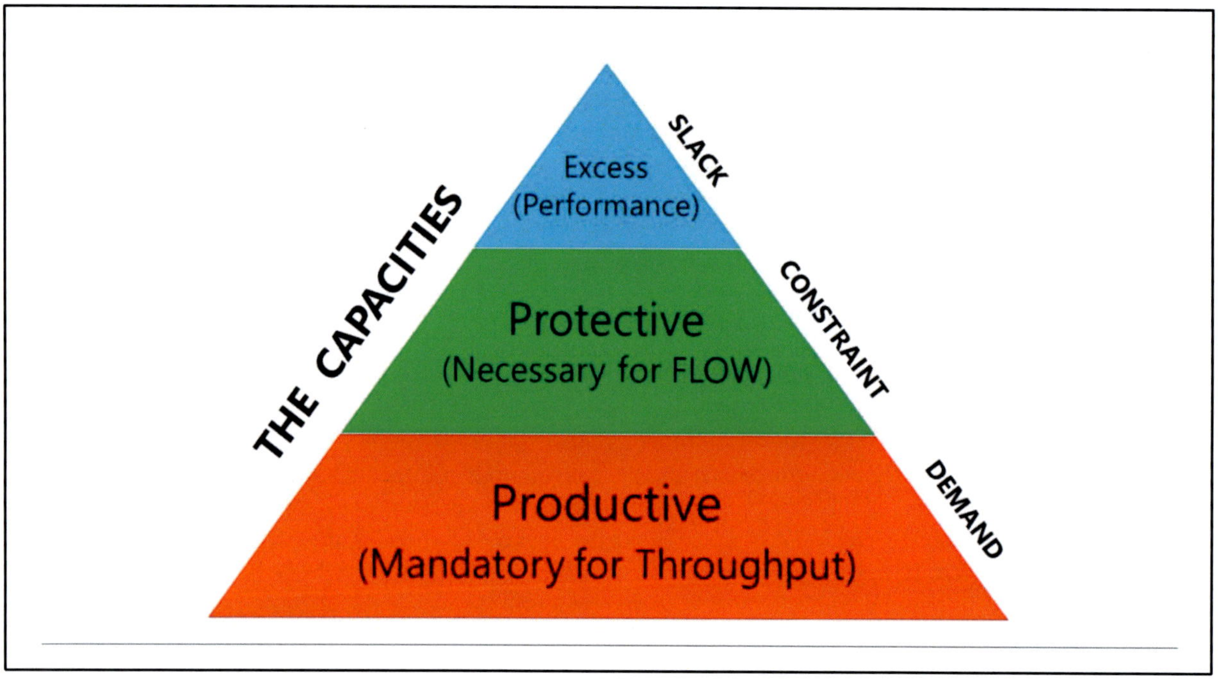

To fully appreciate the discussion below, one needs to assume that we are humming along with Throughput Accounting already and applying the 5 Focusing Steps. Then, new management comes in and takes a different path and introduces Lean.

Lean aims at balancing flow – wrongly - by leveling all capacities downward to the level of productive capacity. (Contrastingly, flow is smoothed by reducing WIP in the ToC world.)

---

[34] A good discussion on the impact of capacity on decision-making in Throughput Accounting is included in Etienne du Plooy's book in the References section. Caspari and Caspari's book on Throughput Accounting devote some chapters on capacity as well with its impact on the constraint

[35] The traditional illustration in the industry is that of Dr Lisa Lang as illustrated in the Novelties section at the beginning of the book. I am using a creation of mine here. The one reason for the change is justified for the blue color at the top. It fits Excess capacity and SLACK better than red in my view. The color red is for me a better conduit to stress that Productive capacity is mandatory in lieu of the traditional green.

Let us see the attractiveness of leveling capacity downward has on management's short term's motivations:

- Cutting capacity slashes costs;
- Which in turn increases profits;
- Which paves the way to a nice bonus!

Sometime down the road, the constraint lies unprotected. The system shows hiccups.

What will happen now?

Due to the lack of protective capacity, overtime is required. If this is the permanent solution – overtime that is – then in theory the amount of inventory required to protect the constraint must be infinite[36].

The trade off between two remedies becomes obvious: either we support a build up of inventory in front of the constraint by straining our resources permanently or we opt for purchasing protective capacity, which is what we walked away from in the first place.

To ease unnecessary pain to those who will always choose the weaker and flawed solution of leveling of capacity to enable flow, the following scientific chain reaction just cannot be avoided:

Protective capacity absorbs variability, if it is removed then:

- ✓ The Flow Time – or Lead Time - variability absorbed by Protective Capacity will be foregone;
- ✓ In lieu, statistical variations will prevail bringing the system into an unstable state;
- ✓ This will be confirmed by the emergence of queues;
- ✓ WIP and Flow Times will increase;
- ✓ Flow Efficiency and Throughput will decrease.

Absence of protective capacity always leads to increased WIP. Always. This applies to Knowledge-Work equally.

The gambit of course is to opt for DBR scheduling on your Kanban boards.

Flawed Mental Model Eight – The DBR and S-DBR Gambit

The proper counter measure to the Corbett sanction just above is to take the DBR gambit when needed for an optimal configuration of your Kanban boards. But first a little story telling from my own discovery of DBR and S-DBR.

Over time, I always listened to explanations of the DBR mechanism on Youtube. Unknowingly, it was in fact the S-DBR mechanism that was always explained! DBR was never the topic and those explaining the S-DBR technology were presenting it as if it were the DBR function. Alas, I thought they operated the same way for too long. But I was getting frustrated as I was

[36] Quoting Mr. Corbett, page 173

walking – mentally - through the progression of work and activating buffer signals in a manufacturing context so as to 'see things' moving.

I did not know then that both were in fact working differently[37] and serving dissimilar purposes. The DBR is meant to protect the internal constraint - the system - and S-DBR to protect the external constraint, the market.

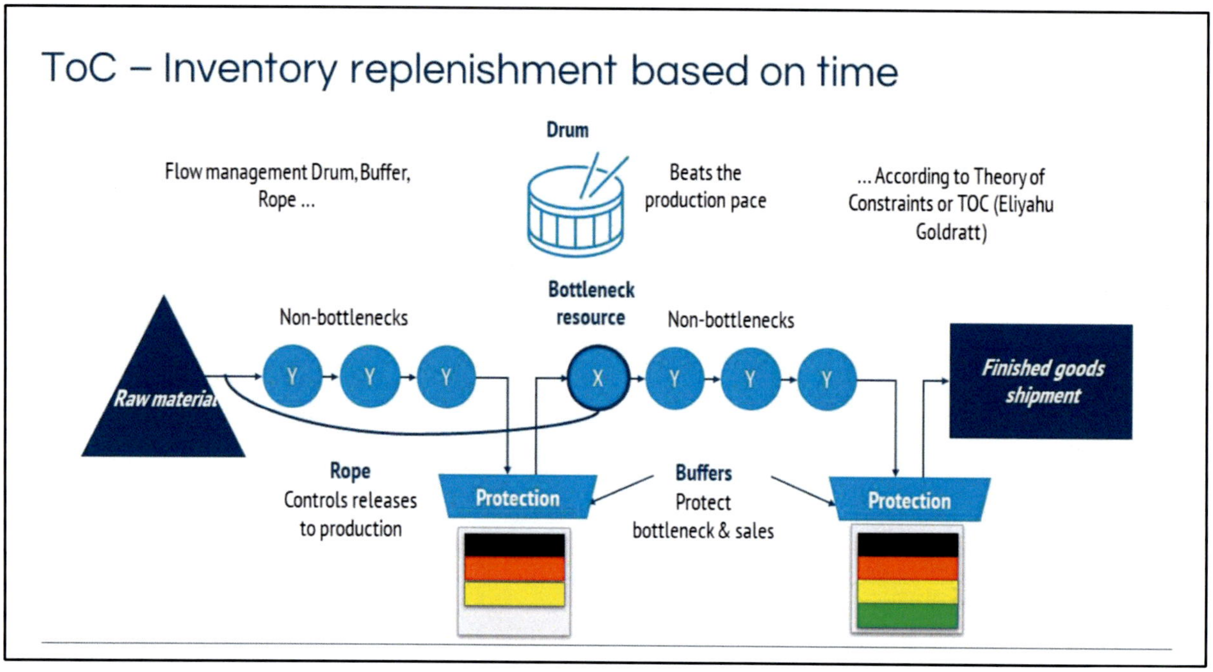

Here are the subtleties:

- The S-DBR buffer – S for Shipping – is located at the exit of the value stream, all the way downstream. The mission of the Rope is twofold: 1) to protect the due date and 2) to protect the market as the external constraint. Good day, bad day, as an item is shipped, a rope signal is always sent upstream irrespective of the Buffer penetration status. Always. If the Buffer penetration states as much, then maybe more than one 'unit' may be requested when sending the rope signal upstream.

- The DBR buffer is the upstream buffer and S-DBR, the downstream buffer. In this case, when we are upstream with DBR, our concern is with the internal or systemic constraint. The rope signal is never automatically triggered for replenishment as a unit of work passes through the internal constraint on its way downstream for shipping. Never. In this case, the Buffer penetration signal will automate the decision and send a rope signal for an extra unit of work to start.

- In all instances, Buffer penetration signals are advanced indicators of the over/under capacity of upstream resources from the buffer location This translates into an exercise to review the state of non constrained emplacements.

[37] That was a long time ago, in early 2020.

The S-DBR construct is not part of Knowledge-Work per se. For that account, I refer the readers to my first book where I mock up the upstream urge to deliver with a CONWIP mechanism. The are described as 'Throughput Boards'.

Flawed Mental Model Nine - Removing and/or planning for Dependencies. Extra Ordinary Popular Delusions and The Madness of Crowds

Increasing the number of layers of indirect – and often times – invisible costs and operating expenses is the fastest way to perdition. It is a reflex. The shortest and surest way to do this is with the total misunderstanding of degrees of freedom and Inherent Simplicity that is foundational to the Theory of Constraints.

Dependencies will be discussed at length throughout this book, notably in chapter 2 and 3. Remove them at your own perils, unless you do so by first being constraint savvy and then by understanding the 3 types of capacity in Throughput Accounting: Productive, Protective and Excess. Don't shoot from the hip and miss. It will have lifetime consequences on the bottom line.

A fascinating note regarding Pareto Law (80-20) in the presence of interdependencies as it becomes the law of 99-1 can be found in the References section. I will spare you the details as Pareto is used in ToC frequency analysis and an article by Gordon Dunbar is quite entertaining to that end. When interdependencies exist, a mere 0.1% of the observations account for 99.9% of the outcomes. Dependencies have enormous managerial value.

Obviously, there are some nuances to be had as I am a ToC flagbearer. A more nuanced and balanced discussion from both Michael Küsters and Jim Benson on all types of dependencies can be appreciated in the references section.

Flawed Mental Model Ten – Death March Project

This is a continuation of flawed mental model number six which targeted inventory level manipulation and its impact on paper profit on the Income Statement. In this scenario, the urge to overproduce is heightened.

This flawed mental model targets capital asset project growth and its impact on asset size on the Balance Sheet. In this scenario, the need to stop producing is nullified.

Cost Accounting creates a strong reinforcing loop that both encourages you to overproduce – the Income Statement effect - and discourages you to stop producing – the Balance Sheet effect.

We will now discuss Software Development Projects and IT Death Marches. (Death Marches are not reserved to IT Projects quite to the contrary.) Whilst your project is going downward and keeps accumulating 'CO$TS', you are not likely to see an accountant complain about this. Death March projects create no incentive to pull the plug from a purely cost accounting basis as (I) increases to find a niche on the Balance Sheet whilst the Income Statement is doctored.

The conclusion here is that no matter what you do, as time passes, the value of your capital projects will go up on your Balance Sheet, killing a key incentive to pull the plug on Death March projects.

As I am reviewing all that is centric to Project Management, I had exchanges where outright disagreement with established thinkers in the field happened. I then came to realize that TA and CA have to be compared across time. My 2 cents are here:

1) When selecting projects – before they actually get initiated – CA will favor projects that target cost cutting or improving in some manner and most notably ignoring all form of constraints. These projects will be hard to stop since they will increase the book value of the asset being build.
2) Throughput Accounting will be orbiting around proposals that bring more money in the coffer and look at the T against OE spread to make sure money is made.
3) Hence optimal ranking choices occur when projects are sorted by Throughput Rate: the speed at which they go thru the constraint.

Flawed Mental Model Eleven – Products do not make profits, Companies do

I often like to remind people that products do not make profits, they generate Throughput. Companies make profits. This is a hard pill to swallow. But it needs to be understood.

Although the selling price of a product is contemporaneous to sales, product costs are unknown and unknowable. For this reason, deriving a profit per product is something that is impossible. The costs derived with cost allocation are not reflective of the company's current capacity or true cost function at the time of sale. Accordingly, the lowest level of granularity for calculating profit is at the corporate level – division, country, state - where operating expenses are a better proxy for costs as they change slowly and are predictable.

This shortcoming in our understanding of business at the daily decision level is again caused by Financial Reporting's granularity. Although it does report on a period basis, which is easy to grasp, all of the details go at the product level, which causes cognitive overload. As managers, let us see if we can easily go up one level of abstraction and contemplate the view from there and the ease with which we can sort things out.

This inherent simplicity lens is key and support all of Dr Eli Goldratt's science that cherished transposing all management quagmires on the time axis, certainly not on the scope or product level as we will entertain in chapter 3.

One needs to live Throughput Accounting at its abstraction level and stop comparing cost measurements as it is envisioned with Cost Accounting. Throughput Accounting's metrics are relevant and contemporaneous to the decisions you are in the midst of taking and show more 'prudence' and adhere more to 'conservatism'; two tenets of US GAAP.

When you use Lean, Agile and Kanban things start to make sense when you get to the top floor of accounting and see the entire spectrum for miles. At the accounting period level – or any period of your choosing – Throughput and Operating Expenses can be matched instantly as they are both contemporaneous to sales and Operating Expenses are always predictable for any given period. Your reflex as a manager should be to validate that T and OE are decoupled at the end of each period.

Throughput Accounting Decision-making Principles[38]

Now that we have exposed some of the most prevalent flawed mental models, we need remediation. This is were rewiring our brains with decision-making principles is indicated.

Principle	Action
Aggregation principle	Inventory and resources are best held centrally because that is where consumption varies least. If you have shared resources like architects, DBA it would be a good thing to hold them and dispatch them centrally.
Buffer principle	Strategically placed units or time for contingencies minimize the spread of disruptions across an entire system (JIT vs DBR) – Kanban WIP limits are like JIT buffers: to be avoided. Instead use buffers to protect the constraint
Capacity principle	Unbalanced capacity is more productive because the Constraint can be used to manage the entire system. When you see actions to balance capacity, do not think it is good. It is bad.
Chain principle	A system can only produce as much as its weakest link, the Constraint, will allow. Many experts in Knowledge-Work claim that constraints move all the time. Allocate one Business Analyst in the design phase and see if the constraint moves.
Conflict principle	Win-win solutions are not only possible, they are the best way to prevent conflict from recurring (DBR & S-DBR). If we all focus on the constraint, consensus driven decision-making disappears and unanimity-based decision-making emerges.
Decision-making principle	The effect of a proposed change can be assessed by comparing its net profit and return on investment to the baseline. Always remember to wear the hat of a Financial Analyst!
Demand principle	Forecasts are usually wrong, but reacting to actual demand is usually right (Rope). I

[38] Adapted from the book 'Reaching the Goal' by Dr John Ricketts

	would say that estimating is even worse than forecasting!
Flow principle	Managing the Constraint manages flow throughout an entire system. When you elect to ignore the constraint, you act to manage the entire system at enormous costs, waste and efforts.
Focus principle	An entire system can be managed by focusing on the Constraint.
Multi tasking principle	Trying to concentrate on more than one task at once decreases performance on all of those tasks. We will show you tricks to detect system overload with WIP ageing, DBR, Buffer Fever Charts and CCPM and more ...
Optimization principle	Local optimizations do not add up to global optimization. The bread and butter of ToC
Pull principle	Rather than pushing work thru a system, setting up procedures that pull work increase the total amount of work done. The basic Kanban rule: Postpone commitment, keep options open etc.[39]
Relay race	Instead of multi-tasking, completing one task before moving on to another accelerates projects.
Replenishment principle	Restocking from a central location leads to fewer stockouts and overstocks than pushing stock to retail locations. In this case it is best that capacity be centrally managed and not financed by projects. This is discussed in the section of the book: 'The first one on the bus pays for the bus' in chapter 5
Time principle	Time lost on the Constraint is time lost on the entire system. An easy baby step approach is the mantra: 'follow idle work, not idle worker'. It is not perfect but it causes discomfort like this very principle.
Utilisation principle	The only utilization that matters is at the Constraint. Why? Because there is plenty of capacity everywhere else. But not so at the constraint. Do not waste it.

[39] Many students ask me how do I physicalize 'postponing commitment' or 'deferring the start of work'! Easy. First you need a capacity constrained system (no more than 5 jobs let say in the system at any point in time). Then, à la queue leu leu, a job can enter the system only after one has left the system. And no, size of jobs does not matter. Capacity restrained systems - like Kanban - absorb variability. Why? Because they are capacity bound!

Conclusion – Down History Lane

While I was learning the accounting profession, all Management Accounting books were written by Charles T Horngren. If memory serves me right, he must have written no fewer than twenty on the topic and is considered the pioneer of Management Accounting.

In 1993, he stated as much, breaking rank with tradition and all his previous teachings:

> "The criterion for maximizing profits when one factor limits sales, is to obtain the greatest contribution to profit for each unit of the limiting or scarce factor**.** The product that is most profitable when one particular factor limits sales may be the least profitable if a different factor restricts sales. When there are limitations, *the conventional contribution or gross margin-per-sales-dollar ratios provide an insufficient clue to profitability*" – *The Measurement Nightmare,* Debra Smith, p21

To this day, this revelation has yet to materialize itself in the business world!

The following heuristics can also be of use to put Throughput Accounting into practice:

1) Act as if you were using the cash basis of accounting in lieu of accrual accounting;
2) Disallow impacts of all transfer pricing when making decisions;
3) Assume that your company is 100% equity funded to eliminate the tax impact of debt financing.

To conclude, all CPA jurisdictions are governed by laws within geographical regions of a country: states in the USA and provinces in Canada. All the laws stipulate that CPAs must help their clients increase their wealth, in addition to providing fiscal, accounting and auditing services.

We can only recall Dr Eli Goldratt's own words: 'Let me help you make more money now and in the future'.

The future is now.

APPENDIX A – HISTORY OF COST/FINANCIAL ACCOUNTING AND CONSEQUENCES ON MANAGEMENT

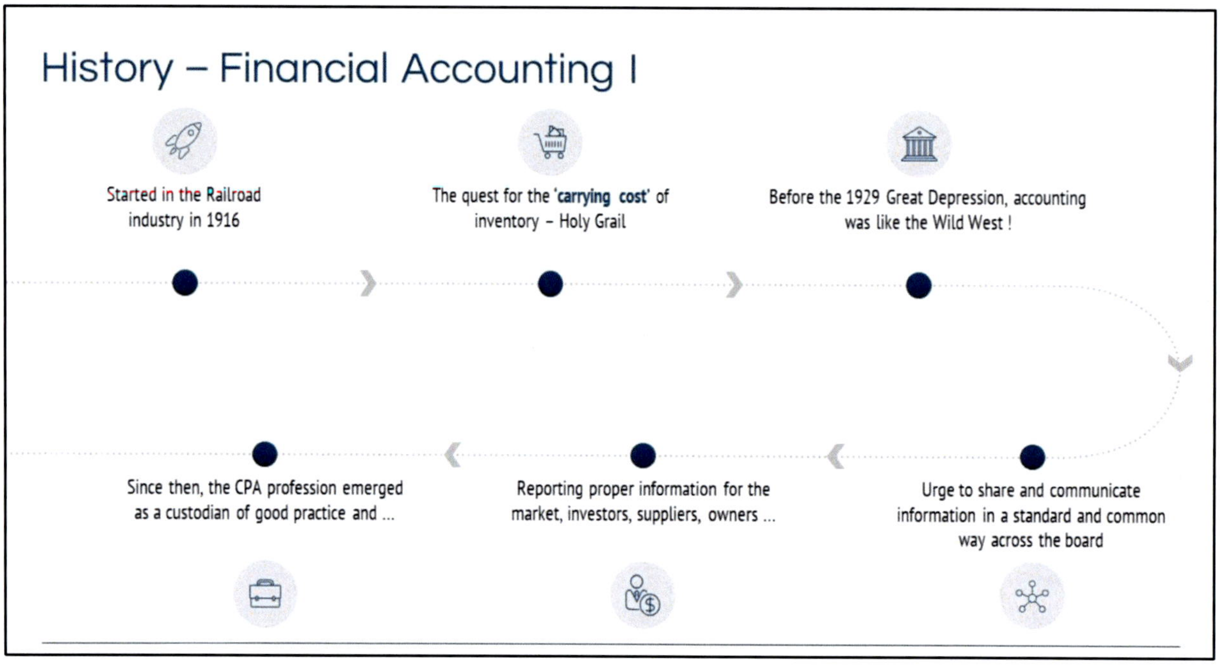

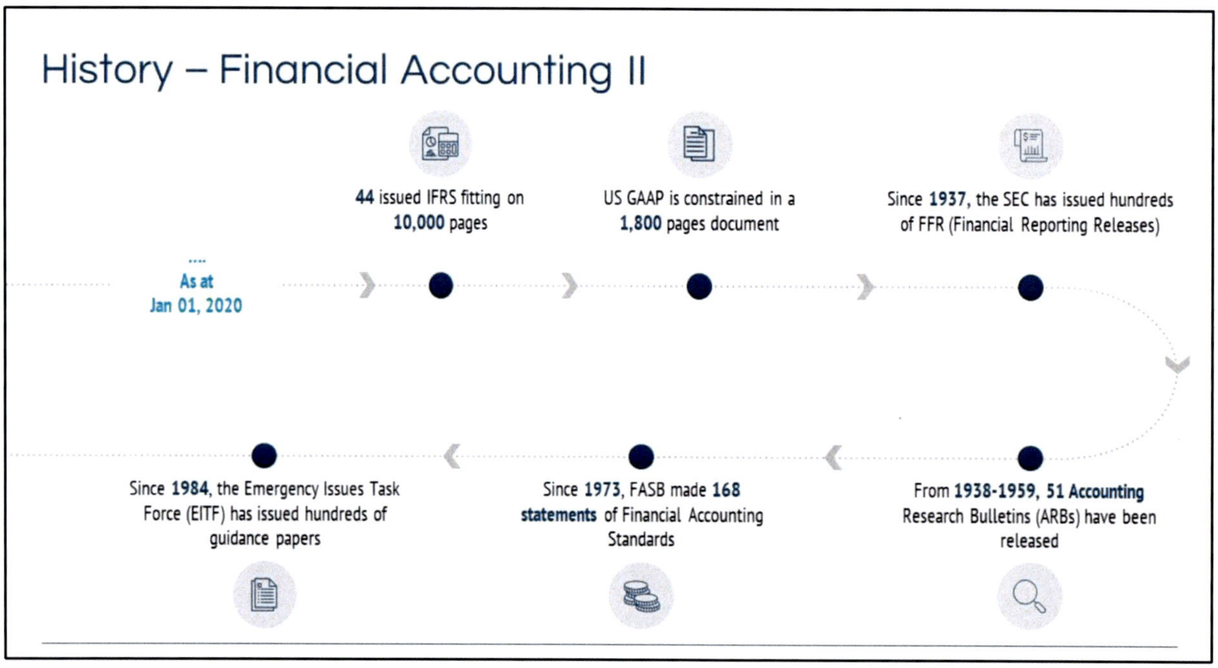

History – Financial Accounting III

All tax laws require obedience to Accounting Standards.

... But ...

To this day, for over 90 years, not a single word has hinted that those principles, standards and rules be followed for managerial purposes

... Still ...

Note: Data from Throughput Economics by : Eli Schragenheim; Henry Fitzhugh Camp; Rocco Surace

Financial Accounting unfit for management in 1916!

... and finally ...

... It is obvious that Maintenance of Way Expenses, which includes the costs of repairs and renewals of the roadbeds and structures of the transportation plant, can only be divided as between freight and passenger service on some arbitrary basis. Opinions differ as to how accurately this arbitrary basis can be made to conform with the facts.

THERE IS NO DIFFERENCE OF OPINION, HOWEVER, AS TO THE FACT THAT NO ONE BASIS FOR DIVISION OR NO GENERAL RULE FOR A DIVISION OF THESES EXPENSES CAN BE MADE WHICH WILL CONFORM TO THE FACTS EVEN APPROXIMATELY UNDER ALL CONDITIONS.

....

Hooper, W. The Accounting System Prescribed for Railroads by the Interstate Commerce Commission. The Annals of the American Academy of Political and Social Science. Vol. 63, National Industries and the Federal Government (Jan. 1916, pp 222-231)

History – Financial Accounting & Throughput Accounting

In June 2005, FASB 151 was issued. Excess capacity may be expensed as a period cost under certain circumstances.

Since 2019, the AICPA has included Throughput Accounting in its syllabus!

CHAPTER II – IMPROVEMENT INITIATIVES

"It's not enough to do your best. You have to know what to do and then do your best." - Deming

Introduction:

Improvement Initiatives come with many established and popular solutions: PROSCI, Lean, Six Sigma, CMMI and many more. All Agile and Kanban flavors can also be categorized as such. The Theory of Constraints has 'POOGI' – **P**rocess **Of** **O**n-**G**oing **I**mprovement. It is exactly the same thing as the 5 Focusing Steps! (And we all know that Throughput Accounting is joined at the hip with the 5 Focusing Steps, making Throughput Accounting an Improvement Initiative method as well as an accounting system, a financial application and the decision-making arm of the Theory of Constraints as we saw in the first paragraph of chapter one.)

There is one thing that separates POOGI from all other Improvement Initiatives approaches: constraint awareness. And so is the focus of all applications of the Theory of Constraints (ToC).

For a better grasp of what the Theory of Constraints offers, here are short descriptions of its basic eight applications[40], the ones that are in **bold** -the first 7 out of 8 - will be discussed in this book:

1. **Synchronous Manufacturing:** Synchronizing the plant using the DBR technique. This gives manufacturers the fastest and most direct path to large-scale, bottom-line improvements. Typical results include reduced inventories, reduced manufacturing lead times, increased service levels/superb on-time delivery, and increased productivity.
2. **Throughput Accounting:** Even the accounting profession has conceded that traditional fully-allocated Cost Accounting causes managers to make wrong decisions. And not just marginally bad.
3. **Critical Chain Project Management:** This is an extraordinarily powerful approach to Project Management that offers results that continue to astonish project-experienced managers. Critical Chain enables organizations to generate schedules that are 25% shorter than traditionally planned schedules, AND to meet the promised completion date 85% or more of the time.
4. Distribution: The TOC offers an approach to having the right parts in the right location in the right quantity at the right time, with a minimum of effort ... while contradicting most of the rules of conventional Distribution thinking.
5. **Supply Chain:** Actually, this and the Distribution application are treated as one, in the formal body of knowledge. The TOC approach to Supply Chain management is so much more powerful than, and so far beyond the conventionally popular and superficial view of Supply Chain, that it really deserves a different name.
6. **Marketing:** There is a special way of applying Theory of Constraints in MOST (not all) manufacturers that creates a major competitive edge – large enough to win a LOT of business even in the most competitive markets, and sometimes large enough to be able to charge more even in the most cost-driven markets. This is the infamous **Mafia Offer** or Unrefusable Offer.

[40] Quoted directly from https://www.synchronix.com/about-theory-of-constraints/theory-of-constraints-applications/

7. **Sales:** The TOC sales approach is necessary for three reasons. One is that the Unrefusable Offer developed as part of the marketing solution has to be sold unconventionally. Another is that the conventional selling model is quite simply very ineffective. And the third is that the sales management set-up in most manufacturing businesses is not capable of generating sales growth at the rate that is possible.
8. **Strategic Planning:** Eli Goldratt turned the world of Strategic Planning on its head with an approach called "Strategy & Tactics Trees." Understanding the S&T approach immediately exposes the flaws in conventional Strategic Planning – and they are huge.

The chapters in this book aim at integrating these applications in a Knowledge-Work context. Most of what will be covered has not made it into mainstream agile thinking as we stand today.

Whenever we address science, the world of Agile raises the shield of 'empiricism' – that all knowledge comes from experiments in your context. That is one solid argument. But empirical evidence from all fields of science across time and industries cannot be discarded. Little's Law is one example; I would not hear of someone telling me that it must first be tried in their environment before vouching for it. There are limits to this popular line of thought as Little's Law will work, irrespective of your environment. So is the case with Throughput Accounting, and much of the body of knowledge from the Theory of Constraints.

In the field of science, everything is beholden to causality. Causality means that if you try that 'thing' repeatedly, you will always get predictable outcomes relatively soon.

Throughput Accounting combines both Inherent Simplicity and causality. If you act on the constraint, you are activating an Archimedean lever whose adherence to the laws of physics need not be proven continuously. A little pinch at the right spot – the constraint – can go a long way. (The lever effect here is that (OE) - Operating Expenses are fixed and predictable. When increasing production, you are in fact using a lever as only TVC – Totally Variable Costs – will increase with additional sales. It is important to stress again that TVC seldom apply in Knowledge-Work, making the OE lever effect even more potent.)

Complexity Divide

The first time I heard of 'Complexity Divide', was when reading Caspari & Caspari's 2004 book on Throughput Accounting. Since then, I have heard Steve Holt – well known in both Cynefin and ToC[41] – use the term. I do not know if the root comes from ToC, Cynefin, or Caspari. But I took it upon myself to find this image of Cynefin that splits its popular representation into the ordered and unordered worlds and drew a red line down the middle showing where the 'Complexity Divide' lies:

[41] Outside of Caspari & Caspari, I cannot find an earlier source of the term 'Complexity Divide' in either Dr Goldratt's work or Mr. Snowden's literature on Cynefin.

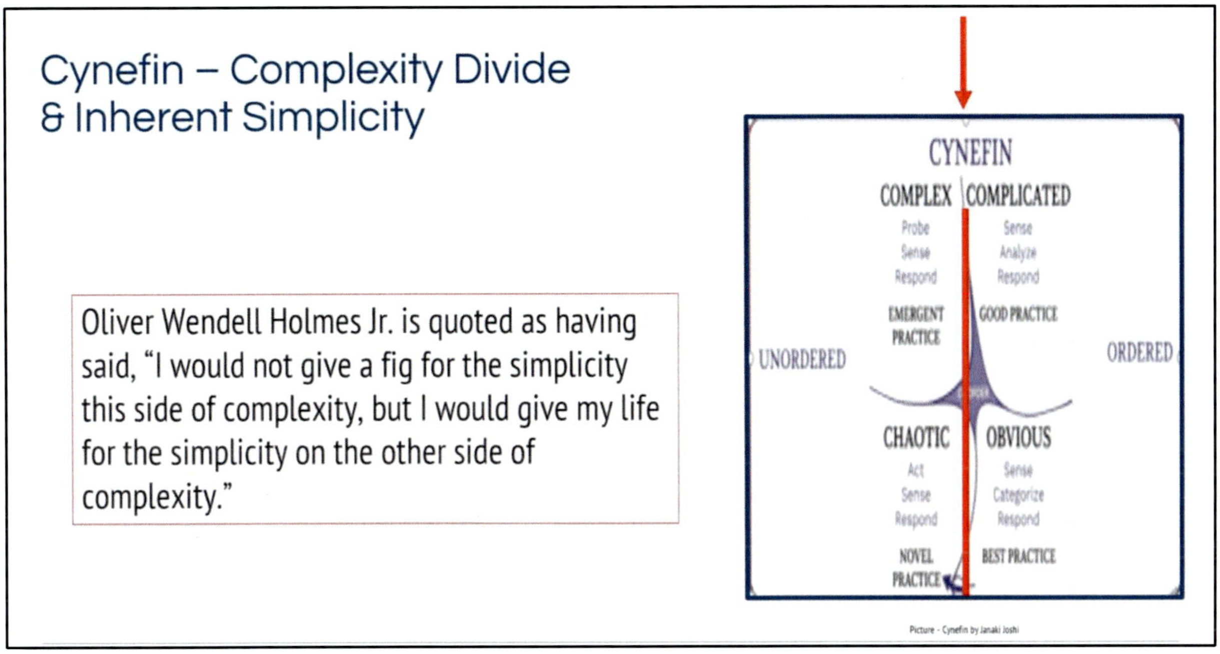

Throughput Accounting lies on the border of the ordered and unordered world. It is a simple solution – to be found in the ordered world - that is within an earshot of complexity.

Buffer management techniques – which we will cover plenty of in this book– are, according to Mr. Holt, directly positioned in the complex quadrant. He makes many a parallel between Cynefin and the Theory of Constraints in the video in the References section.

This is the essence of this chapter: science and Inherent Simplicity. On that note, Dr Eli Goldratt would be of the opinion that 'complexity' is often self-inflicted. But like we say in Scrum, 'I could be wrong[42]'!

Wait Time & Touch Time

1) Flow Efficiency & Wait Time and Touch Time

This chapter is divided into self-explanatory sections all dealing with Touch Time and Wait Time, two components that are added together to yield Lead Time[43]. Lead Time is the denominator of both Flow Efficiency and Little's Law calculations.

---

[42] Like Joseph Pelrine often reminds us, as soon as more than one human is involved, complexity sets in. I concur. But all teams need talent at the individual level. This is the merit of this book. In agile, each member has the onus to improve.

[43] Some call this Flow Time, Cycle Time etc.

Understanding Flow Efficiency as an economic model is of paramount importance in any Improvement Initiative. In fact, it should be considered a business imperative. Flow Efficiency metrics are not to be pursued nor compared. According to many, the Flow Efficiency metric is a 'vanity' metric. I concur. The simple understanding of the formula and its mechanics is all that is required:

$$\text{FLOW EFFICIENCY} = \frac{\text{TOUCH TIME}}{\text{TOUCH TIME} + \text{WAIT TIME}} \times 100$$

OR

$$\text{FLOW EFFICIENCY} = \frac{\text{TOUCH TIME}}{\text{LEAD TIME}} \times 100$$

Note again that Lead Time as the denominator for Flow Efficiency calculations is the same as the denominator that is used in Little's Law! More on this later.

2) Improvement Initiatives - Wait Time and Touch Time

Improvement Initiatives have one thing in common: they aim to change the way you work so that you can deliver faster. All of them require a budget ahead of time that precludes a long journey.

We all know the two components of Lead Time: Wait Time and Touch Time. Wait Time is a state where your work does not make any headway and can be either blocked, idle, in feedback delay, etc.

Touch Time is when the work is being attended to. This is when we actually progress. It is linked to the 'way we work'. Common sense dictates that this is where we make Throughput; operational (more units produced) or financial (more money, more sales).

'Lead Time' – meaning the time that it takes your team to do a job from start to finish – is also the sum of all the 'Wait Times' and all the 'Touch Times' while in process.

If you want to improve and decrease 'Touch Time' – work faster – you need to change your way of working with training, new equipment, investments, processes, etc. It will cost money and time. It is at the core of all Improvement Initiatives.

If you decrease 'Wait Time' in order to deliver faster, you simply have to defer commitment, reduce WIP in the system and exercise your options upstream. Discipline is a must as you decide when to start/stop work, but no investments are required. Reducing Wait Time 'hurts' the brain as in order to achieve it, you need to start work later and thus wait more! The more you wait before starting work (outside the system), the less you wait while doing the work (inside the system)! A managerial quagmire.

In the context of Throughput Accounting, we can conclude that 'Wait Time' does not generate operational or financial Throughput! Therefore, in a Throughput Accounting context, we would love to decrease 'Touch Time' ASAP. But is this another flawed mental model?

Why is this important? According to both Fabok[44] and Forss[45], Flow Efficiencies of 1-5% are the norm in Knowledge-Work. This means that 95% of the time, your work is in some sort of wait state.

Let us now see whether 'working harder' - reducing Touch Time - or 'delivering sooner' – shrinking Wait Time - is the smarter move.

Let's assume that we are in a context where 'Wait Time' represents 95 days of overall Lead Time, which totals 100 days. 'Touch Time' accounts for 5% of Lead Time, or 5 days.

The following illustration tallies the results of a 20% improvement initiative targeting each of Touch Time and Wait Time separately and depicting the resulting impact on both the Lead Time and Throughput of each stratagem.

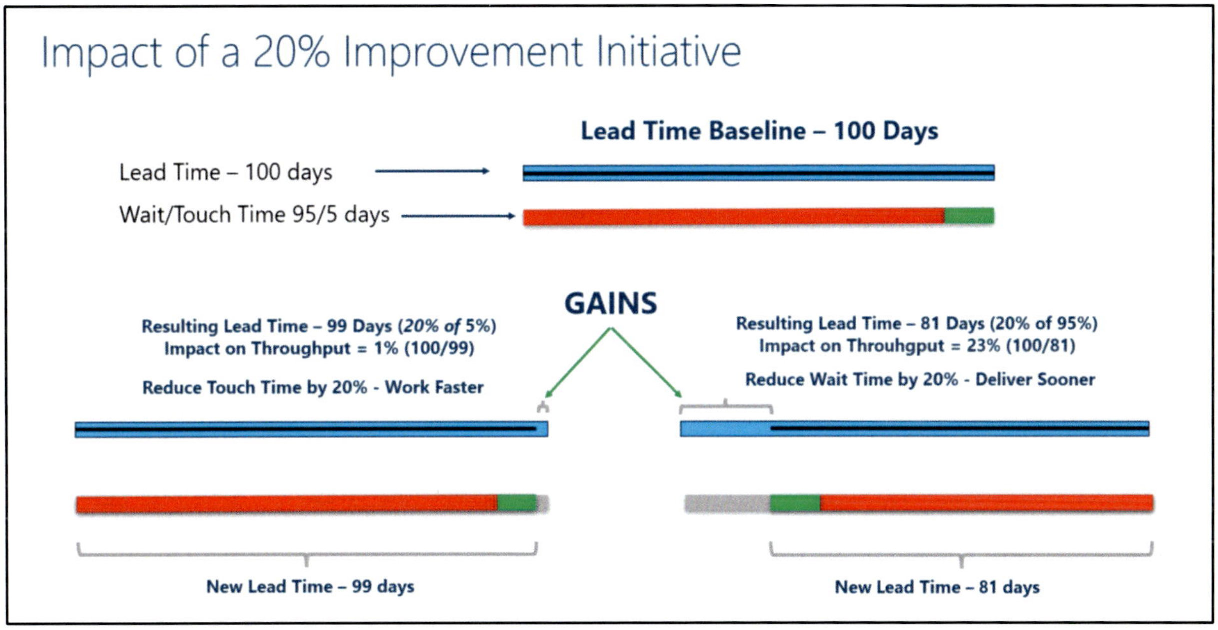

In the above illustration, Wait Time is depicted by red and Touch Time by green. Gray depicts the lead time shaved from acting on Touch or Wait Time.

[44] Zsolt Fabok, Lean Agile Scotland, Sep 2012, Lean Kanban France, Oct 2012

[45] Hakan Forss, Lean Kanban France, Oct 2013

There is no denying that Wait Time reductions – yielding stellar improvements –favorably impact both Lead Time (19 less days) and Throughput (plus 23%). The Touch Time reduction is shaving one day off the original Lead Time and improving Throughput by an insignificant 1%.

Whilst the Wait Time reduction only requires reducing WIP and postponing the start of work, à la Kanban, reducing Touch Time demands impacting possibly two of Throughput Accounting's variables: (I) - Investments and/or (OE) – Operating Expenses. This is done in order to sustain activities such as training and new processes, undoubtedly leading to resistance to change as a by-product while you think you are riding a learning curve!

Reducing Wait Time is a remarkably simple step towards achieving predictability (due date performance) and stability (low WIP).

A stable system is required to reap the benefits of Little's Law. Let us illustrate with two examples of CFDs (Cumulative Flow Diagrams).

At an airport, when too many planes land, the tarmac can get crowded to the point where manoeuvring is difficult and the airport becomes inoperable. On a CFD, the increasing spread between the Arrivals line and the Departures line is a good visual indicator of increasing queue size, a leading indicator of poor performance to come.

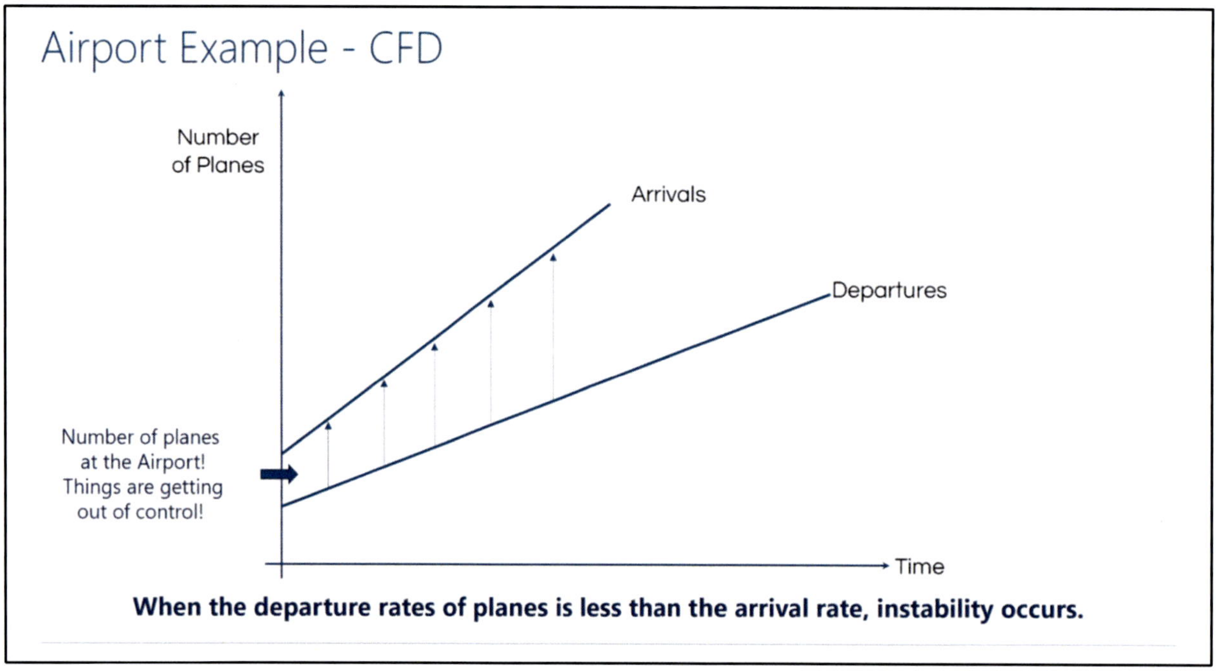

We can now transpose this into a practical assignment for work. It will be self-revealing and should not take too much of your time. Instead of using an airport with planes landing and departing, use the data from your PMO – Project Management Office - and put the number of projects started and finished on a CFD – Cumulative Flow Diagram – like below. A period of 18 months should be sufficient.

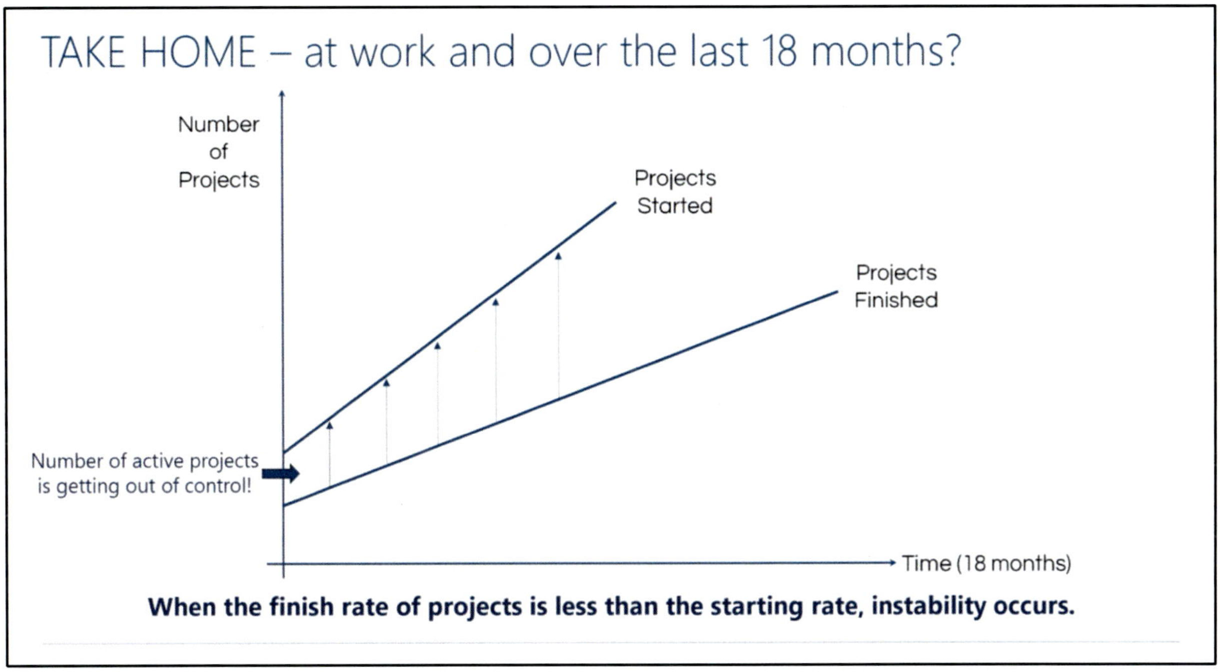

Are you finding some similarity within your organisation? Are the lines diverging? This means that you are in an unstable system and are losing Financial Throughput. The cure is not painful but requires discipline. The two cures described below for Knowledge-Work are variations or the equivalent of ToC's concept of choking the release of work.

A simple and effective remedy for this situation is to use the Two-for-One rule until both project lines become parallel. Only allow one project to start once two have been completed. The improvement will manifest itself as time goes on. If you wish to have a more drastic impact, keep 50% of the active projects only and discard the other half immediately. This is known to quickly yield results, but it is a difficult sale[46].

Some may argue that project sizes are never the same and that this model is moot. But remember these words of wisdom paraphrased and adapted for a project context from Daniel Vacanti:

- The variability in project size is probably not what is killing your predictability;
- The bigger predictability problems are usually caused by too much WIP;
- The frequency with which you violate Little's Law's assumptions, (First In - First Served) etc. is probably what is hurting you the most;
- Generally, those are easier problems to fix than trying to arbitrarily make all projects the same size;
- Even if you were in a context where size did matter, it would be more about queue size (right-sizing) of your work rather than aiming for similar project size (same-sizing) of your work.

Little's Law is important. Let's see some additional reasons as to why.

[46] This is a solution that Mr. Reinertsen is known to practice.

3) Little's Law & Wait Time and Touch Time

Both the Theory of Constraints and Kanban use Little's Law but under different lenses.

- The Theory of Constraints is straightforward and can be associated to a discrete distribution, a histogram. It involves adding up products shipped over time. Using the 5 Focusing Steps is the key to success here. As WIP is reduced, the principal observation is that Throughput augmentation first observed at the operational level will subsequently find its way to the financial level. **(Field of OPERATIONS MANAGEMENT)**
- At its root, and as intended by Dr Little, Little's Law is probabilistic and backward looking. On a CFD, the capacity (output) and demand (input) are drawn on 2 separate lines as seen previously in our example on planes and projects. When the two lines are parallel, and as close as possible to one another thanks to low WIP, we have a stable (delivery rate) and predictable (delivery date) system. It is a law based on stochastic averages observed over long periods of time. The focus in Kanban is to optimize for Lead Times by reducing WIP. **(Field of QUEUING THEORY)**

Little's Law Formulations

THEORY OF CONSTRAINTS	KANBAN
$\overline{TH} = \dfrac{\overline{WIP}}{\overline{LT}}$	$\overline{LT} = \dfrac{\overline{WIP}}{\overline{TH}}$
Increase Throughput	Decrease Lead Time

In Knowledge-Work, reducing WIP is the trigger to unleash the power of Little's Law. What happens next is that, upon reducing WIP, Lead Time will decrease and Throughput increase.

But we have issues. If WIP levels are indeed under our control, what can justify the increase in Throughput as we have not changed the way we work, i.e. Touch Time? The Theory of Constraints is adamant: Throughput augmentation can only be caused by reducing Touch Time and changing the way we work. This does not happen merely by reducing WIP!

It is now time to introduce and apply the 5 Focusing Steps of the Theory of Constraints to shed some light on this.

4) The 5 Focusing Steps & Wait Time and Touch Time

Mastery of the 5 Focusing Steps is essential in getting results with Throughput Accounting. Applying the decision-making algorithm with 1) Δ (T) – Throughput, 2) Δ (I) – Investments and 3) Δ (OE) – Operating Expenses with total disregard for the constraint, would have dire consequences on the potency of your decisions.

All those who have been involved in Improvement Initiatives know that money must be coughed up at the get-go. In most case with the 5 Focusing Steps, you can go from step one to three without spending a penny[47]. The pain might come when changing how you think about when to start and stop work.

There are even cases when step four – Elevate the constraint – does not require any monetary outlays[48]. For example, using existing Operating Expenses to increase capacity upstream of the constraint is a form of exploitation of the constraint, as the sprint capacity – required for outpacing Murphy – has gone up!

A short description of each of the 5 Focusing Steps[49] can be found in the following illustration. For all intents and purposes, they are the same for Knowledge-Work.

---

[47] To identify, exploit and subordinate to the constraints often only requires using existing operating expenses in most cases. For example, in a manufacturing setting, making sure that the constraint never stops at lunch time or between shifts is a simple logistics adjustment that does not require a cash outlay.

[48] Investments are the last thing to consider. All the time. Adding capacity at the constraint could have the constraint move. Adding capacity downstream of the constraint makes little sense. The only place that adding capacity makes sense is for 'sprint' capacity upstream of the constraint where it can have a trade off with the size of the buffer. See Braggs, page 19.

[49] The act of deciding where to put your constraint in a well thought out manner and keep it there in a permanent fashion is a 'step' that should also be taken into account. For the sake of easing the management burden.

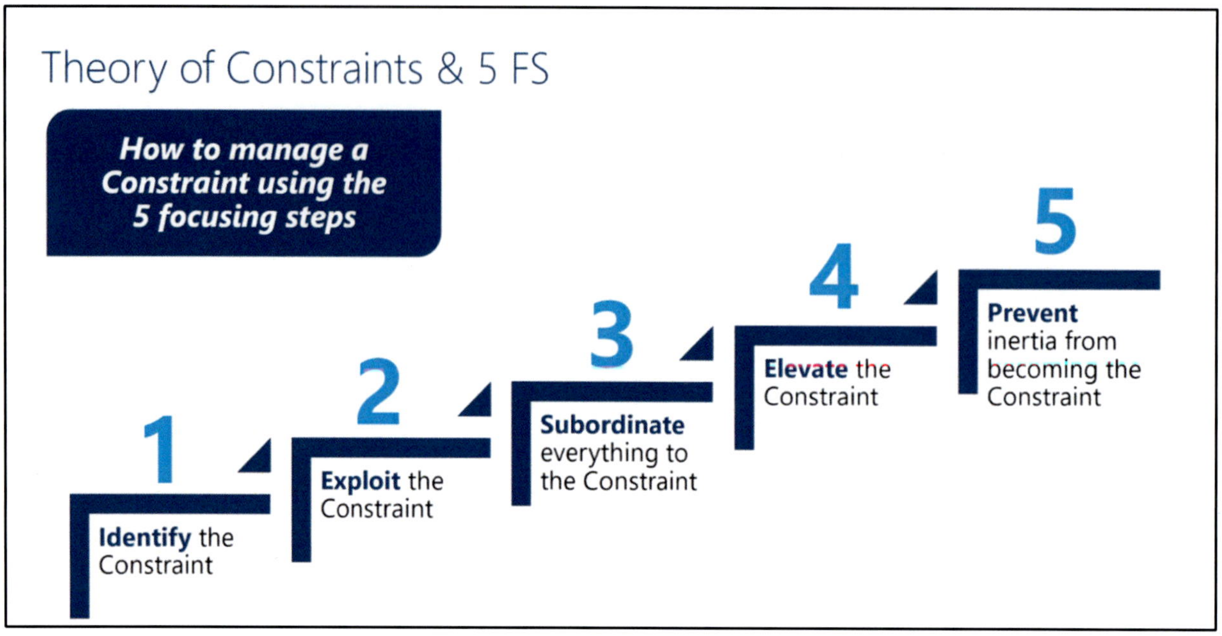

For Knowledge-Work, there is however a twist for Step One – Identify the Constraint - as the constraint is invisible. How are we to proceed at first?

We must invert Steps One and Two as follows:

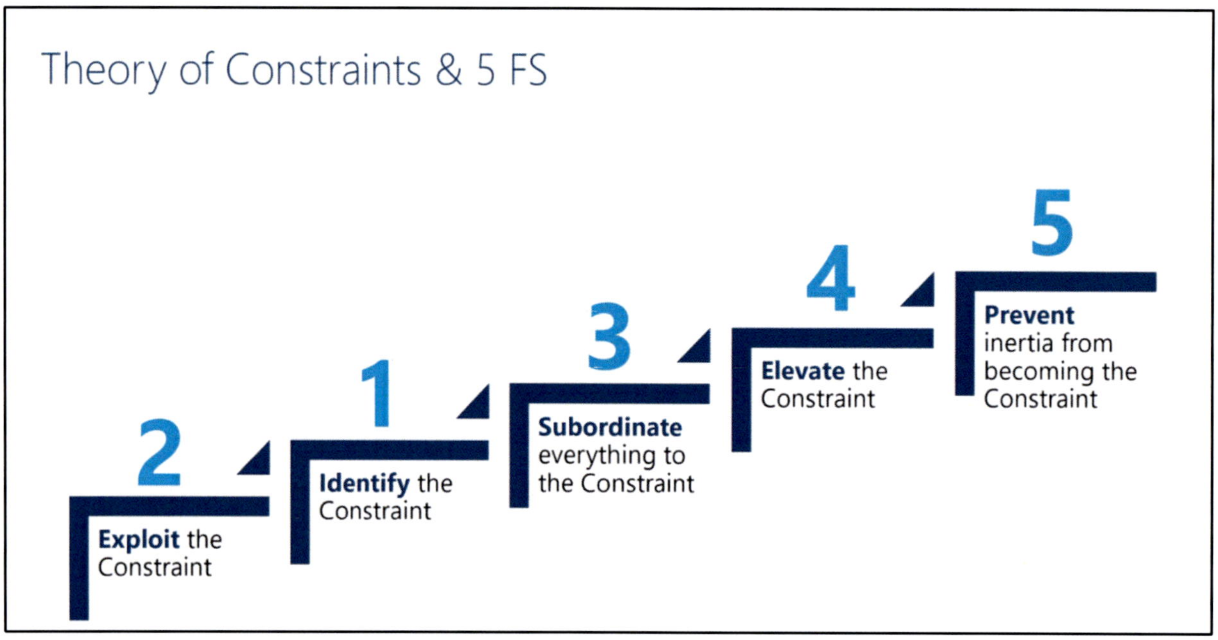

Note: This way of illustrating the situation is valid at first. Once you have done this and identified the constraint, I suggest that you pin the constraint at a strategic place and subsequently apply the 5 FSs in the proper order.

I like the Lean metaphor regarding water levels in a pool and the dangers that lie beneath the surface. Lowering the water level exposes the threats[50].

This is demonstrated in the following photographs:

https://amp.ibtimes.co.uk/paris-canal-saint-martin-clean-pictures-bikes-chairs-trolleys-emerge-sludge-1536564

High WIP is a performance impediment and reducing WIP will show you something very practical in Knowledge-Work: the constraint.

By lowering WIP in Knowledge-Work, we are producing more Throughput. This can only happen if we exploit the constraint from a Theory of Constraints' point of view. As we have not changed anything in the way we work that would affect 'Touch Time', this should not be. And yet, this is exactly what is happening.

Operating with high WIP causes the constraint to be suboptimal. Lowering WIP does not impact 'Touch Time' (in fact, it impacts 'Wait Time') but aids in exploiting the constraint better. It does so in an indirect way as depicted below:

- Anything that allows the constraint to work better is a form of 'exploitation'!
- Reducing Wait Time impacts WIP which impacts multi tasking, which impacts Lead Time, which impacts Throughput without changing Touch Time;
- The constraint wastes less time in multitasking. Capacity is not reclaimed, rather time is!
- The capacity of the constraint remains the same since Touch Time has not been acted upon directly and no improvements on the system have taken place;
- This occurs with no additional (OE) - Operating Expenses or (I) - Investments as if we had reduced 'Wait Time'.

5) Visualisation of Work & Wait Time and Touch Time

[50] There is also a 'pool' metaphor illustrated in Appendix A with respect to Toyota Production Systems.

Kanban[51] boards are immensely popular. They have an interesting construct. The 'Doing' and 'Done' semi columns give priority to 'Touch Time' over 'Wait Time' within a sub process as follows:

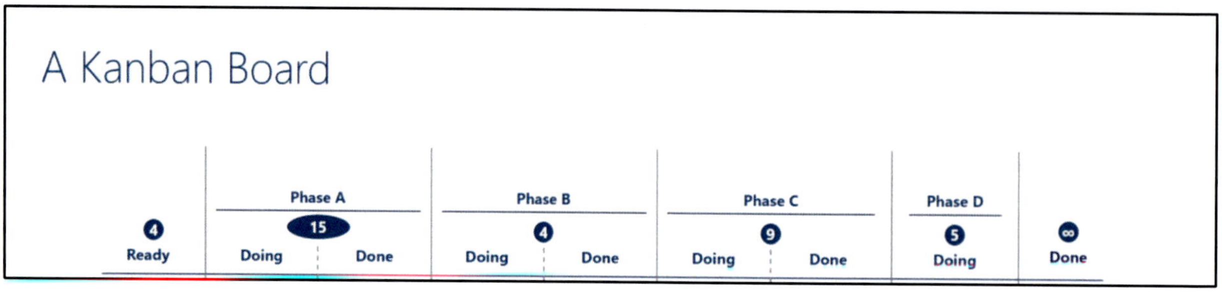

The 'Done' queue is in a 'Wait' state. It has no psychological stressors and is in a passive mode: no one has to attend to it anymore. The work is done here in a sub-process – Phase A - and when Phase B is ready, it can come and pick up a ticket. A worker should have no more purpose with that work. It is 'Done'.

When one looks at a CFD – Cumulative Flow Diagram – the area that would depict Phase B for example, would contain the 'Done' column of the preceding sub process – Phase A – and the 'Doing' column of the current process, Phase B. The 'Done' column of Phase A is not under the Span of Control of Phase B. That is problematic as illustrated below.

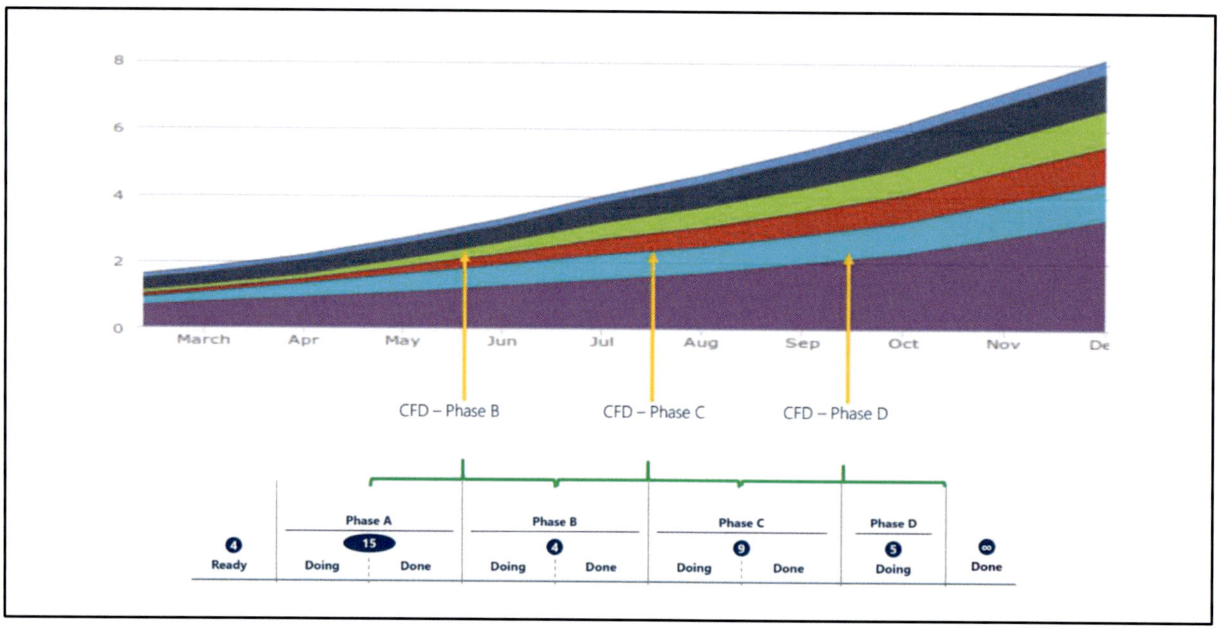

---

[51] There are many flavors of Kanban boards.

Flow efficiency calculations require that you have Span of Control. Flow efficiency also mandates tight coupling between 'Wait Time' and 'Touch Time'. Having the 'Doing' and 'Done' status cross over two phases is more reflective of a 'loosely' coupled situation.

Let us see what a Flow Efficiency board looks like, respecting the process illustrated above. It has the same functionality as a traditional Kanban board.

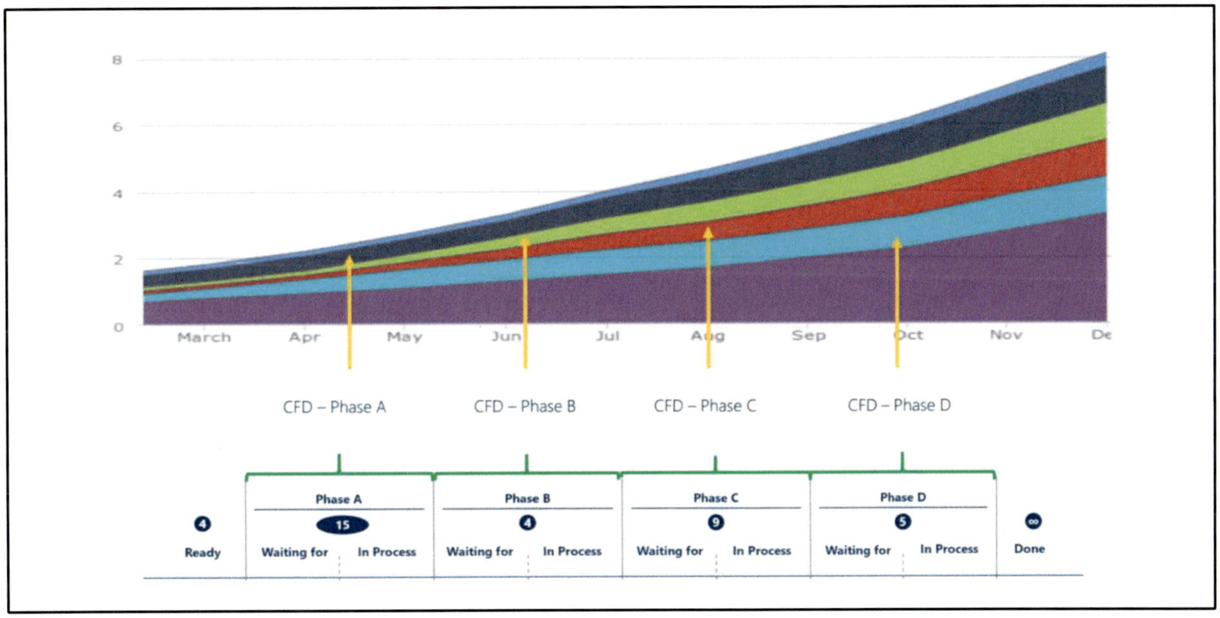

The change in instrumentation is not trivial. It makes 'Wait Time[52]' explicit at the entry point of a sub process, is very precise in tallying the time spent waiting, and engages workers emotionally. Workers understand that work items in the 'Waiting For' semi column accumulate pure wait time. It is under the team's control. Forces will demand that work items be moved as soon as possible to the 'In Process' state. But overcrowding at that location will soon produce a lot of wait time due to high WIP while you are in a 'Touch Time' state in the 'In Process' semi-column. This is not a desirable state.

Arbitrage is now under the Span of Control of the team. This is only going to help Flow Efficiency.

There is a potent tool inserted in this instrumentation: Queuing Theory! In a traditional Kanban board, the wait state (the Done semi column) is in a passive state.

On a Flow Efficiency board, when the wait state is upon entry, you have an active queue to manage! This is powerful. Both queues – Waiting For & In Process – require engagement from workers to manage 'Wait Time' and 'Touch Time'. The 'Done' queue on Kanban boards has no stressors and begs the question: 'who owns this queue and who manages it'?

---

[52] There will always be a fair amount of 'Wait Time' when you are 'In Process'. That cannot be avoided in Knowledge-Work. But by being aware that reducing WIP is under the team's control, the team can improve Flow Efficiency without any form of enhanced calculations.

Constraints and bottlenecks in the manufacturing world are visible and easily identifiable. The same is true in Knowledge-Work so long as you have the proper board instrumentation for actionable visualisation.

6) Transposing a Kanban Board to a Flow Efficiency Board for Wait Time and Touch Time

Doing the transposition from a traditional Kanban board to a Flow Efficiency board is a straightforward process, especially if you use the illustrations below as a step-by-step guide. I make only one recommendation regarding the 'Ready'[53] state: in this upstream activity, make sure that you are 'ready' to go all the way downstream. Why?

Well, this is one of the better ways to manage dependencies that are often of a speculative nature. Some approaches have you draw all of the possible dependencies that can happen in a release using strings and pins. They are all listed as if they happen at the same time in a parallel universe[54]!

This way of thinking is a flawed mental model. Dependencies are not parallel, and depicting them in a 'cumulative' fashion at a point in time before starting work is not reflective of reality. Dependencies grow through time, sequentially. Not all at once, in parallel.

By doing your homework upstream, and being really 'ready' before you start, you can eliminate dependencies downstream!

The steps to migrate from a Kanban board to a Flow Efficiency board are as follows:

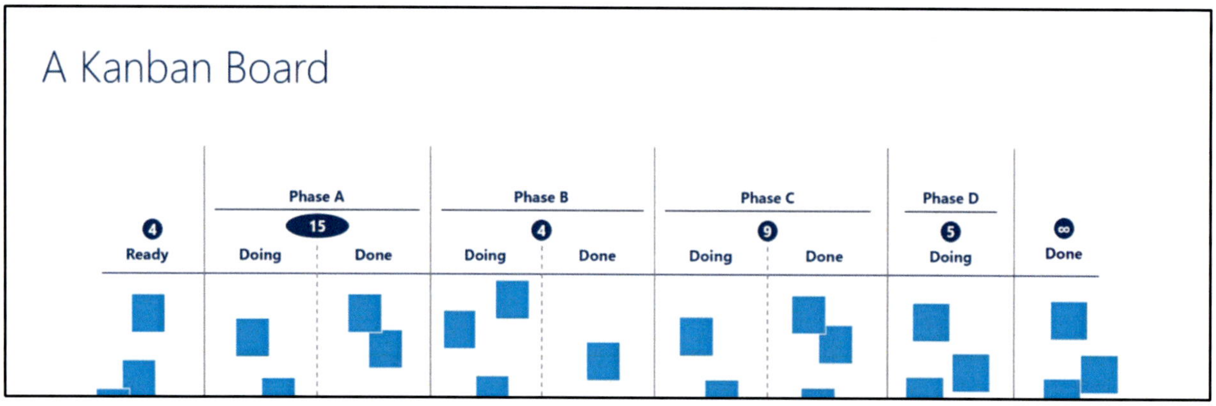

[53] This step is called Full Kitting in ToC parlance. It is a powerful simple step that should always be done!

[54] By parallel universe I mean one where things all happen at the same time for the sake of better planning. This is speculative work.

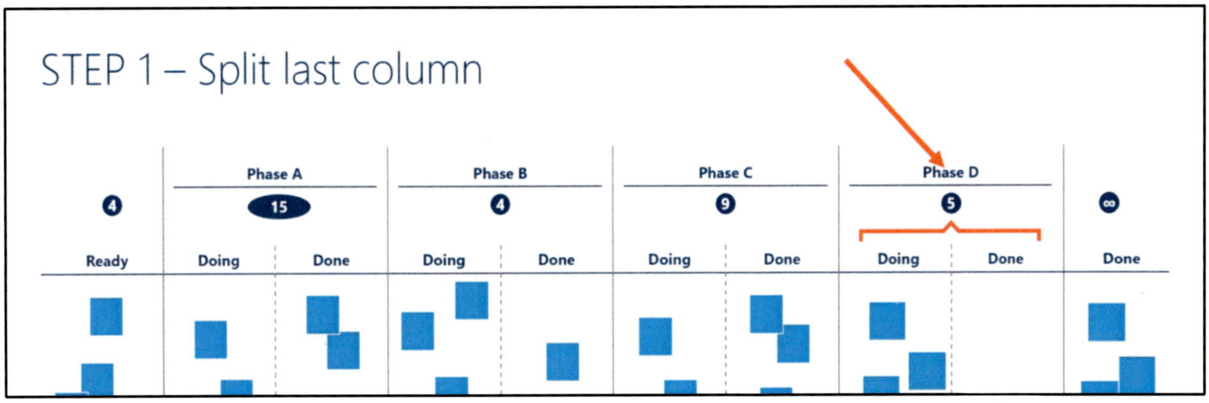
STEP 1 – Split last column
Phase A
Phase B
Phase C
Phase D
4
15
4
9
5
∞
Ready
Doing
Done
Doing
Done
Doing
Done
Doing
Done
Done

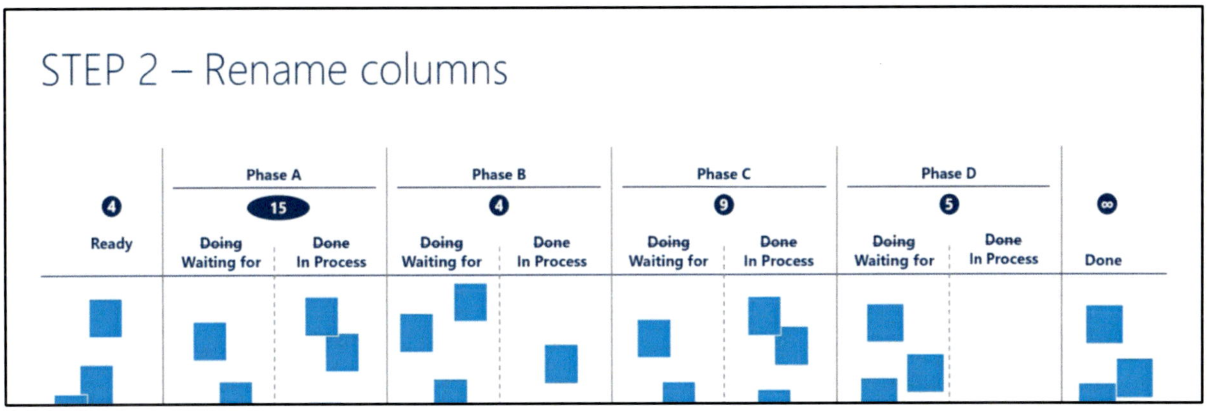
STEP 2 – Rename columns
Phase A
Phase B
Phase C
Phase D
4
15
4
9
5
∞
Ready
~~Doing~~ Waiting for
~~Done~~ In Process
~~Doing~~ Waiting for
~~Done~~ In Process
~~Doing~~ Waiting for
~~Done~~ In Process
~~Doing~~ Waiting for
~~Done~~ In Process
Done

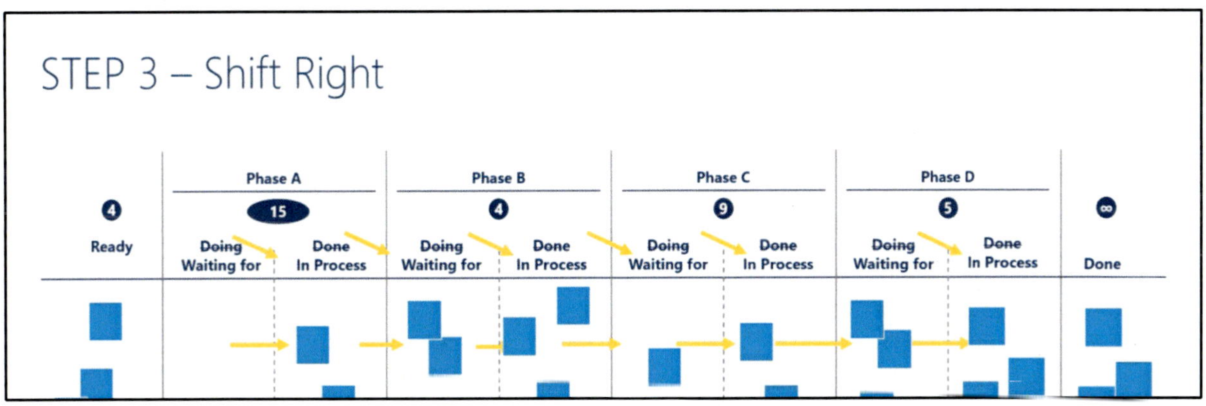
STEP 3 – Shift Right
Phase A
Phase B
Phase C
Phase D
4
15
4
9
5
∞
Ready
~~Doing~~ Waiting for
~~Done~~ In Process
~~Doing~~ Waiting for
~~Done~~ In Process
~~Doing~~ Waiting for
~~Done~~ In Process
~~Doing~~ Waiting for
~~Done~~ In Process
Done

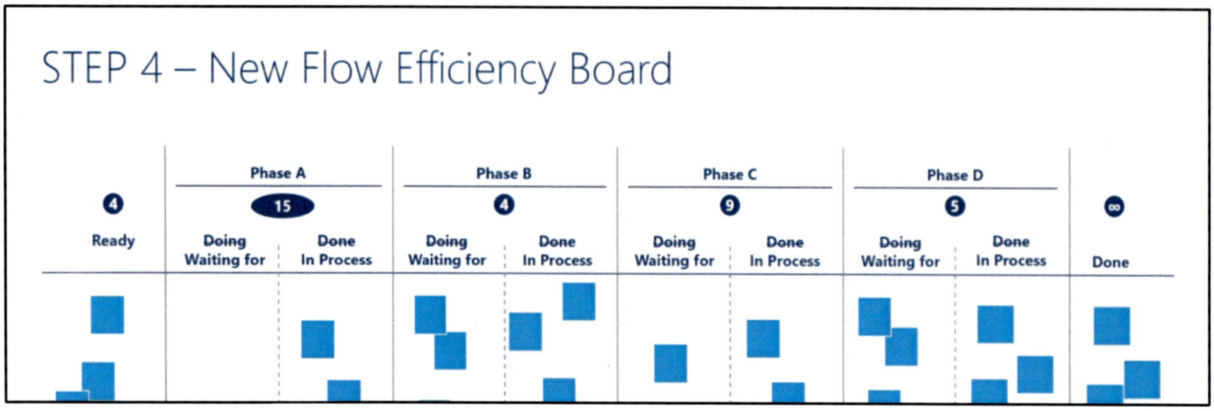

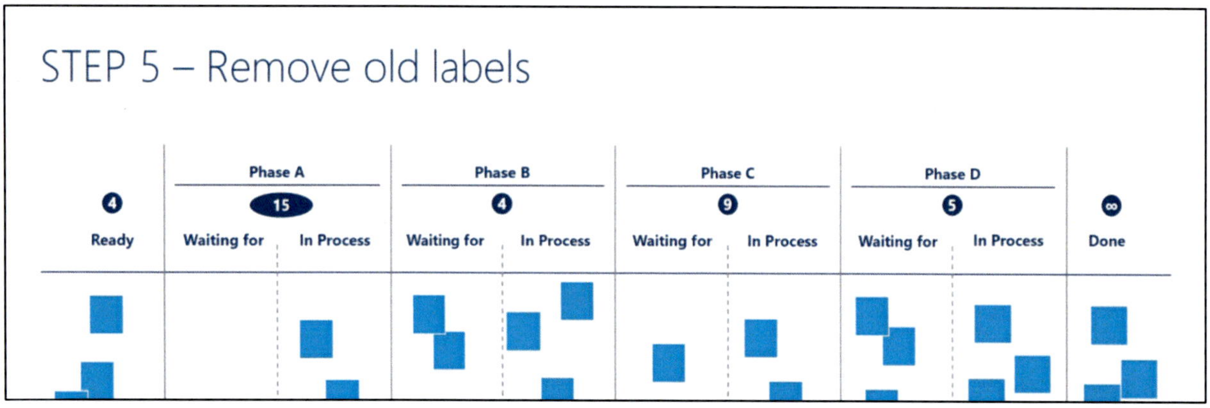

This state is good enough for you to start. However, if you are ramping up immediately with Flow Efficiency boards, you should do without column WIP limits as illustrated below:

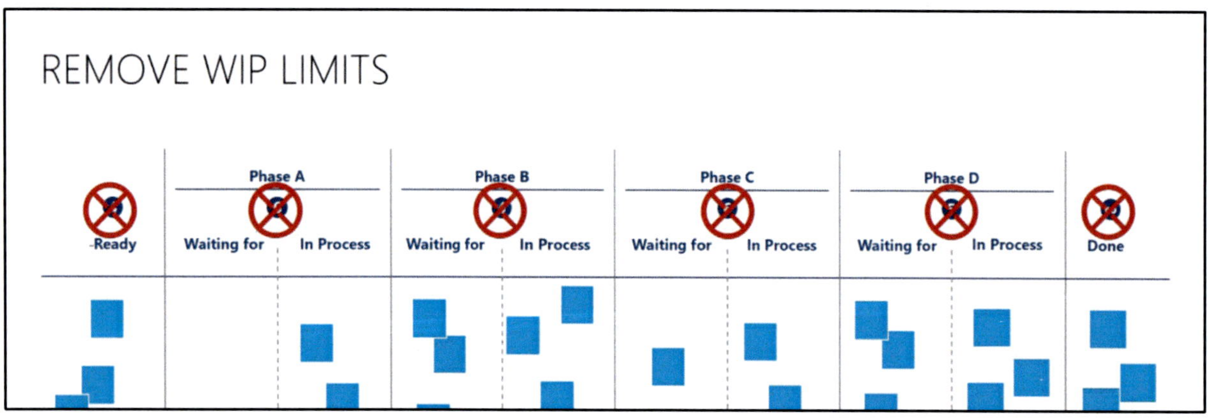

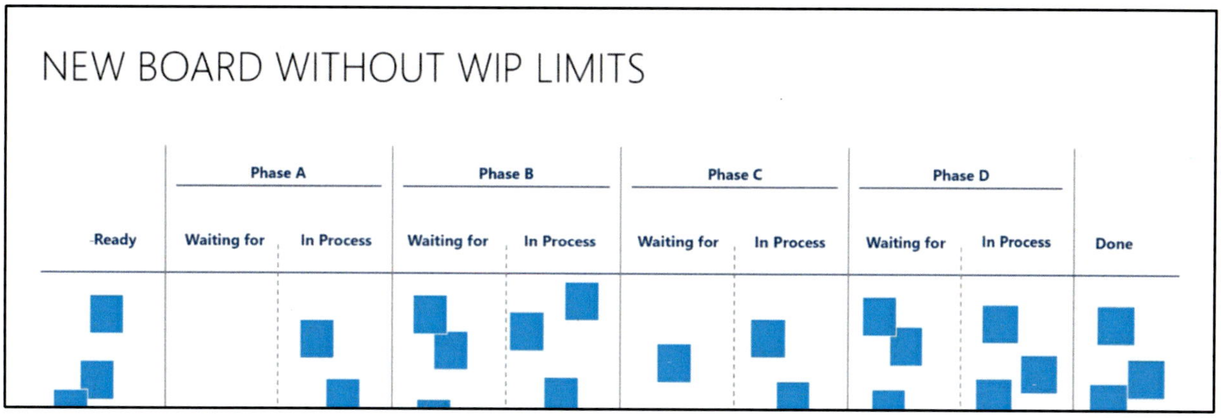

Column WIP limits distort the natural shape of the queues from the Work Load distribution that transit through your Work Process. Additionally, they hide the constraint in the Work Process. Without knowing where the constraint in your Work Process is, it will be impossible to optimize Operational Throughput (production) with the expected ripple effects on Financial Throughput (cash).

Flow Efficiency boards can support identification of the constraint in the Work Process. This is a topic that we will address in a subsequent chapter when dealing with the management of the three constraints of Knowledge-Work: Work Flow, Work Process and Work Execution.

7) Push vs Pull & Wait Time and Touch Time

Many times, I am confronted by the assertion that Flow Efficiency boards are adhering to a 'push' paradigm while Kanban boards are truly 'pull' boards. Nothing could be further from the truth!

In this section, we will encounter for the first time the notion of Common Cause Variation. Those are common and recurring events. They will most likely reveal themselves in your processes, in the way you do things. A count of these occurrences is a sure bet to ascertain their being Common Cause.

Special Cause Variation are those that you can identify and point to easily and most likely reside outside your process. They are not likely to occur regularly.

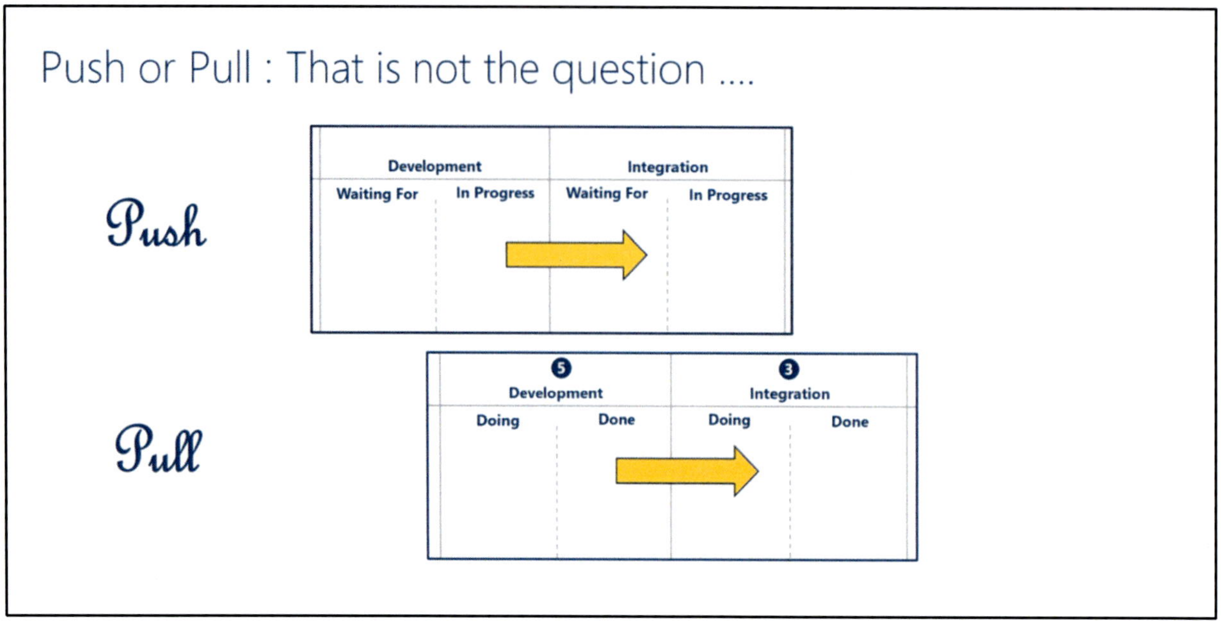

The above illustration from Ian Carroll speaks volumes as it basically aligns the 'Touch Time' semi column – In Progress & Doing - on top of one another. But it is flawed in its conclusion as follows:

1. In a Theory of Constraints paradigm in the manufacturing world, Dr Lisa Lang[55] makes the following observations:
    a. In manufacturing, Kanban is a don't Push system. If the Kanban is full, no one is allowed in. *Space is the buffer.*
    b. In manufacturing, DBR scheduling enables Pull systems. Once the constraint processes a ticket, a new one can come in. *Time is the buffer.*
2. According to DBR – Drum Buffer Rope – one can only pull from the constraint after a signal has been emitted from the constraint. Anywhere else does not make sense according to Dr Lisa Lang. Having 'buffers' with column WIP limits at every process gate resembles JIT – Just in Time - systems where buffers are encountered at the entry point of every phase. These systems are very fragile and kill flow. When a problem occurs, the entire chain is impacted, and Special Cause Variation signals spiral out of control. DBR does not need those 'speed bump'. Problems at the constraint are reflective of Common Cause Variation. The flow from upstream of the constraint is based on *time*, not inventory. If a phase starves upstream and the constraint buffer is in a green state, there is no cause for concern. In a JIT system, that would trigger a chain reaction and be problematic in Knowledge-Work.
3. Finally, pull systems work only when WIP is reduced to a minimum. Good use of Little's Law in Knowledge-Work recommends work must progress on a 'first come, first serve' basis and that the delivery and demand lines be parallel and as close as possible to one another, which reflects on the necessity for low WIP. Automating replenishment decisions is also imperative and made easier in a low WIP system. Having a lot in inventory – acceptable in Lean as it states that enabling flow at the expense of waste by adding WIP is tolerable – disables the precise need to keep minimal WIP and let flow have its way in an unobstructed manner to the constraint. (There are justifications for many 'parking spaces' in Kanban where you can add WIP at will and therefore increase 'Wait Time'.

[55] Dr. Lisa Lang is a renowned Theory of Constraints expert and the foremost authority in the world for applying TOC to marketing. She wrote the book on ToC Mafia offers.

Ghost columns, CCR[56] and NIA[57] bottlenecks, 'Ready for' buffers, etc.) So, the next time you see a loaded Kanban board, don't think of it as a pull system. Nor would it be able to reveal its constraint!

With the tools you already possess, migration of your boards to Flow Efficiency boards can be very easy.

The benefits will be immediate and team members will love the autonomy and the accountability it brings, while raising positive stressors that foster collaboration and cooperation.

8) Cost Accounting vs Throughput Accounting & Wait Time and Touch Time

Wait Time is what it is. But how do you deal with it? What is your perception of it? The more the better, like an asset, or the less the merrier, like a liability?

Wait Time means resource efficiency. In Cost Accounting, it creates excess inventory that is tallied as an asset.

In Throughput Accounting, Wait Time impacts throughput and lead time negatively. It is inventory piling up that is detrimental to operational excellence.

Next time you look at a board – any board – pay attention to the amount of work items, the number of columns, buffers, and swim lanes. If it seems too much, it probably is.

9) The 5 Focusing Steps Quagmire: Step 2 - Exploiting the constraint versus Step 3 - Subordinating to the constraint

Do you recall the Prologue about how professional athletes have to rewire their brain and act counterintuitively to the nature of their sports in order to succeed? Well, there is nothing harder for Knowledge Workers to discern what one's managerial reaction should be at or away from the constraint. They lie opposite to the spectrum all the time but we have tunnel vision: why should I act differently at or away from the constraint? Isn't management science ubiquitous to this?

Therein lies the secret of operational excellence paving the way to exponential returns!

Brain plasticity applies here.

[56] CCR – Capacity Constrained Resource

[57] NIA – Non-Instant Availability

All the actions that we ordinarily would take anywhere in a process are driven by our quest for local optima. This kind of behavior is perfectly suitable at the constraint, but poisonous elsewhere[58]!

Dubious? Well, I took the liberty of putting a test. It is inspired by one of Dr Kevlyn Youngman's work in an article in the References section titled: 'Exploitation and Subordination Reframed as Productivity and Utility'. The quiz is quite fun and educational. Sometimes, you may stand undecided at to which illustration belongs to EXPLOITATION of the constraint or SUBORDINATING to the constraint. The answer to each situation is a type of Boolean test. So, pick one of which you are certain of and the solution to the other illustration will reveal itself.

You can see the test in Appendix B of this chapter. The answers are at the end of the book. For a truly enjoyable experience, do the test before looking at the answers. You will be surprised at how hard it can be to get all the answers right!

For ease of understanding, I am giving the answer to a test where the Exploitation and Subordination contexts are given to you.

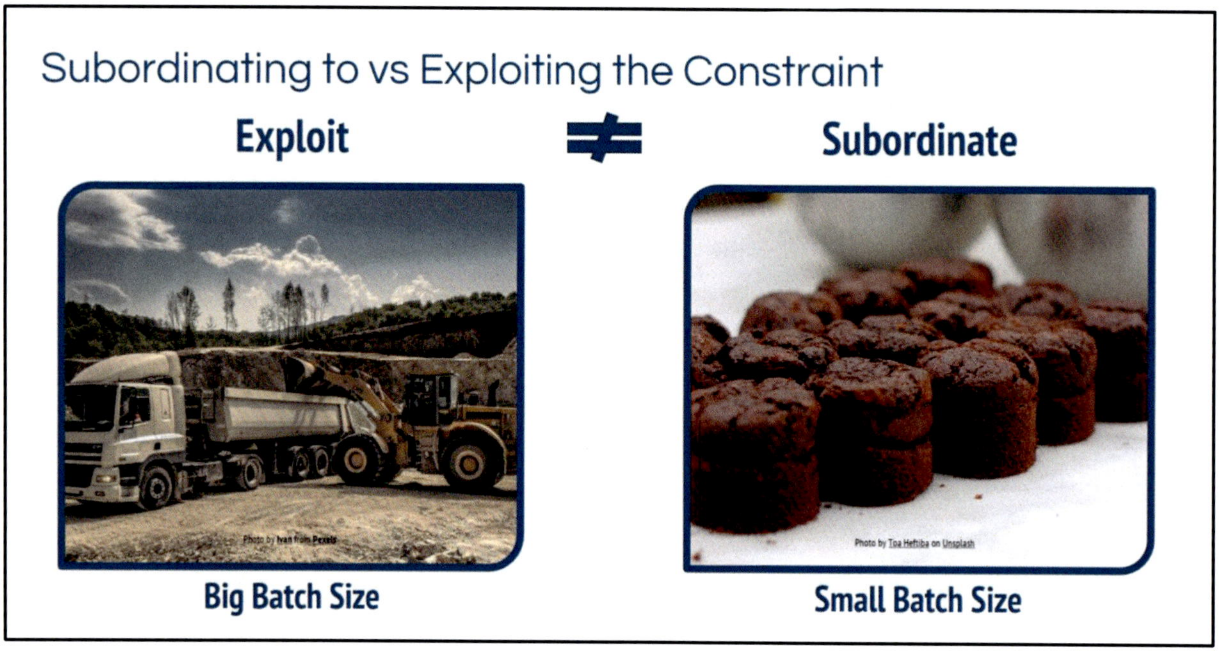

Conclusion – When you see a fork in the road, take it[59]

Making Work visible is a must. Making 'Wait Time' and 'Touch Time' explicit within a subprocess is key to enabling Improvement Initiatives. Using those two components in daily decision-making

[58] Not in all cases, but sometimes U Curve optimizations are ill suited away from the constraint. It is a very complex issue that could be entertained in an upcoming book.

[59] A famous quote from Yogi Berra

engages workers emotionally and serves as a great equalizer as to when work should progress: it is easily understood by all. It is a system.

Below are simple rules of thumb that you could use tomorrow:

HEURISTICS FOR IMPROVEMENT INITIATIVES[60]:

I. Limit Work in Process and Postpone Commitment (Delay Start of Work);
II. Reduce Wait Time for better Flow Efficiency;
III. Reduce Touch Time at the Constraint for enhanced Throughput.

At the origin – before the industry shaping Kanban method was baptized as such – David J Anderson wrote an important book on his original thoughts: *Agile Management for Software Engineering: Applying the Theory of Constraints for Business Results*.

A good part of the book dealt with **Throughput Accounting**.

As he progressed, he moved away from ToC – for some interesting reasons – and in doing so, regrettably left a lot of great ToC content on the table.

Today, many are being drawn back to the Theory of Constraints for Knowledge-Work. Still, very few embrace Throughput Accounting as the decision-making arm of the Theory of Constraints since it must be combined with a deep understanding of the 5 Focusing Steps.

This book on Throughput Accounting will help pave the way toward a better understanding of the benefits of TA at the project level as few IT initiatives really deliver what they intended to do in the first place.

In reality, we need to appreciate the strategic level as well. I think john Ricketts says it best in his book 'Reaching the Goal':

1. Theory of Constraints (TOC) supports all forms of strategic innovation;
2. Critical Chain Project Management for products, services, and marketing transformations;
3. Drum-Buffer-Rope and Replenishment to improve processes;
4. Throughput Accounting to change business models.

When you see a fork in the road, take it.

[60] The Theory of Constraints is an Improvement Initiative body of knowledge. It is the only one that focuses on the constraints of your system. Dealing with waste (Lean) and variation (Six Sigma) really makes sense when being constraint savvy.

APPENDIX A – POOL METAPHOR ANALOGY – LEAN vs TAICHII OHNO – TOYOTA PRODUCTION SYSTEMS

In section 4 of this chapter – The 5 Focusing Steps - we have illustrated the Lean pool metaphor. It states that reducing the water of level in a pool (WIP) really shows the dangers that lie beneath and that reducing WIP enables better flow.

Surprisingly, TPS – Toyota Production System - also has a pool analogy – it is more a container or bin receptacle analogy – and also must be reduced. The caveat is that the pool is always full!

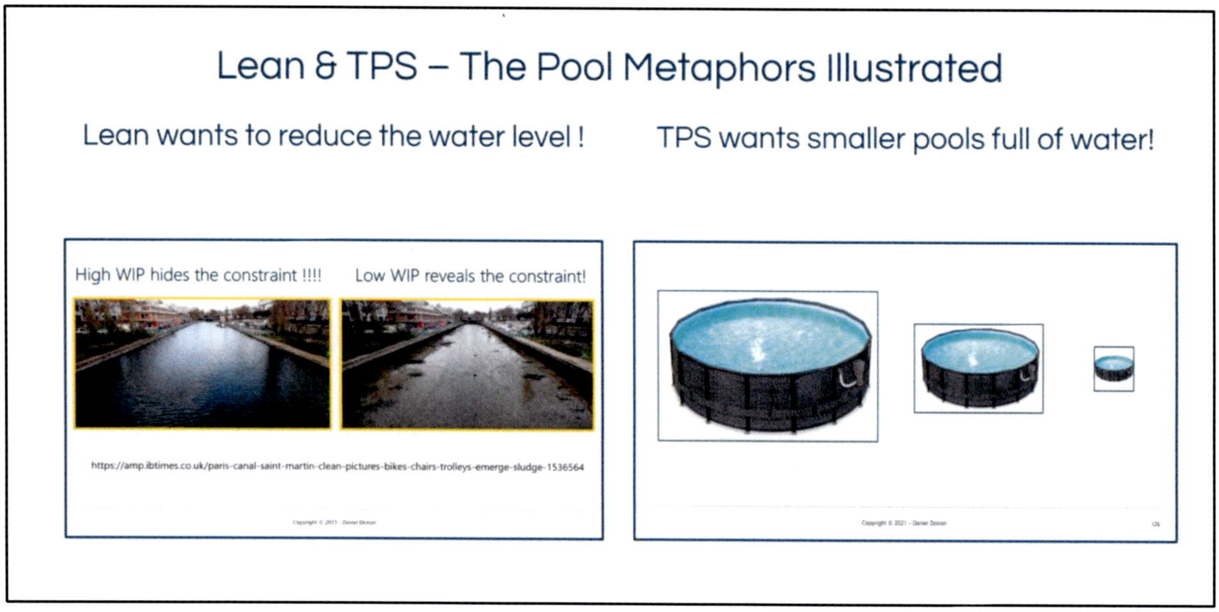

The reader can access Dr Eli Goldratt's article 'Standing on the shoulders of Giants' for a better grasp of Taiichi Ohno as a miniaturist.

APPENDIX B – QUIZ: EXPLOITING OR SUBORDINATING TO THE CONSTRAINT?

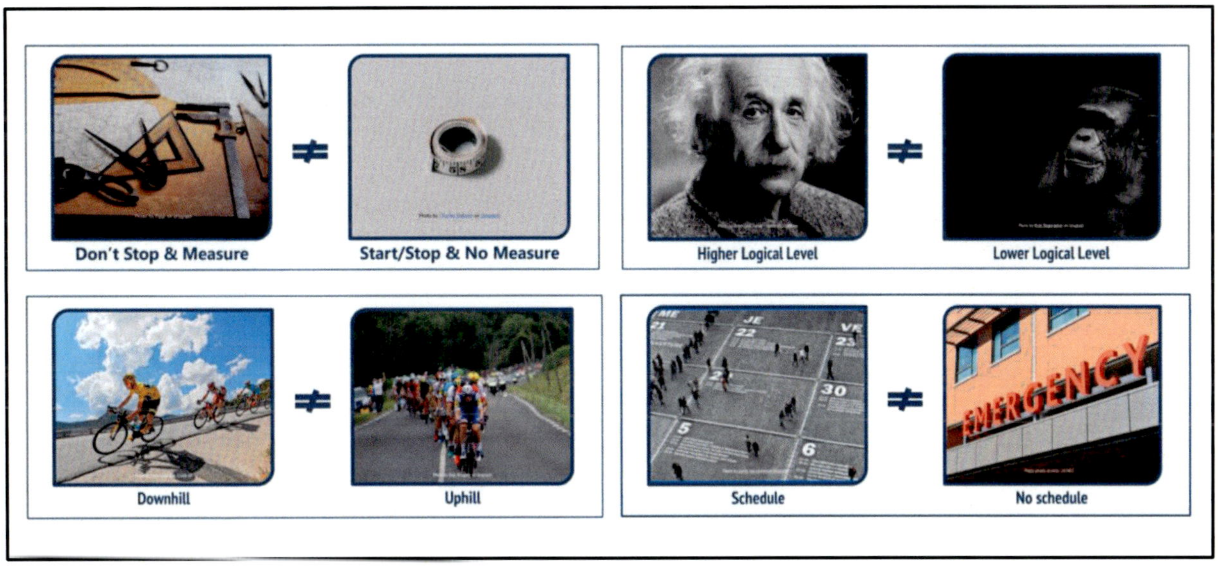

Setup Costs
No Setup Costs
Creating Capacity
Using Capacity
Happy Customers -
Utility
Making Money -
Productivity
Applies to one thing
Applies to everything else

CHAPTER III – MANAGING ON THE TIME AXIS

"Time does not fit, it flows" – Jim Benson

Introduction:

'The passage of time makes a mockery of all of our planning, estimating and forecasting efforts." There are few one-liners I can retrieve from the top of my head, but this quote - from Agenda Shift's Mike Burrows – has always stuck.

The other thing that is important to remember when it comes to time is that it is unidimensional and only goes in one direction: forward. While everybody knows this instinctively, we've only recently been able to prove it scientifically. And of all things, the second law of thermodynamics gives us the 'thermodynamic arrow' of time[61].

This relates to Throughput Accounting and Knowledge-Work in many ways. Managing can be done on two axes: the scope axis or the time axis. Agile – with timeboxing - manages on the scope axis. Dr Eli Goldratt liked to manage on the time axis, transposed in our context as a target scope that is agreed upon and the time required to do it can vary, up to a point of course! The DBR – Drum Buffer Rope – mechanism is filled with 'work' and a signaling apparatus so that the constraint does not starve. The buffer is calculated with material 'work' so that on the time axis, when the rope comes into play - signaling replenishment and limiting WIP - everything that is needed will be delivered on time so the constraint's drum can be maintained. A simple heuristic you can use for your first configuration of the buffer size is:

> If you need three days to process an item at the constraint and it takes nine days for the raw material to get there from upstream, you only need a buffer of three items in front of the constraint to support the traverse time to the buffer.[62]

This is a simple rule of thumb, but it beats the MIN/MAX inventory algorithm hands down. The illustration below will help with the math to give a 50% due time probability:

---

61 This short video from Brian Cox: https://www.youtube.com/watch?v=uQSoaiubuA0 is captivating.

62 The same logic would apply to Knowledge-Work!

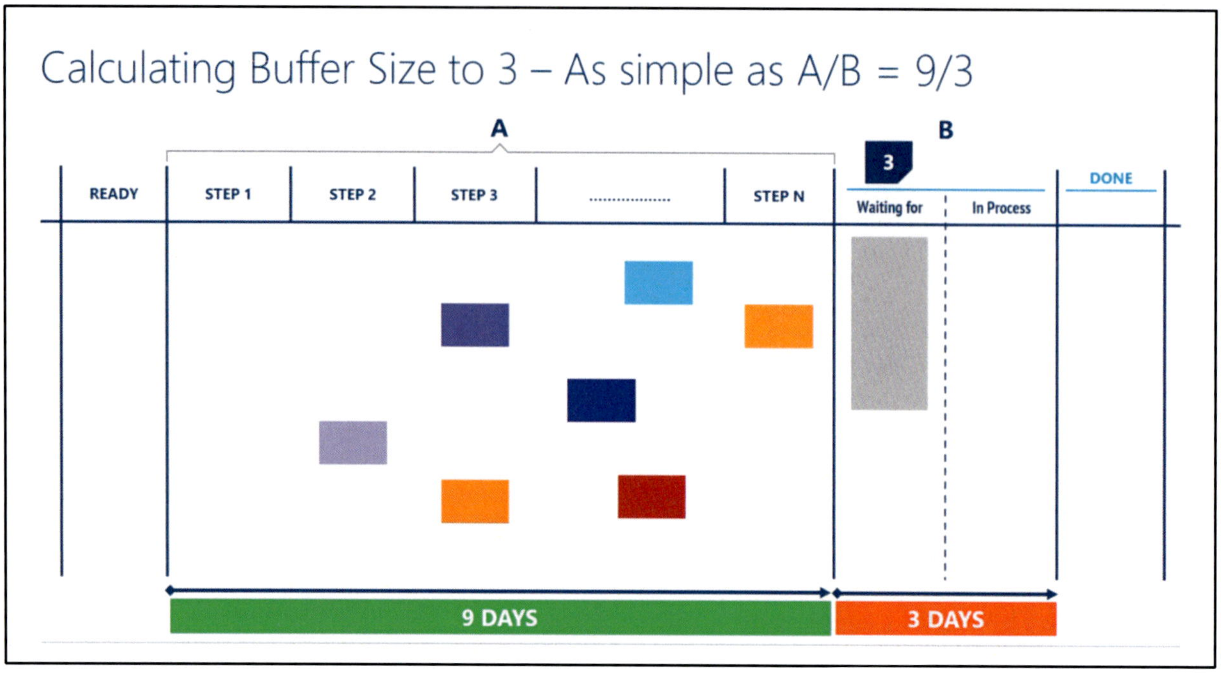

If you were to care for an 80%[63] due data probability – which would make more sense - you would need to increase the size of the buffer to 3*80/50 or 4.8. Rounding the number to 5 will give a better buffer. But there is nothing like experimentation. These rules are good as a heuristic to start. In the long run, these two mantras need to be repeated:

- If you do not get a DBR signal, something is wrong and you might need to decrease the buffer size;
- If you get too many DBR replenishment signals, something is wrong and you might need to increase the buffer size.

Contrary to the traditional column WIP limits – which we discard in a Flow Efficiency board – the DBR buffer does not hint at a maximum quantity but rather a minimal threshold level that serves as an advanced signal that the system is in danger of starving. We are of course talking about management by exception, where automated triggers gently warn us of potential risk materialization. Top management loves to know ahead of time.

Another use of the time axis within the Theory of Constraints is with the CCPM buffer in project management. There as well, time comes into play along with Little's Law. More on this later.

Let's narrow discussions of time down to the scope of this chapter, by examining these concepts as a continuation of the 5 Focusing Steps. We need to dig down and see how the three constraints in Knowledge-Work can be tamed[64]. The three constraints each have a name:

1. The Jungle: The arrival rate of the work that comes toward us, the business domain, **Work Flow**

[63] 75% in fact but it is close enough for 80%!

[64] These three constraints are fully described in my first book.

2. The Jeep: The way we work, the way we do things, **Work Process**
3. The Journey: The things that happen while driving the jeep in the jungle, **Work Execution**

Thus, understanding how to Identify, Exploit, Subordinate and Elevate each of the constraints listed above is part of the 5 Focusing Steps - **and fair game for Throughput Accounting** - as one cannot succeed with Throughput Accounting and having total disregard for the constraints of your systems. And for Knowledge-Work, we need to create visual artefacts to render visible that which is invisible at first sight.

Complexity, degrees of freedom and Inherent Simplicity

There exists a tendency in agile nowadays to get rid of all dependencies. All of them, everywhere, all of the time. So goes the algorithm and the saying.

Dr Eli Goldratt would not approve in all cases.

Let's explore this concept. Which system below is simpler?

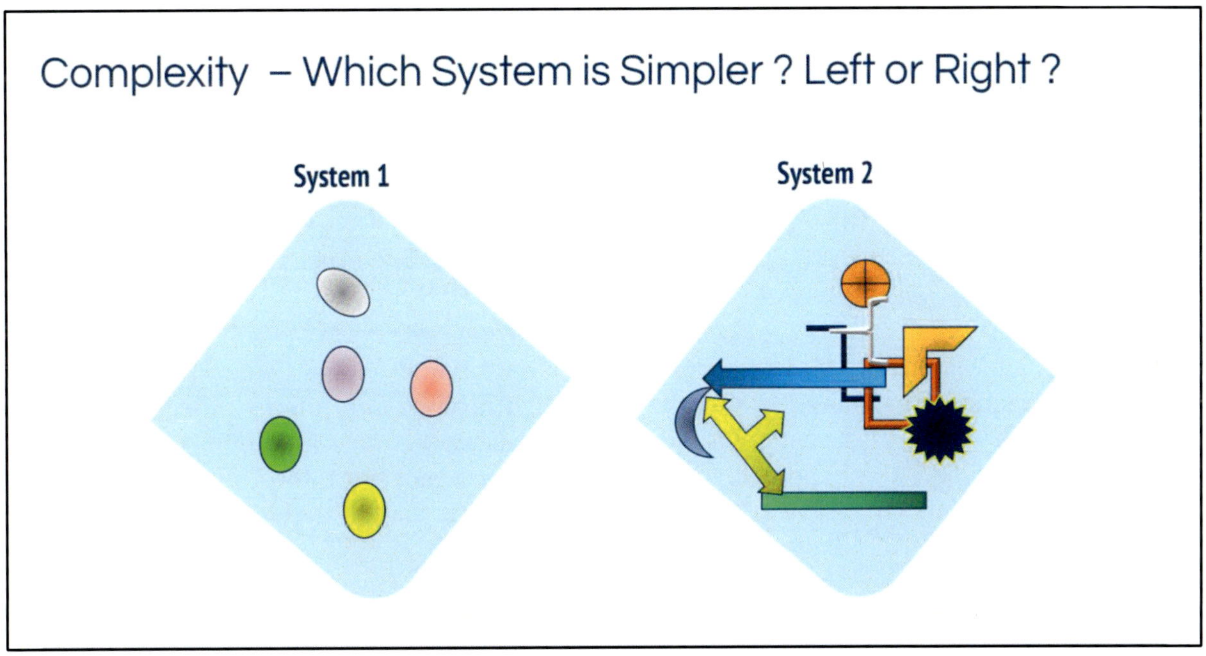

I always get a divided audience when I give this test. The answer is on the right. If you want to manage the system on the left – which is dependency free – then you must act at five different places. It has five degrees of freedom. If you want to impact the system on the right, you can touch it anywhere, once. It will have a ripple effect. That system has one degree of freedom and a lot of dependencies. What a gift!

The BLUF[65] here is that a lot of 'smart' undertakings deal with removing dependencies. They all have merits. My word of advice is to first be constraint-savvy. As you fix dependencies in the hope of improving, you are creating invisible and almost permanent layers of cost overheads. The lack of constraint awareness is the main cause of permanent increases in overhead costs created by Improvement Initiatives. Such is the nature of indirect costs. Do not let that happen. If you make an improvement, make it count on the Throughput of the system and act on the constraint.

If we take the same illustration, we can make a parallel between Cost Accounting and Throughput Accounting:

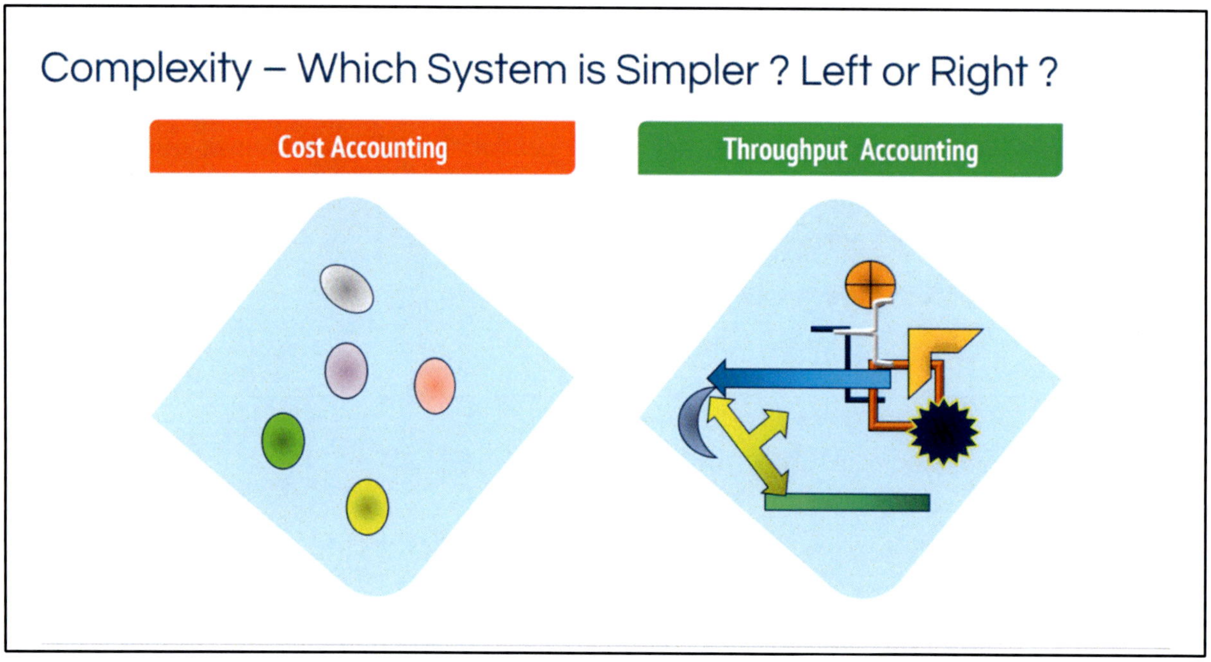

Cost Accounting systems *do not come cheap*[66]. They have tentacles that penetrate every function of the organization. Throughput Accounting is straightforward and can be understood by all once you grasp the marginal impact of each of your decisions on (T) – Throughput, (I) – Investments and (OE) – Operating Expenses. No need for data accuracy but rather relevancy of data. The choice between being **roughly right** or **precisely wrong** is a well-known idiom in the Theory of Constraints!

65 BLUF – Bottom Line Up Front

66 Oddly enough, this can be a reason why Cost Accounting systems are being used for managerial purposes. They are so expensive that management will find a way to leverage them! But they are not fit for decision-making purposes in a daily and operational context.

I could not finish this section without asking: how many degrees of freedom does time have? How many degrees of freedom does scope[67] have? What do you want to manage, the entire system or the constraint? How do you want to manage: through time or scope?

One last word on the much-misused topic of Inherent Simplicity. Inherent Simplicity is a concept that you understand at 3,000 feet in the air. It states that by pushing the right button at the right place, you can get stellar results at little cost. It is a discussion like the one we are having now regarding degrees of freedom and dependencies. You do not go to work every morning with the aim of changing the universe or architecting your environment toward 'Inherent Simplicity'. At times, keeping the constraint from moving – and especially subordinating to the constraint[68] – is not inherently simple and could require you to do some complicated things!

Let's also be fair to Cost & Financial Accounting. They belong to the world of experts. The amount of training required to perform in the world of complexity in the details in not negligeable. Contrariwise, Throughput Accounting's complexity is in causality. When you make a decision and act upon it, the result should be quick and directly connected to the action posed towards T, I and/or OE. Financial literacy is important. Trying to convey such knowledge with Throughput Accounting is the shortest path to enlightenment.

Degrees of freedom - Estimating vs Forecasting

Were we to apply the concept of degrees of freedom and Inherent Simplicity to the agile practice of planning, we would find two extremes: the scrum practice of estimating and the Kanban probabilistic forecasting mantra.

Recently, I think Scrum has backstepped a bit from estimating – or is it story points - and that is a move forward. Scrum with Kanban has embraced forecasting. Whoever is into estimating – with all the costs attached to it – is not really doing agile unless they are under very special circumstances like wading[69] thru waters that have never been tested before. Some people say that they have a new team, new this or new that, but always remember that after 5 observations, the median is revealing itself. A 50% level of confidence can still get you started in the right direction in no time with probabilistic forecasting.

The reason for being a fan of probabilistic forecasting follows. The metaphor of yesterday's weather is all you need to understand. Chances are that the performance of days just passed will be a good indicator of what you can accomplish today. Add to this thinking a bit of odds and a tentative due date, and in fact you have become a weather man and committed to something that is feasible let's say, 85% of the time. No more managerial duties and finger pointing are required.

---

67 I always like to illustrate the topic of degrees of freedom of scope with the Table of Content of a book. Things can go exponential and quadratic quite easily.

68 Smith, Debra. Page 92: 'Measuring subordination is difficult but is key to ToC success'. Page 80: 'Subordination is the basis for 90% of a company's activity'.

69 There are cases when estimating in a group brings social benefits such as commitment to a goal. Fair enough and handle with care. Repetition is not the mother of skills in this case and I would like to remind 'agile' at large that they are all in for empirical data but cannot make the link with probabilistic forecasting with their cycle time evidence and forego estimating altogether.

Once you are done, the empirical data of your last delivery enters the database for future probabilistic forecasting.

On the other hand, look at the chain of events associated with estimating, a process that can suck up to 40% of your budget. The Microsoft XIT case comes to mind![70]

When estimating, you need to gather and dig for information. The longer your estimates collect dust on the shelves, the more that work that you have just done – at estimating – will have to be rejuvenated with recent data as the basis for your analysis would likely change come approval or execution time. And the cost of context switching and immersion, should you redo your work or should someone else try to figure out what you did! And doing estimating is a team sport: you'll have to invite a lot of people.

Then – any half decent estimates – has to be created, presented, argued and S O L D to the client. But at least you get a formal plan, which is in contradiction with agile that plans are waste. But I digress. That is always good because after, you can add more costs to the recipe by looking into the variances from the plan. And it will occur. And variance analysis is counter productive and one of the biggest ailments of cost accounting[71].

In all estimating scenarios, the customer will say, or think:

- You can't estimate properly and you make me waste my time by always being late and charging me more[72] or;
- You are padding so much that you will always deliver sooner than anticipated and you make me waste my time and my money.

The complexity and managerial scrutiny required to support estimating will get the degrees of freedom through the roof. The degrees of freedom with forecasting are well beneath that of estimating.

Kanban does a lot of things right. First starting from where you are and not selling you the red tape and rituals that comes with everything agile to make you think you are doing – or scaling – agile. It is truly designed to get you going, to 'do' agile. Doing more of 'it', more collaborating, more pairing is the way to 'do' and scale agile properly. Not with canned approaches.

To that effect, Jeff Anderson published a book dedicated to scaling agile the smart way with years of on the field experience in the big Toronto banking market. I implore you to read it before trying anything remotely linked to scaling. It is listed in the References section at the end of the book.

Span of Control and Sphere of Influence

[70] The famous case of XIT at Microsoft by Dragos Dumitriu is legendary.

[71] One can think of the purchasing manager getting a good deal on low quality material that will be pushed to operations. Purchasing gets a stellar purchase variance while operations are the ones paying for that great variance.

[72] Estimating and doing the work is often done with Operating Expenses but you can also tax the constraint if you invite workers that are essential at minding the constraint. At which time you are losing sales.

Here are the definitions of both terms in a Knowledge-Work context:

> Span of Control ...
>
> ... is the part of reality over which we have control to change things. Impacting the delivery line with additional Investments is within our Span of Control. We can have it our way here without asking for permission!
>
> Sphere of Influence ...
>
> ... consists of the domains where we have a say. For example, it is here that we can help shape demand, defer commitment, and exercise our options through coordination.

There is a purpose to understanding the nuances. When faced with increasing demand, our first reflex is to add capacity. It lies within our Span of Control!

But the key to reacting to a surge in demand is to postpone commitment, reduce WIP and exercise our options. We are within the realm of our Sphere of Influence and this is where we should intervene. Increasing capacity by buying capacity – within our span of control – should always be the last resort in Throughput Accounting. Always. No matter what. And especially at the constraint! There are ways to increase capacity with existing assets and/or operating expenses[73].

The reason is obvious since (I) – Investments are the denominator of the ROI – Return on Investment metric. It has a leverage effect as per the formula below:

ROI = ((T) - Throughput – (OE) - Operating Expenses) / (I) – Investments

For each of the three constraints, understanding the power of our Span of Control and how to navigate within our Sphere of Influence will be examined.

Collaboration occurs within one's Span of Control or, for example, when this area is shared between teams. Coordination is strictly a matter of Sphere of Influence. Collaboration and coordination with existing (I)- Investments and OE - Operating Expenses is the preferred way to both Exploit the constraint and Subordinate to the constraint, and sometimes the preferred conduit to Elevate sprint capacity in order to better Exploit the constraint.

Purchase of capacity as a first resort should always be toned down by going through this ritual:

1) What to do next? Use selection and prioritization;
2) When to start? Postpone commitment and limit WIP.

Common and Special Cause Variation

[73] Maintenance work on the constraint must be well planned, Quality inspection upon entering the constraint is a must, so is increasing Sprint Capacity (capacity upstream of the constraint) with existing Investments and Operating Expenses, increasing buffer size, T Shape resources, etc.

I don't often get the chance to squeeze in Lucas's critique[74] in my day to day live, but this section is right on the money.

The saying goes in Agile that we evolve in complexity. For the Business Domain this is absolutely true, and Special Cause Variation can be expected. And it applies as well when we are executing our projects as Mr. Murphy is always around the corner. But at execution time, we have systems (CCPM) that can help us tame Common Cause at that level. The color YELLOW is the preferred color to indicate Common Cause. The color RED is reserved for Special Cause.

But for the way we work, the tools we use, the processes we follow, the channels we borrow to communicate with teams with whom we collaborate and cooperate every day: no. There is no complexity here.

There are not a lot of studies and papers dealing with Common Cause Variation in Agile, nor in Kanban for that matter. (The only one to address this topic head on is Donald Reinertsen, whom we will visit in the last and penultimate chapters of the book.)

For this, you need to exploit the Constraint in your Work Process. If a hiccup shows up at the constraint, you are likely to be dealing with systemic issues. This is where the easy money is made. We are talking *big* and *easy* money. Exploiting the constraint in the Work Process is where the goose with the golden egg lives. And it comes at no monetary cost.

No one else in Knowledge-Work renders this better than Donald Reinertsen:

> "In Knowledge-Work, Common Causes have a greater impact than in manufacturing. Therefore, Common Causes should be taken into consideration, especially for finding improvement opportunities."

There is a subtlety that is often ignored from Lean manufacturing with Common Cause Variation and this clause of 'no concern' has been imported into agile. In Lean manufacturing, Common Cause is not a bother[75]. Doing cars serially for years will only have you react on Special Cause – as you pull the ANDON cord!

In Knowledge-Work, the tables are turned: Common Cause will happen assuredly and must be addressed. When Special Cause Variation is observed, it is better to fix it if necessary or let it pass and move on, contrary to Lean manufacturing[76]. But we have fallen into the trap of Lean manufacturing when importing Lean concepts into agile. We must be made aware of this and stop reacting to Special Cause Variation as they do in manufacturing. Being enslaved to the busting of column WIP limits is reacting to Special Cause Variation (flow issues) thinking that it is Common Cause Variation. It is a major cause of tampering with the system.

---

[74] Lucas's critique (1976), states that we often import and apply models out of context. Such is the case with the merits of Common Cause and Special Cause that are totally inverted in their significance from the world of Lean manufacturing to the arena of Knowledge-Work. Lucas pointed out at the time that transposing macroeconomics models to the economics of the firm (micro-economics) was nonsensical. He had to prove it. And he did. With data.

[75] In all fairness, Deming would address common cause when he built a new system. Once humming, he would only react to special cause.

[76] Tallying problem occurrences with the amount of work days lost to fix those that have the biggest impact is an ani-pattern if it does not help the constraint.

When the constraint starves, it is most probably a system issue due to Common Cause Variation. Why? Because we have a system built around that to prevent this from happening! When this occurs, we must act!

Sometimes, it is nearly impossible to distinguish Special Cause[77] from Common Cause[78] in Knowledge-Work. For this reason, many have not bothered to dig further to address this topic.

It would be selling Dr Goldratt short for not coming up with the remedial tools. The Theory of Constraints comes fully equipped to properly classify - in a scientific way - Common and Special Cause with the use of system generated signals, a reason log, frequency analysis, pareto analysis ... and common sense.

The Jungle - Constraint in the Work Flow – The Work that Comes Toward Us

This constraint lies upstream. It is the business domain. Slack that you have everywhere on the value stream can always be repurposed here to help support innovation! It deals with the arrival rate and load distribution of work that is unevenly spread among teams, products, and projects. If you need a meeting to sort things out, have one. Not enough, have ten. Social and human interactions must prevail to tame the 'fuzzy front end'. You should always have SPRINT capacity with plenty of SLACK to support INNOVATION.

One nice way to identify the constraint in the Work Flow with 25 teams is to examine the length of their respective backlogs in man-days efforts. If team B has the longest backlog – based on time to finish the backlog – then that team is the constraint in the Work Flow. This is discrete data that you can transpose to a histogram easily.

Remember the phase of subordination? If you want to properly exploit that team, all the other teams could experience idleness. Slack and idleness are always observable in high-performing organizations. If this is not in line with the way you manage, then a lot of perishable inventory will find its way in terms of stacks of analysis, piles of architectures, outdated designs or untested code that will decay with the passage of time.

Members of teams that are not from the constraint in the Work Flow could literally go fishing. It would not make a difference on Throughput or Operating Expenses. But when they are needed ... they must be sharp. Extra capacity upstream of the constraint is also called 'Sprint' capacity.

Once a team is the constraint in the Work Flow, it must manage its constraint in its Work Process with a DBR board. The other teams can use a simple Flow Efficiency board as discussed in a previous chapter. The change in instrumentation from a DBR to/from a Flow Efficiency board is trivial.

---

[77] Some prefer the term 'assignable cause' - something that you can point to.

[78] Some prefer the term 'chance cause' - something that is endemic or systemic to a process and can be linked to one root cause

The below array depicts how to deal with Constraints in the Work Flow:

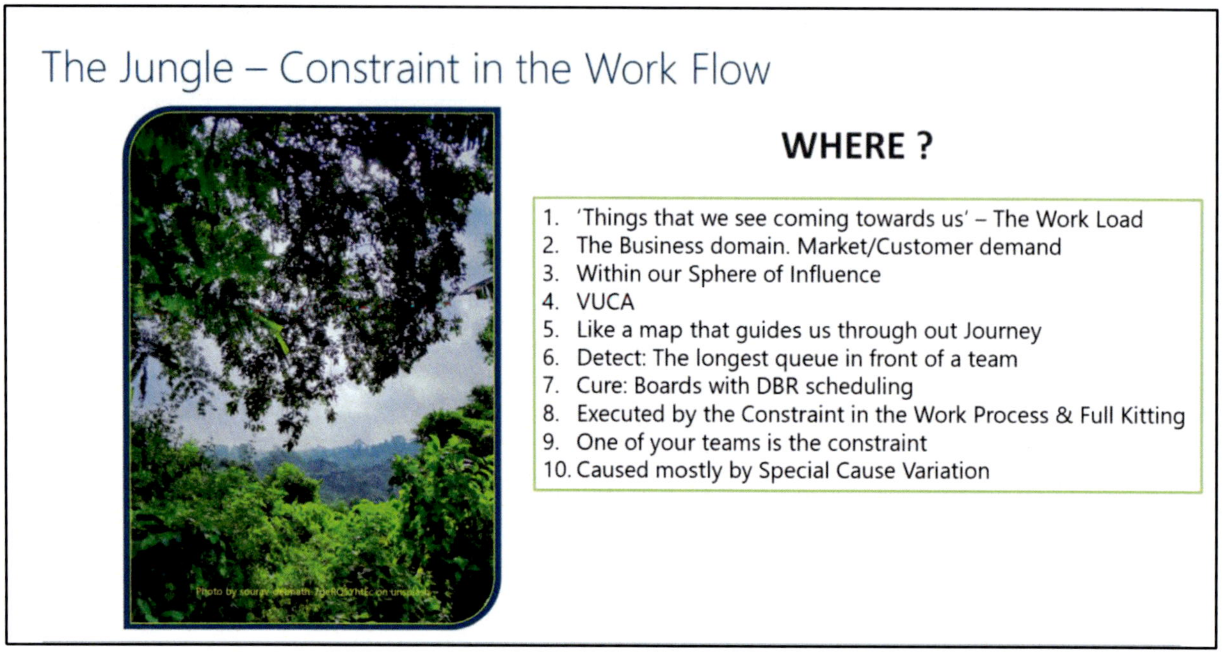

When teams come to you for extra budgets, investments or resources saying that they could go much faster with this or that, just remember, only one team – or some teams upstream of the constraints to enhance sprint capacity - may have a justified need for help. For teams downstream, this is seldom the case unless the constraint could shift as a result or due-date performance is at stake or that lead time could be hastened!

The Jeep – Constraint in the Work Process – The Way We Work

We have covered Flow Efficiency boards in a preceding chapter. We will leverage its use, first to help us discover the Constraint in the Work Process, next to discuss how to exploit that constraint by adding the DBR Buffer to replace the 'Waiting For' queue of the constraining process.

If I were to take a sample Flow Efficiency board, the process with the longest flow time is the constraint in the Work Process as it undoubtedly has the least amount of capacity. Why? Because tickets passing through this specific phase spend more time there than anywhere else.

Let's look at this illustration:

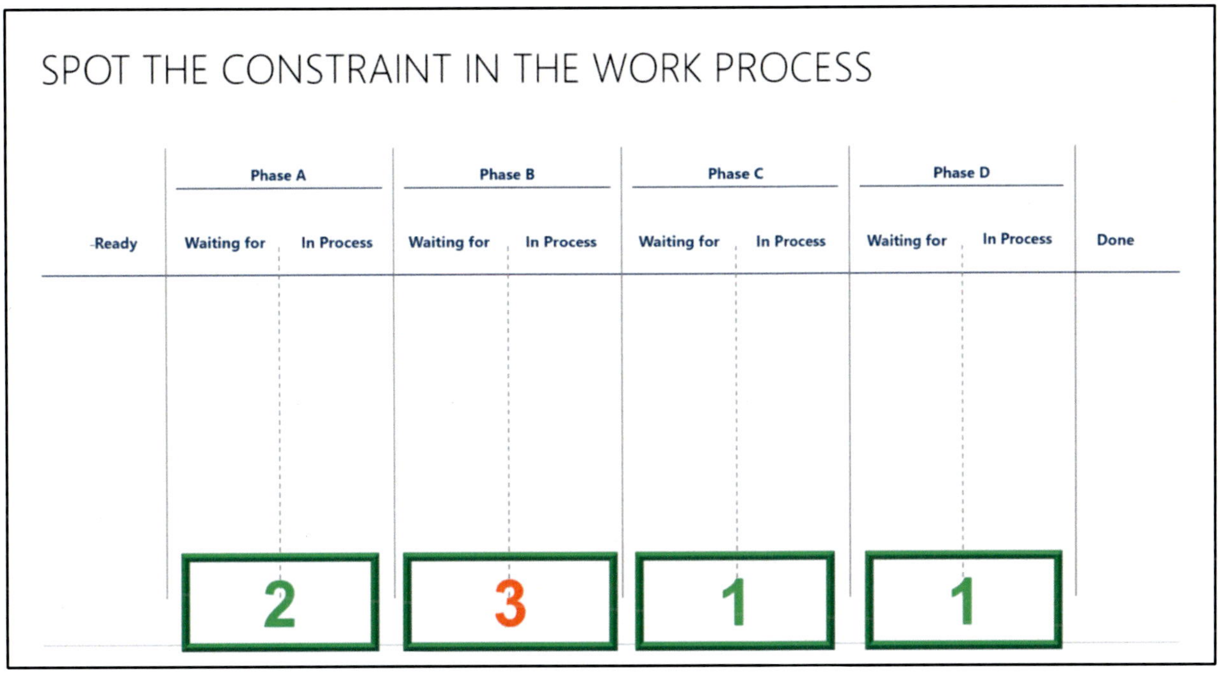

We can see that a ticket spends on average two days in Phase A, three in Phase B and one day in each of Phase C and D.

The constraint in the Work Process lies at Phase B, where the system has the lowest capacity. Let's look at this from a different angle with the three types of capacity we have visited before:

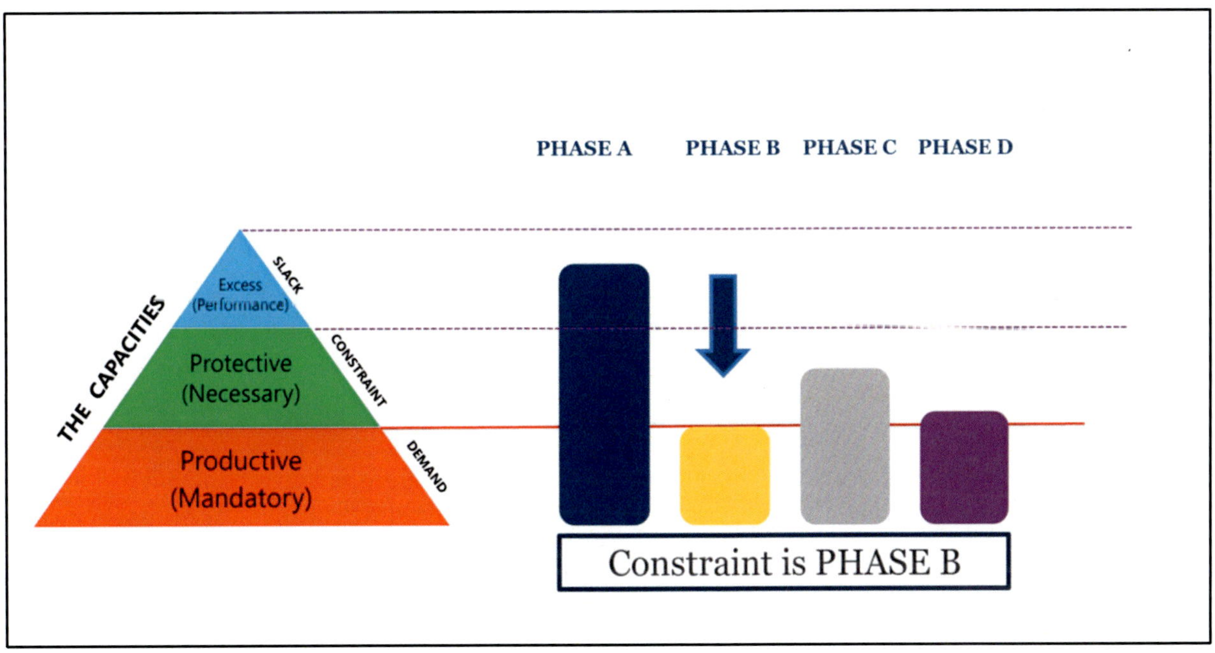

The hidden treasure of WIP ageing to find the Constraint in the Work Process

Explaining this concept is best achieved with the use of similarities and analogies. No matter who I ask, the WIP Ageing chart is the favorite visual artefact of most Kanban practitioners and I assume that you are accustomed with it.

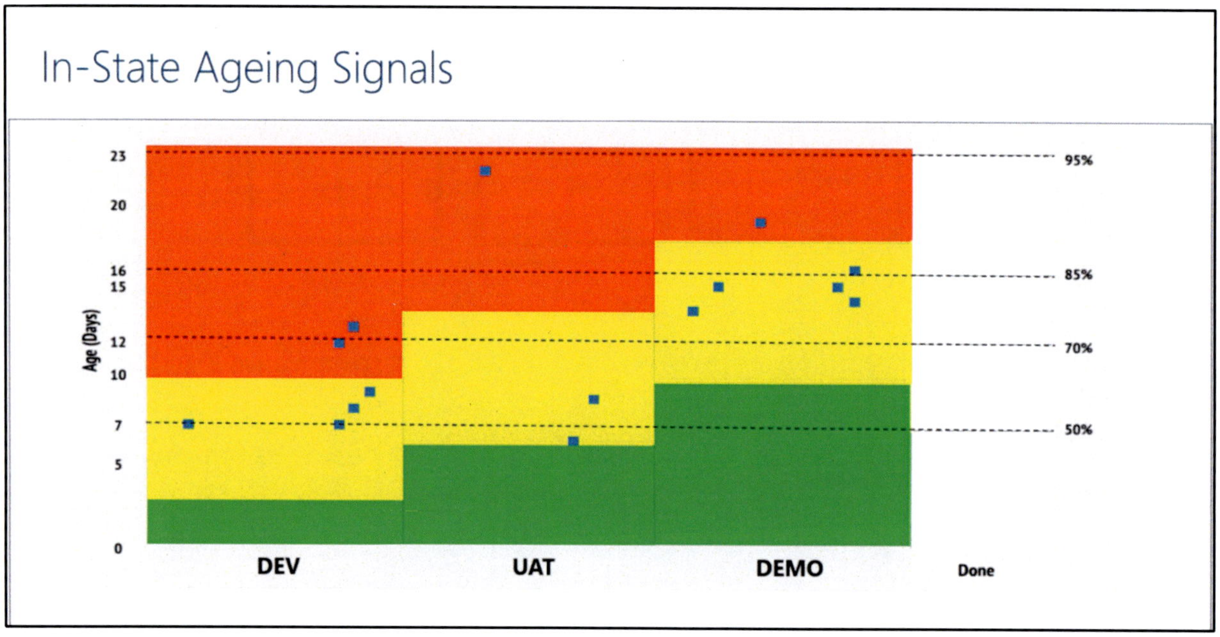

We are all familiar with the Y axis as this is the main use we make of this powerful tool. But what about the X axis? It too can be transposed in terms of days for each of the DEV, UAT and DEMO processes!

Remember the point of managing on the time axis? If it works for the ageing of work items (Y axis), it works for the time spent while in each of the three processes (X axis)!

With the same tool, and by adjusting the parameters, it is easy to extract this data. It allows us to identify the constraint in the Work Process effortlessly. Remember that the team that is the constraint in the Work Flow must manage its constraint in the Work Process. This is important to grasp. The other teams need not worry about optimizing their Work Process. It's key to understand this point, as we do not want to spend money and get nowhere faster by optimizing non-constraint teams. We do not care about their performance, nor should we measure or manage them!

WIP Ageing signals are also leading indicators of risk materialization and enter the perimeter of management by exception. At some point, a WIP ageing signal could very well rippled down all the way to the CCPM buffer penetration level! A topic that we will address soon in this chapter while at the execution of a plan level.

The DBR Buffer

With this information at hand, and having identified the constraint, we can now instrument with the DBR buffer as illustrated below by assuming this time that the proper buffer sizing is three tickets after having experimented and tweaked the system in an operational setting:

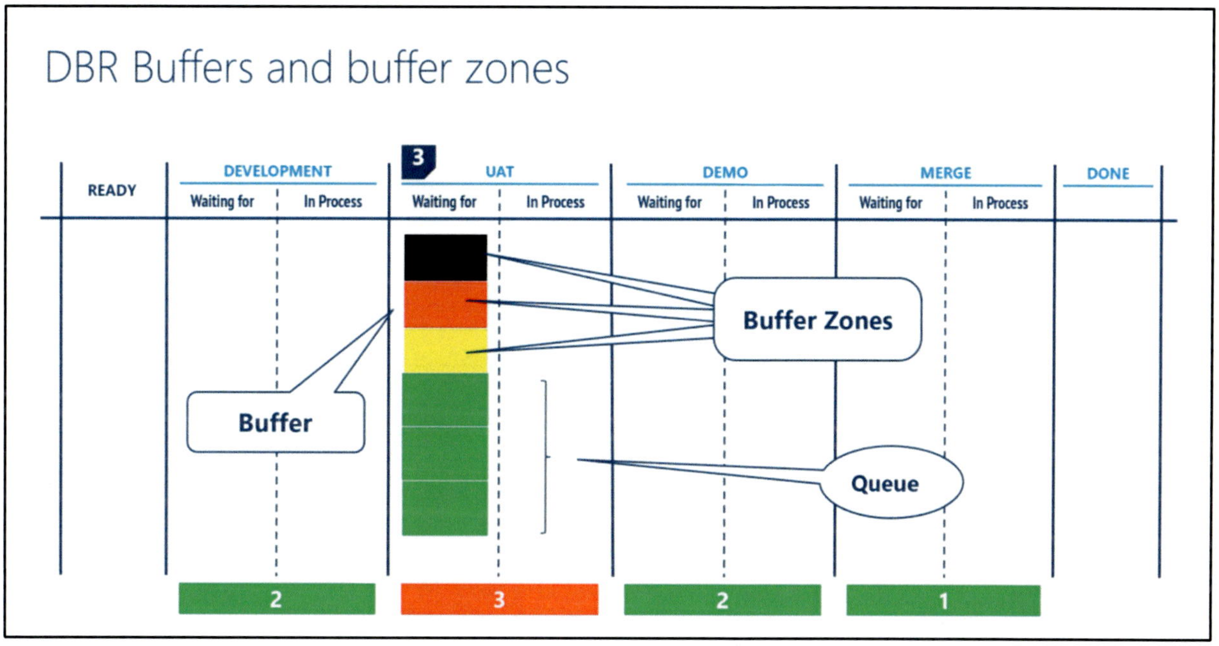

The use of the colors is in conformity with the Theory of Constraints.

1. When the buffer is GREEN, we have no worries. There is no limit to the number of items that can be waiting in the DBR queue. When the GREEN queue is empty, we are not YELLOW yet!
2. When the buffer is YELLOW, or two thirds full, we must keep an eye on the situation as a plausible source of Common Cause Variation alerts.
3. When the buffer is RED, or at one third, the constraint is on the verge of starving and Special Cause Variation could be manifesting itself.
4. When the buffer is empty, or BLACK, we are in an emergency situation. It means all hands-on deck.

The discussion does not render justice to the way the buffer unfolds as the change in color is dictated by the 'emptiness' of the corresponding slot, as shown next:

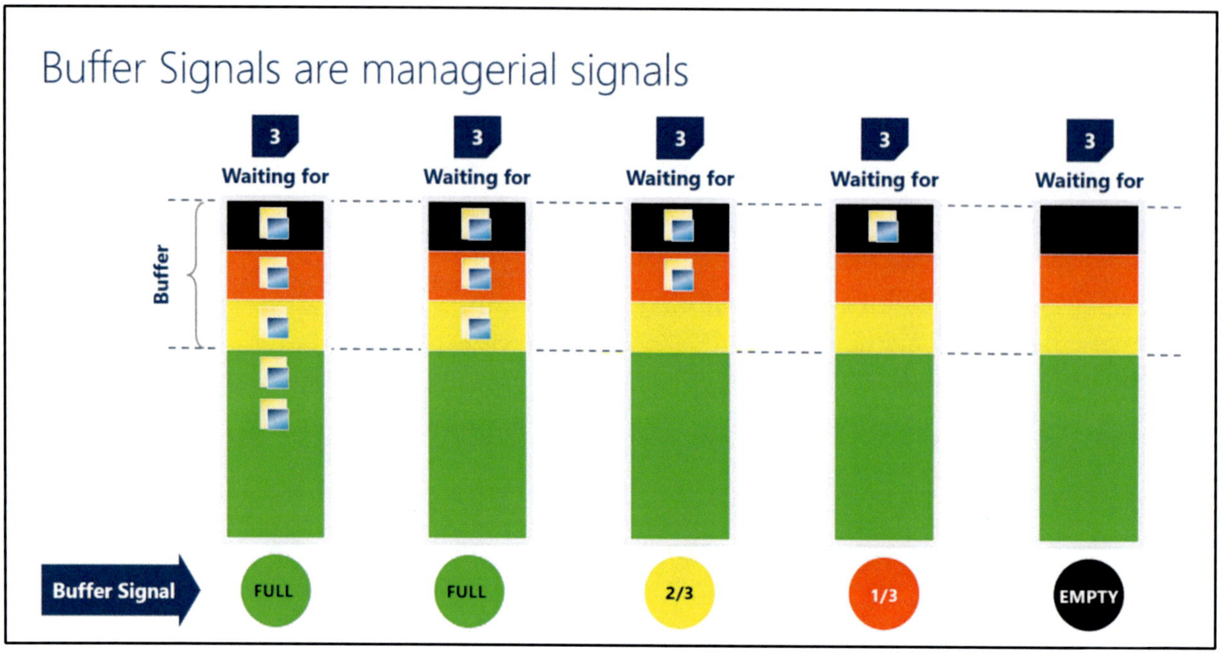

The DBR board is meant to exploit the constraint in the Work Process. It can be invoked by the *only one* team that is the constraint in the Work Flow or by *at least one team* experiencing noticeable constraints in their Work Execution. More on Work Execution signals in an upcoming section of this chapter.

As we did upon ramping up the preceding section on the Jungle, here is a similar array for the management of the Jeep:

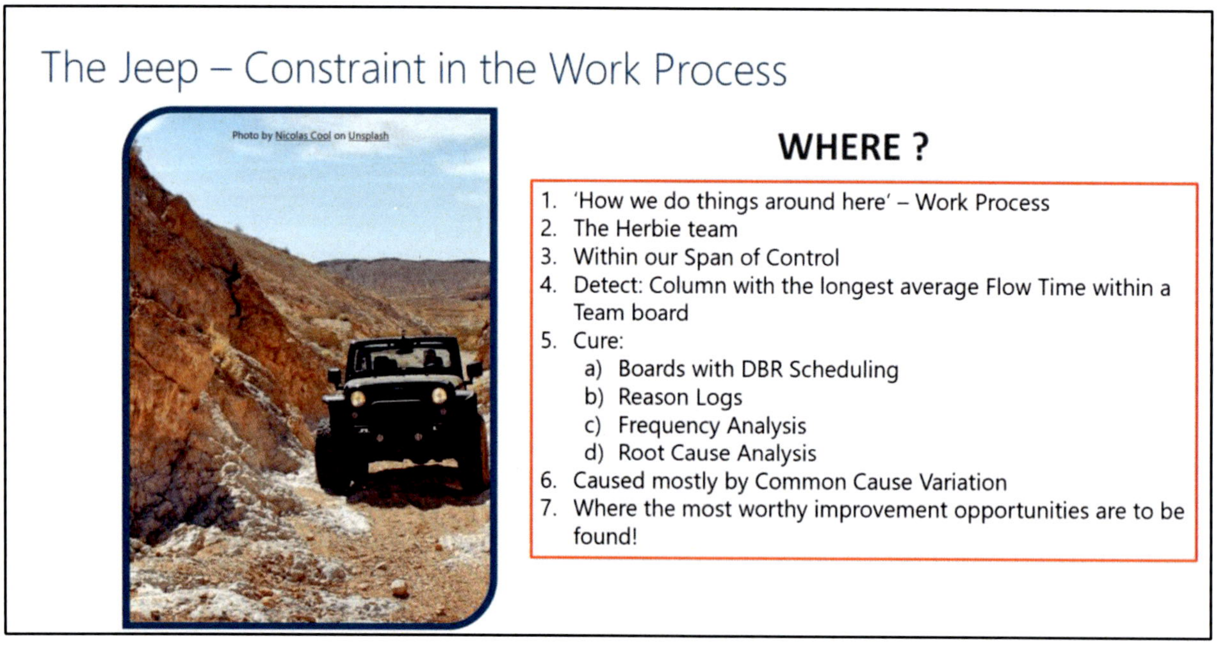

We have covered the first two constraints in Knowledge-Work. Both must be located at a precise 'geographical' point, a place. The third and final constraint, dealing with Work Execution signals, brings us back on the time axis as these constraints are triggered by the passage of time when teams execute projects.

The Journey – Constraint in the Work Execution – The Things that Happen

PMI with CPM and ToC with CCPM

There is a lot of material in CCPM – Critical Chain Project Management – from the Theory of Constraints. Dr Goldratt designed this to tame Common Cause specifically for project management and Knowledge-Work. Engineers are fond of it. It is in stark contrast to CPM – Critical Path Management – from the PMI. The most distinguishing factor is that a buffer is placed at the end of each CCPM project, absorbing variability[79] (not precisely, but I like the metaphor), while buffers are affixed at the end of pretty much everything you want in CPM, leading to local optimization! CCPM's buffers are meant to complete the project on time, CPM's buffers to finish tasks on time. CPM is engineered to start tasks as early as possible, CCPM to finish the project as soon as possible and avoid early starts of tasks at all costs. Very much in line with Kanban's moto of deferring start of work.

CCPM and DBR both focus on the time axis to manage execution risks and have a lot of similarities[80].

Dr Goldratt always believed project estimates were bloated[81], thus the need to perform a few surgical operations before finalizing a project. In normal times, I would point the reader to a case study or an article. But there is a twist for Knowledge-Work when it comes building a CCPM plan that you will find only here. We need to illustrate the mechanics as they stand in a normal context. We will then adjust and see how we can use this CCPM plan and buffer in an agile context.

Both CCPM and CPM are similar in their construct where the scope is relatively fixed but the due date and budget are negotiable.

---

[79] The CCPM buffer is a leading indicator of oncoming risk materialization. Mr. Donald Reinertsen's principle V11 states that 'buffers trade money for variability reduction'. The CCPM buffer comes for free but technically does not absorb variability! It is an advanced signal of upcoming negative variability.

[80] For a complete explanation of this phenomenon, see Sproull, Robert and Nelson, Bruce. Chapters 16-17 and Appendixes 6-7

[81] Parkinson's Law, Student syndrome, sand bagging, inflated estimates etc. are all foes of project estimates. Dr Goldratt accounted for 1) resource contention, 2) then cut all project estimates by 50%, and 3) added a 50% CCPM buffer at the end to arrive at the Critical Chain Plan.

Below is a table contrasting both classical approaches taken directly from Dr John Ricketts' book 'Reaching the Goal':

Single Projects using == >	Critical Path (CP)	Critical Chain (CC)
Tasks are estimated with	80% confidence	50% confidence
Contingency time is planned	In every task	Only around the critical chain
Resource contention is	Sometimes ignored	Always managed
Resource leveling affects	Non critical tasks	All tasks
Work rules allow	Bad multitasking	No bad multitasking
Planned direction is usually	Greater than CC	Less than CP
Early start on gating tasks are	Encouraged	Discouraged
Replanning is done	Frequently	Rarely
Progress is tracked against	Milestones	Time Buffer Penetration
Late completion occurs	Often	Seldom

Crafting a CCPM plan from a CPM plan in a traditional way

Let us now proceed with a traditional PMI like plan of 100 days, free of resource contention[82], created with the project team:

Step 1: Critical Path Management – PMI

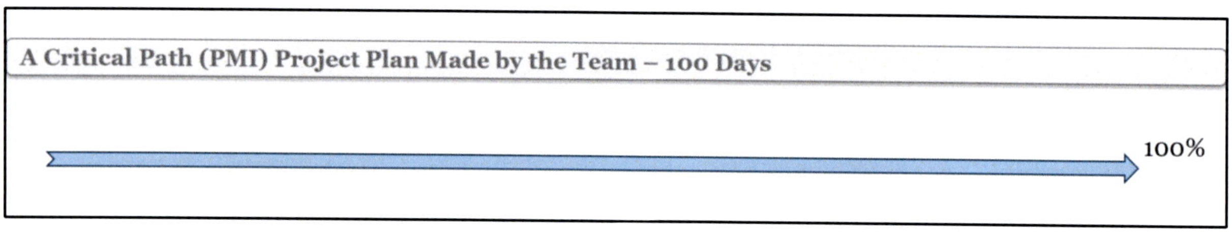

Step 2: Critical Chain Project Management - Cut 50% of Project timeline

[82] Free of resource contention means that no resource can be found in a state of parallelism with itself on another 'branch'

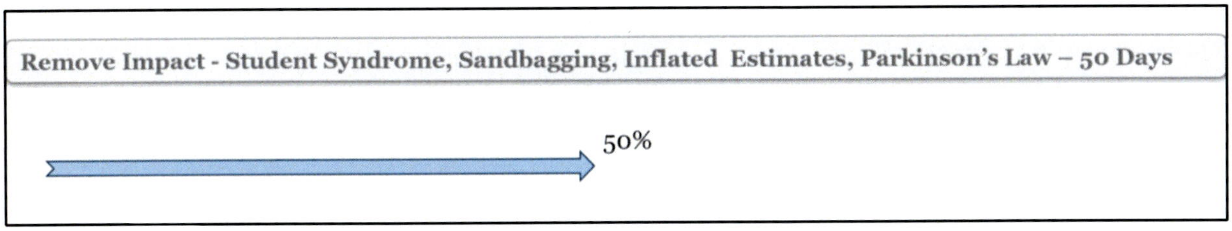

Step 3: Critical Chain Project Management - Add a 50% CCPM buffer on the compressed plan

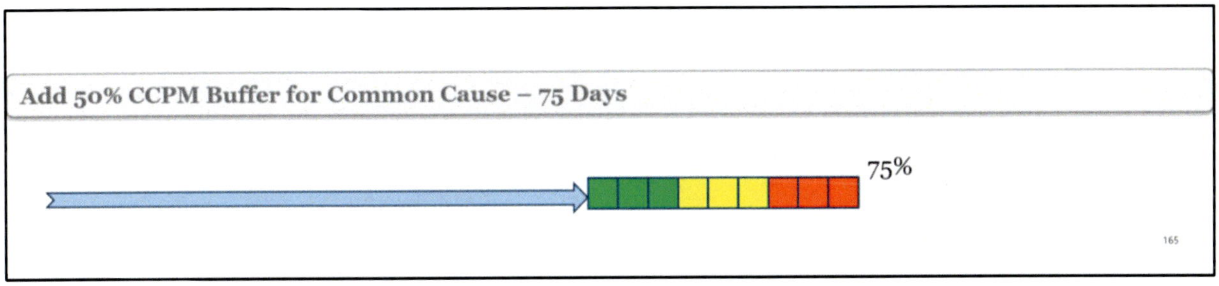

The project duration that is communicated to the stakeholders is 75 days.

As mentioned earlier, Bob Sproull[83] spells out verbally the analogy between CCPM and DBR. I took it upon myself to make the following illustration comparing both concepts as I don't think it has been done before:

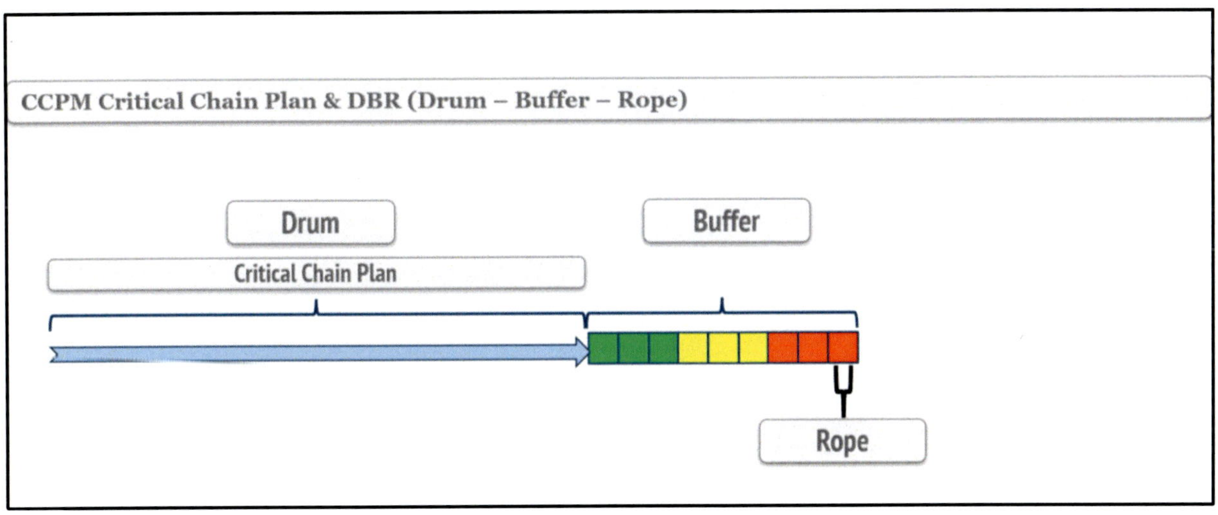

[83] Book: 'Epiphanized'. Page 194 – "The critical chain is the drum, the buffer is the buffer, and the project due date is the rope."

I hope you can appreciate the mechanics in the classical world. Now let's venture into Knowledge-Work, leverage probabilistic forecasting – thereby getting rid of estimating - and get a few Kanban tricks up our sleeves.

Fit of Kanban Lead Time distribution with CCPM plan

The integration between a CCPM plan and a Kanban lead time distribution looks and feels natural.

There has seldom been a case where an image is worth a thousand words!

CCPM Plan at 50% & Lead Time Distribution at 50% and 80% SLA

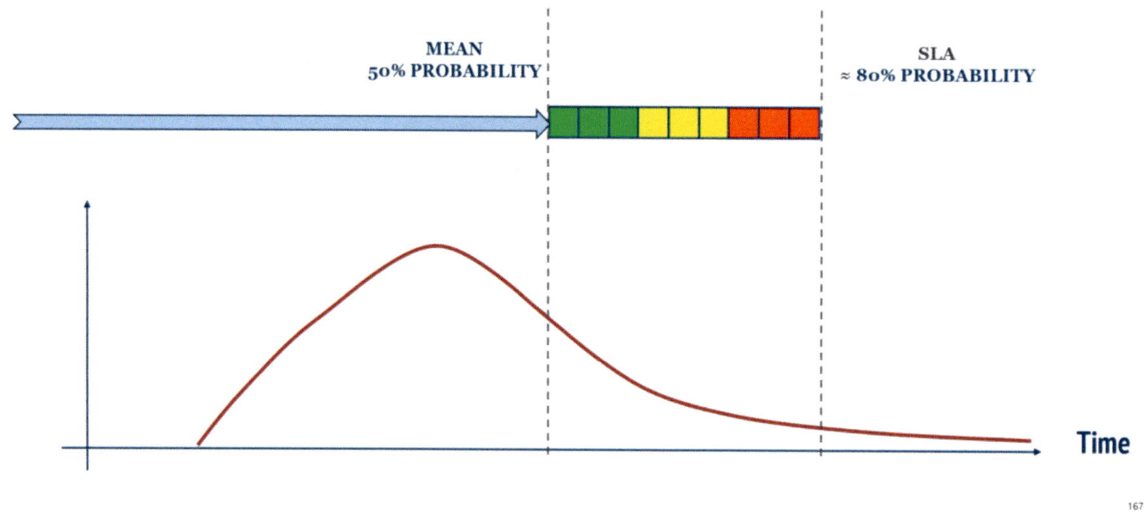

The benefits just achieved are major and twofold:

- We have now a free plan that can deal with Common Cause
- We can now actively manage the 80% SLA with the CCPM buffer progression. In the previous configuration, the SLA was merely a piece of observed information with no actionable management trigger.

The Buffer Fever Chart

The Buffer Fever Chart is as rich as the WIP Ageing chart in terms of information given through visualization with the nuances that it procures us with much more actionable information on a geometric scale. Let me explain.

The Buffer Fever Chart has two relative axes where X = (%Buffer User) and Y = (%Project Completed).

When we see observations on a Buffer Fever Chart, all points are on a relative scale are called BBR - Buffer Burn Rates - and are given by the following formula:

BBR = %Buffer Used / %Project Complete

The BBR metric has this unique attribute in that it is a relative measure, independent of project size, scope, budget or any other dimension you can imagine. Any project/team can fit on a Buffer Fever Chart once it starts execution. It is the greatest equalizer to managing a Portfolio!

Some of the popular visual representations of the Buffer Fever Chart are given below, none of which is coherent with the others! The one that is most acclaimed for its construct sits at the bottom right-hand side and is outlined in green. It is the one we will use as a baseline for our discussions to follow:

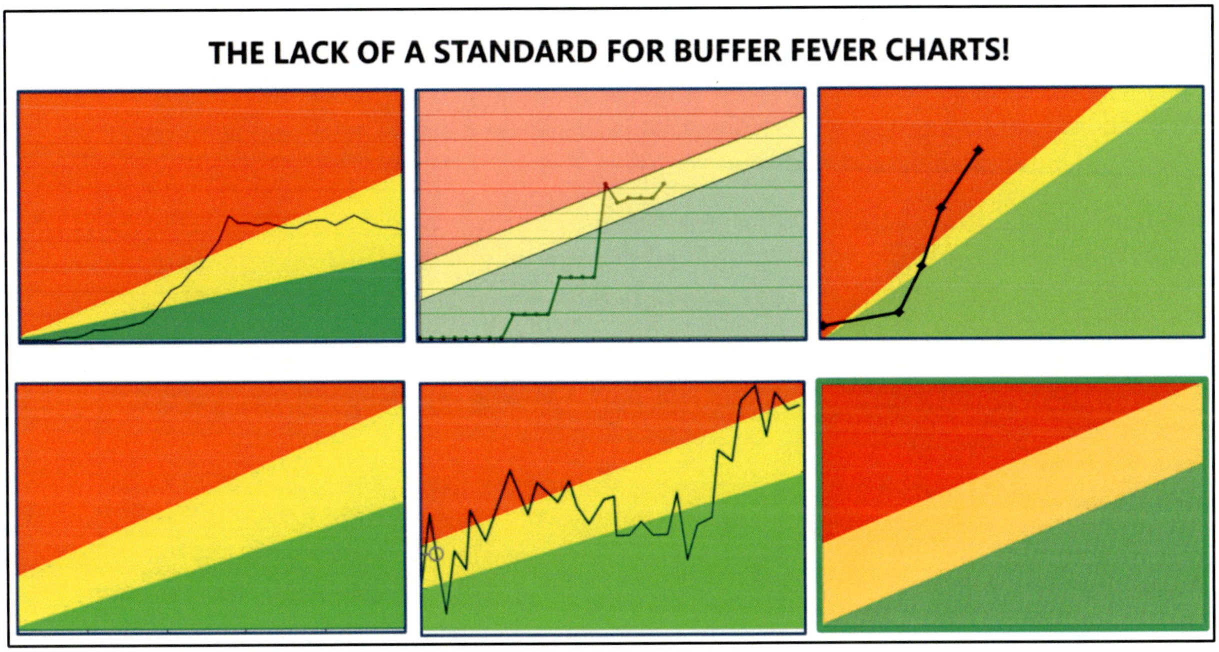

The Green, Yellow and Red area have the usual meaning for managerial purposes.

How is that chart of any help? Well, you can have one hundred projects plotted on a Buffer Fever Chart, each of which with a different scope, budget, team, Product Owner, division, country etc. All that matters is how well they are progressing through time with respect to both the CCPM buffer penetration and adherence to the CCPM schedule.

Imagine the management by exception gift for those governing Portfolios when you can identify among 100 projects those 10 that require preparation for the next monthly meeting! All the wasted time that would usually burden the other 90 teams preparing reports when they are forging ahead safely could be put to better use.

There are caveats. All Buffer Fever Charts have at least

1. one omission (the drum line or the drum beat),
2. one misconception (not properly accounting for downside risk) and,
3. one bad choice of color when it comes to managing psychological flow,

4. one improvement to be done when deciding who comes or not at the Portfolio meeting.

These topics will be developed in the following sections and have never been addressed before in a Knowledge-Work context.

Creating an agile CCPM Project plan without planning

The challenge for agile is to generate a plan that will conform to the 50% cutting of original estimates and adding a 50% CCPM buffer at the end.

And all this must come for free as plans are considered wasteful in all breeds of agile. Kanban as well.

We can solve this.

We will demonstrate how to get a free plan that is already at the 50% mark and upon which we can affix a 50% buffer with data available!

Below is a Lead Time distribution from a standard Kanban team board. I will use the average Lead Time threshold (50% is the mean) and add a 50% buffer. It will take me only ten minutes, which is as close as we can get to a free plan that respects the CCPM constraints!

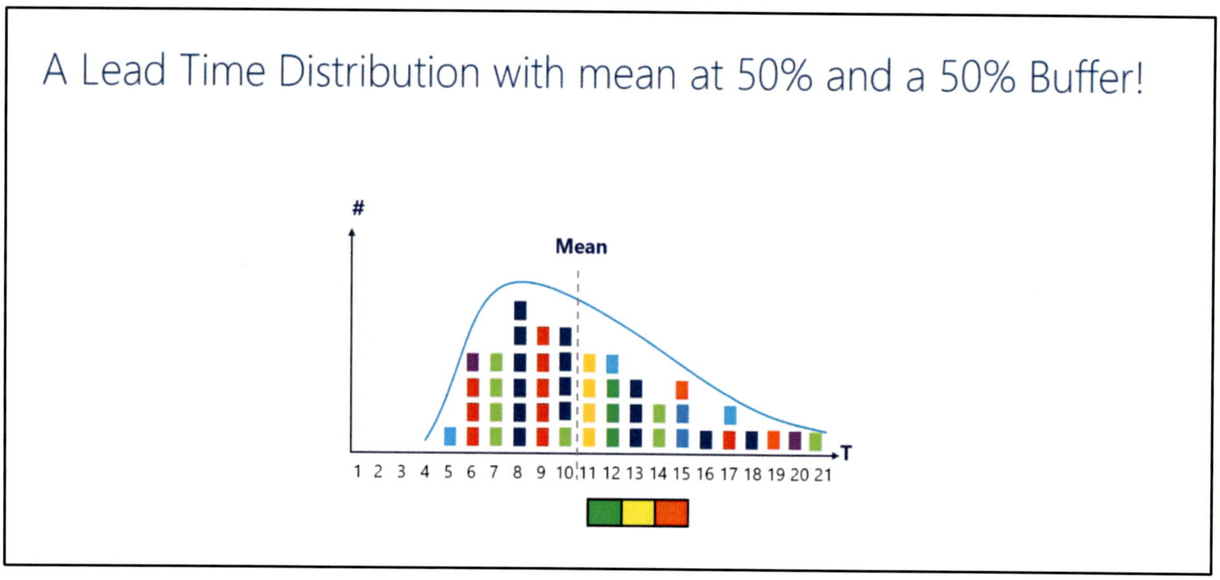

Note: The astute practitioner will also note that pro-active SLA level management is now doable with the CCPM buffer, something that is simply not achievable otherwise. For instance, a plus or minus 80% SLA level is automatically drawn when you take the 50% mean to your lead time distribution and add the 50% buffer to draw your Critical Chain plan. Whenever there is a buffer penetration into the yellow or red zone, you know your SLA can be at stake! We will see later that the CCPM buffer's location and length can be engineered and allow you flexibility toward better SLA results. This trick clearly enhances one's approach to SLA from an observed statistics – where you have nothing else but to gather the data and share it as we all do – to an actively managed metric.

We now have a plan that allows us to use the CCPM buffer and derive the Work Execution signals for each team! If it only took ten minutes, it is deemed a free plan. If it is a free plan, then there is no waste and agile should be 'satisfied' as to the waste issue

We will now activate a real-life situation with Little's Law. Little's Law applies between two points when WIP is equal to zero: at the beginning of a release (target scope project) and at the end.

Let's examine the empirical data we have gathered at work and suppose we have a target scope project of 50 work items. With the empirical evidence of our team, it will take on average 30 days. Time is allowed to slip. We manage on the time axis and the CCPM buffer is there for that very purpose.

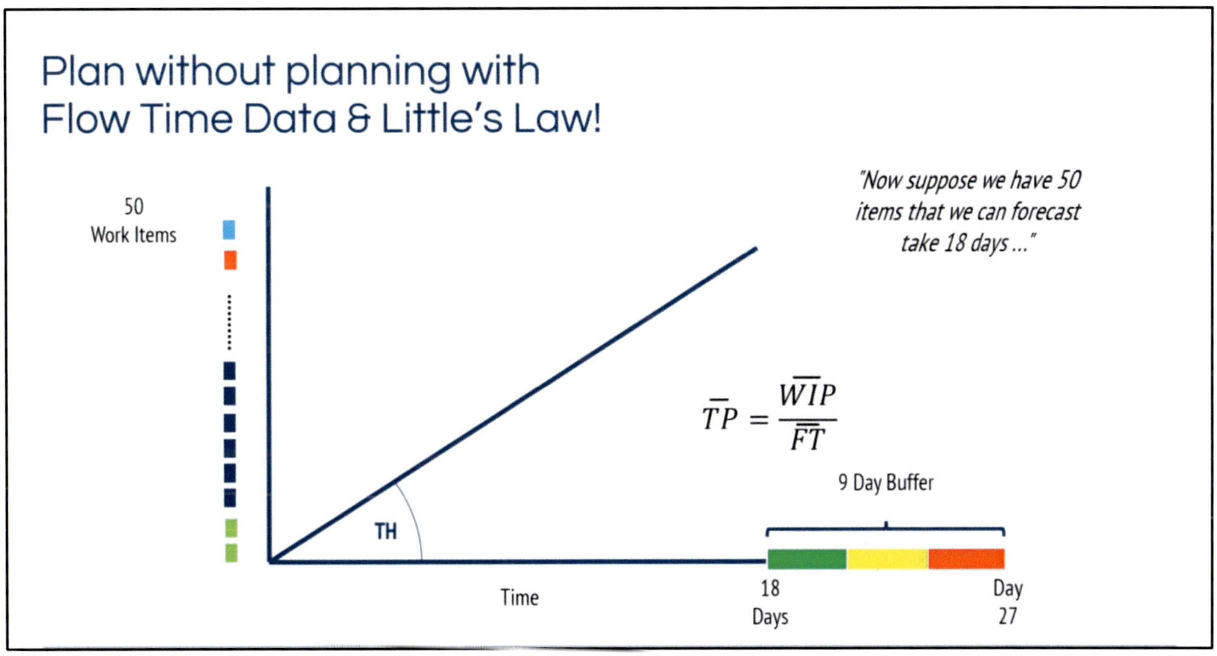

For some dates during the execution of this target scope project, we will observe the progression and calculate three things: the Buffer Consumption, the Buffer Burn Rate, and the revised delivery date:

1) The CCPM Consumption[84] Buffer is indicative of the relative penetration of the CCPM Time Buffer with respect to the work done. This Buffer Penetration is also at the core of

[84] See Appendix A for details pertaining to the traditional interpretation of the CCPM Consumption Buffer

staggering[85], a very potent and visual managerial functionality to help synchronize resources in anticipation of freshly revised delivery dates. The Buffer Consumption works with the usual signals of Green, Yellow and Red.

2) The Buffer Burn Rate[86] is the most important metric and is a relative indicator of lateness or hastiness of a team compared to the progression that is anticipated on the schedule of the CCPM plan. The interpretation of the BBR coefficient is as follow:
   a) If the BBR is less than 1, you are GREEN.
   b) If more than 1, you are RED.
   c) When BBR value is ≈ 1 (very near to one), you are in the YELLOW zone. (Note that when the BBR value is approximately one, you are very near to the relative DRUM rate of the Buffer Fever Chart. We will cover this in the upcoming example that follows where I show a RED BBR and then a GREEN BBR and compare them to the relative rate of 1 of the BBR DRUM. The relative rate of the DRUM with a BBR ≈ 1 – a straight line in fact – has never been addressed explicitly as such before as it never appears in any of the Buffer Fever Charts formats. It is an omission in properly interpreting Work Execution Signals that are in the yellow zone with no distinguishing factors between upside risk and downside risk. This Yellow color will be changed to blue as we progress. For now, we will leave the models in the state we are accustomed to.
3) The new revised date takes into account the projection on the schedule with the data at a specific point in time as hinted by the CCPM Consumption Buffer penetration. Staggering is supported that way and is a powerful, visual synchronization tool that requires no cadence.
4) Sometimes – when project execution goes very well – the staggering information appears to the left of the CCPM Consumption Buffer. This signal is new and its color is blue. It is called the CCPM rope signal. It is a novelty of this book. We will cover it once we enter chapter 6 with a supporting illustration in the appendix of that chapter.

Note: The formulae will be expressed as we go. Note the reference to Little's Law on the top line of the formula.

Managing the execution of a real plan on the Time axis

Let's make it work with a real-life situation:

> We have a target scope[87] project that will require 50 Work Items. On empirical evidence, 50 Work Items will take on average 18 days to deliver. The 18 days is the average and hence is our 50% plan where the CCPM construct and Lead Time distribution meet.

[85] See Appendix B for a detailed representation of the traditional interpretation of staggering, ignoring for now what happens when the project due date lies to the left of the CCPM Consumption Buffer

[86] See Appendix A for details pertaining to the traditional interpretation of the Buffer Burn Rate

[87] The team delivers many types of work items: reports, CRUD, interfaces, queries, ETL and the likes at a pace of (50/30) 2.77 work items per day. (Observation: that 2.77 work items per day sounds like the beat of a DRUM, which is 1 on a relative scale!)

1. The project starts April 1. April 27 is the anticipated delivery date once the CCPM buffer is accounted for. The CCPM buffer will sustain the possibility that the project could be finished any time between April 18 and April 27[88].
2. The buffer of 9 days (50% of the 18 days plan) extends the deadline until April 27th. This deadline is the one communicated to the stakeholders.

The project's critical chain, buffer and key milestones are drawn below:

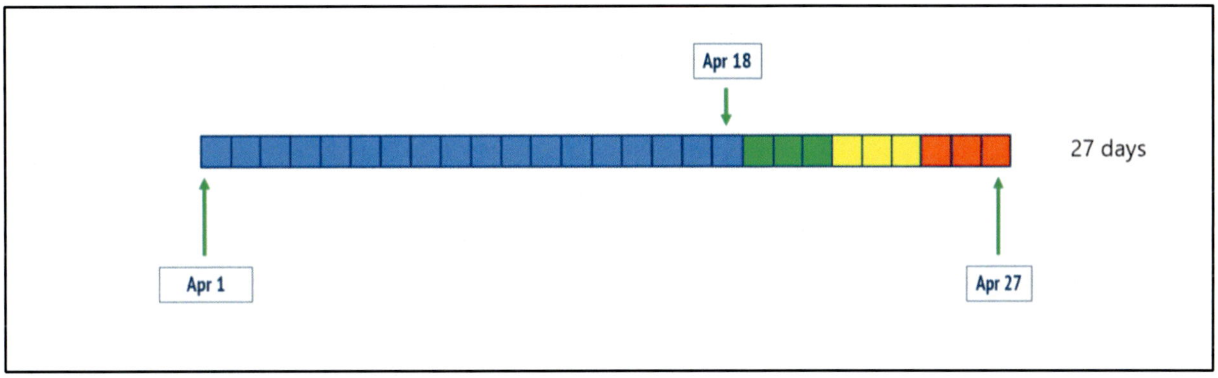

EXERCISE 1 – CCPM and BUFFERS

On April 7, eight work items are completed.

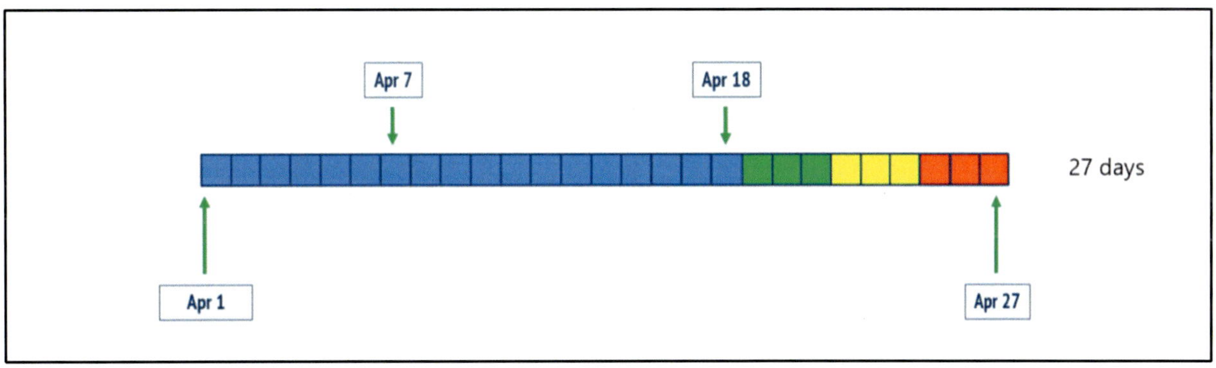

a) What is the Buffer Consumption? (Answer: 77%, represented by the black arrow in the following illustration)

b) What is the Buffer Burn Rate? (Answer: 2.75 in comparison to the Drum rate of ≈ 1, meaning that for a work item that would normally take 1 day, we are busy delivering it over 2.75 days!)

c) What is the new delivery date, the rope? (Answer: April 24 is the new rope, ie the signal for replenishment with a new target scope project!)

[88] Of course, when we revise the new end of project target date, we could even end before April 18th!

d) The relative CCPM planned DRUM beat of 1 is equal to what delivery rate per day on this very project? (Answer 2.75 – see earlier footnote just above)

CCPM and Buffers #1 – Day 7

Little's Law !

Variable	Value
Actual TH = WIP to Date / Lead Time to Date	14/7 = 2.0 work items done per day
Expected Lead Time = Total WIP / Actual TH	50/2.0= 25 days is the new timeline
Lead Time Difference = Expected Lead Time – Average Lead Time	25-18 = 7 days difference – Target date is April 24
%Buffer Consumption = Lead Time Difference * 100 / CCPM Buffer	7*100/9 = 77%
%Work Completed = WIP To Date * 100 / Total WIP	14*100/50 = 28%
Buffer Burn Rate = %Buffer Consumption / %Work Completed	**77/28 = 2.75**

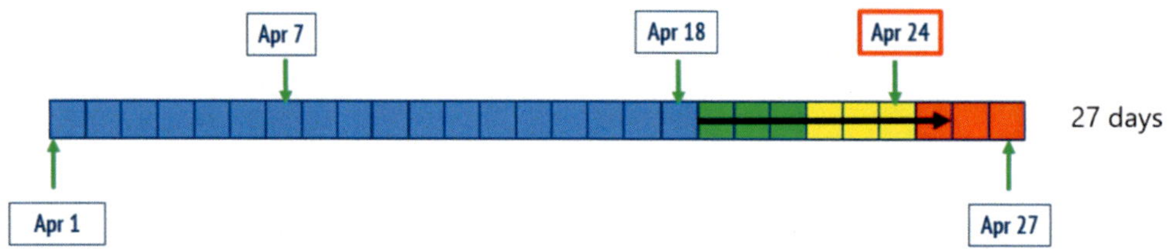

BUFFER BURN RATE : You are consuming the time buffer at 2.75 the amount of work that needs to be delivered. For a work item that would normally take one day (the DRUM), you are spending 2.75 days to do it.

This team should change the instrumentation of its Flow Efficiency board to a DBR board to leverage the constraint!

Also, projects must never get into an early start mode as it is a key tenet of CCPM. This is where staggering comes into play. The new anticipated delivery date of April 24 must be communicated to avoid early start for those who are awaiting that project's completion.

EXERCISE 2 – CCPM and BUFFERS

On April 12, 37 items have been completed.

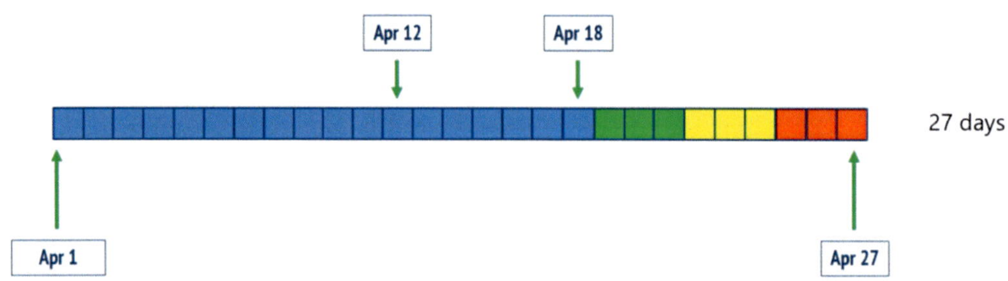

a) What is the Buffer Consumption? (Answer: -13% - CCPM Rope Signal in the white arrow in the next illustration. In fact we have not consumed any of the CCPM buffer.)

b) What is the Buffer Burn Rate? (Answer: 0.175 in comparison to the Drum rate of ≈ 1, meaning that for a work item that would normally require one day of work, we manage to get it done in .175 days!)

c) What is the new delivery date, or rope? (Answer: Apr 16 – CCPM Blue Rope Signal)

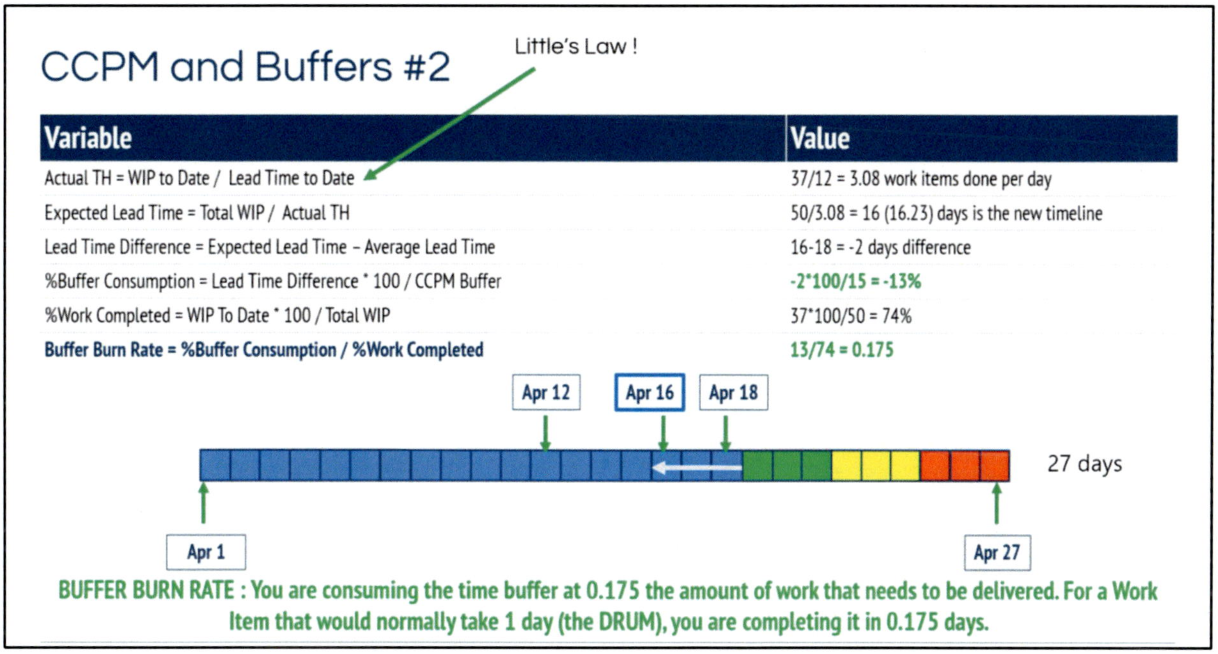

Note the reversal of the previous situation. The CCPM buffer penetration is negative, meaning that it has not been consumed at all. Also, we are progressing at a relative pace of 0.175 days per deliverable when the normal pace of the DRUM is one day on a relative scale on the Buffer Fever Chart. We are going faster than the DRUM rate of ≈ 1.

This team can now revert to a standard Flow Efficiency board. Furthermore, the staggering information given by the penetration of the CCPM buffer would alert all stakeholders that the new revised delivery date of Apr 16 is approaching fast!

Imagine coming to your daily stand-up equipped in this fashion. What do you think the impact on TRUST will be? How do you think the C level will appreciate management by exception with the help of leading indicators of risk materialization on the time axis?

Constraints in the Work Execution - At least one, maybe more!

There must always be at least one constraint in the Work Execution, as we will see shortly[89]. How do we proceed when we start three projects with three teams and not a single day of activities has taken place?

We still need to find at least one constraint in the Work Execution.

This is the procedure, beginning with three projects with their respective CCPM plans:

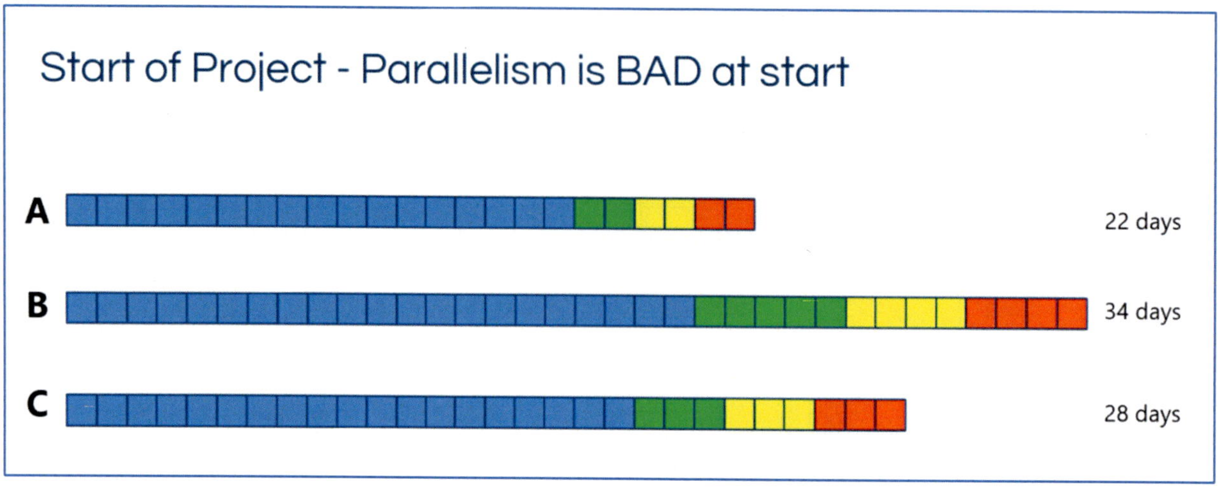

We know that parallelism is harmful and induces multi-tasking. It is a bad idea to start the three projects this way in all cases. We are tackling here a pure synchronization issue – with no cadence - by having all projects tentatively finish on a target date.

So, we must align the projects at a virtual integration point at the end of all the buffers. This way we reduce parallelism to the maximum and protect all three end dates as follows:

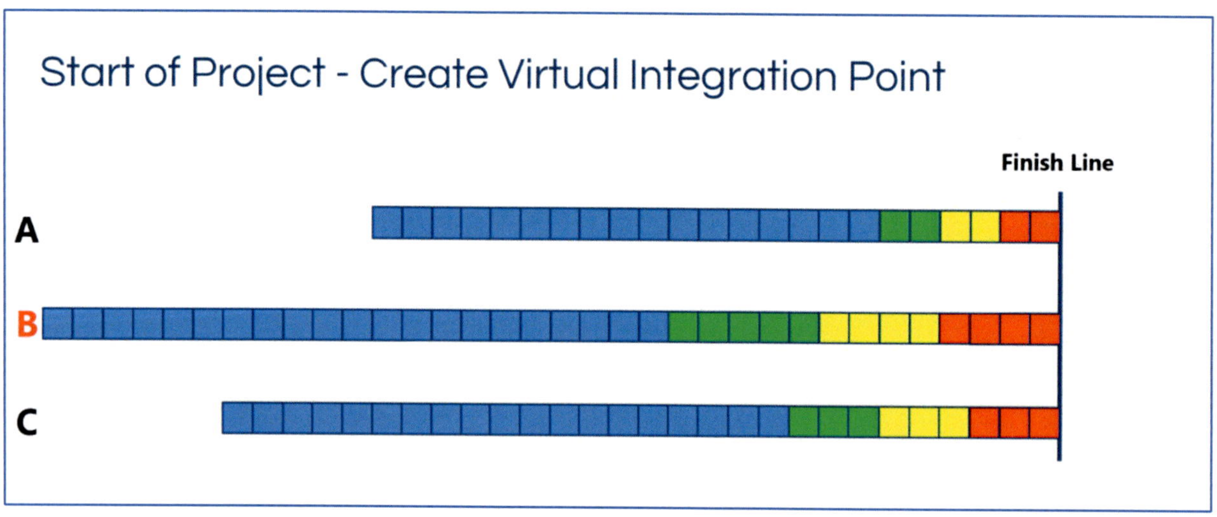

[89] In my first book, it was suggested that there be only one constraint in the Work Execution. This was wrong,

Now that all projects have been aligned and are all green by default since we have not started yet, we must find the constraint in the work execution. It is the one that has the longest path! If until the end of this undertaking, all projects never get to a red status, then Project B will always require a DBR board and be considered the constraint in the Work Execution!

As only one team at a time can be the constraint in the Work Flow, more than one team can be a constraint in the Work Execution with a red indicator. The reason is quite simple as the signal detected for the constraint in the Work Flow is in a one-dimension universe at a precise point in time. (The same is true for identifying the constraint in the Work Process!)

For the constraint in the Work Execution, things occur over time and we operate in a two-dimensional universe with relative time scales. Team A and Team B can be totally decoupled on the time dimension making it impossible to discern who is in worst shape. Let's look at a Buffer Fever Chart instantly by calculating some observations along the DRUM line where the BBR is equal to one (X axis/Y axis):

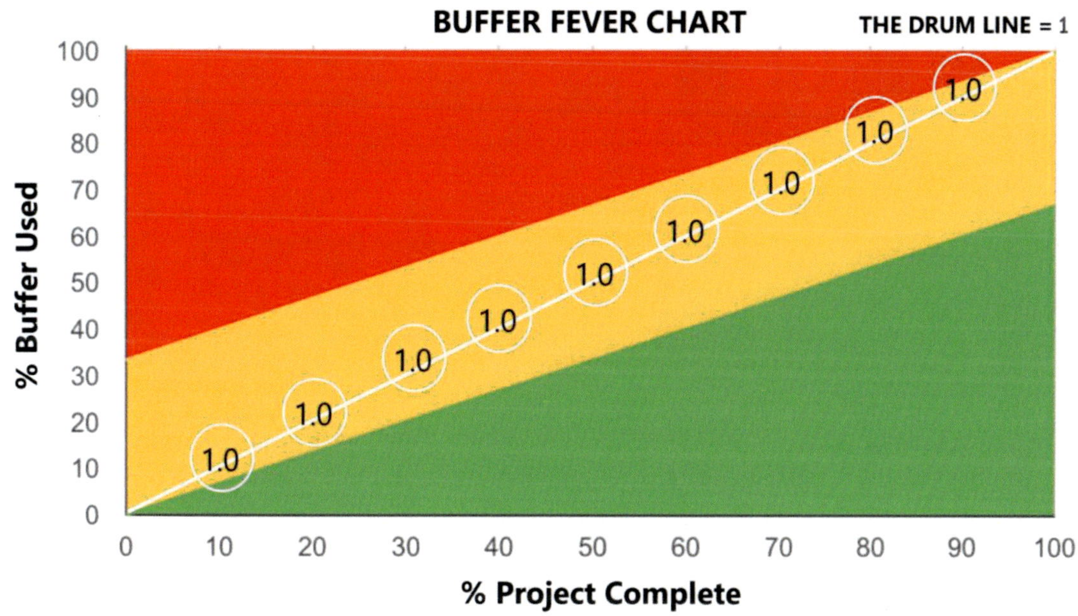

Every point on that graph has a Buffer Burn Rate coefficient. As a matter of fact, the DRUM line has Buffer Burn Rates of 1 all along its line. An infinity if we recall our basic geometry classes pertaining to the number of points along any line! This is the first time I see a Buffer Fever Chart with the DRUM line cutting through it. We will see that this is far from trivial when addressing downside risk and engineering psychological flow.

The same BBR value phenomenon can apply in the red zone as well where we could encounter many teams with a BBR of 2 for example. In this context choosing the 'one team' that is the constraint in the Work Execution becomes a misnomer.

This is why we could have at least one constraint in the Work Execution, and maybe more!

To conclude this section, here is the traditional array depicting the attributes and remedies for the Constraints in the Work Execution! Contrary to the two preceding constraints, this one is triggered by time (when). The other ones are a physical location (where).

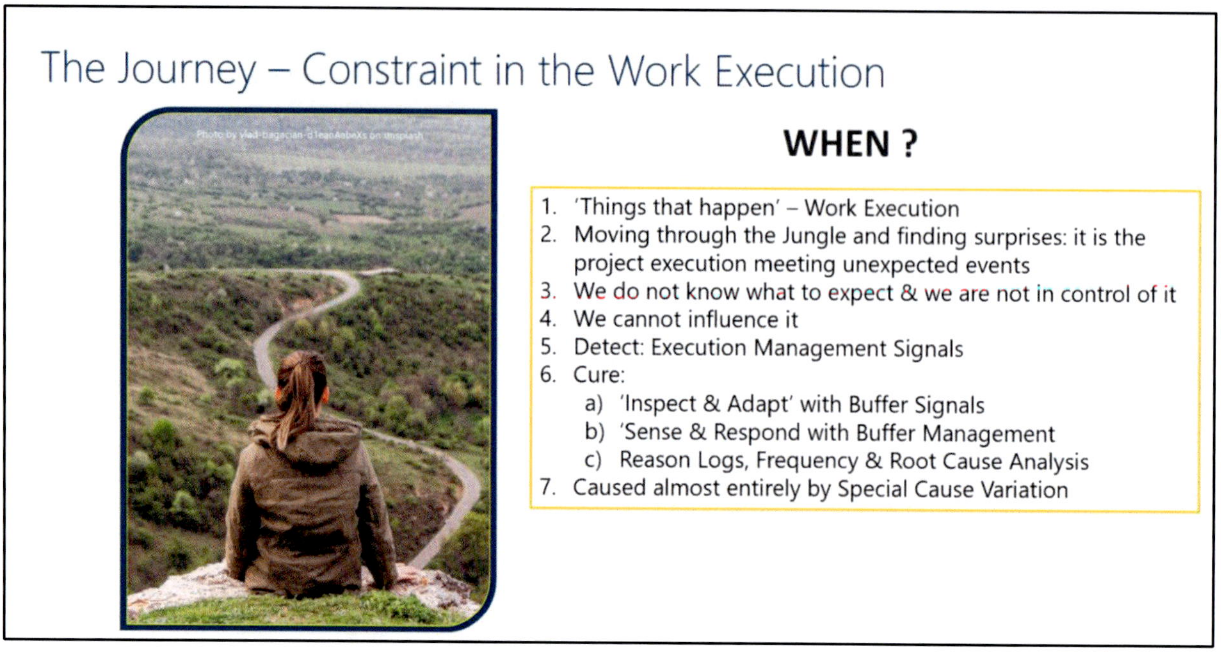

Putting it all together!

We have covered all the materials pertaining to the three constraints in Knowledge-Work and walked through both Flow Efficiency and DBR boards. The former (DBR boards) applies to the *one* team that is the constraint in your Work Flow and as well to *at least one of* the teams that have supporting Work Execution Signals. The latter (Flow Efficiency boards) applies to all the other non-constraints teams.

Here is a table to facilitate the escalation process in a multi team setting once you find a constraint in the Work Flow and/or Work Execution and apply the remedy with managing the constraint in the Work Process for each of those teams:

1. **Constraint in the Work Process**: Identified on a Flow Efficiency Board by the column that has the longest average in-state Lead Time. In other words, the column that has the least capacity. This is based on empirical data fit for your team.
2. **Constraint in the Work Flow**: This is for multi-team environments. It is the *one team* for which you can forecast the longest stack of Work Items awaiting. Note that the queue length is measured in terms of time. This is the team that will face the greatest burden of work ahead.
3. **Constraint in the Work Execution:** This is for multi-team settings. It is ALL THE TEAMS that are "bleeding the most" - i.e. have the same "red" Buffer Burn Rate. It is a representation of the present state, and shows which teams are mostly hit by Mr. Murphy (Special Cause Variation) during execution of the work. Not all teams that are RED need be considered constraints in the Work Execution as we do not encourage tampering with the system. Remember the advice: At least one

team is the constraint in the Work Execution. For the constraint in the Work Flow, it is at most one team!

4. A word of caution. If too many teams have Work Execution Signals with Buffer Burn Rates in a red state, it is an overload signal. Stop allowing work into the system instead. It will be a better cure. If you deem that only a few Work Execution 'red' teams deserve a DBR board, by all means use judgment!
5. For labor liquidity arbitrage and resource allocation, always look for solutions borrowing resources from green state projects.

As an example, let's visualize the relative status of all teams with a Buffer Fever Chart [90]in a Portfolio. Their BBR (BUFFER BURN RATE) is punctuated by colored triangles.

You can easily see here that three projects are in the RED zone. The X and Y axes of the Buffer Fever Chart are both one a relative scale. Being on a relative scale with two axes is far from being on a discrete scale with one dimension as was the case when we tried to identify the Constraint in the Work Flow, which was identified by the team having the single biggest queue of work ahead of it! For this reason, we should allow more than one constraint in the Work Execution.

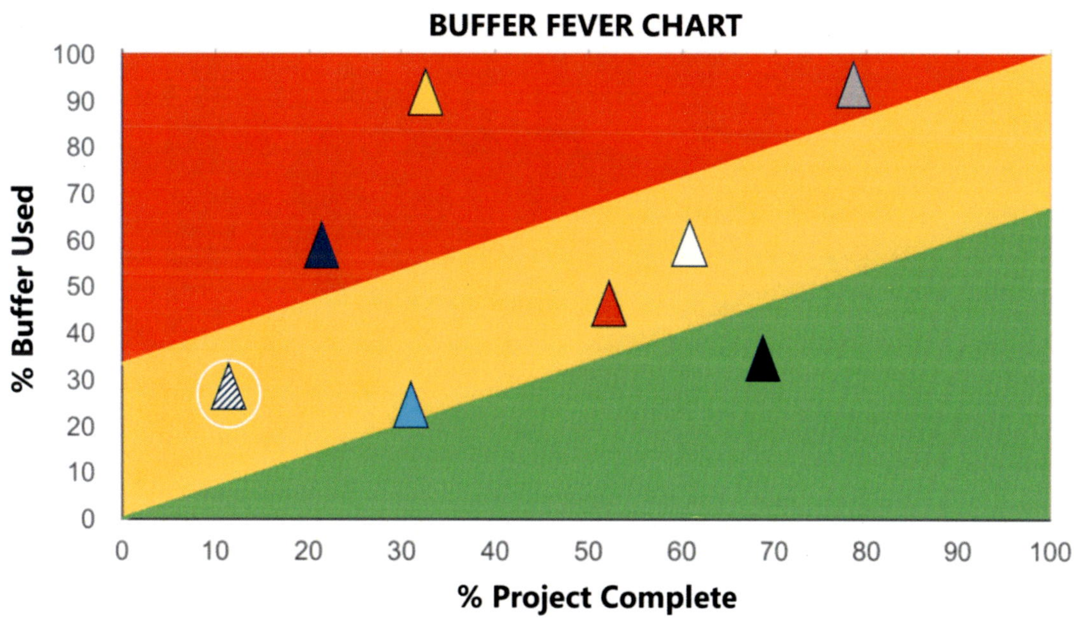

In the situation above, I would not give too much thought to the GREY project as it is near the finish line and has BBR of 1.1. As far as the YELLOW and DARK BLUE projects on the upper left quadrant are concerned, I must admit that picking only one would make me uncomfortable for the simple good reason that they both have the same BBR of 3! I would therefore recommend that both teams instrument a DBR board to manage their respective constraints in their Work Process!

[90] Buffer Fever Charts transpose all projects on a relative scale during execution independent of budget, scope, team, division or schedule!

Another oddity is that the BBR coefficient of the patterned circled triangle in the lower left-hand side of the Yellow zone also has a BBR of 3, similar to our YELLOW and DARK BLUE projects just above in the red zone! All that is red may not be so red after all! Contrary to what was exposed in my first book, you simply cannot choose the one 'reddest' project visually. You first need the BBR coefficient, and then make a decision[91]. As to not overload the system in managerial trivialities, I would choose the project with the longest path to completion, which cannot be deciphered from the Buffer Fever Chart, to be the constraint in the Work Execution.

By looking at the graph that I have made of colliding BBR coefficients below, you can tell that there lies an infinite number of occurrences of 1.0. For a BBR of 2, there can be much more than for a BBR of 4, but too many to limit our thinking that there can be only one constraint in the Work Execution: too many synonyms and collisions! BBR's in circle are all collisions.

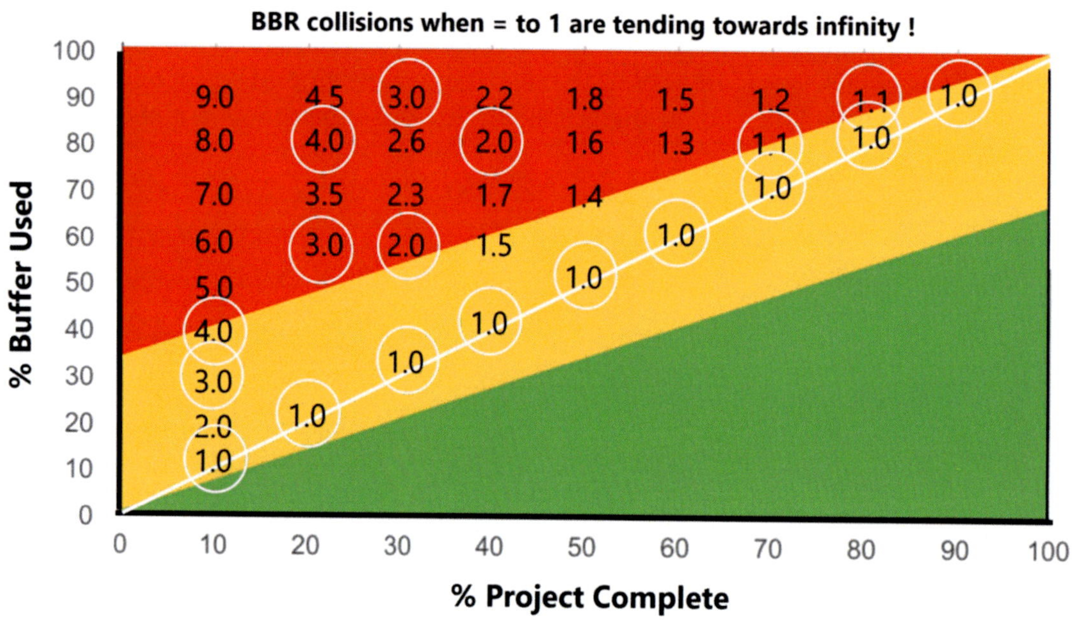

Finding the 'hottest' one can be impossible at times and purely a judgment call, hence the argument to support the possibility of having at least one constraint in the Work Execution. Humans are very bad at integrating and interpreting data. Let's not give Mr. Murphy a say.

The representation of the Buffer Fever Chart above is the one that is most commonly used in the market and the most coherent. Despite this, it has a flaw that we will address in the next section regarding the yellow color.

For now, let us see this illustration and qualify the yellow zone as blue. Things are way too fuzzy in the yellow zone to cause alarm.

[91] Remember this heuristic. When in doubt, always spot the project with the biggest drag on the Y Axis. In this case, the tie breaker from all three BBR coefficients projects of 3.0 would be the one in the **Yellow Zone** that is lagging the most on the time axis. Remember, ToC likes to compete on the time axis!

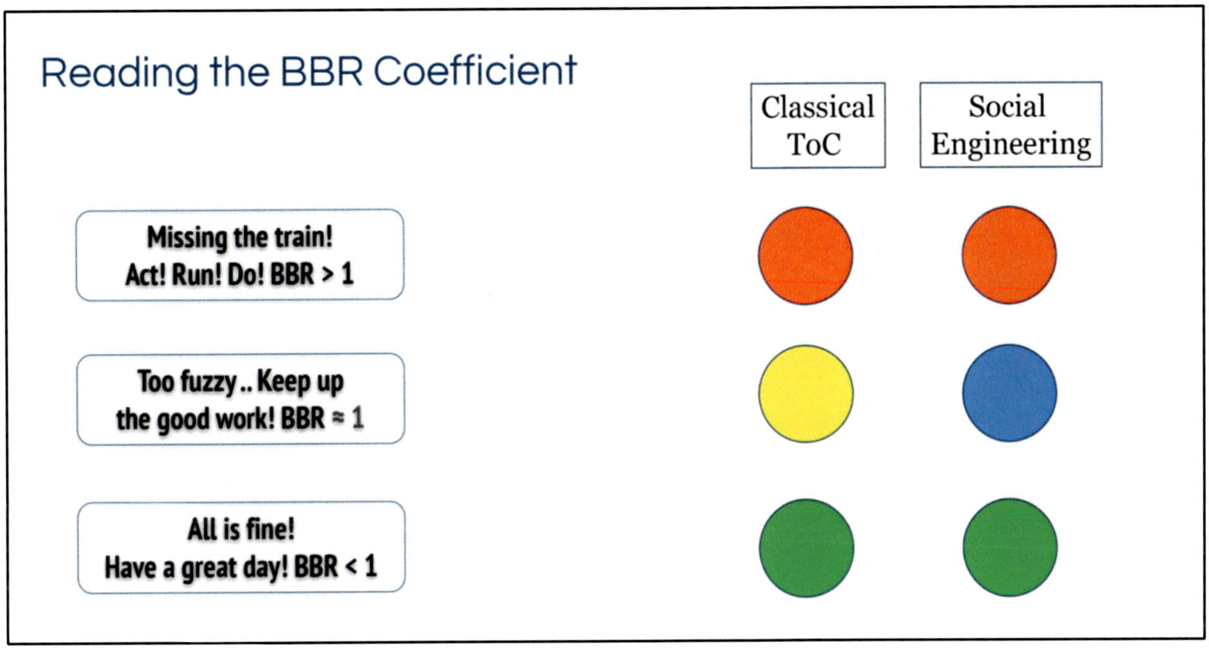

Festina Lente - Psychological Flow, Buffer Fever Charts for Knowledge-Work and Social Engineering at the TEAM or PROJECT level

Psychological Flow

Psychological Flow has been researched extensively by Dr Mihaly Csikszentmihaly. Flow is a state of mind in which a person becomes fully immersed in an activity. Festina lente[92] is the best way I can relate the concept of flow to Agile and Lean and Kanban: sustainable pace at the team level!

Dr Mihaly Csikszentmihaly argues that flow is something that is self-managed for an individual, but the team is the unit of measure in agile – along with management – and in that perspective flow must be engineered on a collective scale. This is what I am trying to accomplish here. Social engineering of Flow at the team/project level.

More than a dozen factors have been tabulated in order to locate FLOW. Two dimensions suffice to derive it: Anxiety and Boredom. Being able to transit at will between these two states is how you manage flow as an individual. When you want excitement, you can go deep into the 'RED' anxiety zone and when tranquility is needed to replenish, you can find a safe harbor in the GREEN zone as illustrated below:

[92] Make haste slowly. A term used by Mr. Donald Reinertsen

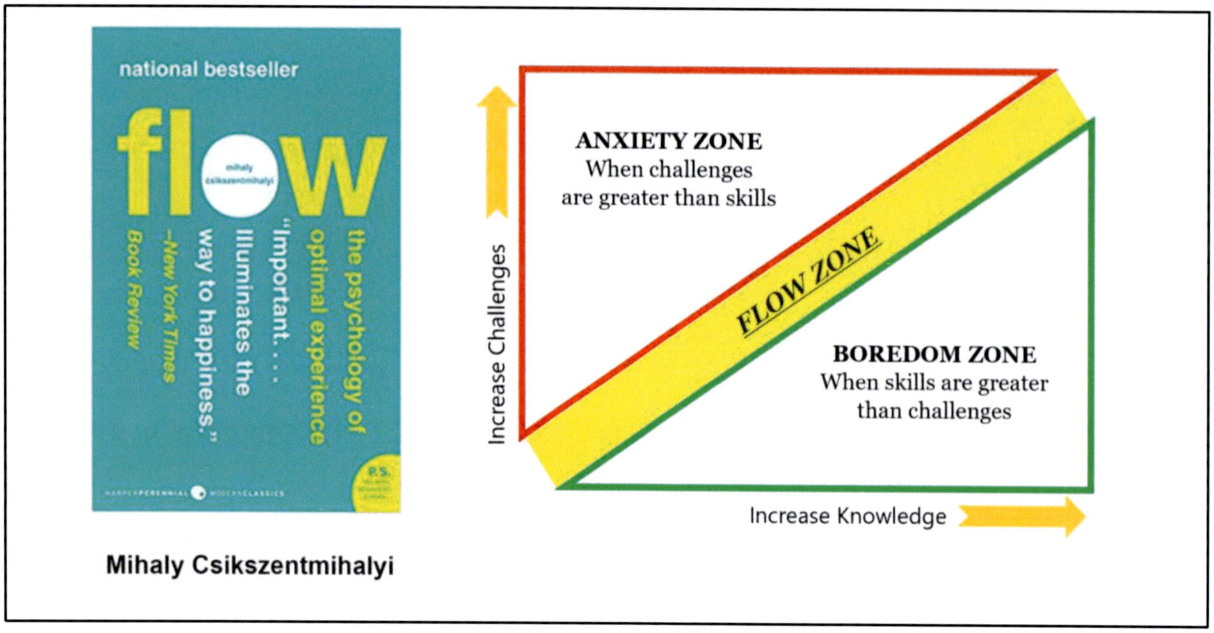

Can you notice the similarities with the Yellow strip of the Buffer Fever Chart and the RED and GREEN triangles that mimic all of the components of a Buffer Fever Chart?

Something peculiar arises when we give second thoughts to the RED and GREEN areas of the Buffer Fever Chart. And something totally wrong lies within the YELLOW area as we hinted earlier.

Let's examine the familiar illustration below:

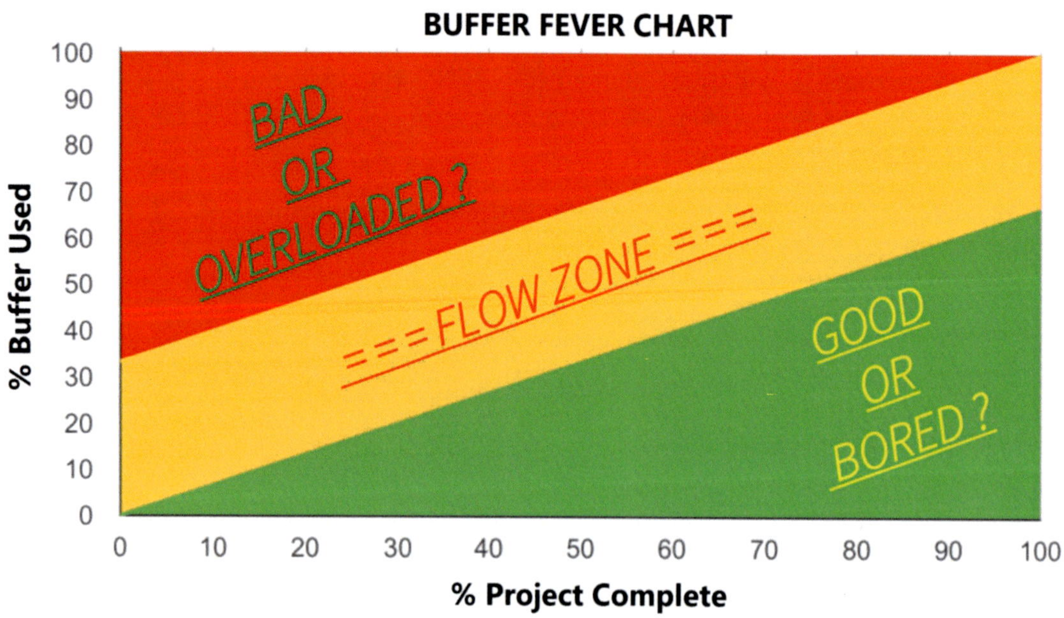

When a team is in the red area, it is performing poorly... or are the team members overloaded, overwhelmed and filled with anxiety? What can be done to rectify the situation and push the team into the yellow zone, the flow zone?

Contrariwise, when a team is in the green zone, is it a great team or one without challenges? A bored team? Is there a solution to resolving this dilemma and moving that team into the yellow zone?

Throughput Accounting has many tenets, some of which is to influence and align behaviors and motivation. Social engineering belongs in that space as well. Combining both of these instruments seems like a must when wading for the first time in the space of Throughput Accounting for Knowledge-Work.

Buffer Fever Charts for Knowledge-Work

Buffer Fever Charts come in many flavors. All of them are wrong for Knowledge-Work! There is a hidden beat in this graph, a DRUM-like beat discussed before when the BBR (Buffer Burn Rate) is ≈ 1. It is never shown on any of the visual representations. But being below that DRUM line – in the next illustration - is not a source of worry. It is what we can relate to downside and upside risk in finance with. We care only about downside risk. The risk that is in the upper part of the yellow zone trending to RED!

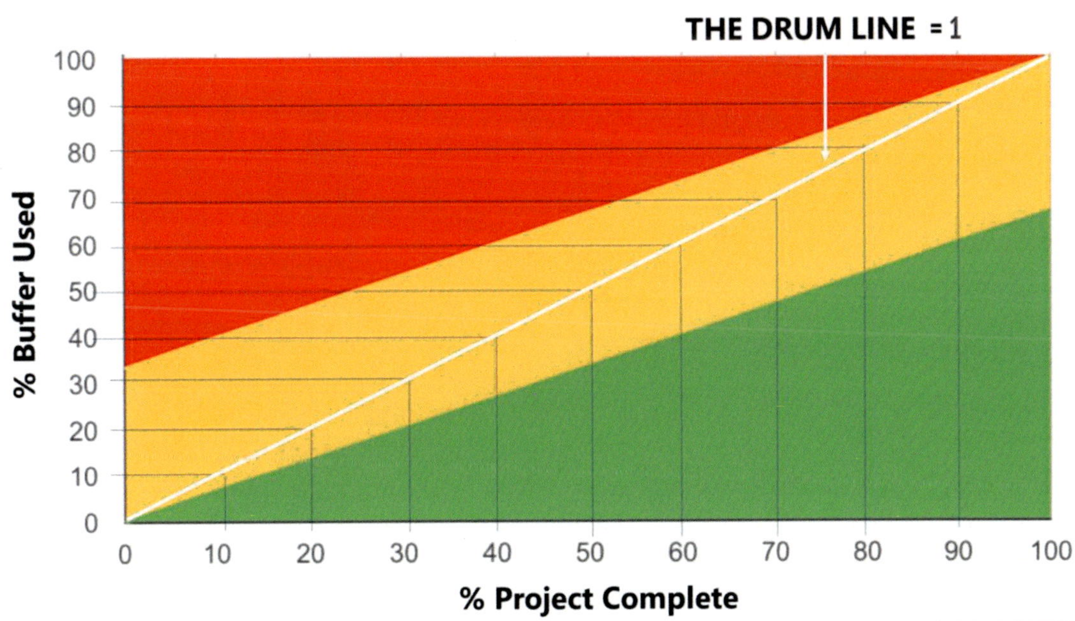

The Yellow zone, attributed as a 'warning zone' when the BBR is ≈ 1, is not actually something to fear. When the BBR is below the DRUM beat, we are in a safe place, at a good pace. Well ahead of the plan. The color Yellow is not appropriate at all for psychological flow.

Blue is in fact a better representation for the flow zone. In the next illustration, the tiny drums inside the new blue flow zone are shaded in blue near the white DRUM line and in light red or light green depending if you are getting close to either the red or green zone.

The downside risk resides above the drum line. Below the drum line, there are really no risks!

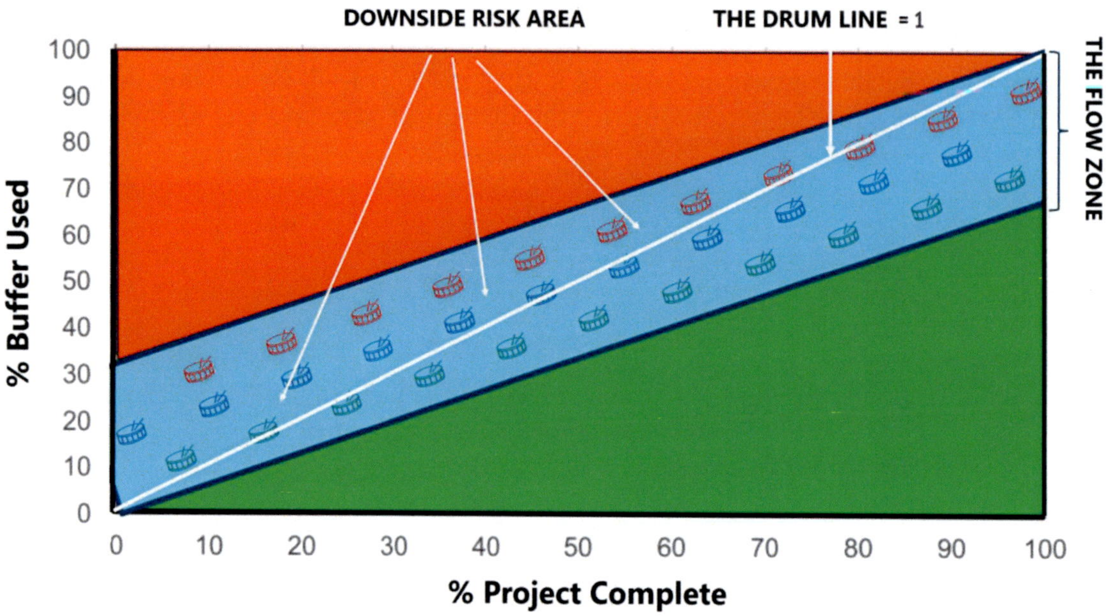

When we are below the white DRUM line, we are perfectly fine. We are not in a YELLOW mode as we all understand it to be. We are nothing short of GREEN, or maybe BLUE!

Social engineering and molding the Work Execution Signals frequency

Let's see if we cannot find some insights in molding the penetration frequency of the RED, YELLOW and GREEN zones of the CCPM buffer that will impact the Work Execution signals generation. (We must revert to the traditional colors now as their meanings are appropriate when considering buffer penetration.)

The size of the CCPM buffer does not have to be 50%. We can orchestrate it to alter the frequency with which we cross into the three zones. This is where social engineering comes into play. It becomes a managerial decision depending on the circumstances. (For example, by next fiscal year end, we may want our development team to accelerate the pace to get some pension fund applications out before January 1st! In the summer we might revert to a slower pace by architecting the CCPM buffer accordingly as we will see below.)

The same project – starting October 01 with a due date of Nov 21 - appears below with three different CCPM buffer sizes:

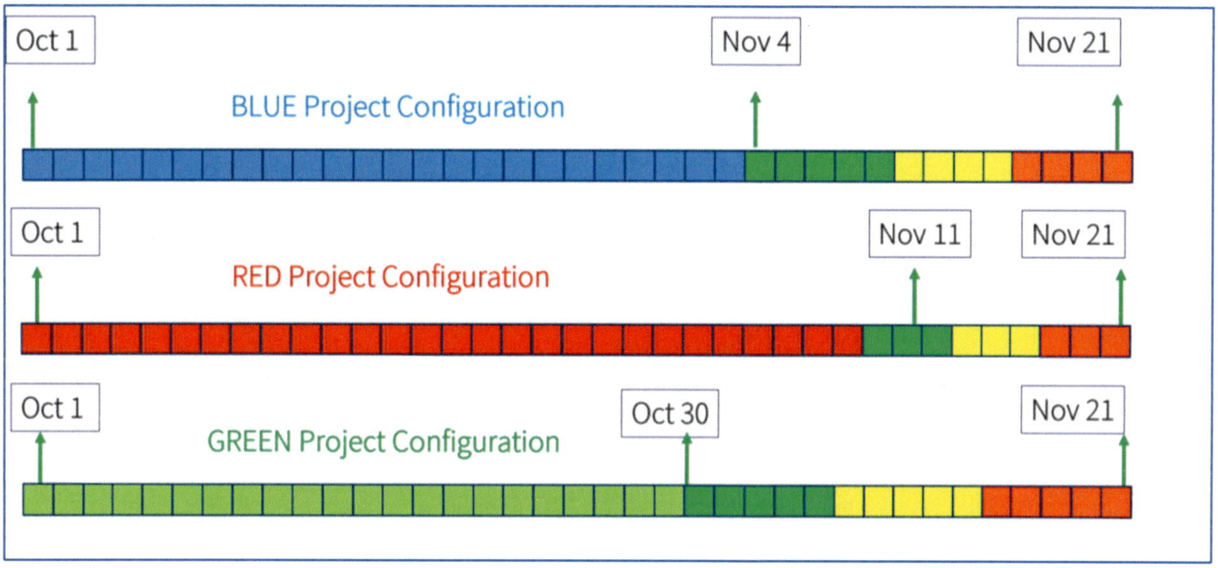

The BLUE configuration is the standard one derived from the customary practice of the CCPM method, the RED configuration aims at hastening the pace, while the GREEN setup slows the beat.

It will come as no surprise that the project with the smaller CCPM buffer will generate more Work Execution signals and that the project with the bigger CCPM buffer will send fewer signals. It is a way to do some social engineering on the flow of the teams with positive stressors. Of course, each project appearing on a Buffer Fever Chart can have different buffer configurations, since they are all represented on a relative scale irrespective of scope, budget, timeline and ... CCPM buffer configuration!

In Cynefin parlance, we often need to 'Inspect and Adapt' and also to 'Sense and Respond'. When you want to 'do' agile, you can refer to the below illustration as well and leverage the buffer signals.

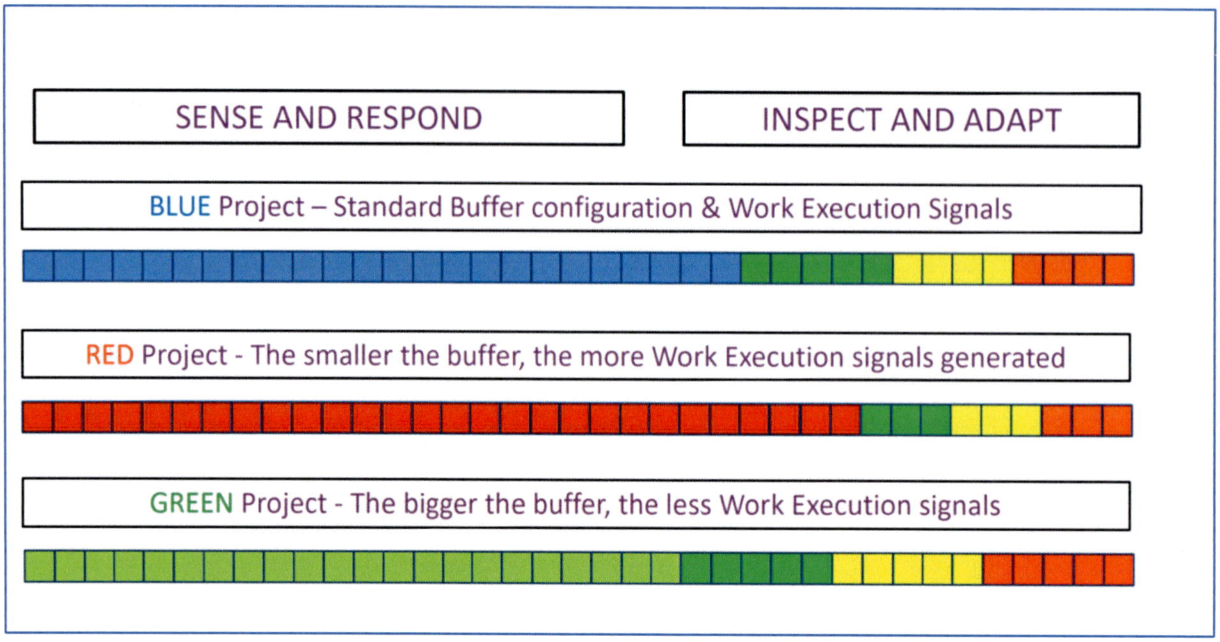

We will now leverage the new representation of the Buffer Fever Chart for Knowledge-Work, with the explicit white DRUM line and the blue flow zone.

The following depicts the same project with the three buffer configurations we have addressed above on the traditional Buffer Fever Chart:

1) Blue line - normal number of Work Execution signals,
2) Red line – increased number of Work Execution signals and,
3) Green line - the lower number of Work Execution signals.

We can see the different configuration of stressors dictating the random walk of the same project into the different zones as shown below:

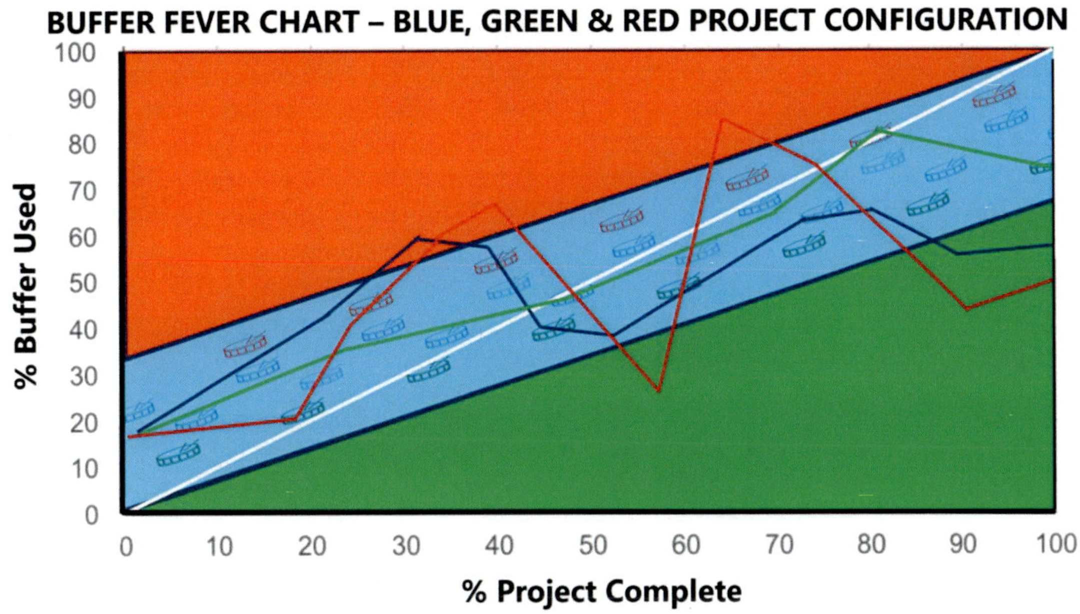

There are a few things to be addressed in this new approach. For example, a yardstick for semi variance to assess downside risk. What is the numerical threshold for a 'RED' BBR? That is to be determined. When the BBR is equal to or less than one, there really is nothing to worry about. So maybe only two zones are needed instead of three.

Conclusion – The Time They Are A-Changin'[93]

The most potent tool covered in this chapter is how to turn your Kanban lead time distribution into a CCPM project plan. Once you have a stable and predictable system as per Little's Law, now is the time to turn Explicit Risk Management into fruition. The resulting trust than can be built with management by exception signals and the staggering function of the CCPM buffer is priceless.

Equally, we have touched on subjects that have never been addressed in Throughput Accounting for Knowledge-Work. Let's review them:

1. The DRUM beat of the Buffer Fever Chart is never shown, yet it exists. Of all the Buffer Fever Charts format used, none show the DRUM line. That DRUM line cuts across the Yellow zone in a non-customary diagonal fashion making visible downside and upside risks in project execution. This is important for decision-making and resource allocation.

[93] Song by Bob Dylan 1964 – If you listen to the lyrics, there is a lot that applies here in the last minute of the song! https://www.youtube.com/watch?v=KOw6ReLIPUc

2. Downside risk is what matters when visualizing a Buffer Fever Chart and the approach of choice to determine it – in the ideal world – is with what is called in finance the 'semi variance'. A perfect solution for getting to a semi variance still eludes us. Maybe the ToC community can come up with this as well and with some guidelines regarding when a BBR measure is to be considered a risk factor. This is important to act upon now as I sincerely believe that 'buffer' penetration signals alongside the YELLOW/GREEN territory OUGHT never to be treated as signals and should be ignored. No dangers lie there. The buffer penetration signals to be put in your registries and analyzed are those crossings on the YELLOWW/RED perimeter. Those are where the low hanging fruits are to be found. They constitute downside risk. The risk you want to keep an eye on.

3. Most of the time, we tend to focus on the 'one' constraint that impacts us, but for Work Execution, we enter into a new computational reality that is the ratio between two relative scales that do not hold time still as when we measure the constraint in the Work Flow. The number of hits – or derived BBR's with the same value showing the same constraint magnitude in many places on the Buffer Fever Chart– can be considerable. For this reason, there is at least one such constraint in the Work Execution.

4. The use of a new Buffer Fever Chart to support psychological flow and using a Blue zone in lieu of the traditional Yellow zone. The Yellow zone is now out of context when we consider that all dots below the DRUM line are really not in a Yellow state. We have also seen how to engineer flow at the team level by shaping the CCPM buffer sizes and molding the frequency of Work Execution Signals generated.

Managing on the time axis should be a strategic imperative. It paves the way to management by exception. It is in line with the essence of Inherent Simplicity and the spirit of the teachings of Throughput Accounting as time lost at the constraint is Throughput gone forever. There is a broad enough knowledge base in Agile regarding what goes right and what goes wrong to embrace the new avenues that Throughput Accounting for Knowledge-Work brings to the table.

I cannot stress enough that nowhere in the Agile Manifesto does it state that timeboxing is warranted.

The science behind CCPM is considerable and has taken aback many agilists, notably the Poppendieks. Simply taking the CCPM buffer and creating free plans at will with your empirical data can lead to project execution excellence that has no comparison in the world of agile. And to paraphrase a quote from my first book:

> "What most approaches fail at is not in the planning itself, but in how the execution is managed. We should stop thinking about the execution of the plan, and more specifically about the execution of the work (work that was presumably planned) with the use of leading indicators and Management by Exception."

Knowledge-Work has yet to embrace constraints awareness. We know without a doubt now that the Work Flow, Work Process and Work Execution can all be subject of constraints. The biggest platitude we hear regarding constraints in Knowledge-Work is that they move all the time. Not so. We can pin down a constraint by limiting its capacity for one thing. We have also gauged in chapter one that discretionary and targeted actions with Throughput, Investments and/or Operating Expenses could prevent the constraints from moving.

The Buffer Fever Chart is a fantastic tool as it brings the panoply of projects attributes down to a relative scale. Just imagine the quadratic time savings obtained when you only need to invite the projects/teams that are in red and let the others work! That is smart execution at the Portfolio level! Also, I am proposing – since the goal is to automate – that only the projects who have a BBR rate that breaks a pre-determined threshold be invited to the Portfolio meeting. It makes no sense to have only one constraint in the Work Execution and invite 10 projects or teams to the Portfolio meeting.

We need to simplify life for top management and embrace the time axis, for the times they are a-changin'!

There are two ways to deal with a BBR coefficient $\approx$ 1:

- The classical way is to associate this state with Common Cause Variation and the YELLOW color. It is customary to think in these terms and totally acceptable.
- The social engineering way where the coefficient can be manipulated with the CCPM buffer to emit more or less signal. In this situation, we think of it as a team improvement mechanism and associate to it the color BLUE.

A closing note. Agilists often times say that we live in a complex world. Things are not predictable from one day to the next. It may be true for the Jungle and a bit less for the Journey. Not a chance with the Jeep which includes our tools, processes, co-workers, technical environment. So not everything changes on a daily basis and for that reason things that are linked 'to the way we do things around here' is the best place to tame Common Cause Variation and get lasting and impactful improvements.

APPENDIX A – CLASSICAL CONSUMPTION BUFFER & MODERN BUFFER BURN RATE

Modern Narrative on Buffer Consumption Penetration Buffer and Buffer Burn Rate

The Buffer Penetration indicates how much of the buffer has been consumed, how many days more (as a percentage of the total buffer) than the original baseline that we are anticipating to finish. It is a dynamic indicator that adapts to the reality. (Can go from Green to Red, to Yellow and back to Green)

If BBR <1, then it is green
If BBR approximately 1 then blue
If BBR >1, then it is red

The Buffer Burn Rate tells you how fast/slow you are progressing to the schedule's original plan (DRUM). It is a dynamic indicator that can go from from Red, to Green to Blue again. It is related – on a relative basis – to the beat of the DRUM, which is equal to 1. Green means you are going faster than the DRUM, RED means slower than the planned beat of the DRUM. BLUE means you are doing OK.

APPENDIX B – CLASSICAL STAGGERING with CCPM BUFFER PENETRATION

Staggering from CCPM is a gift to all stakeholders involved in a project. It deals with the CCPM buffer. When multiple projects run sequentially or in parallel, their start and end dates are adjusted in real time with the penetration level of the CCPM buffer. It allows for dynamically adjusting resources and providing proper communication to all involved. It is also a tool of management by exception: giving us advanced signals of risk materialization on the time axis.

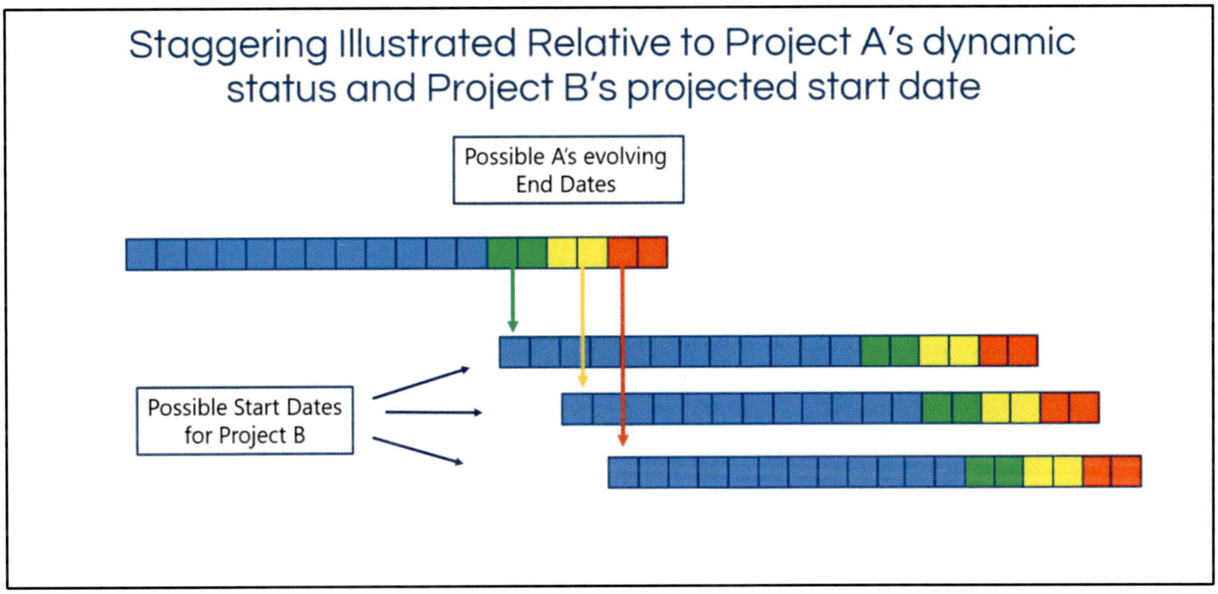

You can control the company's workload in a Portfolio by pipelining and staggering projects to make realistic commitments to deadlines.

CHAPTER IV – THE COLOR OF MONEY‽ [94]

"Down to Gehenna or up to the Throne, he travels fastest he who travels alone." – Rudyard Kipling

Introduction:

Have you heard the story of the CIO that had a $280 million budget and not a penny to spare? There is green money[95] and then there is brown money[96]. What kind of money is your Improvement Initiative 'bringing' in? What kind of money is your Improvement Initiative 'using'?[97]

This is the angle that Throughput Accounting takes with Improvement Initiatives.

Improvement Initiatives of all breeds sometimes will aim to save 'man days' or become more efficient in the back office by closing the books faster (brown money that will not find its way to the bottom line but can nonetheless give you a tactical, competitive advantage).

Being efficient will likely get you more output per input and get things done faster, but it remains to be seen if this will translate into improved cash flows.

---

[94] Punctuation – Acclamation point. A complete array of seldom used punctuation points can be found here: https://www.mentalfloss.com/article/12710/13-little-known-punctuation-marks-we-should-be-using

[95] Green money is money that has been freshly introduced into the system – for example, through new sales. It can also be new money (think financing) that must be found to meet unexpected expenses without taking sums from the current budget. That sort of money requires special approval to obtain or a procedure to follow that is more demanding than simply taking existing and planned-for money from your current budget and assigning it to meet another operational need. This lies within your span of control.

[96] Brown money is 'familiar' money. It can be the predictable sales revenues from your top 5 customers. Year in, year out, it is money assigned to your operating budget: keep-the-lights-on money! Some parts are discretionary and others non-discretionary. It is used at the operational level and if you deem that changing the labor mix or doing things differently will help Identify, Exploit or Subordinate to the constraint, then there is no 'new' money involved. You are within your span of control. The first three steps of the 5FS use that kind of money primarily. In line with the 5 Focusing Steps, there is often no need to increase overall Investments or Operating Expenses to redirect money to the constraint by taking money that is used in vain away from the constraint. It can be a zero-sum game budget and spending wise. Brown money inflows refers to Improvement Initiatives that make you more efficient but do not bring in green money generated by new sales. Money 'saved' in operational 'man days' is often illusionary money that does not make it to the bottom line of the Income Statement. This is brown money as well.

[97] I am often reminded of the story of the $7,000 'cost per day per room' of staying at the hospital. This COST was not a CO$T and was arrived at by allocation of capacity and services. An Improvement Initiative of 1 million dollars aimed at cutting 1,000 days of stay was triggered. It was sold as a 7 million dollar saving! Someone got on the hook for 1,000 green dollars! Altering the rate of consumption of something that is paid for may improve cost per number metrics or resource efficiency but the dollars spent and the impact on cash will not change! The resource is there irrespective of usage.

Those initiatives sometimes show nothing in terms of Financial Throughput, though Operational Throughput is observed. By all means, those 'brown'[98] projects[99] still have merit and are required. You will have your 'savings' but no green money as capacity has not changed and the rate of utilisation that your project has brought about will not alter the economics of what has been bought. One way to spot a 'brown' project is their baseline is on a 'cost per number' metric that they want to target. Efficiency based projects have that smell too. Those 'cost per number' statistics are the fruit of arbitrary allocation drivers that have no relation to reality and in no way are they empowered to change the cash outlays required to pay for purchased capacity.

This is a distinction with a difference. People do not pay attention to the color of money. And they should. Throughput Accounting accomplishes this by having you wear the hat of a financial analyst, base your decisions on the marginal impact of your actions and perform all your accounting on a cash basis. And most importantly, the main driver is money coming from external sources.

The kind of Improvement Initiatives that I want to target are those which have a lot of value, as well as a scientific foundation. Lean aims at reducing waste, Six Sigma at reducing variation. It works best at the constraint!

I am all for immediate gratification in any Improvement Initiative when we can show results early on the path to these long journeys. This is one of the great benefits of applying the 5 Focusing Steps to Throughput Accounting. Benefits are fast coming in terms of green money. In terms of costs, brown money[100] can go a long way.

As I have mentioned in earlier chapters, there are seldom any new cash outflows required with the first three steps: Identify, Exploit and Subordinate. Drawing on existing capacity and operating expenses is not a use of new funds in Throughput Accounting as there is no delta (OE) – Operating Expenses and/or delta (I) - Investments. Green money gets generated very fast and this is a source of new funds.

All decisions made with Throughput Accounting have one driver: money, much more green money coming from outside the firm.

This is important to realize.

In this chapter, we will introduce additional Throughput Accounting principles, formulae and new reports in the context of Improvement Initiatives. But first, let's see how our flawed mental models are causing our own roadblocks.

---

[98] I am using the color brown to distinguish a category of project that creates the illusion that 'savings' of X dollars on improving metrics of the 'cost per number' types will actually be reflected in green cash inflows. It is rarely the case.

[99] A brown project requires green money to finance, but does not change the cash flow situation before and after the fact. Projects that aim to change 'cost per number' statistics or aim for resource efficiency often fall in that category. Some of those projects are required at times, but never should you believe that there will be an impact on inflow of green money.

[100] Performing the first three steps of the 5 Focusing Steps, while not impacting (OE) – Operating Expenses or (I) – Investments, is an example of using brown money. It has great value in this context.

Encore on costs and topics related to chapter 1 and 3

There are a few places where I could have inserted this section. But it deals best with the color of money.

In chapter 1, I dealt with transaction, setup and coordination costs and the impact of those vis-à-vis the constraint[101]. If they take time on the constraint, you need to be smart on that: less is more to a certain extent. Just enough is right. Away from the constraint, we are not concerned as much as there is enough capacity to absorb these charges. There is a caveat. It's about flow. And WIP. If the use you make of your brown money impedes flow and/or increases WIP – you are impacting green money and are not subordinating to the constraint. The bucks stop here and now, whether it happens upstream or downstream of the constraint. Never over produce with brown money.

In Chapter 3, I went all in on the benefits of probabilistic forecasting in lieu of estimating. I even made a bodacious comment on LinkedIn to the fact that despite estimating while using brown money, it can severely impact green money because it can cause FLOW and WIP issues by overburdening away from the constraint the resources associated to those tasks. On LinkedIn, when I saw Joseph Pelrine reacting with a 'curious' emojicon, I said I better take care of this. And I am.

If you review the XIT at Microsoft case, there are a Pleiades of ambushes embedded in estimating. You get to do a lot of activities that impede time, and approvals, and discussions on the backlog sizing and grooming, and permissions, and budget issues, and estimating, looking into code and documentation. And then the deliverables are sitting for a few weeks or months to be finally approved. And once all is done, we need to dance to the beat of variance analysis - (they call those retrospectives in agile) – where we try to find out what went wrong and how we could all be better next time if something of the SAME nature comes around again. The best move is to do your homework properly upstream, clear up the dependencies so that you can take the ball all the way into the end zone. Planning with strings and pins of what could be is just accommodating the ephemeral. It won't happen.

Estimating consumes time. Time is the single most important lever to making money in Throughput Accounting. In the Microsoft XIT case, we were taking 40% of the budget for estimating and much more in terms of stress and unpleasant work. It was not an agile environment to start with so we have to be careful. But I think we can all appreciate.

This is all brown money but it is a bad use of brown money as it can increase WIP (artefacts and ceremonies required in estimating) and impede Flow as a consequence of too much WIP, non needed managerial oversight targeted at resources that should be productive.

---

[101] Size of batches also has no impact on 'management' costs away from the constraint. But batch size WILL have an impact on cycle time that WILL have an impact on Throughput. Throughput is based on speed thru the constraint but speed to the market is also key. This is why we have two buffers in manufacturing: a DBR buffer to protect the constraint and a S-DBR buffer to protect the market! This is a good example of an opportunity cost with DBR (constraint hiccup that definitely causes a loss of revenues that cannot be recouped) and a lost opportunity with S-DBR (potentially a lost sale to a specific client, or not, or ... plenty of scenarios can apply here.) Opportunity costs are hard target. Lost opportunity belongs in the fictitious world as it can never actually be measured for sure.

And always remember the concept of the Jeep – the constraint in the Work Flow: only the team that is the constraint in the work flow needs to plan or estimate if you so wish to. All other teams that would do as such – planning, estimating - are not subordinating to the constraint, are impeding flow and increasing WIP and directly impacting green money's fluidity.[102]

Operating Expenses as a Source of Funds and Motivation

Operating Expenses are meant to 'fund' capacity generally speaking. This is the traditional understanding of the accounting profession and a such, that money would be considered a use of funds[103]. But capacity is malleable. If we were to go into the science fiction movie meme, we could call capacity a 'shape shifter'. There is brown – but real – money hidden in Operating expenses that impacts capacity and turns this into new green money.

Is making money with money a source of funds or a use of funds? This can be tricky. You need to qualify the color of money if you are talking about productivity, growth or expansion as we will reckon in the next few chapters how brown money can generate green money.

Oddly enough, when thinking about it, all Improvement Models tend to operate the same way: you'll have to disburse green money right at the start to eventually make green money down the road. The end state seldom happens in a predictable fashion as none are constraint savvy. At least not in a predictable and repeatable fashion unless you are lucky to hit the constraint every single time. Lucky is the term.

When using the 5 Focusing Steps, need we remind ourselves that the first 3 steps of Identifying, Exploiting and Subordinating to the constraint are key in unleashing new capacity and the inflow of green money. Often time, not a dime of external money is required. We use brown money – Operating Expenses - as a 'source' of funds and shift our managerial attention where it counts.

Operating Expenses are thus a source of funds as well, not only a use of funds. It is incumbent to the participants in the value stream to make it happen.

To conclude this section, there is some discretionary manoeuvring room with Operating Expenses. Allocating funds from low payout activities to new opportunities is making good use of brown money. It is very attractive as normally you can go a long way without getting out of your span of control. This is a good and easy way to shine with good decision-making without asking for permission as opposed to when going to your sphere of influence for your demand.

[102] There is a fine line to be drawn here. Planning and estimating artefacts are for 'execution' purposes, the scope of this book. Using brown money upstream to trace the perimeter of the business requirements, the delivery of the solution and the likes will increase WIP – the number of artefacts – and slow down flow but it is absolutely necessary. There is a reason why we need excess capacity upstream. And it should be used at will. The 'fuzzy front end' has to be tamed.

[103] I am talking figuratively here as sources and uses of funds are provided by assets and liability accounts and certainly not an expense account. But bare with me.

Now that we have established an additional attribute of Operating Expenses, it is important to stretch the importance of this component of Throughput Accounting on morale and employee productivity.

Productivity is linked to capacity. And the reflex of cutting Operating Expenses as the fastest way back to profitability is concerned is the go-to solution. It is also the fastest way to financial perdition. Always remember the launching sequence of Throughput Accounting in the precise order that follows: increase Sales, decrease Investments and reduce Operating Expenses.

In a strange way, Operating Expenses are also the 'money' you give your workforce so that they can perform at work. It is a hidden attribute seldom discussed. But it is important to understand that by first cutting on OE to get more profits is an act of war against the working conditions of the resources. The illustration below gives an alternative view of the components of Throughput Accounting that is indicative of the ripple effect of each component and the overall impact on alignment, culture and goal congruence:

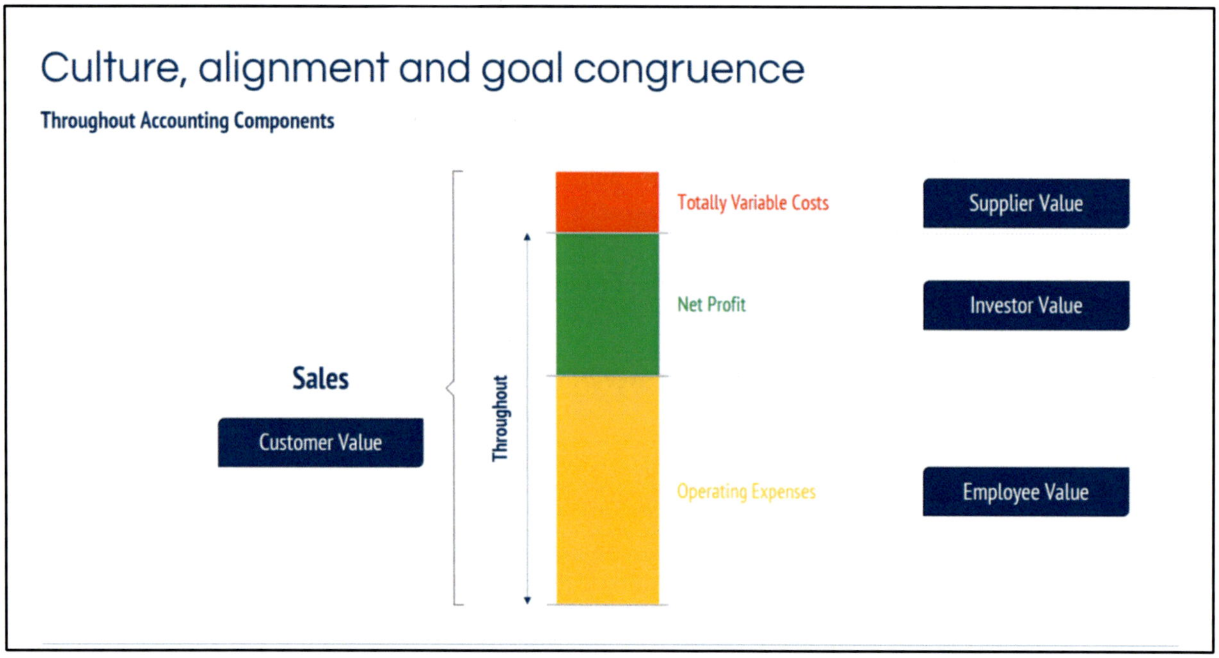

Cash-to-Cash Cycle

Reducing the cash-to-cash cycle is the ultimate lever for generating Throughput in a geometric fashion **within your** company as you build products. It cannot be stressed enough that this is the weapon of choice in the mortar economy.

The illustration below articulates the 3 steps sequential process:

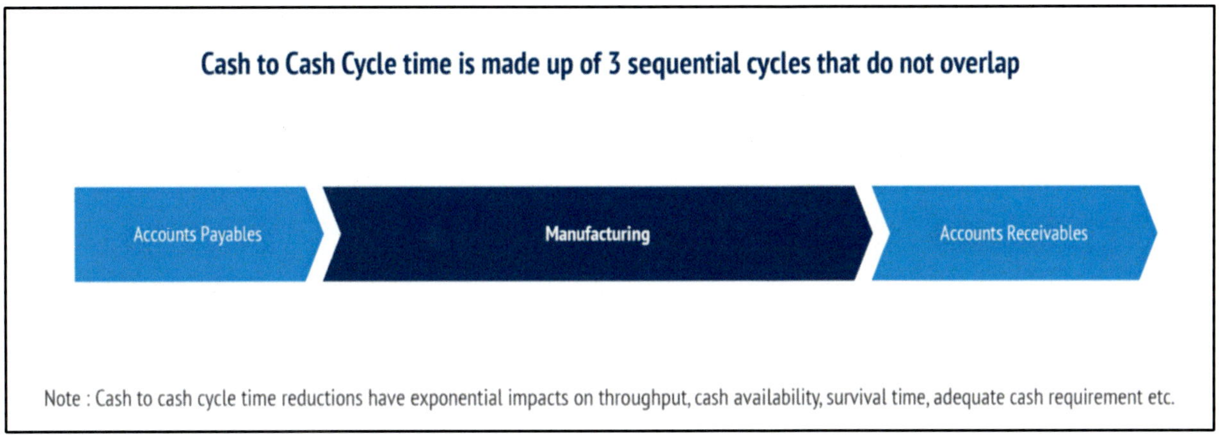

The cash-to-cash cycle deals with green money exclusively. It starts when we pay for TVC – not when we receive the raw materials - and ends when we receive payment from the clients, not when shipment of the goods to the customer happened.

The illustration below shows that the two most potent tools reside first in helping to reduce inventory levels and next, to shrink production time.

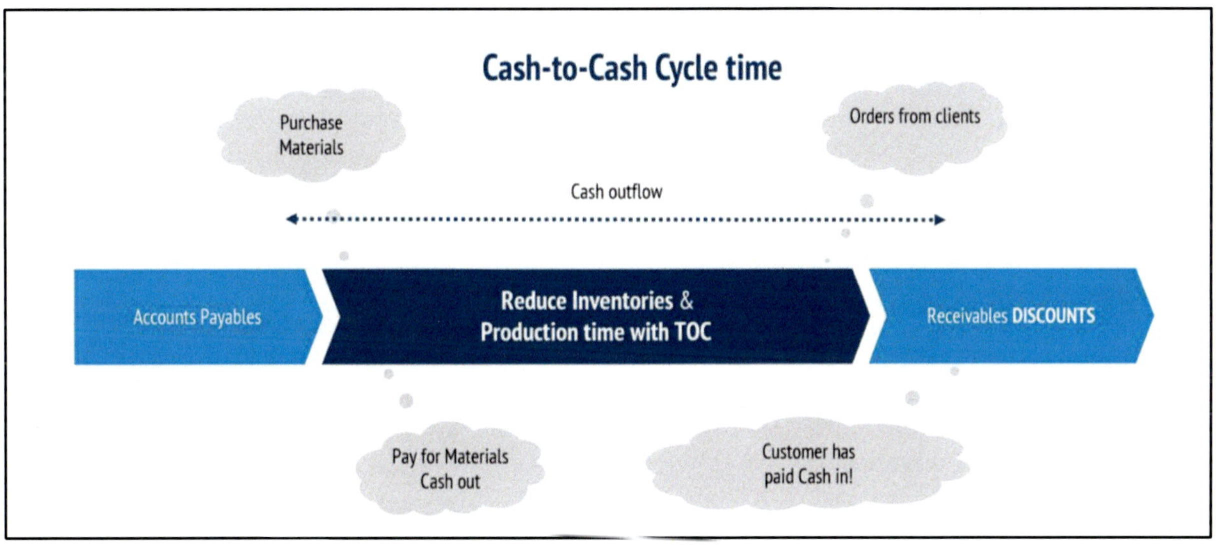

When dealing with the Knowledge economy where TVC seldom exists, we run into interesting issues that we will address soon.

It is important to make a parallel here. Reducing all times – cycle time, production time, lead time, flow time, delivery time etc. – are all considered as valid scope for Improvement Initiatives.

I claim that reducing the Cash-to-Cash cycle time falls into that taxonomy as well in a Throughput Accounting context.

In Through the Out Door

The topics addressed and the way they are tackled in this section are definitely written by an iconoclast, on the entertaining side and edging at the metaphor level as well! A lot of truth will still remain. I wanted to include these topics in the next volume of this series on Throughput Accounting but market imperatives dictate that some market inefficiencies be addressed in the 'job description' market as many agile and/or performance improvement projects make a strong and explicit connection with resource efficiency or efficiency at large. Performance and Resource Efficiency do not belong in the same sentence.

Being in IT for my entire career, being a CPA and having done agile, I am in a unique position to make a 'State of the Situation' address.

Whether you are a head hunter in IT/Agile or Accounting, performance and Resource Efficiency are put in the same sentence. It is unacceptable to me. I have spoken to those who convey these 'job offers' and they are very happy with the state of affair. The status quo is good as it is a shield for protection of their revenues.

The Market for Improvement Initiatives

As I read the keywords for contract work in the Montréal and Toronto markets, I often find content pertaining to performance – aka continuous improvement - and operational efficiency combined in the same add. I wonder how the two halves can be strapped in the same sentence (Performance Improvement Initiatives and operational efficiency). In an efficient market in Knowledge-Work, have we really matured over he last 15 years of Improvement Initiatives? This requires a fix and a visit.

I have entered in contact with quite a few head hunters and consultants in the process. They all plead that they cater to the needs of the clients. I have been down that hatch before and I pledge – as I have been part of that game - that they push what they are best at selling and that working in a revenue protection mode suit them fine. The clients should know better.

These requests for continuous improvement in the Agile market come from big banks, insurance company, utilities and telco. In the manufacturing sector, accountants are sought after to improve performance thru standard accounting operating procedures. Combined, the type of people they look for are accountants, IT/agile professionals and resources having experience in Lean, Six Sigma and/or ADKAR. Often times knowledge of Scrum, Agile, Kanban and SAFe are part of the mix for Agile work. No Theory of Constraints, no POOGI material.

In the months of September to December 2021 – for fun and the purpose of this book – I have been trying to make the case that POOGI – 'Process of On-Going Improvement', Throughput Accounting and the 5 Focusing Steps from the Theory of Constraints were a palatable solution, and I applied a few times to big head-hunters firms in Montréal and Toronto for such continuous improvement, performance, agility, operational efficiency etc. types of jobs. I targeted accounting firms and the traditional IT firms. None of them knew of Dr Eli Goldratt's legacy. None of them showed any interest in searching any further.

Regularly, those who lead such undertakings are more enamored with resource efficiency - which is bad for flow and ideal for fostering high inventory levels and the proliferation of queues - and unbeknownst to them, they are losing money! I hope this section will be of use. Not only to them but to those who embark, or even sponsor these death marches and suffer the consequences in the process. Remember, every inch you travel on a path of improvement may change the way you work and increase operating expenses and layers of overhead costs - which are invisible to the most astute - and difficult to remove once in place. Unless you know where the constraint is and can then arbitrage the use of your operating expenses.

If you act every month and consume resources on fixing things that are not in line with Throughput Accounting and the 5 Focusing Steps, you are digging yourself into a permanent hole.

We have visited some of the flawed mental models that are part of the fabric of society in the first chapter. But to what end? Making money is the goal. And nothing gives you more of that than reducing the cash-to-cash cycle time. It is a specialty of Throughput Accounting[104] and no one else can go as deep and as far into resolving this dire situation.

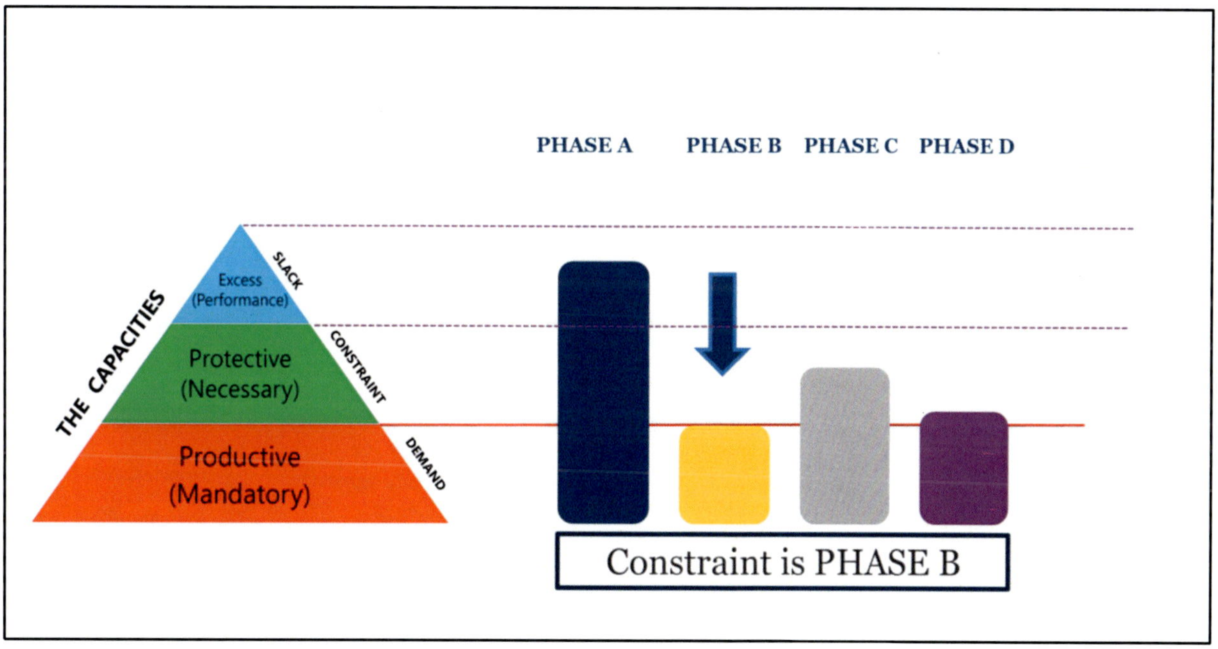

[104] Of all 'Financial' accreditations such as CA, CPA, CMA, CIMA and CFA no one has a formula for getting out of a severe cash constraint with cash velocity. It is unique to Throughput Accounting and a potent tool to optimize the cash-to-cash cycle. Here it is: CV = ((S/TVC)^(1/n) -1). I go at length on this formula in my Throughput Accounting class for CPAs.

Money Talk - Resource Efficiency vs Flow Efficiency[105]

Remember the illustration just above from chapter 3? One thing that is never mentioned is that resource efficiency and flow efficiency reflect your affective predisposition toward the color of money. If all the money flowing in your company is 'green', you are high on Resource Efficiency. You are color blind. Not a penny to spare and to create value, you need green money as an input. Let's build up WIP, create local optima, queues and Wait Time. The more we buy, the lower the unit cost and the more profits come selling time, if and when sales come.

Busy hands and busy feet are all you see because no work gets done.

This is how money is treated in a resource efficiency environment. It need be spent. If not, it will be taken away from you in the next budget cycle. A resource efficiency environment treats all components of the enterprise – Phase A, B, C and D as per the illustration above - as having equal weight, hence the significantly bigger amount of green money to have the organisation perform. By contrast, the Theory of Constraint (ToC) recognizes that plenty of brown money and slack capacity lies upstream and downstream of the constraint and that they can be used to have the constraint located at Phase C and humming – the only part of the organisation that matters for bottom line results.

Still doubting me? One thing is a sure give away. Resource Efficiency metrics fit nicely in a traditional accounting environment and accompany status reports and financial statements like a side dish.

Get up, go a few staircases up and ask the PMO for the metrics they show upper management. The PMO serves at the pleasure of upper management and no one else. The truth between Resource Efficiency and Flow Efficiency lies there if you were not convinced with my first argument.

See if they have brown money – at no charge off of your systems – on Flow metrics corresponding to the ones in the illustration below. If not, you are running high on Resource Efficiency, hinging on irrelevant historical costs with no predictive value and burning green money!

---

[105] I have included in the references section a series of articles on the topic by Johanna Rothman. They cover a wide array of topics

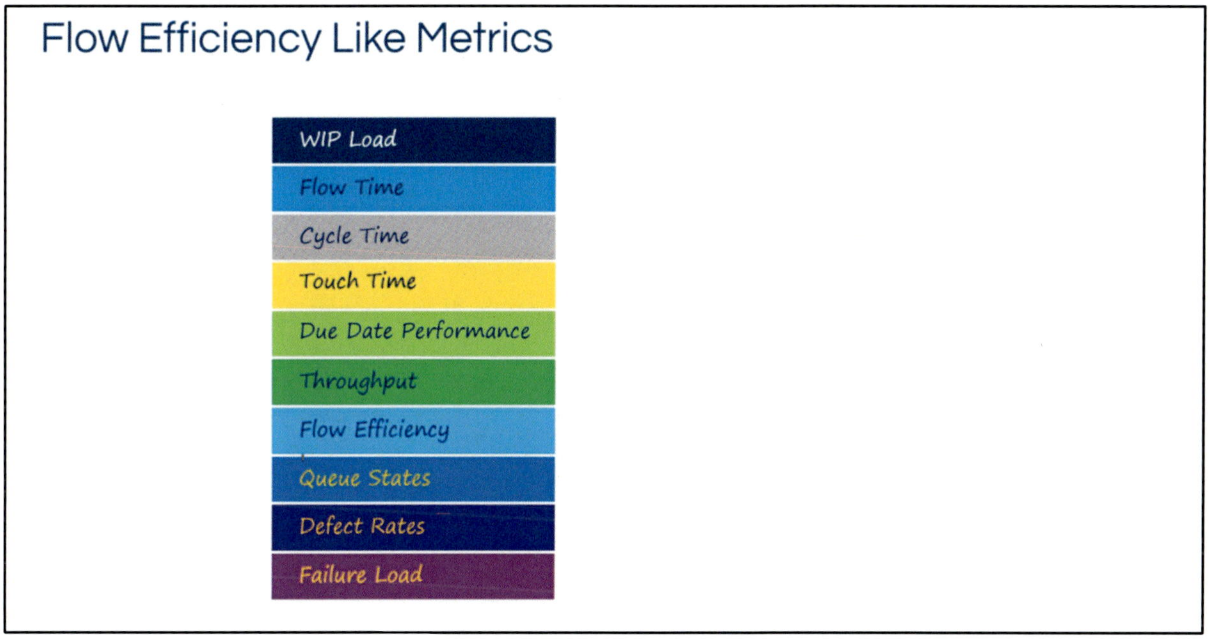

But what is the issue with comprehending Flow Efficiency? When I was very young and had to 'do' with physical toys made of wood and in 2 dimensions, I enjoyed this game on Resource Efficiency and Flow Efficiency. You can have one – Resource Efficiency or Flow Efficiency - but not both![106]

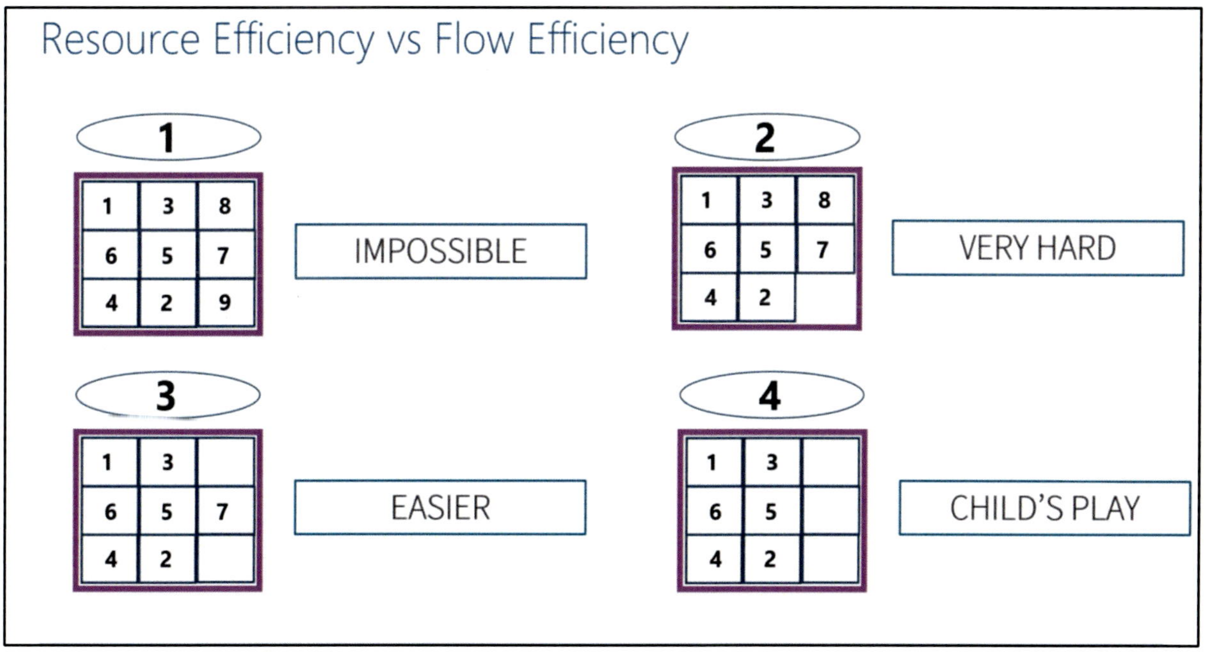

[106] You can have both. But this is an advanced topic on your way to Lean Nirvana!

The game is easy and important to understand. You have to arrange the numbers in ascending order starting at 1. The game is simply impossible to play in quadrant 1 where Resource Efficiency is at 100%. There is simply no room. But you have your 100% Resource Efficiency: there is no space to spare and nowhere to go on the wooden surface and zero performance to be had!

Scenario 2 is still quite hard to resolve timewise as configuration 3 gets easier with more slack in the system.

Come configuration 4, where Flow Efficiency is king, and this become child's play as the ranking from 1 to 6 can be done in seconds. Resource Efficiency is very low as a trade off and it has the smell of brown money with free capacity. But you can get this assignment of ranking the digits in less than 2 or 3 seconds if you are wearing mittens, and you start raking in green money!

People always ask me what is the point of this demonstration in real life. I simply tell them that when work arrives within your span of control, you can exert some control and trade off between Resource Efficiency and Flow Efficiency. And the message that follows is very potent. There will always be unlimited demand on your capacities (external) but you control the speed at which things get done at your end (internal use of capacity).

What people fail to understand is that if you manage at your end, then people only wait outside. Once they are in your system, things go very fast. But there is always the second option, do not manage your Flow Efficiency and have people requesting your services wait a long time outside the system and a long time once inside the system. The choice exists. It is a discretionary choice. It is entirely up to you.

This is what Improvement Initiatives should be all about: Flow Efficiency and performance. Nothing to do with Resource Efficiency. Ever. But it is what most of them aim for and strive to achieve.

For the final twist. Which do you prefer:

- Idle People – People wait for work? (Flow Efficiency/Throughput Accounting)
- Idle Work – Work waits for people? (Resource Efficiency/Cost Accounting)

If you opt for resource efficiency, work will wait to be serviced for quite a long time. Resources and queues will tend to build up and appear in front of the work. System performance will decay while everybody works extremely hard at getting nowhere fast!

This is the worst scenario and the one we have grown accustomed to recklessly adhere to. Such is the resource efficiency trap, and still today my brain falls for it. But not as often as it once did.

I had training like the top performing athletes must receive as we discussed in the Prologue. My brain is now rewired.

Idle workers are essential and the trade mark of high performing organisation. When work shows up, it is serviced immediately.

It is hard for conventional managers to conceive of this trade-off. In those instances, I like to point them to the Queen event of the Olympic games: the 4X100 relay!

Race	Resource Efficiency	World Record Time - (Flow Time)
400 meters	100%	43.03 seconds
4X100 meters	25%	36.84 seconds

The table above says it all. At any time during the 4X100 race, resource efficiency is topped at 25% as only one runner out of four is active. Flow Time – or Flow Efficiency - is observed by following the baton, not the runners.[107]

Money Talk - The Cash-to-Cash Cycle in a Knowledge-Work Context

We covered already the normal and traditional cash-to-cash cycle as a propellant for Throughput generation in the traditional economy. In a scenario applied to the manufacturing world, it is absolutely necessary to spend green dollars to pay for all of the material under TVC – Totally Variable Costs - needed to transform the stuff we sell to collect green dollars as a result. The context of the cash-to-cash cycle here is to produce goods. There is no brown money.

What if we were to take that cash-to-cash cycle time as an improvement model for Knowledge-Work where TVC seldom applies? Would that mean that there are no more tracers as to when the cycle time begins since there are no cash outlays for TVC? This is an interesting point of view as all that counts now is to collect the client as fast as possible.

I am taking an awkward stance in this section and dissecting the cash-to-cash cycle out of its original context and applying the 5 Focusing Steps lens on it as a candidate for an improvement initiative model which it is never labelled as such. It was confusing when I contemplated the idea, and I think I have narrowed the perimeter I wanted to trace. There is still a bit of work to do to deliver a clearer message and I will revisit the topic in my next book. We are in the world of metaphors for the sake of looking at things from an angle they were not intended to be looked at. We can draw some interesting lessons from that.

Some would argue that comparing the cash-to-cash cycle amongst different improvement initiatives is fruitless unless we share a common yardstick which is green money and refrain from using the term 'brown' money anymore. The traditional clock for the cash-to-cash cycle starts once you pay for the inputs – not upon reception of raw materials - and ends when you receive the money from your outputs - not upon shipping the goods to the customer. Easy, cash-to-cash in the context of increasing Throughput by shrinking the length of the cash-to-cash cycle in the material world of manufacturing.

I agree, and you asked for it. Here is the ca$ch22[108]:

- In Throughput Accounting, the cash-to-cash cycle always deals with green money!
- In Throughput Accounting, when using the 5FS as an Improvement Initiative, we can go a long way with brown money in order to get green money.

---

[107] The agile adage: 'Focus on idle work, not idle workers' still eludes most managers today!

[108] Of course, catch 22 is implied ….

In a Knowledge-Work context, the cash-to-cash cycle loses its starting and ending markers. It then becomes closer to a POOGI model, which aims at reducing lead time, a foundational pillar of the cash-to-cash cycle.

And if you were to collect the money from the customer before actually doing the work? Then both markers of the cash-to-cash sequential process are gone!

We need new yardsticks for the cash-to-cash cycle and to that aim, I think it should merge with POOGI!

Money Talk - Duration

I will not delve indefinitely on the concept of duration as it requires a start and end state for reaching the break-even point. There are just a few plug-in variables that are not available when using Throughput Accounting's deltas for additional Investments or Operating expenses. Most of the time, they would not apply. When they do, you can use duration. One such scenario would be once you reached Step 4 – Elevate the Constraint. Most of the time outlays of green money is required, but not always.

Again, be careful with the Cost Accounting's 'contribution margin' approach which has similarities with Throughput Accounting's break-even point in calculating duration. The break-even point from a contribution margin approach will always require more sales volume to break-even showing again that traditional accounting always places additional hurdles and burdens on optimal managerial solutions. Your duration calculations will be skewed. The contribution margin – like all traditional accounting models – uses allocation which sets the bar higher and include head office salaries under the false lens that it is a variable cost. Throughput Accounting only uses TVC to truly represent the cost of a unit linked to its sale.

The illustration below shows the difference in the breakdown of components from both statements.

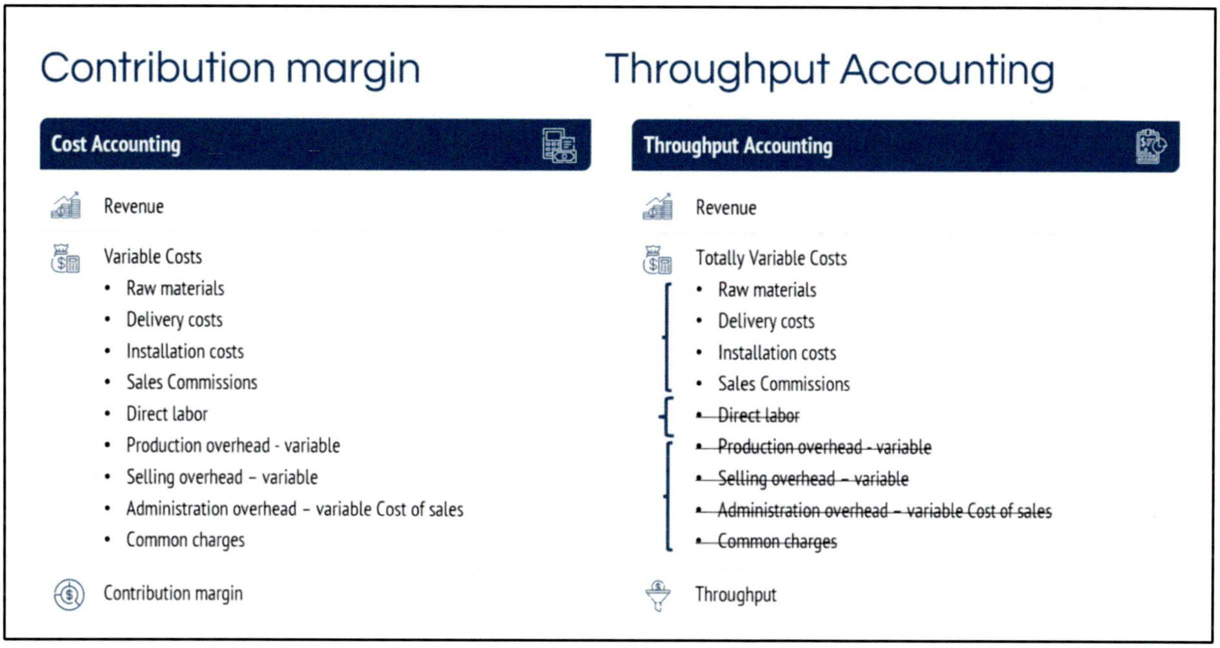

Cost Accounting's Contribution Margin two main concerns are to look at the links between the relevance and the directness of all that contributes to a product cost. In so doing such items as labor costs and depreciation would make the cut. Under a Throughput Accounting lens these two expenditures would be viewed as period expenses instead of costs: labor costs definitely being under Operating Expenses and depreciation – a non fund expense – below the Throughput tally and the cash flow items of the TA Income Statement.

Throughput Accounting would only be preoccupied with the TVC of the product as it goes thru the supply chain to the end user with sales as being the only factor under visibility.

Money Talk – Inflation and Deflation

Now this may come as a bit of a stretch. I want to use deflation (to demonize Cost Accounting), and inflation (to praise Throughput Accounting) to convey my message as both concepts are easily understood by all and carry some overtone of emotion, which is seldom done when discussing accounting. For simplicity we will link inflation to growth and expansion, and deflation to economic depression. Borrowing the words and adjusting their meaning in this discussion will bring life to the concepts I wish to convey.

One needs to understand that in times of inflation[109], prices are likely to go up, hence your motivation to purchase sooner rather than later. In a deflationary environment, prices will spiral down. You can wait before purchasing; the odds are on your side and in all likelihood, you'll have a better deal tomorrow.

[109] Inflation has its 'pains' but we know what they are. Of all evils, government would rather deal with inflation than being caught in a deflation or a situation where they would have to raise taxes. Raising taxes is the last thing governments want to do.

I am definitely mixing inflation with Throughput growth and deflation with Operating Expenses augmentation or better yet as a swing when one is outpacing the other. It is an easy association to make. T and OE have this relationship we need to be made aware of. The ratio between T and OE are key indicators of performance of operational excellence and absolute profitability.

Improvement Initiatives that linger on for too long and miss the constraint WILL show a loss. It will never be disclosed as such and will assuredly be disguised in some sort of 'efficiency' romance after the fact, a 'brown project' of kind now aimed at a different target where all partakers are just extenuated and bored. The start state fared much better. Ah, the good old times ...

It is a deflationary model. One where the value of the system was greater at the beginning than at the end. There is no 'easy' cure known for deflation. When it comes around, things will get a lot worse before they get a lot worse. Morale is just as bad in a cost cutting environment as growth decline is observed with Operating Expenses cuts outpacing Throughput generation. The Faustian bargain version of sustaining profits – cutting costs! Need I remind one that cutting interest rates below zero is unthinkable? So is cutting Operating Expenses, yet it is a path that we often engage on.

When the current price of an asset is higher today than what people think it will be in the future, nobody buys hoping that they will get it cheaper in a while. They wait for it to get even lower. Unknowingly, increasing the number and amount layers of cost overheads thinking you are fixing things will never reveal itself to you until it is too late. The value of your firm has gone down. It's not on the accounts nor on paper; you are just much worst at turning inputs into outputs. It has the same perverse effect as deflation to the extent that it is quasi-irreversible and lasts a long time. These costs are sticky and enduring. They will chew your profits, despite the fact that your revenues are on an upward trend. Imagine the distress. The first reflex now becomes: slash operating expenses!

Avoid Improvement Initiative projects that will decrease the value of your firm! Stop ignoring the constraint. Or better still, keep using your favorite Improvement Initiative approach to have fun and work the way you like. That stratagem was adopted by Bob Sproull who was a big fan of Lean and Six Sigma before he ran into Dr Eli Goldratt's universe. When he found the Inherent Simplicity of the Theory of Constraints, he never looked back and walked straight up ahead always carrying his Lean and Six Sigma tool box as he did his entire career. Do as such, as changing the way people work and taking away their favorite tools is a recipe for disaster. Dr Goldratt's teachings are just to be considered a 'firmware' upgrade to your brain. No new roles, no new responsibilities, no new artefacts. A lot like the Kanban method. Respect where people are and what they have done to get there, and start improving.

Now comes inflation, figuratively speaking. Increasing revenues are always easy to tally as they are contemporaneous to sales. Not so with costs as they are unknown and unknowable. Finding out which cost increase/cutting is healthy or not is near impossible. So, every month just make sure the spread between T and OE keeps growing a bit like a healthy inflationary measure, except that growth is carrying this rise, not inflation in the traditional meaning of the word. The spread between T and OE is called Net Profit – or absolute profitability - and its growth is linked to operational excellence. When T and OE are not decoupled, you are in a stagflation or deflation state. It is imperative that T and OE decouple through time and that their curves diverge.

This should be witnessed every time Income Statements are generated. Traditional accounting does not have anything similar to monitor either absolute or relative profitability. System Productivity (T/OE) is also a mandatory metric to calculate the lever effect of your capacity on Throughput at financial statements generation time.

The fastest way to a deflationary state is to Elevate the constraint by spending green money before having resolved the first 3 of the 5 Focusing Steps[110]. The best you will achieve is linear results. Expansion of current production: ten times the sales for ten times the increase in expenses. Productivity and growth have nothing to do here and will be out of the question.

Why inflation? Inflation is how our brains are wired. It is how governments like to work. And inflation is its own cure as "there is nothing like high prices[111] to fight high prices!". But we are not using inflation at that level, just he fact that seeing increasing prices is healthy over time. Declining prices are very dangerous.

Now back to deflation.

No one wants in on a deflationary sinking boat. But if you do not mind your constraint in your next Improvement Initiative, your operating expenses will skyrocket. And operational complexity will follow and hindered decision-making processes will tag along a long time. But you just asked for it. Now you know. And the last thing you want as a constraint is operational complexity.

Money Talk – Estimating and Probabilistic Forecasting

This section deals with brown money and green money with a new twist. It is pretty short. But very important. Whenever you are using resources from the constraint and taking them away from their work, you are using green money.

We need to acquiesce to the fact that when estimating – as we conceive of it as a group exercise – you will need someone from the constraint. That may impact Throughput. It is not difficult to imagine as those at the constraint should be spared managerial duties so that they can focus. Estimating is in nature speculative and such an activity is not the best choice to divert resources from the constraint to such an exercise.

I often get the rebuttal that probabilistic forecasting is just as speculative and unprecise as estimating would be. Absolutely! It is a matter of cost and time to get there. Maintaining the full control loop of an estimating cycle can chew up to 40% of your budget as demonstrated by the Microsoft XIT case. Probabilistic forecasting is done on a totally different scale. It takes almost no time to leverage your data that was generated with your operational systems – for which you already paid for - to make a target scope-based plan.

---

[110] It is possible to Elevate the constraint with brown money. But at some point, green money is needed after all!

[111] In the early 1980s, when high inflation and high unemployment were rampant, the Trudeau government imposed a freeze on prices and salaries. Those were not the right proxy variables to use. The right move is to let the market balance itself out and act on fiscal and monetary policy instruments. Raising interest rates is always the best move governments can take to tame inflation. Other variables are not as potent.

Probabilistic forecasting always uses brown money. Estimating – by the mere fact of mortgaging constraint resources – uses green money.

A proposal for an Improvement Initiative – Where to improve

In a Knowledge-Work setting, we need to maximize each of our value streams for Throughput. After showing discipline as to when to start and stop work, a fictitious company was ready to move on to the next step.

Everybody was pleased with the 100% Flow Efficiency metric now that all the Wait Time in the process was eliminated. It was time to focus on an improvement initiative to 'work faster', shaving time off the eleven days process' overall time. Green money needs to be sourced in this very instance as improving will require outside help to 'change the way we do things around here'. It's Touch Time's turn.

To that effect, the VP of operations asked for two Improvement Initiatives to be provided ASAP. Mike and Jane are assigned to the task.

The Lead Time of the three-step process, which takes eleven days, is illustrated below:

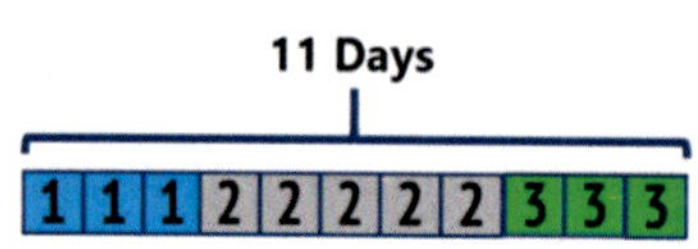

Mike and Jane's proposals are highlighted below:

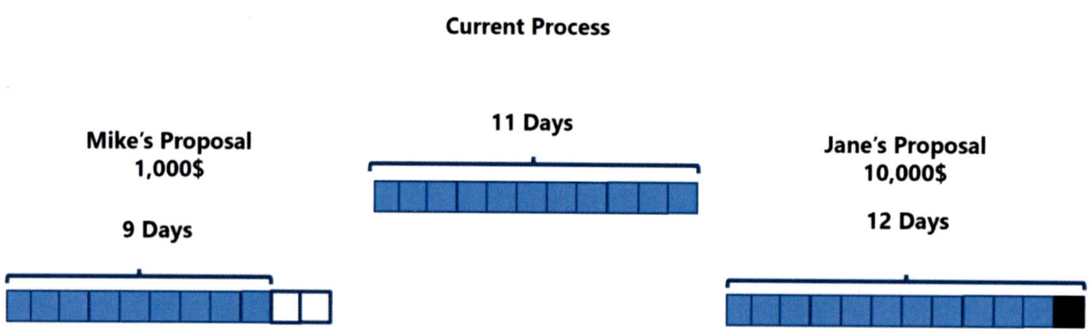

Mike's proposal cuts two days off the baseline at an external cost of $1,000. Jane's project adds one day with a cash outflow of green money to the amount of $10,000.

Jane and Mike were summoned to the executive floor to meet with upper management once their reports were completed. The meeting did not take long, as the C level executives were all about to leave for a retreat. Mike met no resistance from the board, and his proposal was retained and to be implemented in earnest. (Jane could not attend that meeting for personal reasons and would return to work in a month.)

Mike was directly impacting step three, which meant the delivery step was truncated by two entire days! Jane's alternative increased step three by a day, a solution that will no doubt frustrate customers. No half-decent Lean Improvement Initiative can afford to further alienate the market with an additional day of delivery.

A six-iteration cycle takes 36 days to complete as reflected in the CFD - Cumulative Flow Diagram - below:

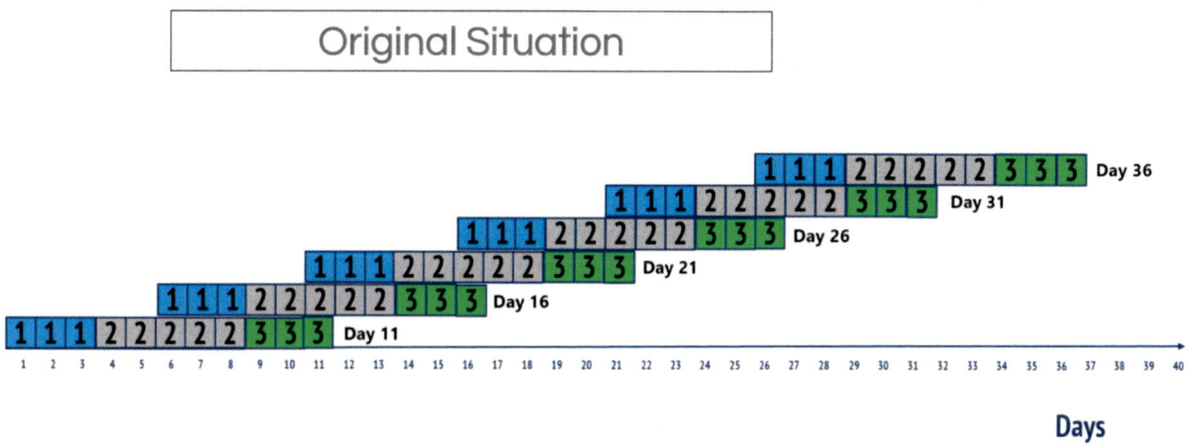

The following CFDs – Cumulative Flow Diagrams - show the impact of Mike's two-day Improvement Initiative as contrasted to the baseline:

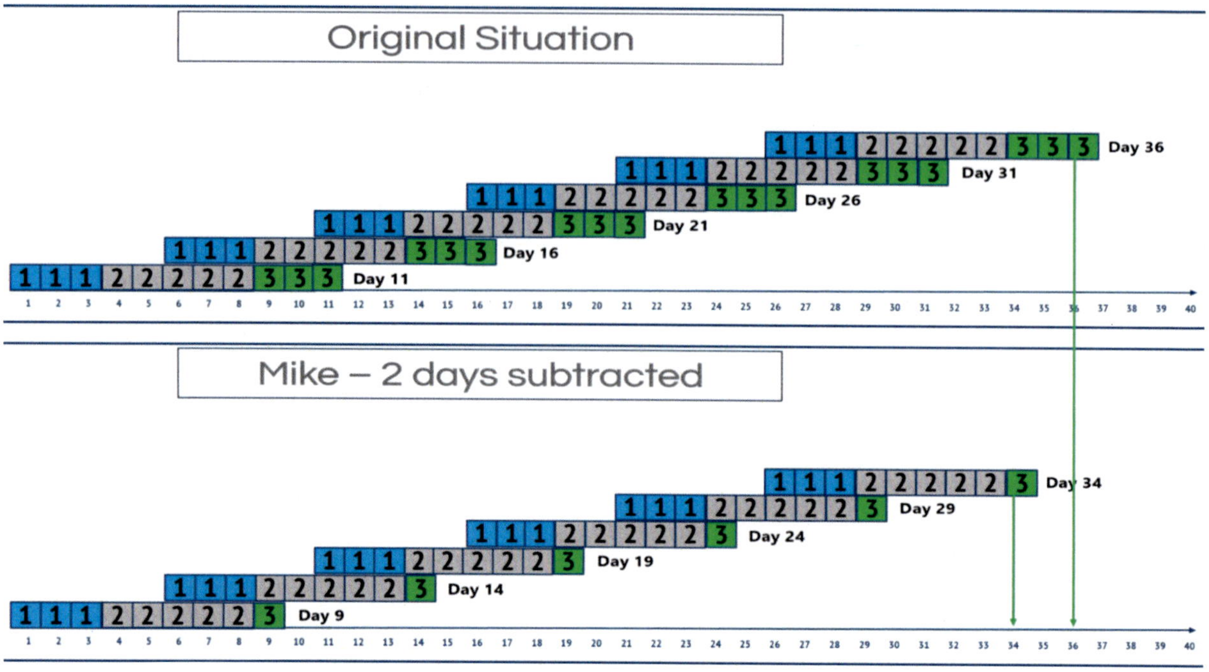

The problem with dealing with initiatives that bring end to end Lead Time down is that they are not evaluated on Throughput. Jane's proposed solution of increasing overall processing time by one day would be considered as waste under Lean, as additional time is always considered waste. Mike, by shaving off two days, falls within the boundaries of Lean's thinking as delays and wastes are directly proportional. Two less days of Lead Time are days of waste eliminated.

If we remind ourselves that the constraint is always the place in a process that has the lowest capacity - or longest cycle time - we can see that step two is in fact the constraint.

Mike is shaving off days from step three, away from the constraint.

Let's consider Jane's proposal which in fact reduces one day at the constraint despite increasing overall Lead Time by one day. Both steps one and three are upped by one day!

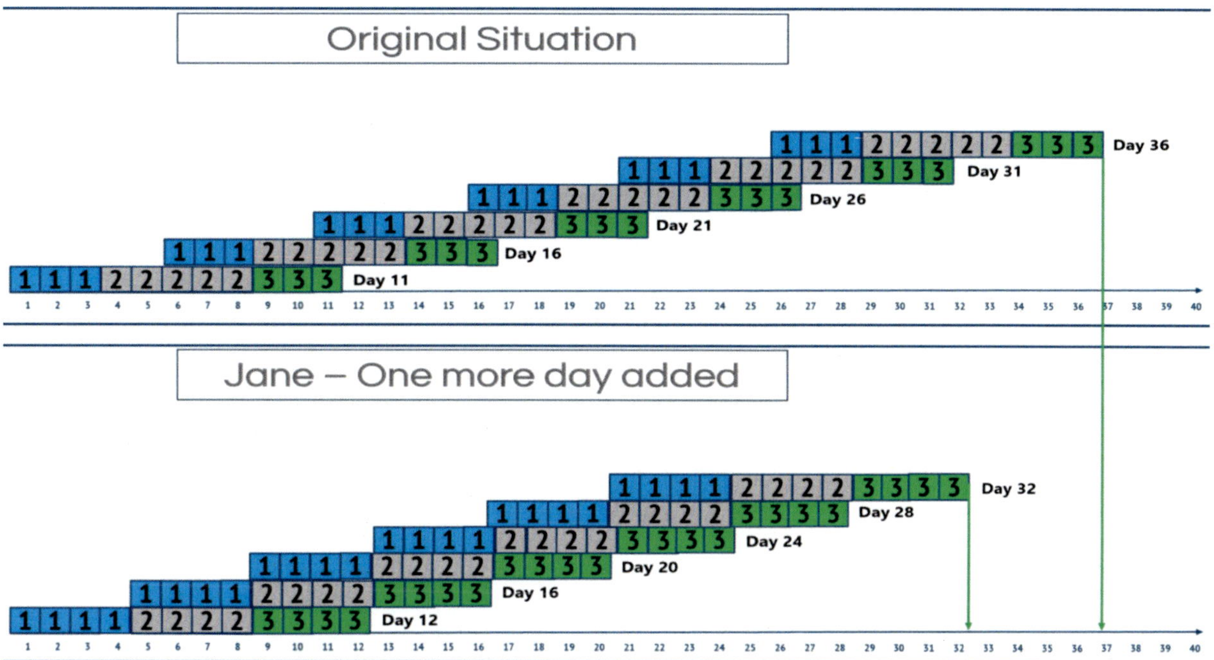

We can see that four days are saved in lieu of Mike's two days after six runs!

But this is selling Jane short. Let's project these savings through 50 runs.

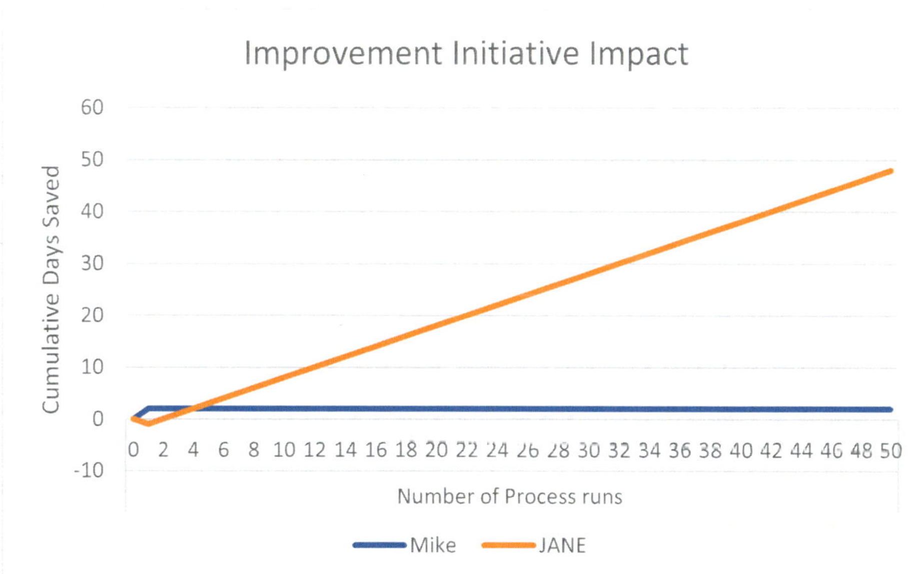

We see that Mike's solution, costing $1,000, is saving two days and this is the cumulative impact. However, Jane's approach saves 48 days after 50 runs! An impressive feat compared to the two-day, noncumulative improvement that was approved. And after 100 runs, results will still be felt.

But there is something unusual in Jane's solution. She is elevating the constraint! We now see that all three processes take four days! Are we faced with three constraints? Weren't we told that there is one constraint?

1	1	1	1	2	2	2	2	3	3	3	3

Jane is a Throughput Accounting specialist and her answer is worth listening to. In fact, we are in a situation where we have three bottlenecks, or no bottleneck.

Let's bring back what the definition of a constraint is:

> **Constraint:** The bottleneck (maybe one of many) that shows longest Lead Time or the smallest Capacity.

We can finesse this definition further to justify the situation:

> **Constraint**: The bottleneck (maybe one of many) that is actively managed!

What Jane is confessing to is that the constraint before the Improvement Initiative was at step two, and that it will remain there and be actively managed for the time being! Steps one and three are not actively managed and therefore cannot be considered as constraints.

In retrospect, Mike's solution is simply left-shifting the delivery line by two days. There will never be a cumulative effect. Two days is all there is.

Jane is augmenting the slope of the capacity line and will gain an extra day from the third iteration onward. The rate of delivery is always dictated by the constraint, which Mike did not take into account.

Cost of Delay vs Throughput Rate vs ROI

The mechanics of Throughput Accounting are unique as it is the only branch of accounting that totally bans cost allocations. It is also the only accounting discipline that does not have a Handbook, an oddity! Recently, Etienne Du Plooy[112] provided a list of nine Throughput Accounting concepts that are key to shaping our understanding and that I will provide verbatim:

1. **Systems Focused:**
    a. Performance measurement is focused on improving the system's performance *at* the Constraint
2. **Cost Variability:**

[112] Du Plooy, Etienne. 'Throughput Accounting Techniques'. General Media Press. 2016. Pages 57-63

   a. A system's operating costs and expenses are *either Operating Expenses (OE) or Totally Variable Costs (TVC)*[113] as determined by their correlation with units of products and services at a discriminant of R =1.0
   b. Clarity in *cost classification* is a major feature of *Throughput Accounting*
3. **Constrained Systems:**
   a. Every system has *at least one* Constraint that determines the system's performance
   b. Without a Constraint, a system is *incapable* of generating Throughput
4. **TVC Inventory:**
   a. Inventory is valued at Totally Variable Costs (TVC)[114] in order to *avoid* unrealized profits and align motivation of participants of the systems to preserve cash
5. **Pre-Determinable Cost:**
   a. Products and services are integral to a system whose costs and expenses are largely pre-determined irrespective of volumes the system produces or sells
   b. A fair portion of costs and expenses will be incurred no matter what the level of production is and for *that reason TVC and OE should never be allocated to products or services*
6. **Throughput rate:**
   a. The throughput rate is a function of a system's Constraint processing time for Throughput generation
   b. This concept is linked to the system's response to the market demand as determined by the system's Constraint
   c. The *slower* the response time, the *longer* the Throughput rate and thus the *lower* the profitability of the system
7. **Absolute profitability (Net Profit):**
   a. T-OE - Throughput less Operating Expenses determines a system's Net Profit from operations
   b. In addition to Net Profit, it depicts the speeds of total System Throughput and total system Operating Expenses
   c. It is also relevant to the change and progression of profits *through time* due to decisions, strategies and tactics
8. **Relative Profitability - (Throughput Rate):**
   a. The *rate* at which a system's products and services contribute money relative to its system's Constraint utilization determines the relative profitability of a system
   b. *Throughput rates* are additive in a system. In that regard, *Throughputability* is the sum of all aggregated Throughput of a single customer, group of customers, divisions, systems etc. for the purpose of marketing analysis.[115]
9. **System Productivity (T/OE):**
   a. T/OE - Throughput per (divided by) Operating Expenses determines the *productivity* of the system
   b. Is a measure to ascertain if the system is moving towards the goal

[113] The concept of TVC – Totally Variable Costs seldom applies to Knowledge-Work

[114] Inventory at TVC in Knowledge-Work is a moot concept as far as Throughput Accounting is concerned. Capital asset projects – case in point - always include labor costs. In that regard, historical data regarding past projects are useless for decision-making!

[115] This sentence is mine. Note that ROI and IRR are not additive, which makes the Throughput rate a fascinating tool to arbitrage and rank projects within a constrained system!

A Business Case – Throughput Accounting

FAK CHEK is a fictitious company offering credit ratings on customers who have double citizenships[116]. In recent years, the international market has seen an increasing amount of fraud and 'abuse' from borrowers having double residency status, taking loans in more than one country and increasing their risk of default. The ADDA – Anti Double Dipping Act – has been enacted as law on an international scale and the penalties for both lenders and borrowers of funds are severe. Now, all borrowers must indicate all their nationalities on their loan applications.

FAK CHEK has a unique process and value proposition. It is forwarded these applications the world over from lenders of funds who subscribe to the contract free service on a monthly bill, based on the number of cases processed. It offers an SLA of less than 12 hours, which they always respect. The GOAL now is to generate more operational Throughput as world demand is exploding.

FAK CHEK's CEO, Mr. Bounce, calls two consulting firms to provide alternatives on forging ahead. The winner will be awarded the contract.

CoD[117], the first company, sends their representative Charles. The other company, ToC[118], will be represented by Tanya.

FAK CHEK is small. Managerial expertise at the operational level is thin. But Mr. Bounce is not afraid; what he lacks in terms of expertise on the floor is more than made up at the financial level by the CFO, Mr. Frik[119], a Middle Eastern businessman who used to run the biggest bank in the world.

The current process is depicted as follows in four phases:

- ✓ CATCH: This step deals with receiving all the information pertaining to the case under review from the lending institution. A passport picture of each applicant will be used in facial recognition.
- ✓ STOP: The mission of this subprocess is to search for all aliases, next of kin and neighbors with shady pasts, as well as the criminal history of all contacts on social networks. Passport validation is a key subprocess, and one of FAC CHEK's secret weapon, is its ability to validate passports from all countries instantly!
- ✓ FRISK: This step searches the records of all the top criminal and secret service agencies in the world to flag borrowers for past mischiefs.
- ✓ RELEASE: Here, the information is forwarded in an encrypted manner back to the source. The messages not only encrypt the names of the applicants but also the amount of the requested loan and the terms. This encryption process requires a lot of mathematical and computational power.

---

[116] Not only is the company fictitious but so is the story and the family names!

[117] CoD for Cost of Delay

[118] ToC for Theory of Constraints

[119] Pronounce 'fric' à la française. *Fric* means *Money*

Operational Throughput Data

The process was presented and explained to both Charles (from CoD) and Tanya (from ToC) after they had signed an NDA. Both consultants were given full access to technical, process and data volume information.

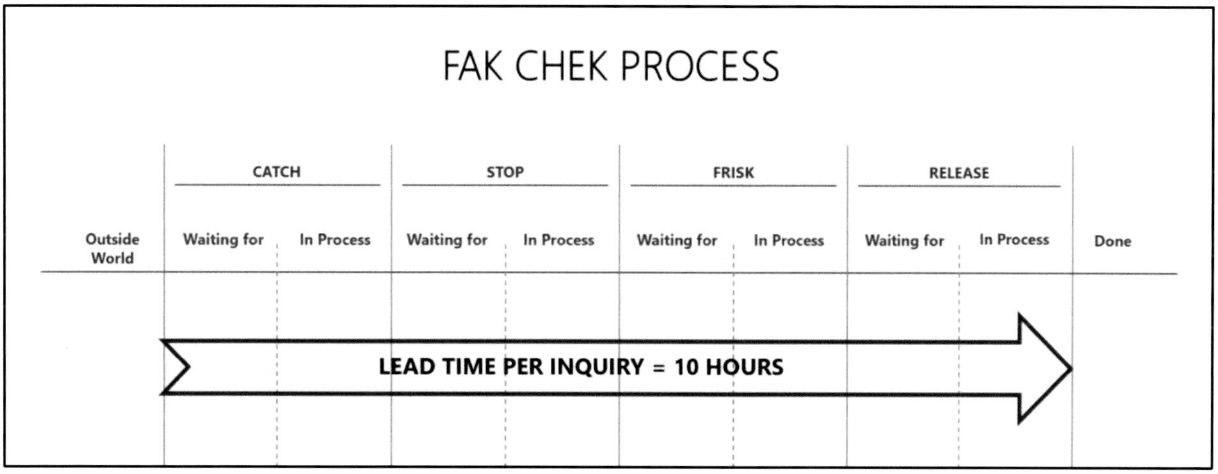

The Lead Time per inquiry was ten hours and Flow Efficiency was excellent. And never in the history of FAK CHEK was the SLA of twelve hours violated. This had to be a constraint for both consultants; Charles and Tanya.

Another constraint was that the capacity of 5,840 hours per year be maintained as adding capacity was an issue with the current application portfolio.

Charles and Tanya presented their respective plans as follows:

	Baseline	Charles (CoD)	Tanya (T0C)
Lead Time per Inquiry	10 Hours	9 Hours	11 Hours

Everybody is impressed with Charles' proposal as it would further secure their twelve hours SLA. This gives him the spotlight, allowing him to present his case first. Tanya will present the next day.

	Baseline	Charles (CoD)	Tanya (TOC)
Capacity per year (hours)	5840	5840	5840
Average Lead Time (hours)	10	9	11
Requests per year	584	649	531
Variance	N/A	65	-53

In terms of Operational Throughput, the additional cash inflow from 65 inquiries per year is a very good scenario, as opposed to Tanya falling short by 53! Mr. Frik, the CFO, is smiling after the presentation. Mr. Frik never smiles. But he knows that the basic formula that Revenues are equal to Price x Quantity! That means 65 additional requests per year. At the price FAK CHEK is charging, everybody – including Mr. Bounce – is happy.

The next day, Tanya presents additional data to the attendees. Mr. Bounce and Mr. Frik are not impressed with the additional day that her proposal would impose, but are willing to listen anyway.

Tanya starts by thanking Charles for his presentation and salesmanship acumen.

She knows how to handle Throughput Accounting's counterintuitive paradigm. 'Brain pain' must be served first. Otherwise, the battles linger for too long. She likes the nuclear approach.

She begins her meeting with a shocking sentence: 'We live in a constrained world. If such was not the case, we could not make a single sale!'

Tanya knows what she's doing. She first must unyoke them all. Set them free from their flawed mental models and cognitive biases.[120]

She lets them scramble for a while to show them what she means.

She argues, "When Mr. Frik said yesterday that Revenue = Price x Quantity, he was roughly right and precisely wrong.[121]"

Mr. Frik is known for one thing: he likes challenges and never turns one down. "Humor me, Ms Tanya."

"Sir, we live at the age of speed. Would you not agree?"

Mr. Frik never likes to concede, and gives his favorite elusive answer: "I am not saying yes and I am not saying no."

> Tanya answers: "Fair enough. Let me illustrate. All systems have one constraint and the speed at which you go through the constraint per unit of time dictates your Throughput. So, in fact, Revenues are equal to the selling price divided by the speed at the constraint

[120] From Dave Snowden, 23 August 2021: "Mental models are not supported by cognitive neuroscience as they arise from a poor metaphor that does not understand the diversity of human decision-making."

[121] This quote is attributable John Maynard Keynes. It is used frequently within ToC circles.

per unit of time. The Quantity variable is not as good a predictor of revenues as speed and value at the constraint are!"

Mr. Frik is listening while searching the web on his phone. But one can tell that he is paying attention despite his 'laissez-faire' demeanour.

Tanya presents this table, assuming that all requests for investigation are priced at the same amount and are indistinguishable from one to the next in terms of size, complexity or time to solve. She is right.

She points out that the additional Throughput rate[122] at the constraint for Charles' proposal is 0.16 (973/5840) requests per hour while hers is 0.25 (1460/5840), significantly more!

Mr. Bounce interrupts after noticing Charles' dubitative posture and says: "Tanya, we are CPU bound here, our brains are not machines. Could you put your logic on equal footing with Charles' and make your case on a similar table? That would make things easier for all of us."

Tanya then presents her analysis comparing Charles' proposal in one column and hers in the right column. She breaks down the value stream to show that the constraint is at the STOP phase where a request would spend five hours to be processed.

	Baseline	Charles (CoD)	Tanya (TOC)
Average Lead Time (hours)	10	9	11
Process Steps (hours)			
CATCH	2	1	3
STOP	5	6	4
FRISK	2	1	2
RELEASE	1	1	2

She indicates that any improvement that would not generate more Throughput would only increase layers of overhead costs and that her solution, despite adding one hour to both the CATCH and RELEASE phases, was beneficial. What counts is reducing the time spent at the constraint.

She then recycles Charles' table to make her point:

[122] The Throughput rate is the speed at which you go through the constraint. Classical economics have us thinking in the of Price x Quantity to derive revenues. Throughput Accounting ascertains absolute profitability with the time that you mortgage the constraint per unit produced. The faster a product passes through the constraint, the better!

	Baseline	Charles (CoD)	Tanya (T0C)
Capacity per year (hours)	5840	5840	5840
Constraint Lead Time (hours)	5	6	4
Requests per year	1,168	973	1,460
Variance	N/A	-195	292

Charles' alternative is discarded and Tanya has to prepare the Financials. The increase in Operational Throughput of 292 requests per year (or 4.5 times more than Charles' 65 additional requests) is palatable, but they still need to know what they're in for. Mr. Frik is still smiling. And every body at FAK CHEK knows what that means.

Financial Throughput Data

Mr. Frik congratulates Tanya and tells Charles he will not be retained. He then asks Tanya to come up with a complete financial perspective now that he understands Operational Throughput. Still, he needs to see the other side of the coin - Financial Throughput - and a schedule to implement. He reminds her that once a project begins, the criteria for profitability are the projects' duration[123] and ROI over twelve months rolling calendar starting at the beginning of the development phase.

Tanya is told to contact the Board once the reporting is done.

Before seeing Tanya off, Mr. Frik says: "I don't know how you are going to get the Financials in order since you did not even bother to see our monthly cost function and allocation practices. So, before you call and ask me for the relevant information, I printed out the basic figures so that you don't bug me later. I am a busy man."

He hands the following data sheet to Tanya:

Rubrique	**Montant mensuel**
Salaires	80,000$
Energie	10,000$
Dépréciation	5,000$
Téléphone	1,000$
Commisson	2,000$
Marketing	3,000$
Autres	1,500$
TOTAL	99,500$

[123] Duration is the time it takes to break-even.

Tanya noticed that the information was about Operating expenses and in French but that would not matter. What would ultimately count would be the marginal impact of her analysis on T, I, and OE. The following Throughput Accounting data is gathered for the project:

Financial Info – Throughput Accounting	Amount
Number of months of exploitation of solution over a year	8
Sales Revenue per requests	1,000$
Duration of Project (months)	4
Number of additional requests received over 8 months (292/12*8)	195
Throughput per month – (T)	16,250$
Cost of Server (one time charge) – (I)	15,000$
Consulting fees per month of project – (OE)	10,000$

The Income Statement is ready in no time![124]

Income Statement – Throughput Accounting	Amount
Variation in T – Throughput (8 months out of 12)	130,000$
Variation in Operating Expenses – (OE) 4 months out of 12	40,000$
Variation in Net Profit (NP) 12 months = T-OE	90,000$
Duration – (Month when Break Even is Reached)	6
Variation in Investment – (I)	15,000$
12 month ROI - Return on Investment NP/I – 90,000/15,000	6,000%
Absolute Profitability (or Net Profit)	90,000$
Relative Profitability – Throughput rate per month 8 to 12	16,250$
Relative Profitability – T/OE (130,000/40,000)	3.25

Tanya also prepares a break-even[125] analysis to support the duration calculation (the period of time to the break-even point, which occurs when Net Profit reaches zero).

[124] There are no predetermined formats to report Throughput Accounting data as opposed to Financial Accounting statements where form is important.

[125] The astute reader will notice that a traditional cost accounting's contribution margin break-even point always lies to the right of a Throughput Accounting's break-even Point. Showing again that countless imaginary hurdles are created with allocating sales and head office overhead to the final tally of traditional break-even analysis. The presence of fixed salary expenses masked as variable costs add to the confusion and to the hurdle that must be met.

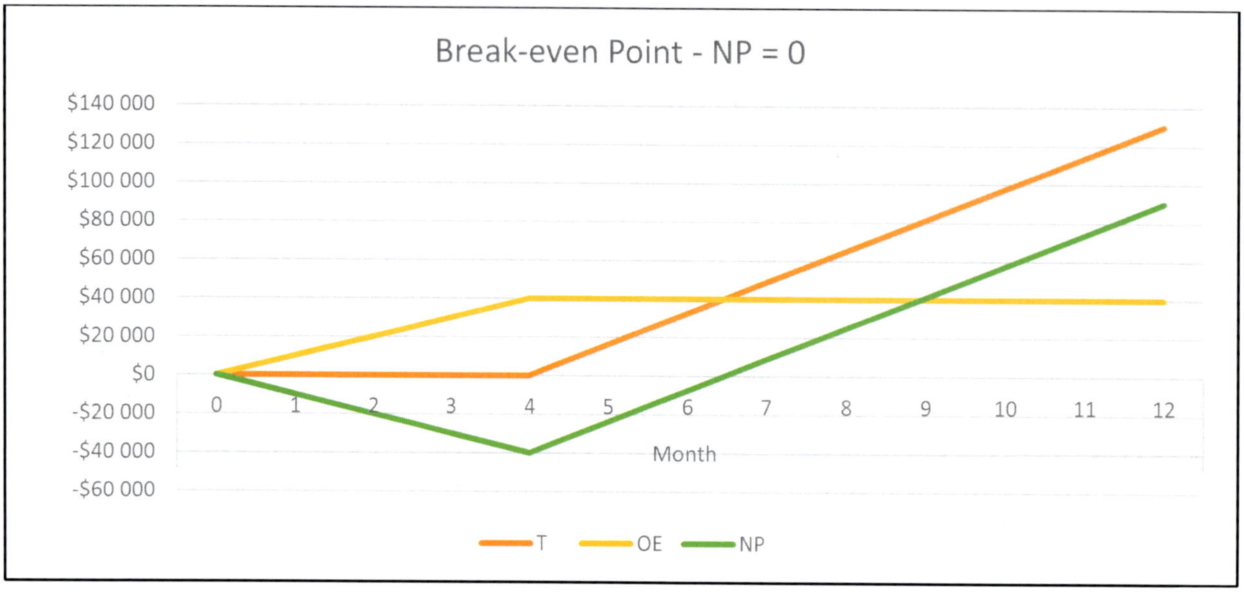

Days later, Mr. Bounce, Frik and Tanya look at the proposal.

Tanya starts her presentation with the break-even data just above[126].

She explains that the project has a duration of six months and a Net Profit of $90,000 for the twelve rolling calendar months starting at the beginning of development.

Mr. Frik says that he had hoped for Financials that were more in line with the best practices of the industry and that this worries him. The math does not add up. He shows her a set of Financials that would pass the smell test for any CPA. Hers would not.

"How could you, Tanya? How could you forget to deduct the salaries[127] of the full-time employees from the project's projection? They will be working on that project! And the Variable and Fixed overheads as well. And commissions! I have never seen in my lifetime a COGS section that was, well, not there at all! By COGS, I mean Costs of Goods Sold! I can't accept this Net Profit of $90,000."

He continues, "Let me show you a pro format Income Statement like it should be done with our modus operandi. How can you expect our respect if you do not want to understand how we work and how we are financed?"

Tanya asks: "Would the numbers you've just tallied be the same if they were done by another CFO ? "[128]

---

[126] Just as was the case with Flawed Mental Model Four, the break-even point in Cost Accounting is always to the right of the one derived from Throughput Accounting showing again that additional illusionary hurdles are imposed by Cost Accounting putting more stress on the organisation. Likewise, Cost Accounting would set the duration metric discussed in earlier higher than that of Throughput Accounting's.

[127] Remember, salaries are to be tallied as brown money and part of Operating Expenses.

[128] Punctuation – Doubt point

"Of course not. This is an art as much as a science. This is why we have a Handbook! Finding the right cost drivers to allocate expenses is simply impossible!"

"Exactly my point." Tanya answers. "We are more concerned with data relevancy than data accuracy. And when the IFRS, FASB, FFRs, EITF guidance papers, ARBs and GAAP guidelines combined together take up more than 20,000 pages, I would choose another name than Handbook⸮ [129]

Tanya pursued on a more assertive tone: "Form is the least of our concerns, while for Financial Accounting, it is mandatory. We are worlds apart when discussing decision-making."

When Mr. Frik hears technical terms that could only be known to a CPA, he searches for her name on the AICPA members repertory. She's in it! She's one of ours! Not a good day to get a bloody nose. He changes tactics. His mission now is to extract her knowledge.

Tanya continues: "But Mr. Frik, your technical points are right on the money. And I have prepared for you a bridge from your GAAP Income Statement to a Throughput Accounting Income Statement[130]. See for yourself that the bottom lines balance. No spilled milk and no expenses have been omitted. This way of presenting data makes you focus on growth, not expenses. The more you see expenses, the more you are motivated to cut them. So, upon receiving your Throughput Accounting Income Statement, develop the following simple reflex:

- ✓ Validate if T is greater than OE!

This will allow you to evaluate the consequences of increases in Throughput and decreases in pricing. You never want to decrease prices. Ever. But this is programmed into our DNA as CPA's."

Mr. Frik is listening but knows he needs to get out of this meeting ASAP, while leaving the impression that he has the upper hand. "I see. The bridging algorithm is nothing short of clerical.

Would you not agree, Tanya؟ "[131]

"Absolutely. And understanding that, you have already figured out that you will not need two sets of books. This is an unfounded concern that 'would be' adopters of Throughput Accounting express. [132]But I get the feeling that this 'pricing across the board' you're practicing is a legacy of a bad habit this company has of covering costs that are unavoidable. In your case, I would strongly suggest you find a more diverse approach to pricing. For example, Throughput generators are the newest thing in Throughput Accounting. There is also a great potential here to be more creative with pricing. And the sales force would love it as your 'one size fits all for pricing' takes the wind out of all marketing efforts."

---

[129] Punctuation – Irony mark

[130] This bridge appears in Appendix A and B

[131] Punctuation – Rhetorical question

[132] Punctuation – Certitude point

Mr. Frik understands that they should not focus only on operational issues but on sales strategies as well. He asks Tanya to take this extra dimension into account.

Tanya looks at Mr. Bounce. "I need more money for that!"

"Write your own ticket and send me a proposal," says Mr. Frik. "And don't forget the operational purchase discount[133]."

Tanya suspects something is amiss and is willing to engage. "What makes you think I would offer such a discount ‽ [134]You'd have to pay me upfront!"

"I know that, Tanya. I saw the depth of your bench at head office. It seemed pretty crowded to me! I want to help you manage your Inventory. Telling me that TVC do not exist in Knowledge-Work is one thing, but making me believe that Inventory does not apply is deceitful, would you not agree?"

"Bravo Monsieur Frik," says Tanya. She's surprised but she's been here before. "Indeed, our fleet of consultants at head office - or the employees at your company - is our Inventory in Knowledge-Work. It is a novelty in the field of cash management that I will be happy to share[135]. You have been busy reading, Mr. Frik."

"I am not saying yes and I am not saying no," Mr. Frik replies, very seriously.

They both could not stop laughing♡[136]

My ex[137] and I – Opportunity Cost or Lost Opportunity?

Weeks after the deal was approved, and on a routine trip up a crowded elevator at FAK CHEK's, Tanya overhead a conversation from two employees from her firm. She never saw them before, but they were wearing the company's pin as is the tradition while on assignment on customer sites. This assured the best of behaviors.[138]

They were talking about the fact that the opportunity cost of not choosing Tanya's offer would be the differential between the 65 inquiries that would have been obtained from the wrong scenario and the 292 that turned out to be the optimal solution. A big opportunity cost of 227 unit of sales!

---

[133] Throughput Accounting treats discounts differently. If they are of an operational nature for quick shipment to get cash immediately and inventory out the door, they are called operational purchase discounts. These discounts do not show on the Income Statement and are deducted from Net Sales. The other kind of discount is for quick financial settlement once the goods are received at the customer's site, they are commonly referred to as terms of payments. They are of a financial nature. They are accounted for under General Expenses after Net Profit and before EBITDA.

[134] Punctuation – Interrobang: equivalent of a grimace or a shrug of the shoulders

[135] This topic will have its own chapter. It is inspired from the work of John Ricketts at IBM

[136] Punctuation – Love point

[137] Ex-ante and ex-post

[138] EDS had such a corporate procedure for all its employees

Tanya was not stopping on the same floor, but decided to hop off to chat with the two young recruits as the analysis they provided were based on two figures that had different baselines!

"Hi young fellows", Tanya said. "I guess you must know me, Tanya, and I was on the back of the elevator when I overheard you both".

"Hi!" both of them shouted back. "Nice to meet you".

"Same here", Tanya replied. "I do not have much time as I am already late for a meeting with Mr. Frick, but I will say this as succinctly as possible".

"First, the notion of opportunity cost in Throughput Accounting is an ex-post event". When Tanya saw their eyes in a dubitative state, she pursued on: "You can only have an opportunity cost when the constraint has missed a beat[139]. You have definitely lost money in that case. What you were discussing has never happened, or has it?".

Both recruits said: "Indeed, you are right". Then the taller one asked: "How would you qualify our discussion then. Like an 'ex-ante' proposition. Does it have a reference in the Theory of Constraint?"

Tanya obliged: "If you want to use 'ex-ante' here in the sense of before the fact, you would be right. But it does not apply here. What you were engaged in is pure speculation. Why? Because it is not likely to ever happen that any two scenarios would occur concurrently because only one was retained. Ex-ante means before the fact of an event that has occurred, the assumption we made. From that angle, I would give you an A for effort, if nothing else!".

She added: "What people mean is a potential for a 'lost opportunity' when a bad scenario is discarded just in time for a more profitable one before any damages are done. Capiche?"

Tanya made sure she used the 'Big Smile' routine to deliver her message. It needed to sting, but only for the time of the blink of an eye, which she always coupled with her 'Big Smile' routine!

"You see, what you are confusing is the conclusion reached by the 'Reality Tree'. The decision we have reached. Comparing this decision in contrast with what could have been with other discarded scenarios, is pure speculation and is not something we fathom. It has nothing to do with an opportunity cost under all circumstances, but people think that way. It is a cognitive bias. The 'Reality Tree' is for 292 more sales! Period. All other scenarios are out not only for discussion purposes, but from a trivial point of view as well!"

Upon hearing the bell ringing for the next ride up, she ran for the elevators and left two now much smarter employees already discussing the merit of what they had just learnt while texting, chatting, discussing - ignoring each other as it were - while trading crypto and engaging in parallel activities of all sorts. The future is theirs.

[139] This was addressed in Chapter 1 – Flawed mental model four

Conclusion – Brown Money is Smart Money.~ [140]

Improvement Initiatives that do not take into account the constraint of your system will increase layers of permanent costs, which in turn will cause your demise. Understanding the deltas is key in differentiating between green money and brown money. It is often not understood but I like the analogy made just above. Accepting solutions that shrink lead time is a flawed mental model.

It is an inheritance of Lean manufacturing that has no place in Knowledge-Work! [141]

The Theory of Constraints, the 5 Focusing Steps and Throughput Accounting are also packaged together under another ToC term: POOGI – Process of On-Going Improvement. POOGI is as legitimate as ADKAR, CMMI, Lean, Six Sigma and the other avenues to lead to improvement. POOGI focuses on the constraint, the others do not.[142]

It covers a wide array of topics that are beyond the scope of this chapter, the most fascinating of which is the bonus remuneration system to align motivations and behaviors; a key tenet of management accounting and culture.[143]

As humans, we are creatures of habit. Letting go of your favorite Continuous Improvement method is asking for too much as they all have merits. Just include the knowledge rendered in these lines and you should be able to do better at no extra cost and continue working the way you are accustomed to and stop the outflux of green money at the get go. Agile should not impose new roles, structures, responsibilities at the get go. Only Kanban seems to understand the tenets of resistance to change⸮ [144]

Many people wonder if they must keep two sets of books to leverage Throughput Accounting. It is possible as reconciliation from any accounting system to another is straightforward. In truth, very few people keep two sets of books. It is best to keep your current systems to fulfil your Financial Statement reporting obligations under GAAP or IFRS. Those are the more complicated systems to maintain as they have a much more detailed level of granularity.

Migrating to a strict Throughput Accounting system would require adjusting your inventory accounts[145] to tally the TVCs and the overheads separately. Much ado about nothing.

The preferred avenue is to stick to the Throughput Accounting Income Statement preparation only. Bridging to that statement from any other accounting system is quite easy as the only thing required is to remove the allocated overhead costs buried in your Inventory accounts and put them under (OE) - Operating expenses at period end.

---

[140] Punctuation – Snark mark: This is used to indicate that a sentence should be understood beyond the literal meaning.

[141] Punctuation - Authority point

[142] Those paths all lead to better Flow Efficiency, which is a proxy of both operational and financial Throughput.

[143] Culture is a reflection of our systems and our systems are a reflection of our culture. When in doubt, start with system changes by adopting Throughput Accounting. The results will come fast.

[144] Punctuation – Irony mark

[145] Raw materials, Work In Progress and Finished goods.

Next, assemble the relevant Throughput data at the constraint, and focus on mastery of the 5 Focusing Steps. Then comes the Throughput Accounting decision-making algorithm of delta (T) Throughput, delta (I) - Inventory and delta (OE) – Operating Expenses in that precise order. Once you have that in hand, you're ready!

I am also compelled to add a qualifier to Operating Expenses (which are constant and predictable in the short to medium term for the sake of this argument[146]) as a source of funds for Improvement Initiatives on top of the traditional view of them being strictly a use of funds, as sometimes we may use brown money (source and use of funds) or green money (use of funds). It would add value in the analysis when we displace money (brown money to generate green money in the first 3 steps of the 5FS) or get green money right away (Step 4 to Elevate the constraint) when we need to actually cough up cash.

Some critics of Throughput Accounting state that it omits Fixed Costs, CAPEX and OPEX; to which I respond there are two categories of costs. One is TVC, the other one is OE. It if does not fit in TVC, then it has to be OE![147]

There are many ToC metrics for manufacturing. For Knowledge-Work, visualization is king and it is sufficient to instrument both the Flow Efficiency and DBR boards interchangeably when context demands it. The flow metrics between process steps is more than enough. Removing column WIP limits is mandatory as it impacts flow.

I would suggest only one metric on top and above the ones that are intrinsic to your Flow Efficiency and DBR boards regarding Lead Times and in-process times. That one additional metric is to count the frequency of yellow, red and black signals from the DBR buffer. When they are too frequent, it's time to worry: increase the buffer size. When you are not receiving any replenishment signal, it's time to worry: you may have too much WIP in the system.

Like Rudyard Kippling said, you can go alone and fast with no external help like the other improvement initiatives would entail. And get an influx of green money very soon instead of spending it on new approaches that ignore the goose with the golden eggs.

---

[146] I want to cut the oxygen to those who would slash into OE to disguise it as a source of funds. Cutting OE is cutting the life line to the quality of work of your employees: the tools they use, the level of slack they enjoy etc. It is never recommended in TA. You focus on generating Sales first, second and third.

[147] Saying that there are two categories of costs: TVC and non-TVC is approximately right but precisely wrong! It will not pass the smell test whilst discussing with a Throughput Accounting expert! Experts only consider two categories: TVC and OE. I learned the hard way when exchanging nonchalantly with Etienne du Plooy!

APPENDIX A – Getting to GAAP Net Profit – Full Absorption Costing vs TA

1) Validate if TH is greater than OE
2) Such a quick conversion also allows us to evaluate the consequences of increases in throughput and decreases in pricing.
3) Dr Goldratt's consistent admonishment is not to decrease prices.

Full Absorption Costing	Throughput Accounting
Sales	**Sales**
Cost of Goods Sold	**Totally Variable Costs**
• Materials	• Materials
• Direct Labor	• Sales Commissions
• Variable Manufacturing Overhead	
• Fixed Manufacturing Overhead	
	= Throughput
Stock Movement	**Inventory Change at TVC**
• Opening - Closing	• Opening - Closing
= Gross Profit	
Operating Expenses	**Operational Expenses**
• Selling Expenses	
– Commissions	
– Others	
• Administration Expenses	
	• Selling
	• Administrative
	• Fixed Manufacturing Overhead
	• Direct labor
= Operating Income	**= Operating Income**
Income Taxes	**Income Taxes**
= Net Profit (GAAP)	**= Net Profit (GAAP)**

APPENDIX B – Getting to GAAP Net Profit – Variable Costing vs TA

Getting to GAAP Net Profit – Variable Costing vs TA

1) Validate if TH is greater than OE
2) Such a quick conversion also allows us to evaluate the consequences of increases in throughput and decreases in pricing.
3) Dr Goldratt's consistent admonishment is not to decrease prices.

Variable Costing	Throughput Accounting
Sales	Sales
Variable Manufacturing Costs	Totally Variable Costs
• Materials	• Materials
• Direct Labor	• Sales Commissions
• Variable Manufacturing Overhead	
	= Throughput
Stock Change	Inventory Change at TVC
• Opening - Closing	• Opening - Closing
= Manufacturing Margin	
Variable Selling & Admin	
• Sales Commissions	
= Contribution Margin	
Period Expenses	Operational Expenses
• Fixed Selling and Admin	
• Fixed Manufacturing Overhead	
	• Selling
	• Administrative
	• Manufacturing Overhead
	• Direct labor
= Operating Income	= Operating Income
Income Taxes	Income Taxes
= Net Profit (GAAP)	= Net Profit (GAAP)

CHAPTER V - CASH GENERATION, T GENERATORS AND MAFIA OFFERS[148]

"There is no team in a masterpiece" – Jurgen Appelo

Introduction:

In Throughput Accounting, everything starts and ends with cash. You are done once you have collected cash. Cash can be a resource, a metric as well as a constraint. When cash is a constraint, nothing else matters. It becomes the only active constraint!

We all know what to do when we are short of cash[149]. What all of us have forgotten is how to make cash. This is the gist of this chapter, and the gist of Throughput Accounting[150].

There is a cycle to cash that goes thru the entire array of systems in a company. It has been illustrated by the most respected authors in the field of Throughput Accounting[151] with the 'Flows and Pools of Money[152]' diagram. I inspired myself from all of the drawings of this diagram to come up with mine just below: [153]

[148] Mafia offer could be a bit threatening. You can substitute it for a term that is more suitable to your context. Sweet offer, Pirate offer etc.

[149] For those interested in the topic, a great article by Eli Shargenheim and Ravi Gilani can be found here: https://elischragenheim.com/2017/05/11/evaporating-an-active-cash-constraint/

[150] The content of this article is inspired in part from the writings of Dr Kevlyn Youngman and John Ricketts, whose works are included in the References section. The adaptation to agile and MAFIA offers is entirely mine.

[151] Henry Camp and Ravi Gilani, Dr Kevlyn Youngman and Eli S Schragenheim have all used this fundamental model in one form or another in their work.

[152] 'Pool' is meant to note the static nature of assets trapped in the company's Balance Sheet, as opposed to 'Flow' which describes movements of money, represented on the Income Statement.

[153] Please find in Appendix an explanation for all the arrows and the colors

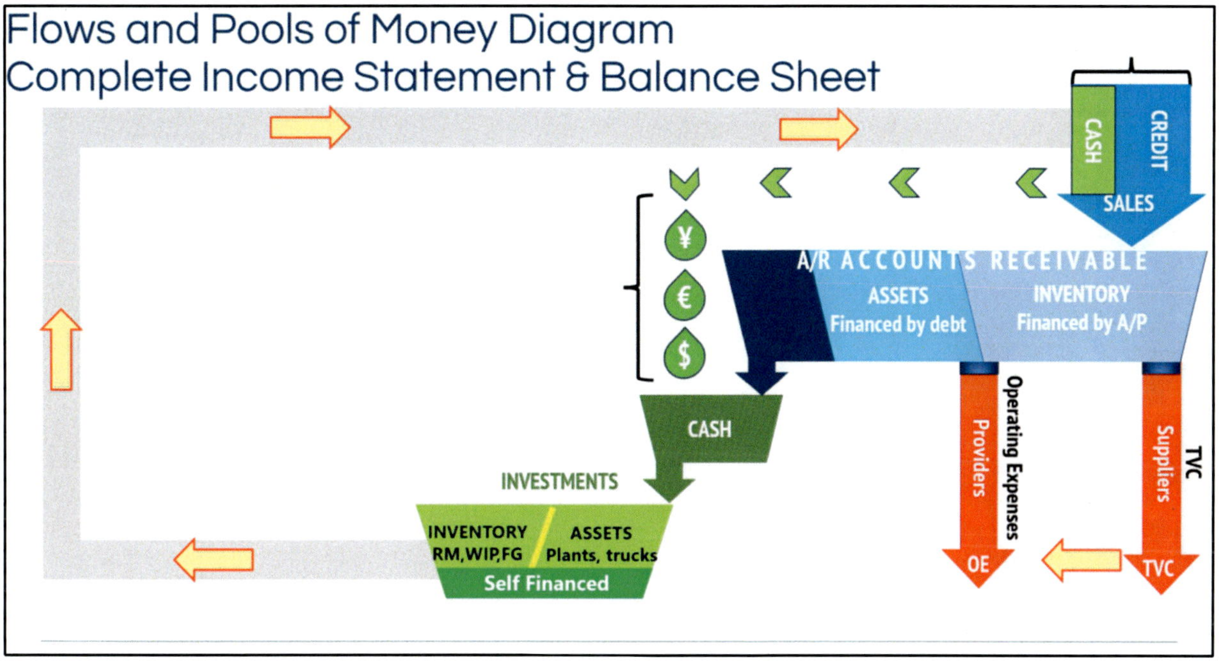

The journey we take to create this diagram leads us to a complete picture of the asset and liability pools, some sources of funds, flows of money, as well as the Income and Balance Sheet Statements![154]

Although all authors are coherent within their own variation of the traditional 'Flows and Pools of Money' diagrams for manufacturing shown above, there are a few – sometimes important – discrepancies or omissions across them. I am sure my version also has its own flaws. But I am definitely the first one to venture with a 'Pools and Flows of Money' diagram for Knowledge-Work as we will see soon![155]

The illustration can apply to companies in almost every sector of the economy that manufactures or creates physical goods. It can also work - at times - in the service industry and Knowledge-Work with some adjustments depending on context.

We must now cover both the Accounting System and the Financial Application facets of Throughput Accounting, the aim of which is to leverage brown money[156] and 'launder' it into green money! The mechanics and reflexes and rewiring of the brain requires getting physical with the model and do some easy math while applying to the letter the 5 Focusing Steps and their positioning with green and brown money. And all this while mastering the 'Flows and Pools of Money' diagram.

---

[154] The color densities also have significance. For a short explanation, see the details in Appendix.

[155] There can be many variations of the 'Pools and Flows of Money' diagram in Knowledge-Work depending on your 'ownership' of the resources. Do they work for you? Are they contractors? Are you the middleman as a head hunter or a software company like IBM?

[156] Green money and Brown money were discussed in the 'Color of Money' chapter.

Expansion or Growth? – The 5 Focusing Steps again

In this first section, we need to revert to the visible and physical world. Of course, we will dive neck-deep into Knowledge-Work, but some key principles need to be clearly explained using a brick-and-mortar example.

We all know that the most challenging step for the 5 Focusing Steps for Knowledge-Work is to Identify the constraint as it is invisible. We have discussed remedies to this problem. When we are in more traditional and visible contexts – where inventory is actually palpable – subordinating to the constraint is most difficult as it requires us to change mental models. This applies to Knowledge-Work as well. But at this point, efforts with existing budgets, or brown money, prove to be adequate to Identify, Exploit and Subordinate to the constraint.

But isn't Throughput Accounting all about making more money rather than subordinating to the constraint[157]?

This is where the Exploitation[158] step comes in. In order to increase sales by a factor of five, the most commonly used path is to multiply by five your capacity, your workforce, and operating expenses. The profits will increase by a factor of five as well. A bland linear scale model no more! A zero-sum game no less.

This solution has everything to do with step four: Elevate the constraint. This can be pricey. But it may come to that at some point and require financing.

Or we can go for a free ride and Exploit the constraint with brown money – using existing capacity (I) and operating expenses (OE) - and get five times the bang and ride a quadratic curve.

Let visualise this:

[157] Subordinating to the constraint prevents us from overproducing and keeping WIP in check!

[158] One of the better articles contrasting Subordination and Exploitation is by Dr Kevlyn Youngman in the References section.

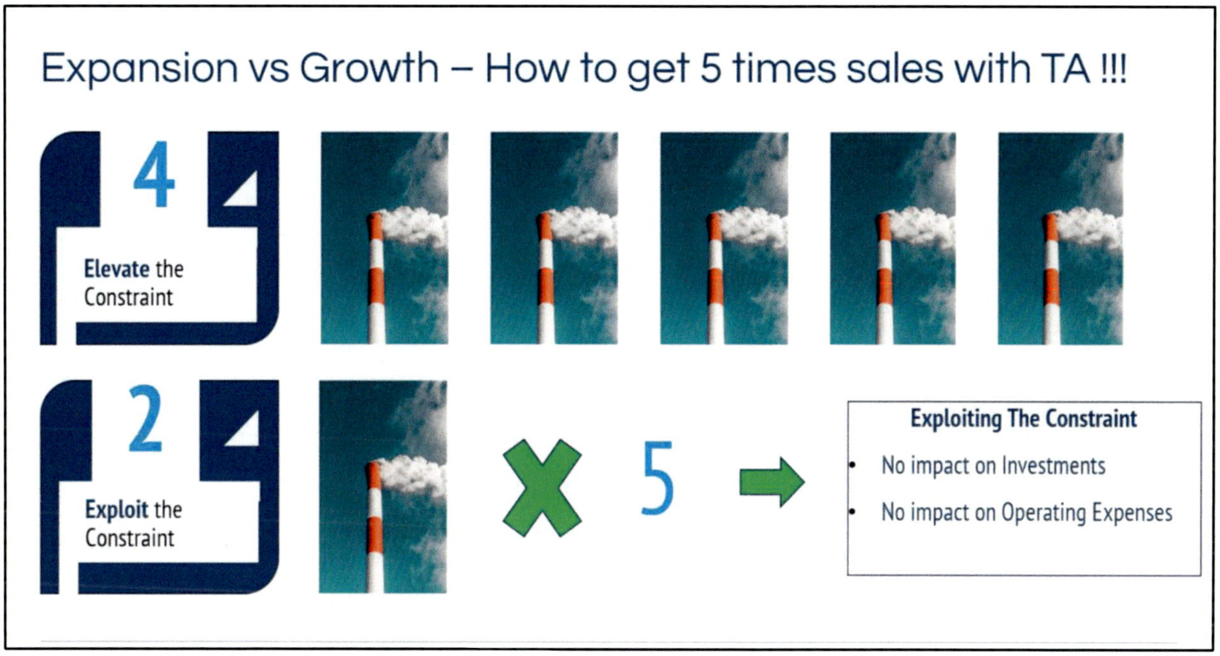

Why did I not think of that, you might ask!

Well, this has everything to do with a flawed mental model that is deeply rooted in the fabric of society. I will explain this by adapting Albert A Bartlett's[159] words of wisdom:

> "The greatest shortcoming of modern management is our inability to understand the capacity function."

Earlier, we discussed how Cost Accounting has a habit of changing the behavior of the capacity function, whose function is ALWAYS a flat horizontal line. Capacity is expressed under the (OE) – Operating Expenses - component of Throughput Accounting. It is the sum of the resources that you put at the disposal of your employees to help them perform, to provide them with a decent working environment where they can foster! Quality of life at work in other words. After understanding this fact on capacity, one would ask: "Why should we cut there to increase productivity, which leads to profits?"

Throughput Accounting views capacity as a financial lever[160]. That truism has unfortunately been forgotten by the accounting profession. Indeed, Cost Accounting distorts input capacity – which is paid for – and output capacity, which is free to use. In doing so, Cost Accounting tightly couples Operating Expenses with Sales. Nonsense!

This brings us back to our Expansion vs Growth discussion of a few paragraphs ago, where we aimed to get five times sales at no extra monetary outlay. To do this we need – in our heads only – to decouple (T) – Throughput, from (OE) – Operating Expenses, as shown below.

[159] The original quote being: "The greatest shortcoming of the human race is our inability to understand the exponential function."

[160] All accountants understand the power of capacity financed by debt. It is a basic knowledge in fiscality.

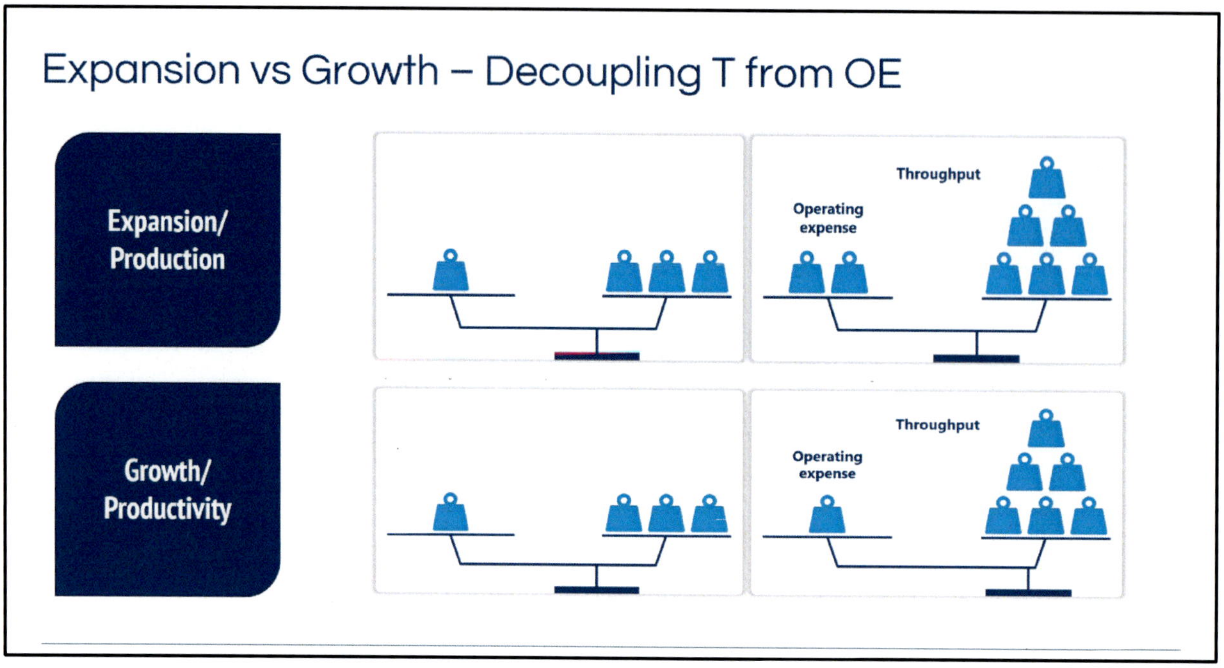

The illustration above demonstrates that simply moving the fulcrum to the right (as in the bottom-right corner) achieves greater productivity (which leads to prosperity) by using brown money without affecting the current level of Operating Expenses![161]

The path to exponential growth lies not in increasing Investment (as we are first inclined to do since it is within our span of control!). It resides rather in sticking to the first three steps of the 5 Focusing Steps as shown below:

[161] This should be a major selling point for pushing the adoption of TA. You can get green money with brown money. I just can't figure out why this is not stated and overstated more often.

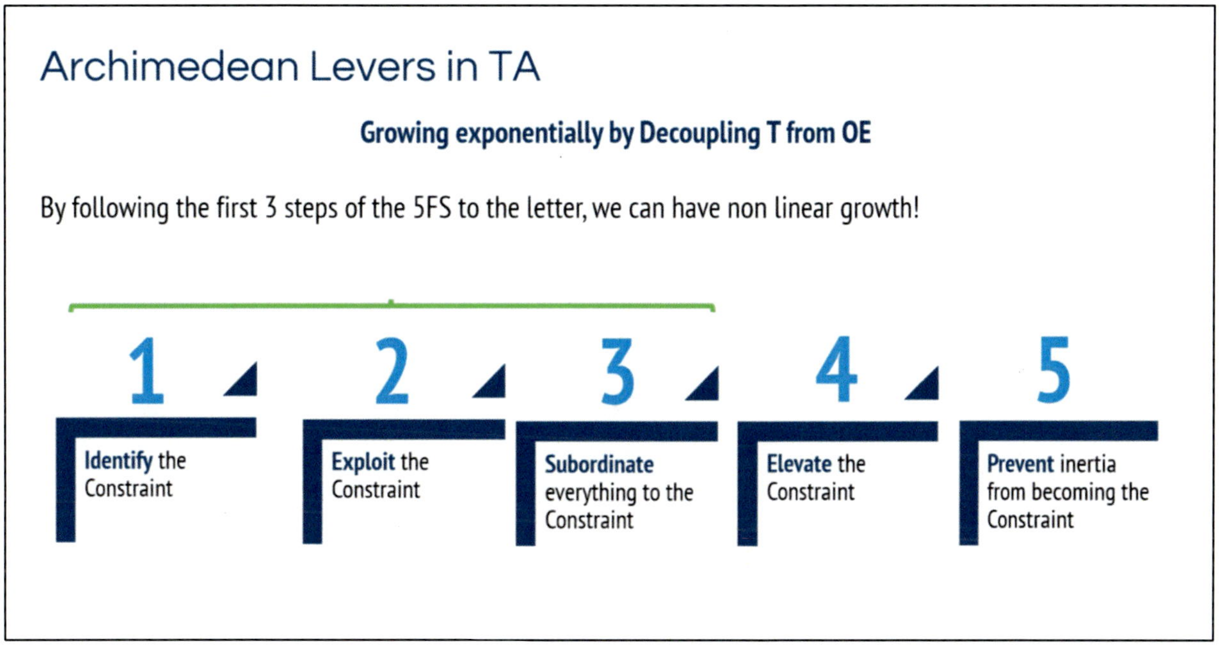

Exploiting the constraint is the cash cow. Especially for Knowledge-Work enterprises. And managing through the time axis as explained in a previous chapter is key to provide tools to tame Common Cause variation. Need I need repeating again the words of wisdom of Mr. Donald Reinertsen to the fact that removing Common Cause ailments is the low hanging fruit of stellar financial performance and immediate returns. This is happening at Exploitation.

The power of Operations on Cash generation

Remember the first illustration? It will be shown again just below with a purpose. With the single use of the first two or three Focusing Steps, we have now created an increase of 24% in sales in the service industry (Banking, Hospitality) with the following operational parameters:

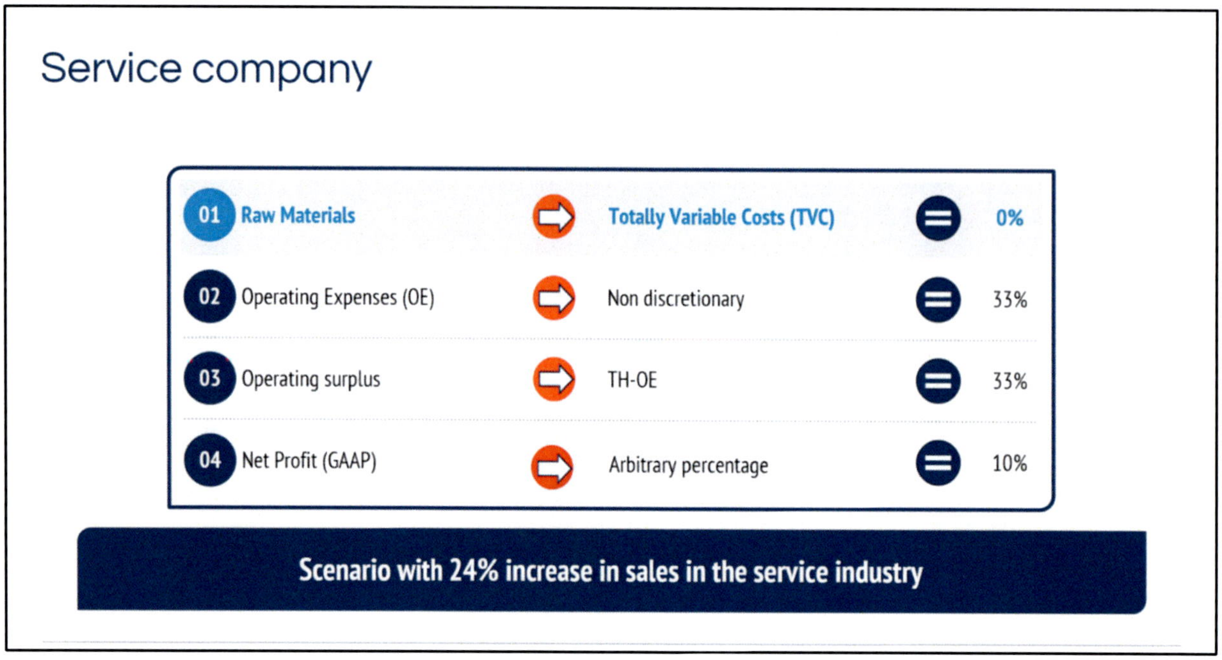

Let's see what an increase in sales of 24% does to Net Profit under GAAP.

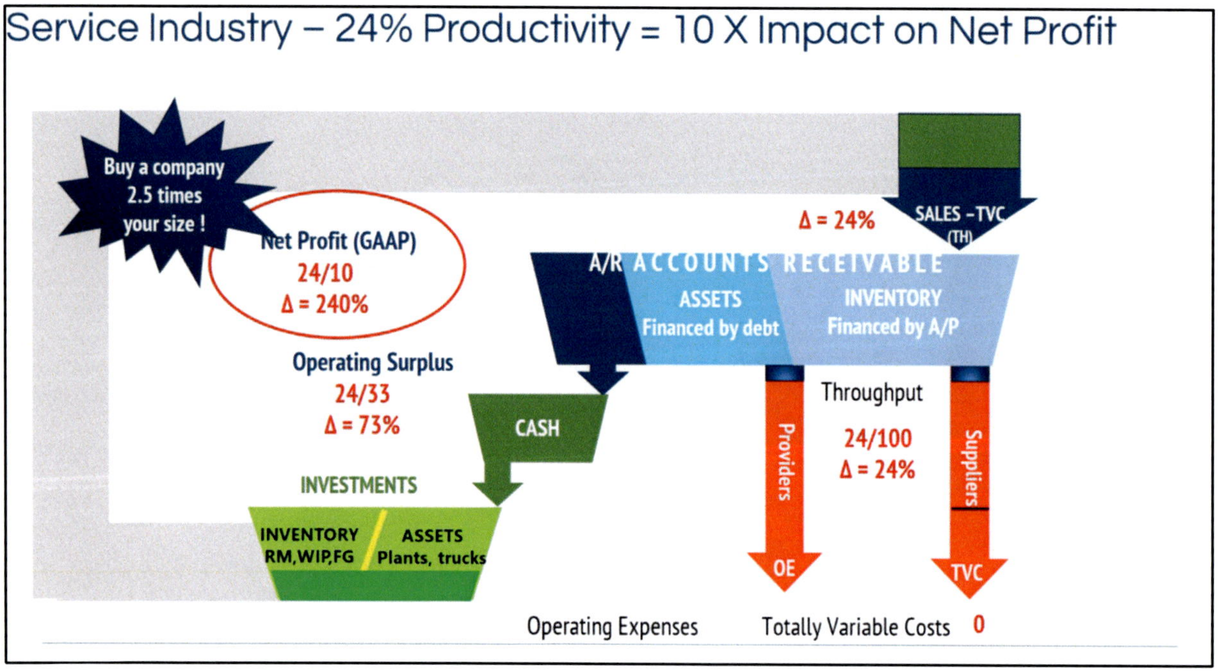

This diagram illustrates the case for a company without TVC[162] - as it seldom applies to Knowledge-Work - that increases sales by 24%. The results? Net Profit under GAAP goes up by 240%.

You can self finance your way to acquire a company 2.5 times your size!

The detailed calculations are shown below.

Service Industry – 24% Productivity = 10 X Impact on Net Profit

	%	ACTUAL	NEW	DELTA	% DELTA	
Sales	100	100	124	24	24%	
Raw Material / TVC	0	0	0	0	0%	
Throughput	100	100	124	24	24%	
Operating Expenses	0.33	33	33	0	0%	
Operating Surplus / Improvement	0.33	33	91	24	72.73%	More than 3 times sales
Net Profit GAAP	0.10	10		24	240.00%	10 times sales. Enough to buy 2.5 companies your size.

The results seem impressive. But if this enterprise wished to acquire a company 2.5 times its size, it could do so thanks to its TOE spread! (Difference between (T)- Throughput and (OE) - Operating Expenses). We will address the significance of the TOE spread further down this chapter, but for now suffice it to say that it is a measure that puts internal growth in the forefront by keeping an eye on capacity.

Going through the ten or so steps required to build the illustration at the beginning of this article is time consuming. It requires attention and intellectual effort. The Powerpoint link to Henry Camp's and Ravi Gilani's succinct 'build-up' of the 'Flows and Pools of Money' diagram is provided in the References. The well-articulated article by Dr Kevlyn Youngman on the same topic can also be found in the References. They are both worthy of the best 'walk-thru' of cash in a company. Dr Youngman's work is at the core of the essence of what we have covered so far in this chapter.

Set aside time to digest the material in Camp, Gilani and Youngman's articles if you desire a detailed analysis.

[162] TVC in Software could include commissions, performance bonus and **sub contractor fees** – a dimension we will leverage very soon.

You will also find my new 'consolidated' model in Appendix A where I took the liberty to assemble a more recent version based on all the existing artefacts available. I took some items out, left many untouched and added a lot of my own thinking. And for the finale, at the conclusion of this article, we will create a 'Flows and Pools of Money' diagram for our business case where TVC will be of paramount importance, a feat that is not very common in Knowledge-Work! To that aim, we will use sub contractors as TVC!

We now have to see how we can change the market participants' motivation and behaviors in the agile coaching market with Mafia offers. Once this is done, we will come back to drawing the proper 'Flows and Pools of Money' diagram where a head-hunter serves as the matchmaker between the client and the agile coach, who is a free lance consultant.

Mafia offers[163]

There is a lot of money trapped in the agile coaching market. Unfortunately, we all operate in a Time and Materials model. The time has come for clients to dictate how business is to be made so that a bigger share of the pie becomes visible to all market participants. It is not an easy task to detach yourself from a cost-plus billing model to something more equitable for those who can perform.

Well, I have a newsflash for you. We will not be able to unleash the enormous potential of Mafia offers by using agile technologies dating back 30 years, especially when the trendy ones are mimicking three decades old knowledge with a different candy wrapper.

This section challenges the current, flawed mental model of the agile coaching (with or without a team) consulting market. It will be painful for some readers but at the end, we will be reminded of Ravi Gilani's words of wisdom: *Make more* and *more rupees* over time.

Mafia offers have characteristics[164] of their own:

- The offer must be explicit, detailed and targeted to the customer
- The offer must be built to mitigate risks for the customer
- The right customers must be pursued
- You must short circuit your competitors' lead time – when they are on a month's scale, you go on a week's scale
- You must destroy their DDP – Due Date Performance
- The offer must improve operations almost immediately

[163] Mafia offers are a formal topic in Throughput Accounting. Dr Lisa Lang is the world's expert on this topic. It is the subject of chapter 22 of the ToC Handbook. Some links

1) https://www.slideshare.net/enterpriselithuania/building-mafia-offers-for-sm-bs-presentation
2) https://www.slideshare.net/enterpriselithuania/how-to-prepare-mafia-offers-under-lithuanian-circumstances-red?next_slideshow=1

[164] "A mafia offer is an offer that is so good that your customers can't refuse it and your competition can't or won't offer the same." Dr Lisa Lang

A Mafia offer is not/does not:

- Based on innovation and new technology
- Based on predetermined price
- Require new products/markets
- Built on comparison with competitors or market practices

To develop a Mafia offer, you need 3 things:

- Your competence and capabilities compared to the market
- How your industry supplies the services/products
- The state of affairs in your industry and the impact your supply can have on the customer

Let us now proceed with the matter at hand. In the coming discussion, I am not entertaining the case of agile coaches being hired in a context of 'staff augmentation'. The agile coaching resources that are part of this discussion are 'specialists' hired to provide value for a new, in-development context or project. Too often, clients hire consultants with the 'unconscious' aim of controlling OE – Operating Expenses. It is a cognitive bias that is innate in the industry. When hiring agile coaches, one should do so in a revenue growth perspective. We need to get there. This onus is on the client.

I will focus here on the Agile coaching consulting market, a subset of IT consulting. There are 3 partakers[165]:

- The client – Who hires external help to reduce risk and increase revenues. They do not care about the length of stay of the consultants – they just want the job done, but the sooner the better. The VP of Human Resources – and in some places the legislator – do not like having hired help that linger on and that are disguised as full-time employees. The effect on the morale of permanent employees when they see someone doing their work at twice their salaries impacts their engagement. No matter the angle you take, this is bad management. This market participant – the client - loves fixed-bid engagements that are predictable in outcomes, costs, and less on duration were we to be explicit on revenue growth.
- The head-hunter, consulting firm or IT outsourcer – Who makes a match between the client and the consultants available on the bench or the market. They are looking for a predictable revenue stream. Every time a mandate ends, their revenues are impacted. They want a thin bench and long-lasting mandates. There can be binding contracts at times between the client and the providers of consultants. Taken from any angle, this is mainly clerical work (matching consultants to clients) and the margins are thinner as some clients now will not give more than 5% of the consultant's earnings as commissions for their role as a go-between. This is a linear revenue model. This model applies to the 'staff augmentation market' when you come to think of it. The head-hunter is more likely to go on a time and material option. The IT outsourcers can do fixed-bids, but usually only when they must.
- The consultant (agile coach with/without a team) - Who has the ability and track record to do the job and who is often recommended based on the duration of their past contracts, which for all intents and purposes, is a weak predictor of future performance. It becomes a self-enforcing feedback loop, motivating consultants to stay as long as possible to secure their next job. They are in revenue protection mode as time between mandates is to be avoided. Their interest lies in

[165] I have spoken with numerous head-hunters and consulting firms about the solution that I am presenting. I got the cold shoulder as my approach would destroy their business models. Consultants as well. The change from the market must come from the clients who pay and must demand Throughput! I know the clients would welcome the change as I have spoken to many of them but the status quo is the constraint here.

extending their stays as they cannot command a higher rate than the market can bear. They are always on a time and material billing business model.

We operate in a market where Revenues = Price x Quantity. This is a linear model. If only there was a way to change all that and make the pie bigger. This is where ToC Mafia offers come into play. Everyone ends up with the upper hand, and better off financially.

The core problem is revenues. When you work in a revenue protection mode - as head-hunters and consultants do – you are in fact operating under a 'cost-plus' scenario. Cost-plus scenarios do one thing extremely well: passing inefficiencies onto the payer and providing a motivation to extend services for those who invoice.

Nobody likes to be on the short end of fix bids. The consultants do not want to bear the risk of being paid on a deliverable basis. The head-hunter, outsourcer or consulting firm that has managed only one such fix bid contract is not crazy enough to do it again and enter a bidding war. The catchphrase 'out of scope' comes from this model. Plus, the business relationship with the client is fragile and difficult to maintain in fix bid mandates that linger on for too long.

Clients and fix bids? They love it. Their business risk is shared. The more the better.

The only way we can all get around this illiquid market is to generate more money for all participants by competing on short time horizons and revenue/benefit sharing. That is only possible if you have a recipe that works, that is repeatable, that has causality. A bit like science. The essence of to 'do' agile.

Throughput Accounting and the Theory of Constraints have these traits. They are based on science. Once you start, you are already near the finish line. Results are repeatable and predictable.[166]

So here is the Mafia offer. Everybody wins in the end. And especially the talented workers who, for lifestyle reasons, enjoy permanency and stability offered by full-time employment. They will learn from the best consultants in short bursts, after which those consultants will then move on to the next, more rewarding mandate, putting an end to their main stressor which is the 'in between' mandate idle time.

The key is to understand the revenue and/or cost function of the client (the client must be forthcoming). Then one must find out how much cutting Lead Time by more than 20% in one month is worth. That is the first fix bid mandate. Risk sharing means revenue sharing. That is problematic for the clients as they are not used to spending money that way nor revealing their revenue and cost curves to outsiders.

---

[166] Many agilists tell me they have to try it before they adopt it. This is frustrating. Little's law works. Try it if you like, it will be time wasted. I like the analogy of the medical field. When you consult for an illness that requires time for a cure, then time is needed in psychiatry or pediatrics. Knowing the patient and 'social' skills, rapport and trust have to be built over time. I am all for that. But for a heart surgeon - or any kind of surgery - I have often seen last minute replacements. The specialists look at the X-Rays, and on she goes to operate. Not even a need to talk to the surgeon you are relieving nor to the patient you are operating on. There is expertise in the agile field that can get things fixed in no time - and quickly - with flow metrics and visualization. The Theory of Constraints, DBR, CCPM and Throughput Accounting come to mind as tools that give predictable results time after time without having to ride a learning curve.

When the first month has shown great success, then a second mandate of two months can be contemplated with, let's say, an increase in Throughput of 30%. If things did not work out, the adventure comes to a conclusion.

Finally, a three-month mandate can seal the intervention with more of the same, while focusing on more details of the 5 Focusing Steps and Throughput Accounting.

Then, on to the next customer.

The client has paid in a matter of weeks what was usually spread over years but earned the economic rewards now; the consulting firms now have a new business model based on repetition of high margin gigs; and the consultants can live a 'stress free' career as they know they simply need to show up and step up to the plate to hit a home run. The friction between mandates when they are short on revenues is more than made up for by the enhanced revenues they actually make while working half as hard.

On this account, the head-hunter or IT outsourcer can now enter into fix bid contracts at no risk. The number of contracts is multiplied, and by not doing clerical work but participating in finding value in proposals that show understanding of their clients' path to prosperity, the quality of their revenue stream goes up, which is what they are ultimately looking for. But the accounting – and 'Flows and Pools of Money' diagram - would look different for each of them for the following reasons:

- For the IT firm, the increase in Throughput comes by turning over their (I)nventory – their full-time consultants - tenfold at a higher markup. We are including the concept of (I)nventory and (T) management for that market segment. The employees' full-time salaries are OE.
- Accounting wise, the situation is different for the head hunter. He has no (I) and no full-time employees. The billings he receives from the agile coaches, acting as sub contractors, he passes on to the clients are in fact TVC. In his case which he is marking up at a much higher rate than before. No more 5% profit margin. This is a big win. His OE – Operating Expenses – are of no help in transforming anything into Throughput, TVC are!

The results are anticipatable. So are the revenues, which is what is sought in the first place. There are plenty of clients who want these kinds of results in a short time span.

This is doable. But the lead must come from the clients as the head-hunters and consultants cherish their business models as it stands. Clients want growth and risk sharing, not an extra layer of overheads. And HR wants happy employees who can better themselves and increase their market value. HR does not want consultants disguised as full-time employees at twice the salary of their regular workforce for mandates that last years. The impact on their morale is real and invisible being released thru passive aggressive behaviors.

The current business model offers linear results. It cannot be otherwise. Let's embrace geometric growth and prosperity for all by using the alternate Throughput Accounting formula for Revenues:

Revenues = Quantity / Time spent at the constraint per unit of time

The money is there! We just need to convert it faster and do more repetition in the same timespan.

We will address the new "Pools and Flows of Money" diagram for the head-hunter in the next section. There are significant changes to be made compared to a standard 'made for manufacturing' diagram!

One may wonder what is the connection between Throughput Accounting and Mafia offers? I asked that very question to Dr Lisa Lang – who is the creator of the Mafia Offer topic – and she told me that TA can help you determine who you should target your offer to. A Mafia Offer is built on an operational decisive competitive edge. It's how we EXPLOIT a market constraint.

Building up a new 'Flows and Pools of Money' diagram for Knowledge-Work in the Agile Coaching Consulting market

In this section, I will submit a different 'version' of:

> Operating Expenses turn Investments into Throughput.

And replace it with:

> TVC generates Throughput. (Albeit I have repeated many times that TVC does not exist in Knowledge-Work, but when the coaches are paid by the head hunters who acts as a go between with the clients, they become sub contractors!)

The change is of course due to the peculiar model that we have developed. Also, OE – Operating Expenses – normally conceived of as the conduit to turn I into T does not apply to the head hunter.

Transformation of 'Flows and Pools of Money' diagram for Head-Hunter

When I was juggling as to how I would 'sketch' the diagram for the agile coaching market, I came up with a few variations. But we are all heading for a 'cash generating' business with the use of T Generators[167], in the true spirit of Throughput Accounting. We will use the context of the head-hunter and not of a consulting firm – which would yield a different diagram altogether, believe it or not!

Something haunted me while I was deciphering how to illustrate the situation without destroying the original intent of the 'Flows and Pools of Money' diagram. Then I remembered that OE, I and TVC and T are all subject to variations in their descriptions. I was reminded by both Mr. Du Plooy and Gilani that T is not additional sales – like I attribute it in this book – but rather "the rate at which 'contribution rupees' are coming into the organization".

---

[167] T Generators are discussed at length in: Schragenheim, Eli and Camp, Henry and Surace, Rocco. 'Throughput Economics: Making Good Management Decisions'. Routledge, A Productivity Press Book. 2019

For instance, the definition of 'I' has significantly evolved to the point where it is nowhere near what it was at the beginning when Dr Goldratt first coined the term.

I recall one such variation on TVC. An authority, whom I cannot recall the name, said that OE turned TVC into T. It irritates the mind at first and for a while. But it is just as true as OE turns I into T. Not as good, but just as right. At least in the manufacturing sector.

This is what I will do. I will go so far in this example as to say that OE – for the head-hunter – in no way helps in turning anything into T. Rather it is entirely TVC – the billings from the agile coaches – that acts as the lever in this particular case. Let's see how this develops. In the traditional sense, Investments only involve the devices own by the agile coaches and the infrastructure of the client. The head-hunter provides no help at all in terms of 'physical' or 'intellectual' Investments. We can even go so far as to say that the Operating Expenses of the head-hunter in no way helps into turning anything into Throughput, except for the fact that his mere existence is what makes all of this happen. But there is not enough to make an 'operational' connection. Throughput Accounting is at the operational level, may I remind you.

Below is the 'Flows and Pools of Money' diagram stripped off from the unnecessary components.

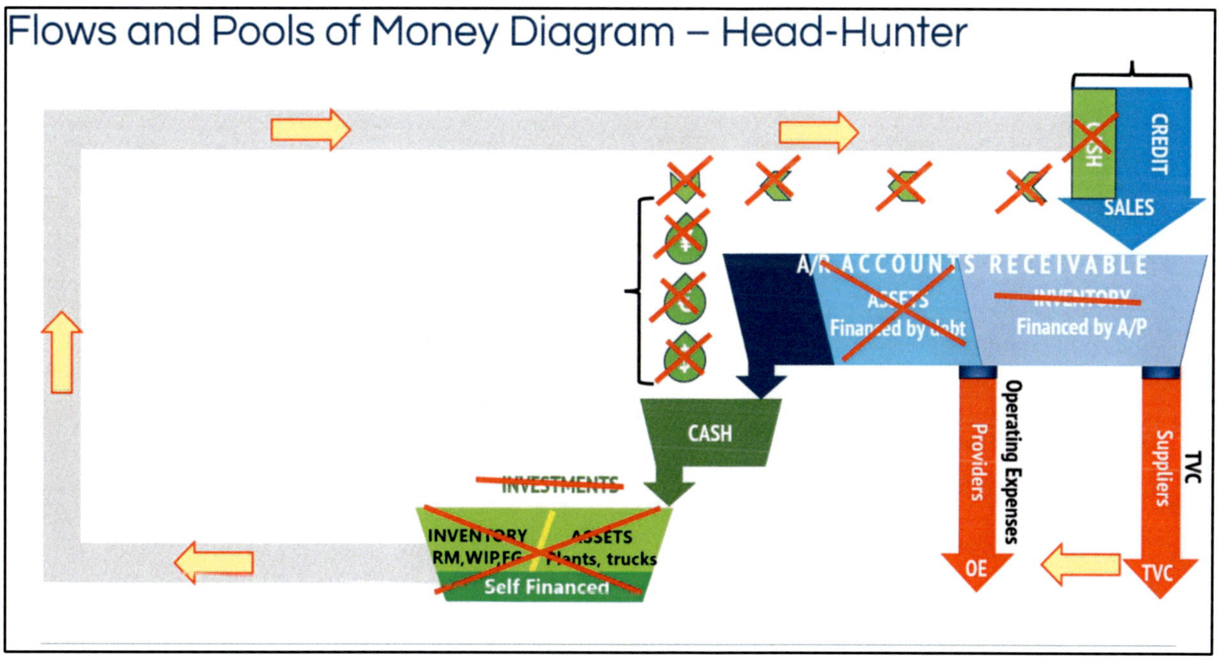

- Cash inflows will be replaced entirely by Accounts Receivables. Once the head-hunter bills the clients, payments will be wired or sent by cheque!
- Accounts Payable will be required to support the timing difference between the billings from the agile coaches and the receipts from Accounts Receivables coming from the clients. The traditional model dictates that consultants are remunerated by the head-hunter once the clients has paid. Since Mafia offers do not change the manner in which we usually work, this will remain intact.
- There will no longer be a need for debt financing in this context as we do not acquire or develop any kind of overly complicated assets or intellectual property.

- The Operating Expenses would be the salary of the head-hunter and other services provided by banks etc. However, in this context, the Operating Expenses would not turn I into T. In this situation, TVC represents the billings for the work of the consultants and would create T directly with a hefty margin.
- INVESTMENTS in Throughput Accounting can consist of both tangible and non tangible assets. 'Out' we are with the green box with physical goods and fixed assets. What I intend to do is replace the green INVESTMENT box with what Eli Schragenheim, Henry Camp, and Rocco Surace label as 'T Generators', as in Throughput Generators. This will constitute the knowledge base that is required to do the work. It is for all intent and purposes carried in the head of the consultants, except maybe for some RFP templates and pricing models, which are in the physical domain. Those would not be significant and could be treated as Operational Expenses.

In our case, the INVESTMENT box would be replaced by intangible assets linked to knowledge of the Theory of Constraints, Throughput Accounting, MAFIA offers, 5 FS etc.

T Generators

T Generators (Throughput Generators) apply in all context. It is a new concept that hit the market in 2019. Through this new optic, no links exists between the inputs, the processing, the outputs and how it is sold and how much it is sold for. It fits Knowledge-Work like a glove when you match it with Mafia offers! Every situation requires a new mind set. They remind me of Mafia offers.

This is exactly how we should label the old green INVESTMENTS box. There are of course tangible assets that can be developed such as pricing models, RFP templates and the likes and they do fall under the category of 'tangible' assets.

Throughput Accounting has passed the test of time and works pretty well for the service industry as well as for manufacturing. For Knowledge-Work, we may be exposed to challenging hiccups.

In the case that we are building, is centered on Mafia offers for a head-hunter that hires all of the resources he requires to make a markup. In fact, he is like a software distributor that would have no warehouse, no trucks, no ownership of the assets he sells. In fact, his product generating green 'INVESTMENTS' box in his 'Flows and Pools of Money' diagram would simply be a plain 'markup' engine! Our software distributor is just a pivot. So is our head-hunter; a mere facilitator.

T Generators are discussed at length in the book 'Throughput Economics' that can be found in the References section. We have also a pretty good idea of what a Mafia offer is. They have so much in common that I believe that this is what creates value to our new 'Flows and Pools of Money' diagram in the invisible world of Knowledge-Work.

Each Mafia offer is different and priced as such. T Generators are also to be considered products that are different between themselves in terms of market value.

Strikingly, in both cases it is mandatory to differentiate between what is produced and what is being sold. The perceived value of the product for each market condition is more important than the process or its inputs!

In both cases, that which is sold is referred to its name: Mafia offers and T Generators[168].

But the one thing that is interesting with T Generators is where we 'make', 'assemble' and 'build' products. A bit like our old INVESTMENTS green box. The difference would be in the scale of the selling price. You can only add so much value to transforming a piece of wood, but shaving off 30% of Lead Time is a different value proposition each and single time a Mafia offer is made to a client! There is no common denominator!

There are so many affinities between the 'products' being created with Mafia offers in our agile coaching market and T Generators that the 'INVESTMENTS' green box in our diagram needs to be labelled as 'T GENERATORS'.

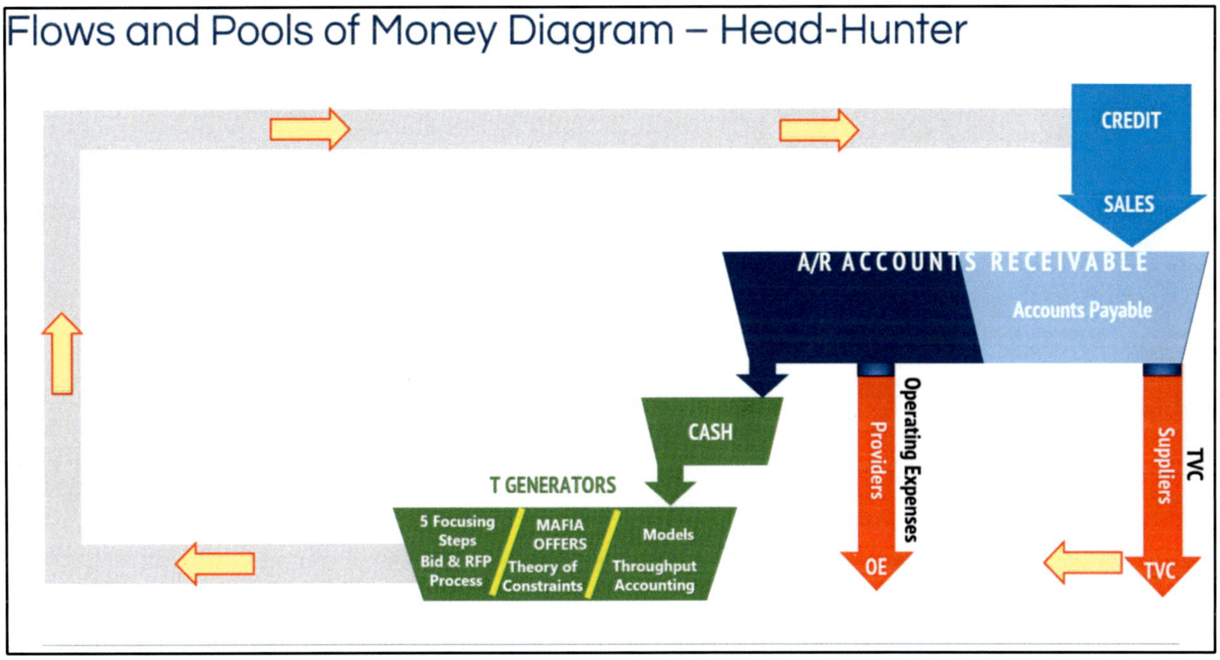

As one can see, the model has been stripped off to over emphasize the fact that we are heading into a near 'cash' business. Every time an opportunity occurs, the forces prevailing in the market take over to curtail to the Mafia offer.[169]

Also, the T GENERATORS box is fully financed by cash, hence the dark green color.

[168] I am surprised that the creators of T Generators did not pick up some 'similarities' they share with Mafia offers. But after contacting Eli Schragenheim, he had this brilliant and succinct bit to share: 'Thinking on what we sell (T-generators) from what we produce (our products) is a good way to create mafia offers. Still, most T-generators are not mafia offers, but every mafia offer is a T-generator.

[169] There are no investments in working capital for the head hunter to finance the first month of operations as it is customary to await the receipts from the clients before paying the consultants.

The conclusion is simple. The middleman – head-hunter - has to be able to target clients and master the concepts of Mafia offers and T Generators. This is the new model.

Investments - The First One on the BUS pays for the BUS

The expression above comes from Glenn Menzies, a colleague whom I worked with in the Insurance industry a while back. I never heard it before I met him, and I really think it illustrates the case I am trying to make.

We have addressed in length (T) – Throughput and (OE) – Operating Expenses, but where does (I) - Investments fit in all this? Curiously, there is an 'I' link with T and OE!

But first, we need to come back to the 'material' world and take the example of companies that work in project mode to acquire new capacity. The banking, utility, cellular, and insurance market come to mind.

We have addressed the fact that capacity is a flat line. It is, until we need to augment it. At this juncture, the capacity function is better represented as a staircase:

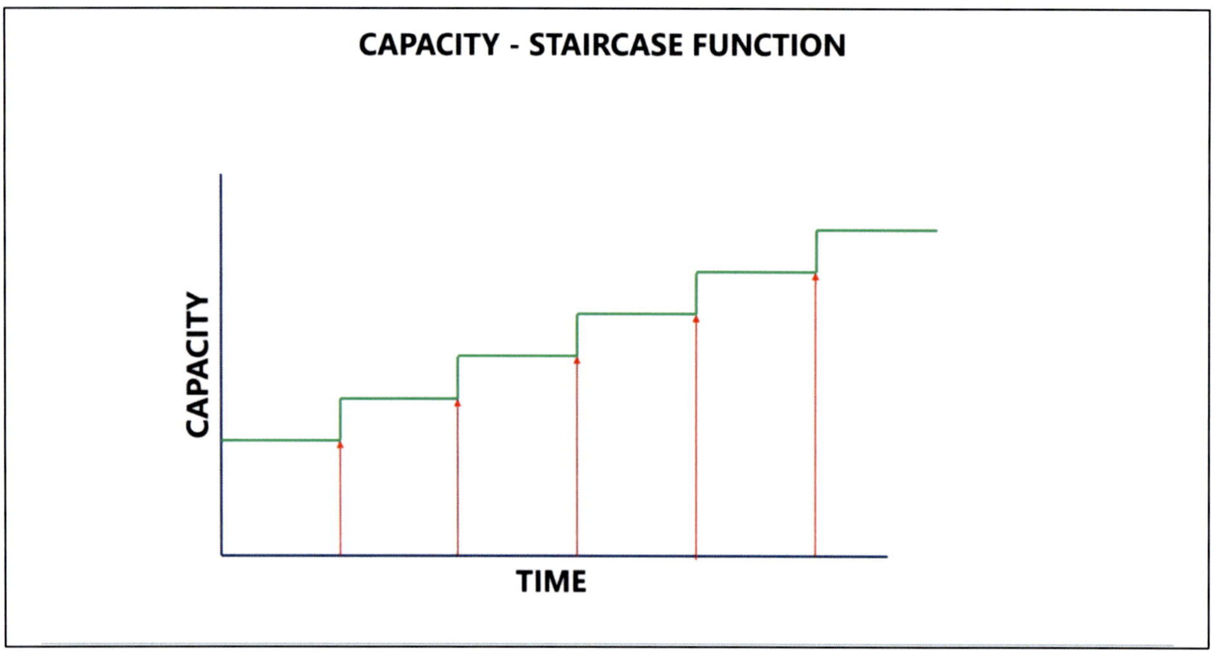

When the need arises to increase capacity for servers when the bank or insurance company hits the 'red arrow' points above, one project must find the money to purchase the capacity that suits the corporate needs. If a project needs a bit, it has to buy a whole lot of capacity for everybody else. This is the way that corporate architecture guides the growth of overall capacity. This makes sense. Up to a point.

The negative impact of such an approach is that when the time comes for adding capacity, projects that are less 'fortunate' will hide in the hope that someone else will find the money. This creates accounting f(r)iction[170].

This scenario is not well suited for Throughput Accounting as the economic life of the incremental (I) - Investments or (OE) – Operational Expenses must be matched with the additional (T) – Throughput generated in the targeted period. Buying capacity for the entire bank does not serve the Throughput Accounting model. What are we to do?

The spread between T and OE – usually referred in TA as absolute profitability (Net Profit) – is the answer as to where to look for finding the money for I through **internal growth**, something that we have forgotten since the time we started to transform fixed cost (capacity) into some sort of variable costs variations!

As T is decoupled from OE, new money is injected into the system. As T is decoupled from OE, the index of productivity (T/OE) goes up in a non-linear pattern as well! Herein lies the key to Elevate once you have done all that could be done with the Archimedean lever of the first three steps of the 5 Focusing Steps! Now is the time to invest in capacity with the TOE[171] (T minus OE) spread and give some thoughts to increasing (I) in that fashion and not resort to individual projects to get delayed and lose Throughput as a consequence. Now is the time to Elevate. Resorting to external financing should be contemplated when the TOE spread, read internal growth, is lacking.[172]

Accountants understand taxation and the benefits of debt financing. The tax shield is a form of financial lever. Capacity is a lever as well. It has gone into oblivion by our insistence on transforming fixed costs into variable costs for the rightful need of cost allocation for Financial Accounting reporting. We need to acknowledge that and step sideway to give room for internal growth.

Conclusion – Smart Money and Cash-to-Cash Cycle

No one becomes Albert Einstein overnight, not even Albert Einstein! Today, we all benefit from his knowledge, thanks to the advances of society. No need to travel the path of relativity.

---

[170] Accounting F(r)iction is a play on words that I created a long, long time ago. Fiction first. Balance Sheet and Income Statements can de window dressed and to that extend, they represent 'fiction'. When you come to play the accounting game, always bring a Cash Flow statement as those cannot be gamed. While this is going on, the road to 'friction' is paved. Let say you have a purchaser. He buys you more servers than you expected for the budgeted amount. He has a favorable purchase variance. Then, when the Operations managers puts the servers into Prod, the lack of quality emerges after a few months. His operating variance is hit hard. He gets fired and the purchasing manager gets a raise. In cost accounting, variances are often done in a Win-win situation: one participant will get the big W the other one, the small w.

[171] TOE spread. A new term of mine to indicate how increases in Investments ought to be financed and also give an incentive to decouple T from OE!

[172] Ravi Gilani and Henry Camp provide every answer to these questions with their common work in the References section.

The same applies to the teachings of Dr Eli Goldratt and his many followers today.

The GOAL, the first book published by Dr Goldratt, included this sentence: "Make more money now and in the future".

It may have a negative connotation, but it was spoken to a friend who in the early 1980s – where stagflation and record interest rates were intolerable – was struggling financially. Later, he would admit that all his work was made to help humanity achieve better economic prosperity, so we could all have better lives at home, at work and within society.

This body of knowledge is within reach for all of us. The time to reap the benefits is quick. This knowledge is the 'software' that runs the T Generators in the new 'Flows and Pools of Money' diagram since intangible assets must take the place that is owed to them.

It is time to realize the unrecognised positive impact of the Archemedian lever operations exerts upon finance by decoupling T – Throughput from OE – Operating Expenses to pave to way to finance more I - Investments. The TOE spread is the secret to the self financing of (I).

When I noticed this decoupling the first time, I also realized that Kanban decouples its inputs from its outputs with the use of Cadences and measurements. I like decoupling. It works and makes things a lot easier to understand and manage.

You will also pick up that T Generators decouple the inputs, the processing, the outputs and how it is sold and how much it is sold for. This is management accounting!

Mafia offers – which are always T Generators – are also cash engines built on decoupling.

Financial Accounting and Cost Accounting being tightly coupled cannot serve both at the pleasure of external reporting and internal performance. It is plainly not doable and hope this book will pave the way to the CPA profession to meet its obligation of maximising the value of the patrimony of its clients.

The lack of TVC in Knowledge-Work makes a mockery of the cash-to-cash cycle. I have shown in previous chapters that its boundaries in Knowledge-Work simply collapse as there are no TVC to trigger the beginning of the cash cycle and that with the use of Mafia offers, you could technically collect the money before even starting the work! There goes both the markers of the cash-to-cash cycle and the sequential construct of the model.

It is also time for participants in the agile coaching market to think about exploiting the constraint for growth and productivity – as we have debated in the first section – instead of thinking in terms of cutting Operating Expenses and using agile coaches as workforce augmentation for a mere markup.

One last thing, when making Mafia offers:

- You should always stress why your client would benefit from doing business with you and;
- Making outrageous guarantees are often – not always - part of Mafia offers!

It's time for Mafia offers. Let the ~~market~~ clients decide. It will take courage, but it can be done.

APPENDIX A – The 'Flows and Pools of Money' Diagram – Explanations of colors and arrows

Please find below the most complete Flows and Pools of money diagram. At this point, I simply want to explain the colors and arrows and every thing that will help to decipher the illustration:

Flows and Pools of Money Diagram
Complete Income Statement & Balance Sheet

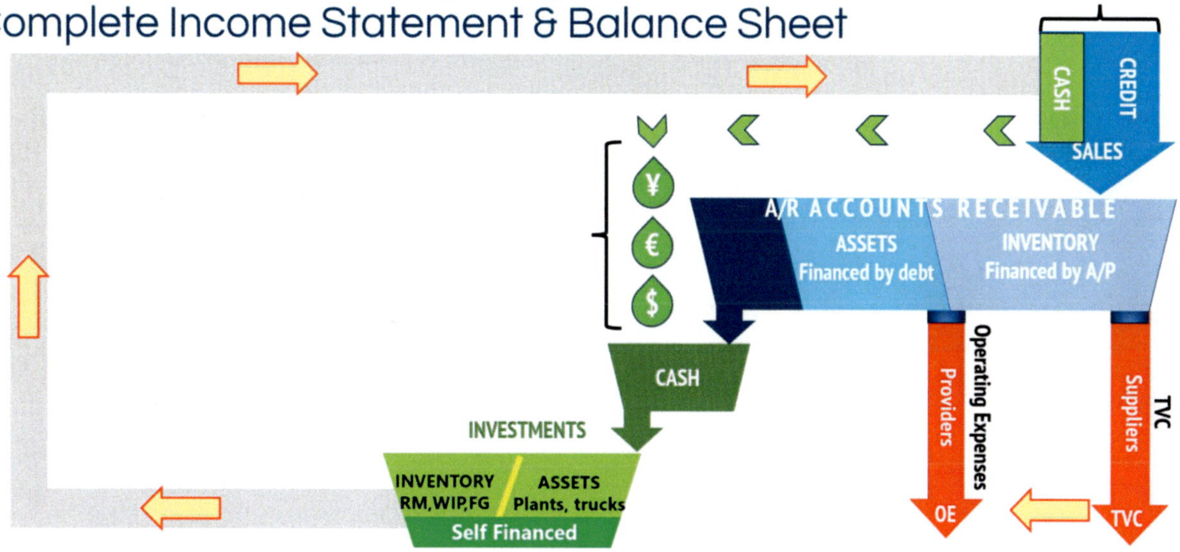

- Arrows are meant to be Flows of money. Pools of money trapped on the Balance Sheet are represented by throughs.
- The yellow arrow that we see in the contour represents TVC – Totally Variable Costs - to be paid. It starts from the Suppliers.
- The red color associated with the fat arrows for OE – Providers and TVC – Suppliers is simply meant to represent an eventual cash outflow.
- The dark blue area represents Accounts Receivable. Unnoticeable to the naked eye, this dark blue area occupies all of the geometric form that it sits on. The reason that a light blue (Assets Financed by Debt) and light grey area (Financed by A/P – Accounts Payables) overtake it just goes to show that these Accounts Receivables are not 'clean of debt'. The money trapped in A/R – Accounts Receivables is are used to finance Assets and Inventory thru debt (Providers) and Accounts Payables (Suppliers).
- All bold areas are assets

APPENDIX B – Building The 'Flows and Pools of Money' Diagram

This appendix deserves a bit of history. The 'Flows and Pools of Money' diagram is a major artefact in Throughput Accounting. It is not given the light and importance that it should have and, frankly, all CPA and CxO level executives ought to understand its mechanic.

If you Google 'Throughput Accounting Flows and Pools of money diagram' you will get nowhere. As a CPA I did not know of its existence and found it challenging to master. I am trying here to create an awareness and provide and easy guide to understanding this major accounting artefact.

It is the best kept secret of the accounting profession. I have taken the time to integrate the words and wisdoms of all those, who up until now, have produced a version of the 'Flows and Pools of Money Diagram'. I am indebted to their original thinking.

Changes are required on the evolution of this diagram. It will come in due time. For now, it is good enough although is may have some flaws.

A Sale is made either a) for cash or b) on credit.

- PLEASE NOTE THAT THE SCALE, SIZE and FORM of the various geometric figures in the following pages are for visualization purposes only.
- **It bears no meaning to the actual size of one Flow or Pool over any other.**

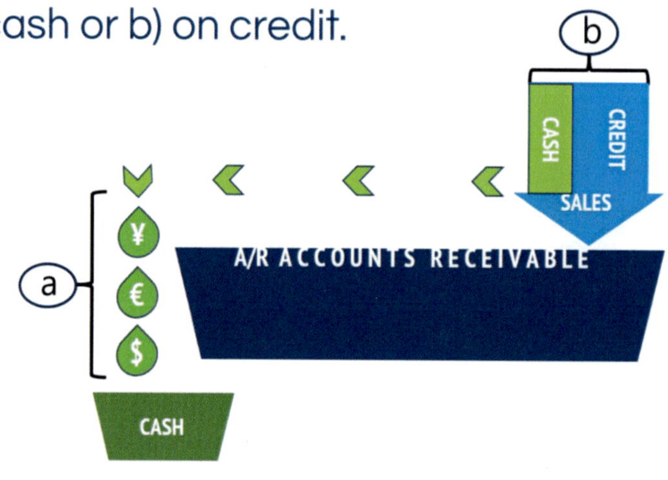

Note: Arrows represent FLOWS. All other forms represent POOLS of Money.

A Sale is made either a) for cash or b) on credit.

- Payments received in various currencies are translated to CASH immediately.
- Sales on Credit find their way into Accounts Receivable.
- Net Sales (money coming in) is what is considered in Throughput Accounting. Gross Sales have to be adjusted for discounts, commisions etc.
- Once TVC – Totally Variable Costs – are subtracted from Net Sales, we arrive at Throughput.

Once Sales are converted into money, they flow into 3 directions: c) Company, d) Providers and e) Suppliers

- Providers encompass employees, banks, Insurances, Utilities, debt service. (Operational Expenses)
- Suppliers are paid for raw materials, components, supplies used to support the production of goods. (Totally Variable Costs)

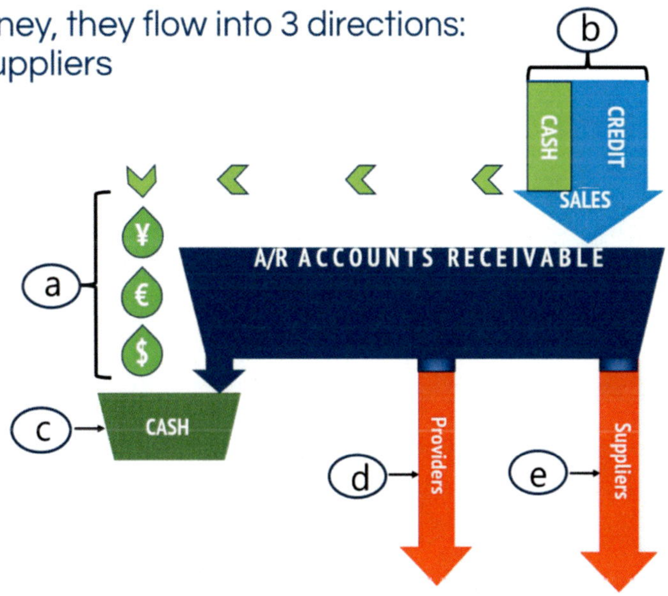

A nuance on Profit and Net Profit !

- Any receipts left over from Net Sales once Suppliers and Providers are paid, is called a **Profit**
- Anything else is a **Loss**
- We need to be careful, as in a Throughput Accounting world, notes payables for the growth of the business, dividends to shareholders and payments to owners are not included in Net Profit as they are not Operational Expenses. (Concept 6 – Throughput Accounting – Etienne Du Plooy).
- The notion of Net Profit and Profit have key differentiating factors in Throughput Accounting.
- The bottom line for Profits, in both Financial Accounting and Throughput Accounting, would reveal the same amount!

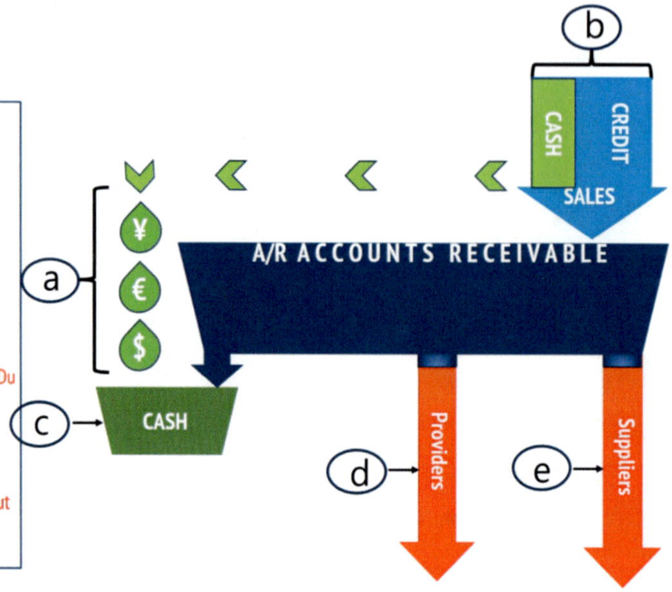

Note: For example, purchase of land for future growth or building of a new plant are not really operational assets yet!

One Financial statement at a time !

This illustration depicts the :

- Income Statement
- Accounts Receivable
- Money in the bank

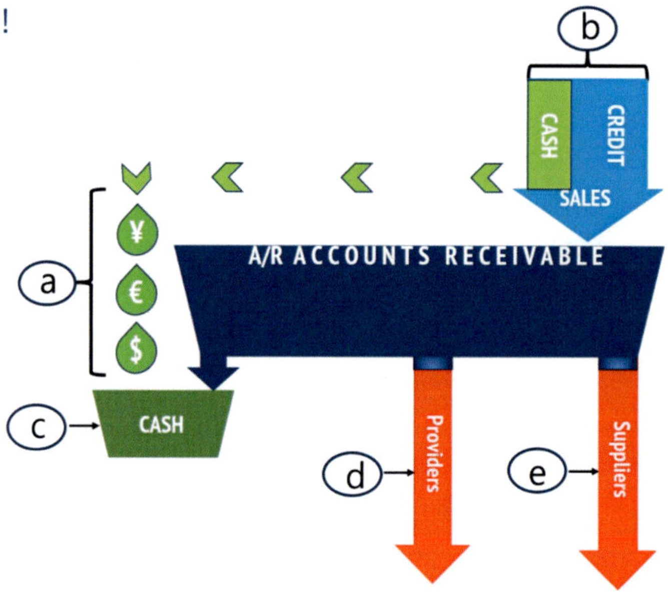

We can add one more Asset Pool – f) INVESTMENTS

- Investments and Accounts Receivables are monies that are trapped inside the company.
- Cash isn't stuck and can be readily spend and is not part of INVESTMENTS
- All asset pools except CASH can be considered INVESTMENTS

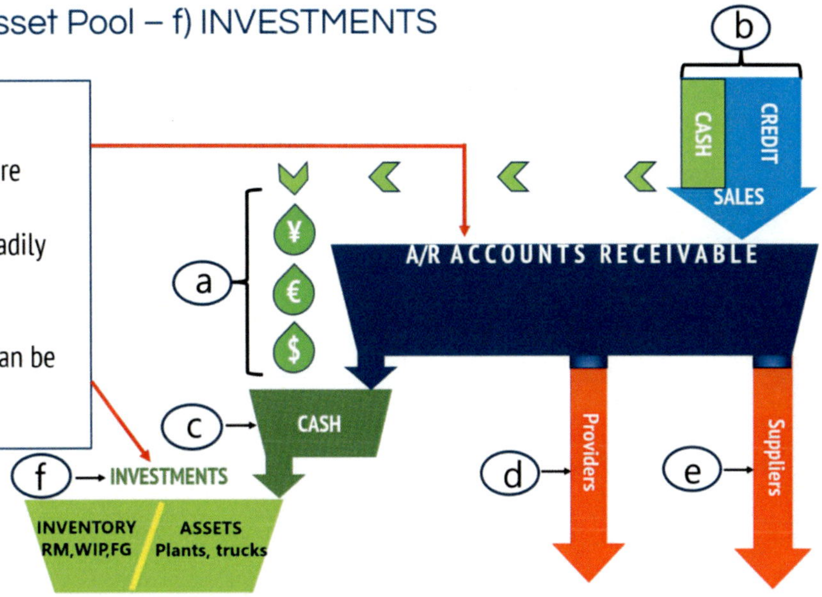

Note: There are nuances to be made with CASH as the definition of INVESTMENTS has evolved over the years. We will address those as we progress.

Investments represented with Inventory and Assets

INVESTMENTS includes anything which could be sold, including

a) **INVENTORY**: Raw Materials, WIP, Finished Goods at cost plus freight-in

b) **ASSETS**: Warehouse, Trucks, Equipments

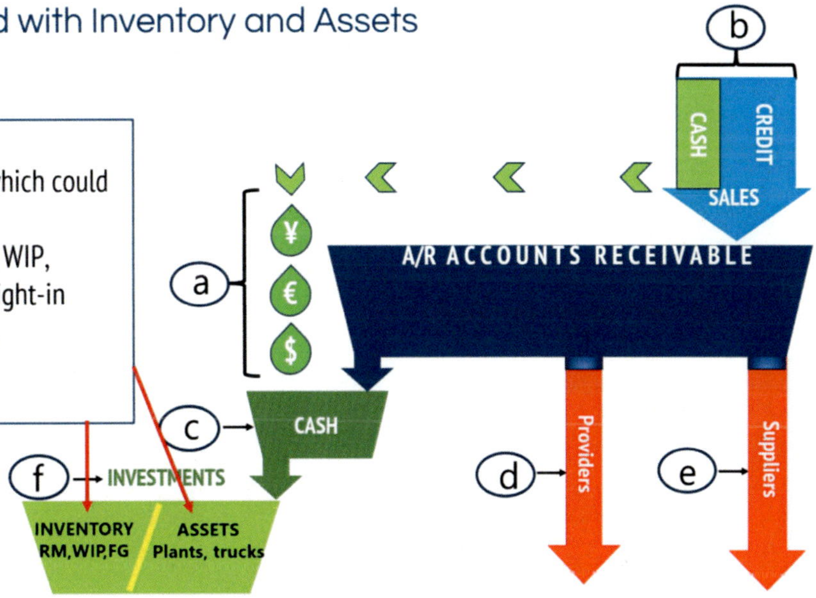

Note on Inventory: RM = Raw Material, WIP = Work In Progress & FG = Finished Goods valued at TVC – Totally Variable Costs – (Purchase price plus freight-in)

Flows and Pools of Money Diagram – Source of Sales of Goods

This 'Flows and Pools of Money' diagram shows the source of the goods which are sold in a manufacturing context. Their provenance must be from **INVESTMENTS**

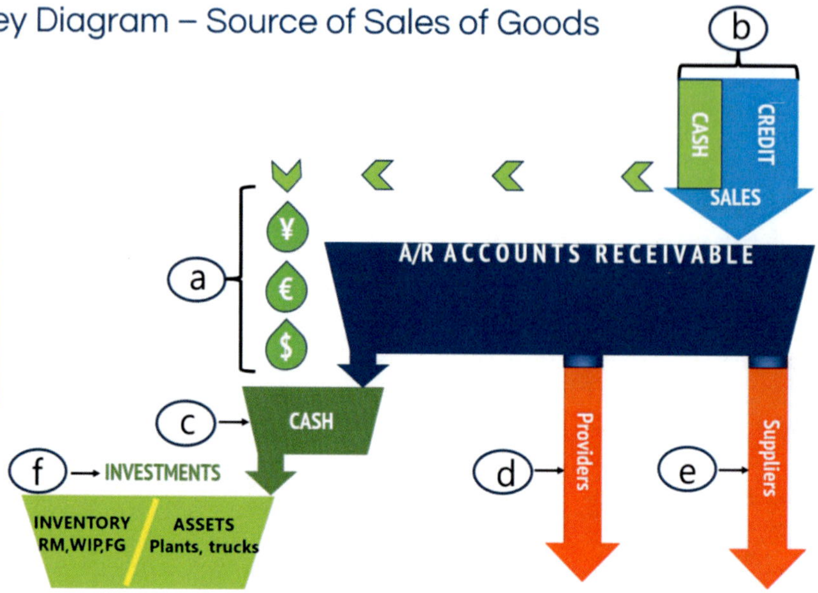

Note: **INVESTMENTS** include INVENTORY and ASSETS in the context of production of goods (Throughput). Operational Expenses turn INVESTMENTS into THROUGHPUT

More Financial Accounting artefacts

The diagram now shows the:

- **Income Statement**
- **All Assets**

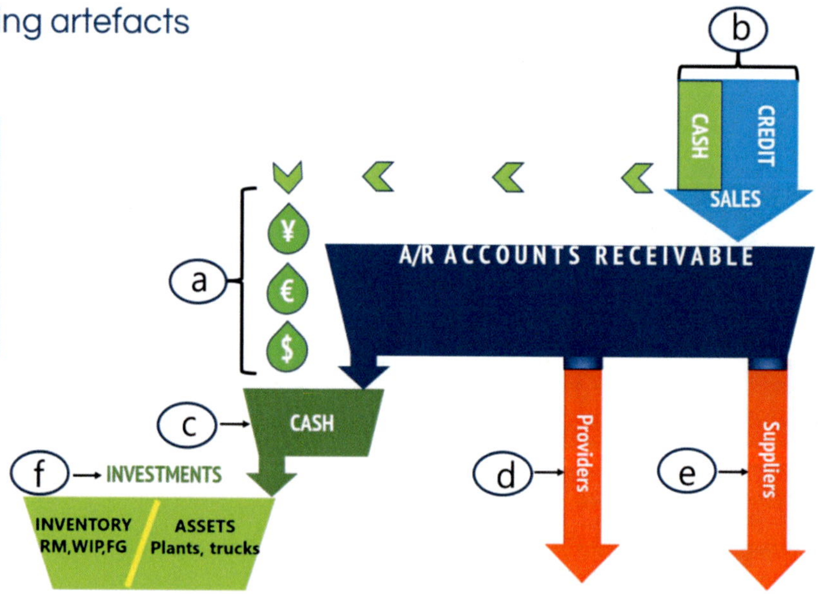

INVESTMENTS POOL DEFINITIONS – 2 MOTIVES

(INVESTMENT)- THROUGHPUT GENERATION PERSPECTIVE

Under this lens we can include the evolution of what (I) meant over time:

- Inventory
- Assets + Inventory
- Assets + Inventory + Investments
- All the money in the system

All money in the system = Things purchased by the system with cash (Dr Eli Goldratt)

(INVESTMENT) -THROUGHPUT ACCOUNTING VIEW THE GOAL : Make more and more Money

Under this lens, the definition of Investment then becomes:

- All the money in the system except CASH

The goal of any commercial organisation is to make more and more money as measured by money in the bank. The purpose of considering all assets - other than cash in the bank - is to reduce them to increase cash in the bank.

The typical assets that Throughput Accounting tends to focus on to reduce are Accounts Receivables and Inventories. Not cash as it is something we aim to maximize!

(Paraphrased from Ravi Gilani)

INVESTMENT is all the money trapped inside the system that belongs to the firm, but has not yet been converted into cash (Dr Kevlin Youngman)

Note: I was really inclined to give 2 definitions to INVESTMENT... One for Throughput Generation (I) and one more in line with Throughput Accounting and attaining the GOAL of maximizing cash and keeping to a minimum all other assets (I) in the more traditional sense. Keeping (I) to a minimum – except cash – allows the system to funnel more CASH in the bank.

Income Statement and All Assets Pools – Adding OE and TVC to Providers and Suppliers

Arrow d – Providers & OE – Operating Expenses:

- All the money that the organization spends in generating production units

Arrow e – Suppliers & TVC – Totally Variable Costs:

- Everything that varies with a correlation R =1 with sales

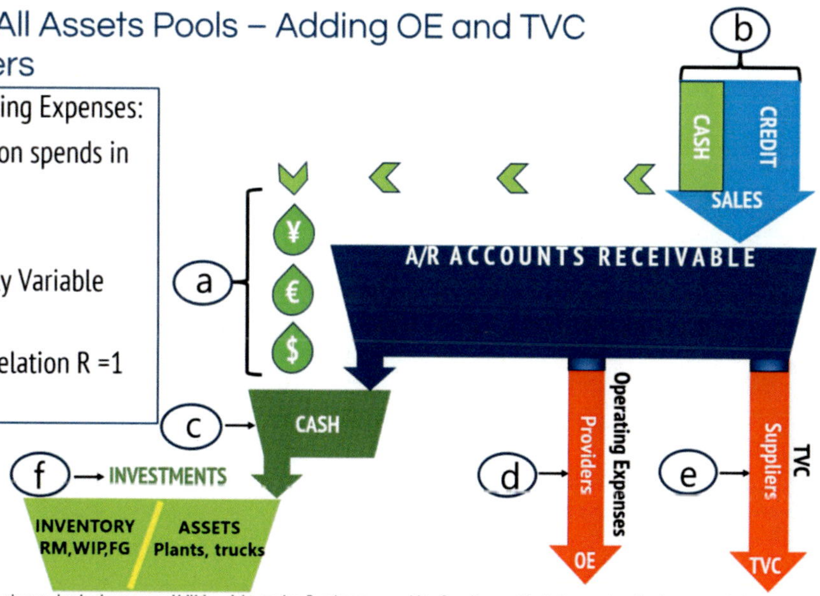

Note: (OE) – Operating Expenses are paid to Providers: employees, banks, Insurances, Utilities, debt service. Purchases are paid to Suppliers and include everyting that has a correlation coefficient of 1 with sales.

TVC, Non TVC and Operating Expenses

We hear many times that Throughput Accounting eases the understanding of expenses with a simple two pronged classification:

- TVC and Non TVC - WRONG
- TVC and Operating Expenses – RIGHT

'Non TVC ' is not proper as it never appears in any Throughput Accounting statements as an 'official' label used anywhere!

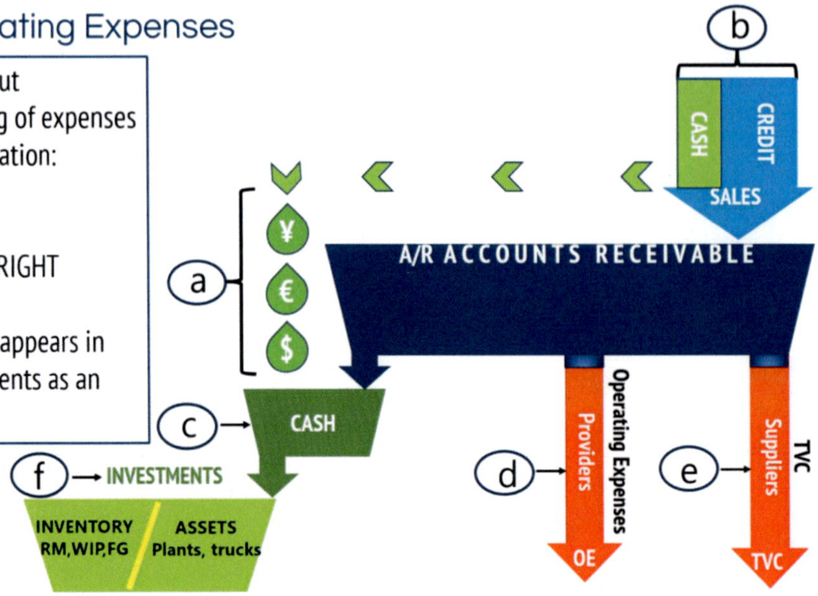

The TVC pipe

The grey zone where the yellow arrows flow represents the amount that must be paid to suppliers.

The width is represented by the letter X which is exactly the same that we find at the bottom of the red Supplier arrow at the far bottom right

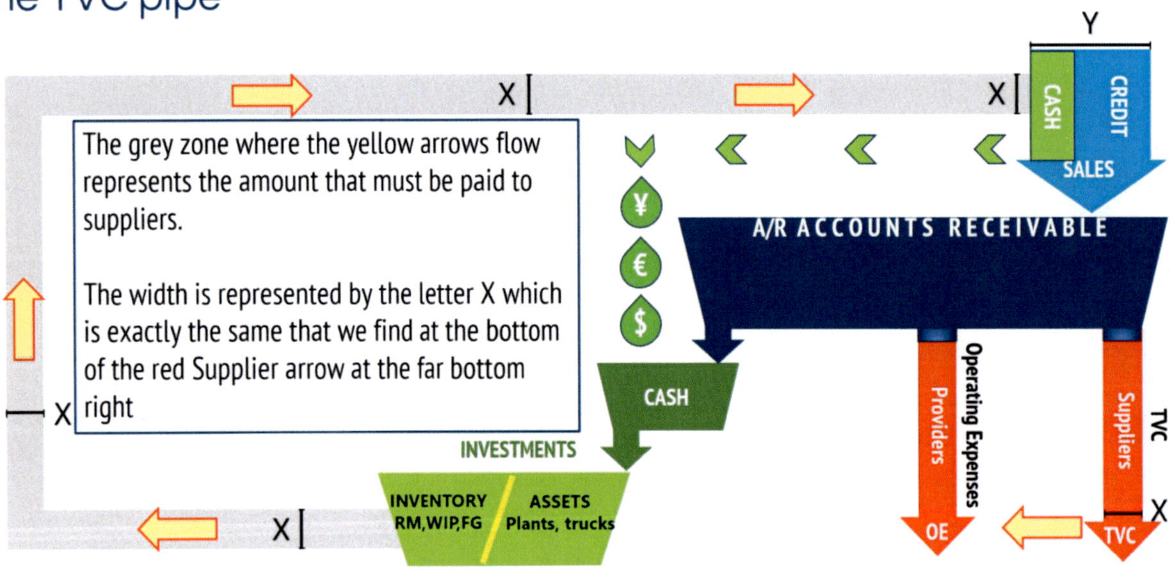

Totally Variable Costs (X) is subtracted from Net Sales (Y) to arrive at Throughput

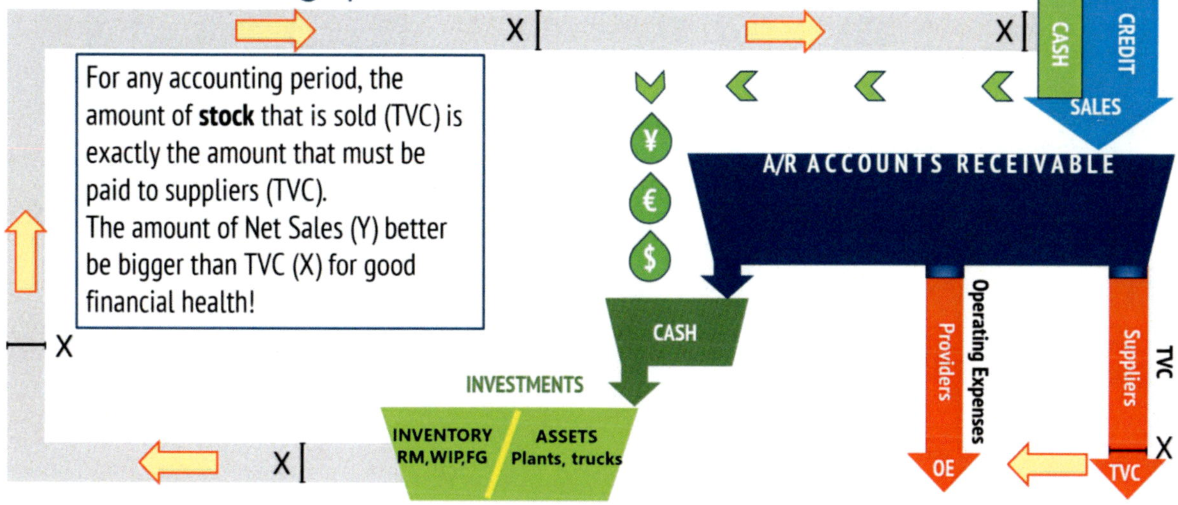

Where are we ?

We have covered:

- Income and Loss Statement
- All Assets Pools on the Balance Sheet

What is next :

- Liabilities
- Free Cash Flow, Operating Surplus
- Net Worth of Company

g) Inventory under Investments - financed via A/P

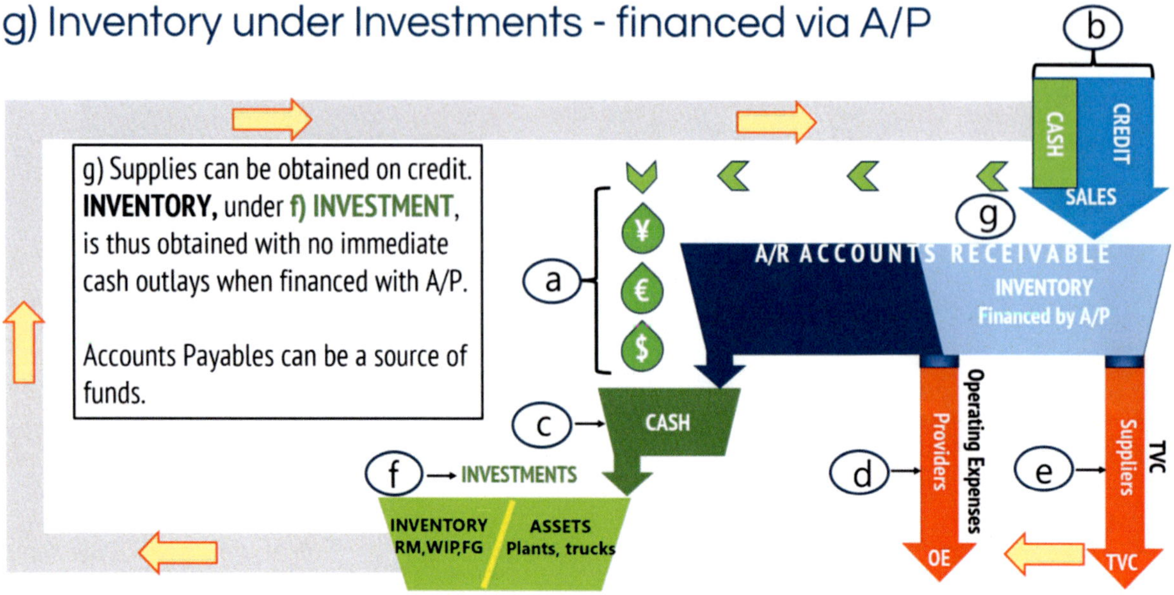

Note: Companies that cannot afford to pay for goods at the moment can always get them with Accounts Payable.

---

h) Assets under Investments - financed with debt

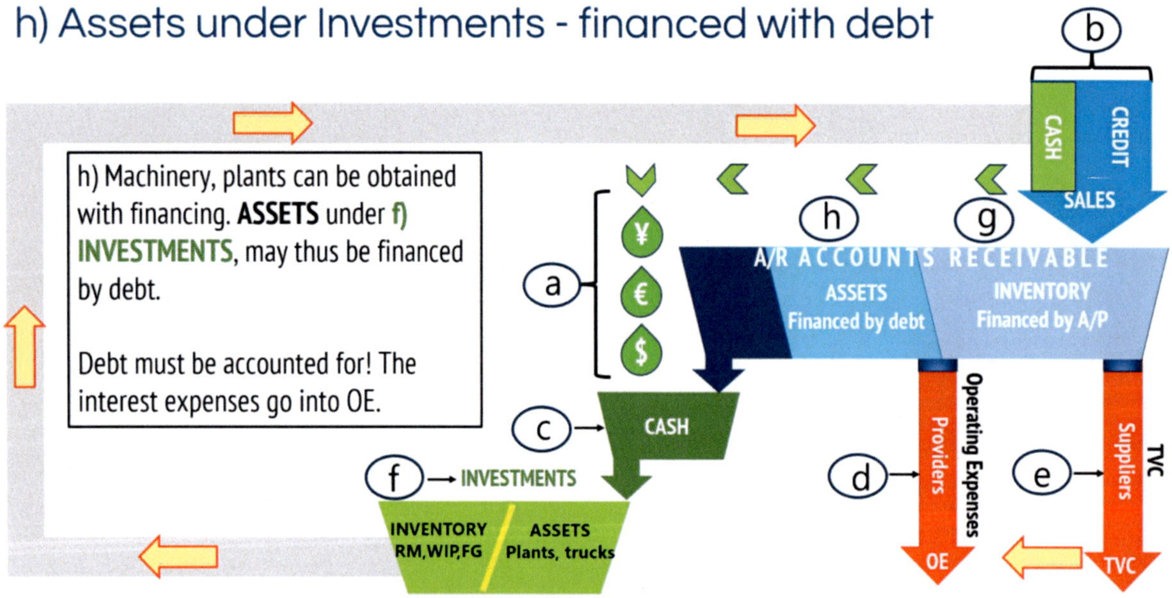

Note: Companies in good financial health can also but more assets than they can afford with debt.

Payment to Suppliers and Providers

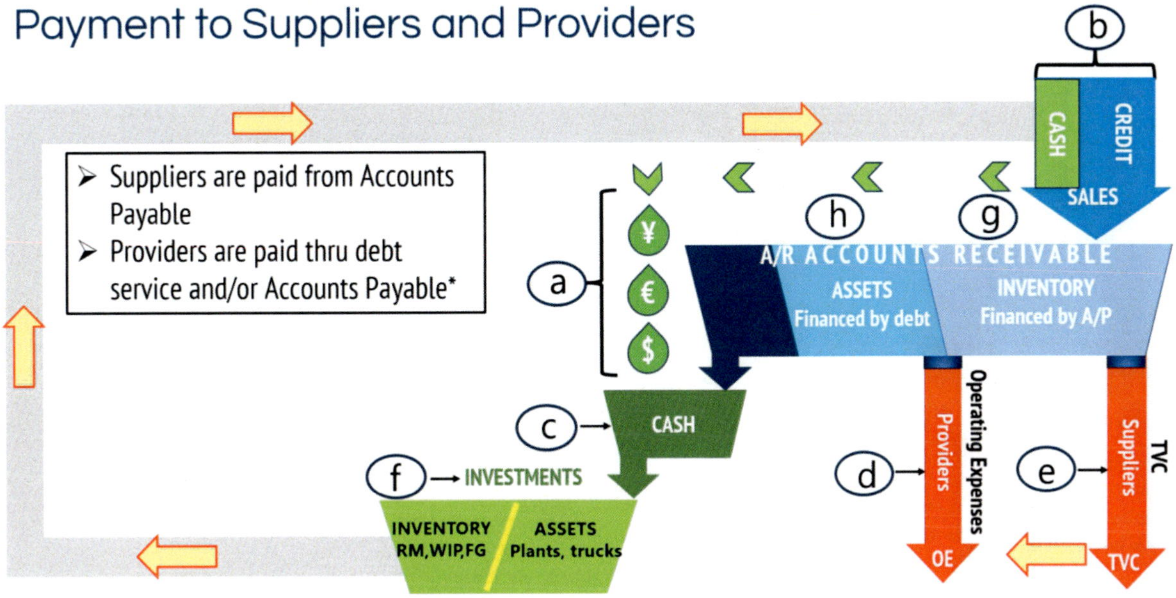

Note: This explains why the top of the Providers' red arrow straddles over Debt financing and AP financing. (the 2 light blue areas)

Self Financing of Investments

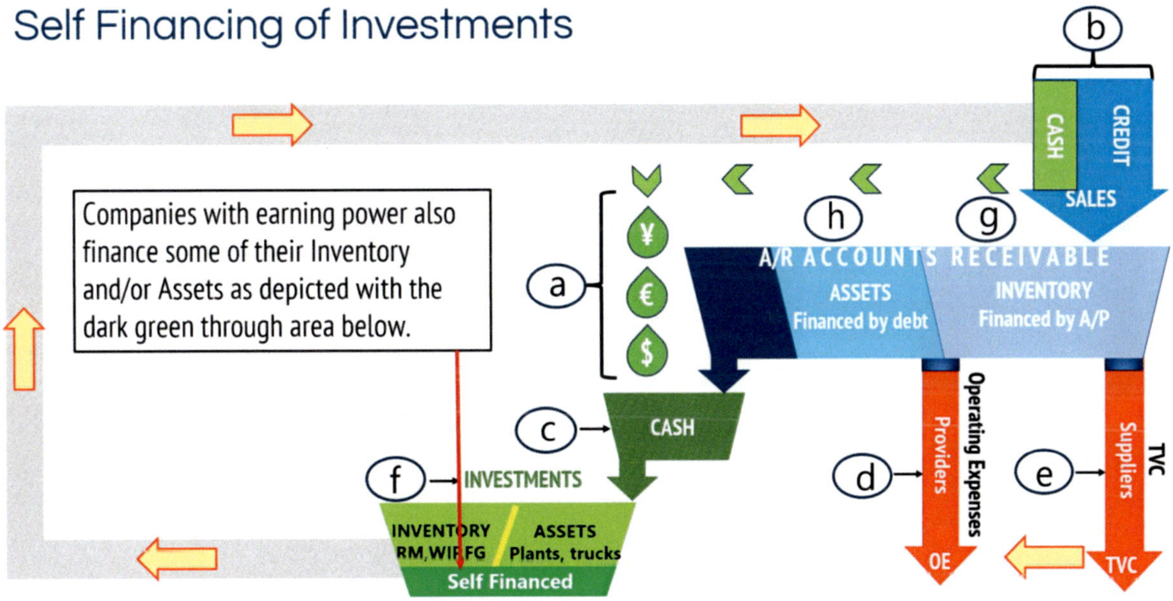

Freely Owned Assets – Bold Green areas

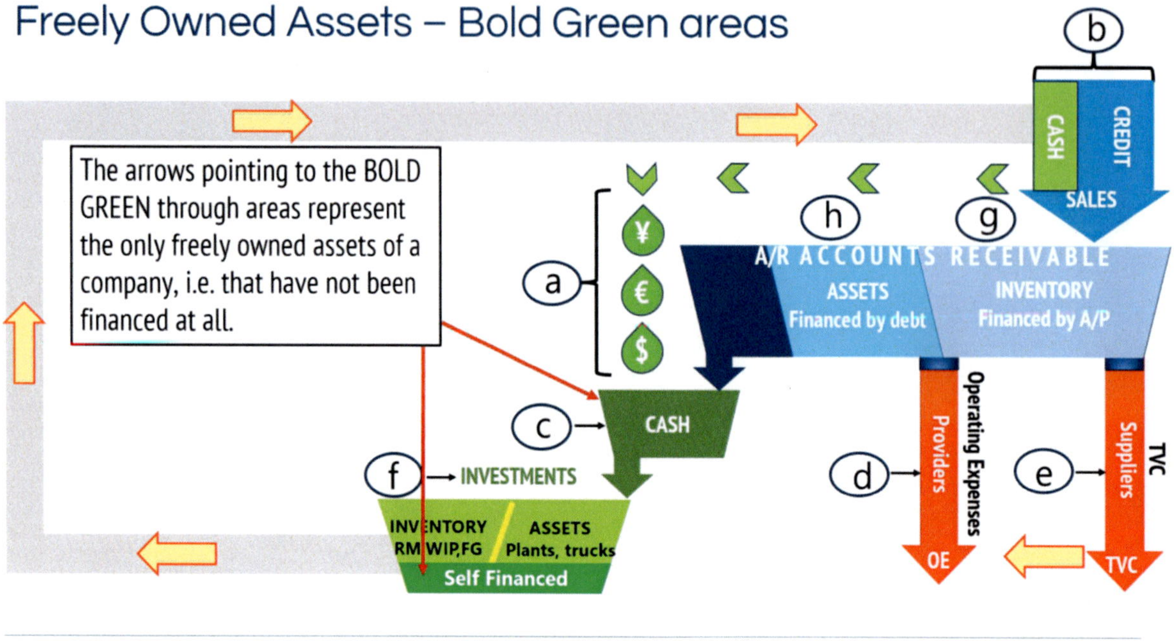

Flows and Pools of Money Diagram
Complete Income Statement & Balance Sheet

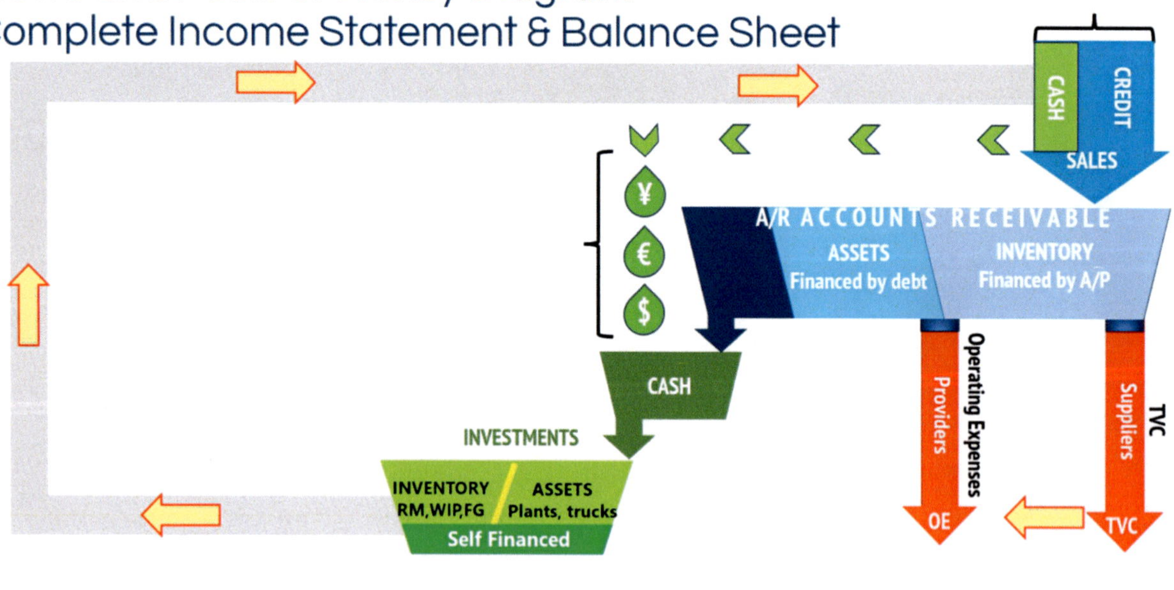

Additional Metrics

"It's better to **be approximately** right **than precisely wrong.**"

Eli Goldratt.

Net Profit from a Throughput Accounting lens

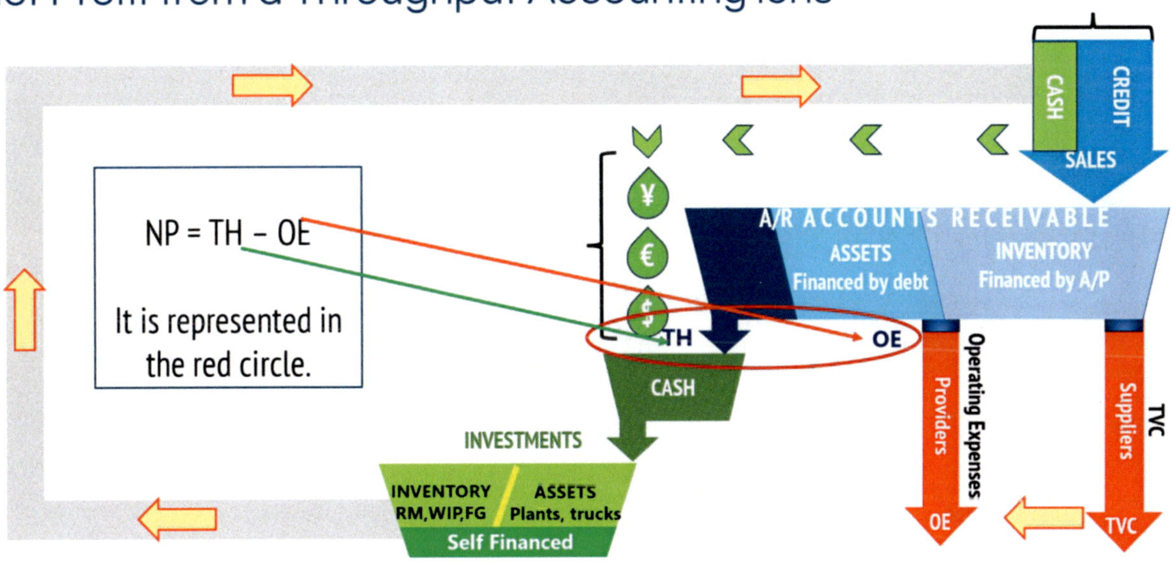

Net Worth

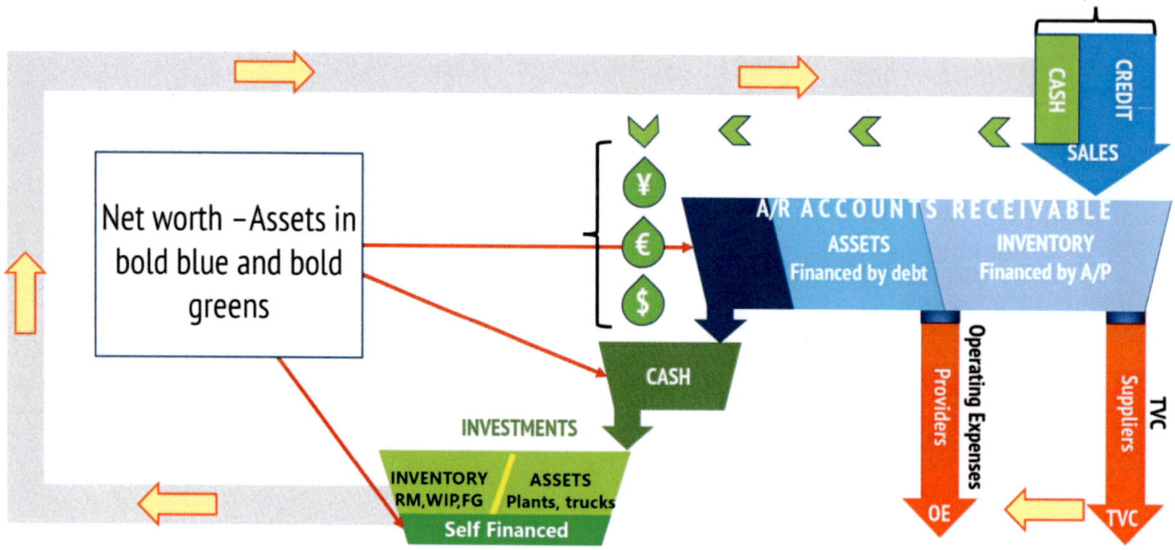

Freely Owned Assets

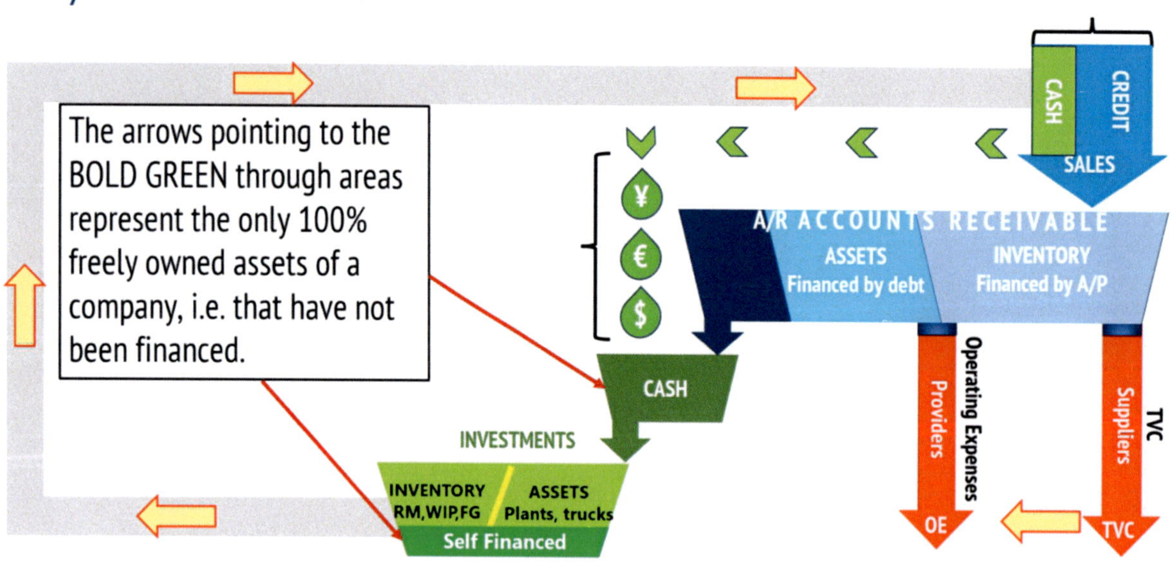

Note: A/R is not 'freely owned' as a sales can be under Accounts Receivable, even paid for, with TVC that have yet to be paid to the suppliers and still under A/P!

Free Cash Flow

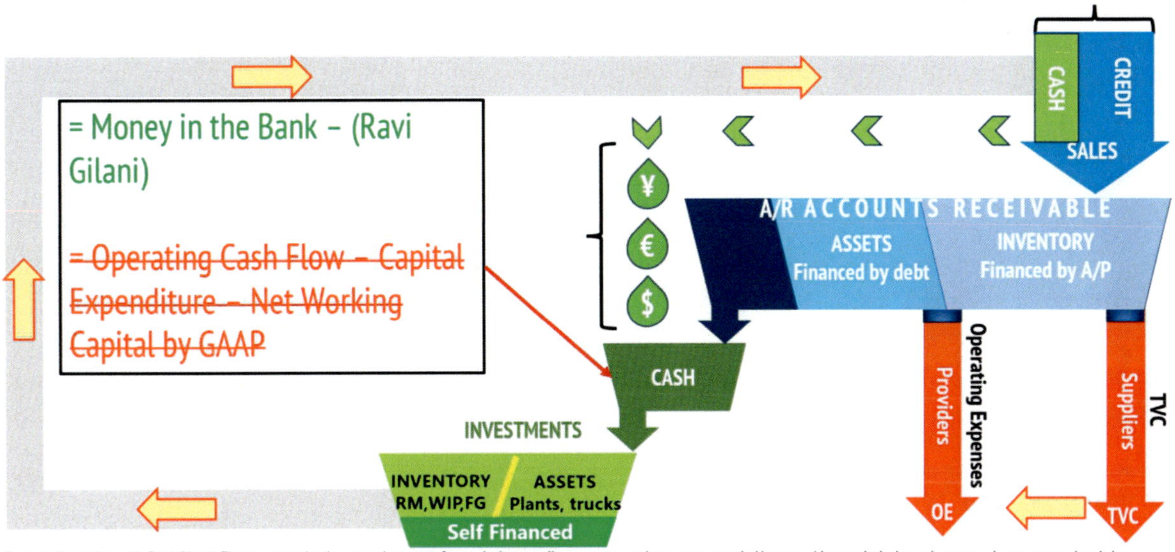

From a discussion with Ravi Gilani: First no organisation spends money for capital expenditure every week or every month. Next, working capital, throughput etc. change every day. It is just simpler in a Throughput Accounting context to ping the balance in your cash account!

References

Du Plooy, Etienne. 'Throughput Accounting Techniques'. General Media Press. 2016

Gilani, Ravi and Camp, Henry. 'The right metrics and when'. http://bit.ly/2AH9KZs

Schragenheim, Eli and Camp, Henry and Surace, Rocco. 'Throughput Economics: Making Good Management Decisions'. Routledge, A Productivity Press Book. 2019

Dr Yougman, Kelvyn. 'The Unrecognised Positive Impact of Operations Upon Finance'. https://www.linkedin.com/pulse/unrecognised-positive-impact-operations-upon-finance-youngman/

CHAPTER VI – VARIATIONS ON A THEME BY MR. DONALD REINERTSEN

"95% of performance is attributable to systems" - Deming

Theme by Mr. Donald Reinertsen

- Principle V11: "Buffers trade money for variability reduction"
- "In Knowledge-Work, Common Causes have a greater impact than in manufacturing. Therefore, Common Causes should be taken into consideration, especially for finding improvement opportunities."
- "Cadence is the use of a regular, predictable rhythm within a process. This rhythm transforms unpredictable events into predictable events. It plays an important role in preventing variability from accumulating in a sequential process."
- Cadence can be used with or without synchronisation
- Synchronisation can be used with or without cadences
- It is best to use both cadence and synchronisation
- Some of the 175 Flow principles.

All quotes are from Donald Reinertsen's book 'Second Generation Lean Product Development'

Note: This chapter is the longest and one may be curious at to why the work of Donald Reinertsen is occupying so much space. When you compare all of Throughput Accounting's decision-making principles discussed thus far – by Etienne Du Plooy and Dr John Ricketts - they lodge at the 'macro' level. Mr. Donald Reinertsen's 175 principles are at an operating level and have these attributes that link them directly to Throughput Accounting as follows:

- They can be used for decision-making at the individual, team, project, product level etc.
- They are short and to the point and have this idiomatic quality that makes them easy to master, remember and apply
- They support decentralised decision-making and are actionable
- Most of them impact directly either (T) – Throughput, (OE) – Operating Expenses or (I) – Investment
- And first and foremost, most of them have this **causality** attribute that is so obvious and necessary to Throughput Accounting that it would have been a serious omission to have side stepped them in a book about Throughput Accounting for Knowledge-Work context.

Introduction

Songs, movie titles and many one liner are dedicated to time. Occasionally, you have more than enough, other times not. In extreme cases, you can even trade your life for it or borrow some!

Great negotiators make of time their greatest weapon and fear it as well when they draw the short straw.

I wish to raise some paradox regarding time and find some common denominators:

- CCPM is built to favor late starts in order for projects to finish early, yet we allow time to slide when executing a fixed scope project.
- We want to reduce time: cycle time, cash-to-cash cycle, time do delivery to show that we are improving.
- Time is a great cause of concern for variability accumulation. Sprints kill that variability every two weeks by pulling the plug while Kanban lets it go for the sake of flow and introduces cadences – with or without synchronisation – to serve as a heartbeat to mitigate the accumulation of variability. These systems do not provide for Common Cause variation and use something similar to an ANDON that you can pull **in real time**.
- Some systems simply do not bother with time, they have been engineered to tame Common Cause variation and are meant to 'resist' the passage of time. In these cases, problems will be revealed to you **ahead of time or correct themselves automatically!**
- Causality is also a phenomenon that uses time as a yardstick. When you act following a decision made with Throughput Accounting, the results must be assignable to that which you just did. The effects should be immediate. Time matters. We will not get too far deep into the axiomatic causality between A and B as per the scientific notation ($A \Rightarrow B$) only if ($\neg B \Rightarrow \neg A$).
- The management by exception signals covered in this book emit beacons through time but randomly. Once a condition occurs, the signal is emitted irrespective of the passage of time or since the last signal was sent. (No need for cadences or synchronisation like all other phenomenon that link variability to the unregulated passage of time)
- The longer the time span, the more variability is to be expected for system that do not tame Common Cause.

Linearization of topics has proven difficult in this very chapter. Therefore, let's start with two unusual suspects and how they can at times be connected to time: Common and Special Cause Variation.

> Note: This introduction is loaded. But so is this chapter and both early exposure and late repetition are needed.

To the trained, and untrained eye alike, there is an oddity in the following statements regarding the unattended passage of time and the accumulation of variability:

- **Let time go unmonitored and variability, the bad kind (linked to Special Cause variation), will occupy the space.**[173]

[173] I have included in Appendix the 1,000 coin tosses illustration that Mr. Donald Reinertsen likes to abord when tackling variability associated with the passage of time

- **In ToC and Knowledge-Work, when the moment comes to choke the release, time does not matter. It will take the time that it takes to stabilize the system. (Taming Common Cause)[174]**

What is it with time and the variability attached to it? Does it work in any specific way? Do we need cadences and synchronisation if we manage on the time axis? We certainly do if we manage on the scope axis, I will grant you that much. Are Special and Common Cause dimensions of this quagmire?

I will give the answer right now as it is anyway from the thinking of Mr. Reinertsen. Variability is both bad and good. And there are two kinds. First, variability caused by the business domain is unavoidable. It is undiversifiable. There are no needs to qualify it as either good or bad. We need to conquer it and accept it. This is how we get new information and create options to develop better products.

On the downside, variability caused by system flaws are bad. To tame those, you need good systems. The best ones are those that can address Common Cause variation. Systems that are centric to tame Common Cause will lead you to lasting improvements, to the land of the goose with the golden eggs. Some systems cannot resist the passage of time and to that extent, the mix of 175 principles offered by Mr. Reinertsen offers remedies to that ailment specifically and frankly, a bit more.

I often get into arguments when I dare associate variability, passage of time, Common Cause, Special Cause and systems. Then tell me if the following statement is true or false?

When a system is in an unstable state, most variability will come from Special Cause Variation.

Systems can resist the passage of time are said to be robust. Systems that support management by exception like we have covered are such like systems.

Mix those systems with constraint awareness and Throughput Accounting based decision-making that adhere to causality – meaning the benefits are quick to come and directly linked to the actions just taken - and you are on your way to the richest. Oh, always bring along a pinch of the 5 FS!

Few options orbit the agile universe to provide Common Cause remedies, inoculation to the passage of time and the variability accumulation attached to it. The Theory of Constraints does. CCPM from Dr Goldratt was meant to address Common Cause in project management. You can't get any closer to Knowledge-Work than that!

In this chapter, I will quote passages from Mr. Reinertsen's book on Lean Product Development. They are all perfectly sound rest assured and have all passed the test of time! When taken together, I think I can make strides to serve my purpose. This chapter is evidently all about integration of knowledge and I intend to use what is in Mr. Reinertsen's opus and propel it to my

[174] Identifying the constraint is a key finding in choking the release. A fantastic and compelling article by Justin Roff-Marsh is on the References section and deals with Step 1 – Identifying the Constraint and Dr Goldratt's stroke of genius behind this. I included it in an Appendix of this chapter.

aim in supporting Throughput Accounting – which need I remind you is the decision-making arm of the Theory of Constraints - and to that end, can pretty much use everything that the Theory of Constraints body of knowledge encapsulates.

Mr. Reinertsen's work is all about to 'do' agile. There is no WAIT time when you apply the remedies of the 175 principles. The same stands for Throughput Accounting.

The scope of this entire book is as well. Those who are in the business of aspiring to 'be' agile often take the long way home. It is at times necessary as we all think and progress along different axis and premises. But there is way too much of that and not enough of this, of which I am certain. To 'do' agile requires one to apply science ad nauseam.

It is time for excellence at the execution level and exploit all the science required. It is also demanded to inoculate our systems from the passage of time[175], be Common Cause savvy and get help as to when - and if - intervention is needed.

This is why we have this chapter, and this book built on management by exception with the use of leading indicators of risk materialisations. We also need decentralized potency and reflexes, be able to rack up small decisions without thinking and to that extent, we will see how well Mr. Reinertsen's 175 Flow principles of more than a decade ago fare with modern Throughput Accounting's principles developed by Dr John Ricketts. All those principles will be confronted from a Throughout Accounting lens and evaluated for excellence to use in today's world.

And causality is a tenet of Throughput Accounting. If you operate in Knowledge-Work at the execution level and do not fully understand all 175 Flow principles from Mr. Reinertsen, you are a bit off and need to take stock in mastering them.

Common Cause and Special Cause

> Donald Reinertsen: "In Knowledge-Work, Common Causes have a greater impact than in manufacturing. Therefore, Common Causes should be taken into consideration, especially for finding improvement opportunities."

We have discussed earlier on that Common Cause Variation has never been given much space by Mr. Deming[176] in Lean manufacturing, whose thought leadership has been migrated without any challenges - nor changes - to agile mainstream, and I am including Kanban here.

In Lean manufacturing, having predictable demand to mass produce cars with little variability and in vast quantities will expose you to Special Cause Variation only and if such an event were to occur, you – or someone else - simply pulls the ANDON in line with Event Driven Risk management. (As you see something odd on your Kanban or Scrum board, you figuratively pull the ANDON as well!)

No need for plans, estimates of any sort as they would be considered waste in a Lean manufacturing environment not so much that they are not needed, but mostly because they cost

[175] Short target scope projects of less than 6 weeks are a must. Those projects need not abide by any rule. You can have short, medium or longer target scope projects. Do what makes sense!

[176] In all fairness, Mr Deming did care about common cause when building or ramping up an assembly line. Once it was humming along, he had no more concern for common cause and acted on special cause signals exclusively.

money and that planning is not required as pulling dictates production alignment. Deviations from plans are therefore trivial. This line of thoughts has been exported to Agile and Kanban for Knowledge-Work and seldom do we see a plan from which deviations could be observed and suggesting some systemic flaws that could be attributed to Common Cause Variation. Once those system flaws fixed, the goose with the golden egg shows up with tangible rewards!

We are now entering the construct of Explicit Risk Management, where variations to the plan trigger managerial scrutiny. (Variations to the plan in this book being CCPM and DBR buffer penetrations into the Yellow, Red or Black zones at the Execution of the plan level. (Note: WIP ageing signals could be an early precursor of things to come for an individual work item.))

As a remedy to this, I went all in and showed you how to create a free plan – free therefore means no waste - that can trigger alerts with both the CCPM consumption buffer and the CCPM Buffer Burn Rate signals. Chapter three of this book contains all of the mechanics to get you started next week. So that there are no misunderstandings as to the motivation of Dr Goldratt to create a Project Management application – CCPM (Critical Chain Project Management) - let it be said one more time that it was designed to tame Common Cause Variation in Knowledge-Work.

At this point, all I wish to accomplish is link formal plans to deviations from the plans to enter the arena of Common Cause Variation, the terrain where Mr. Reinertsen suggests we find the low hanging fruits to lasting improvement opportunities and financial prosperity.

Take stock of this note: if you want to tame Common Cause at the quantitative level, then you need a system based on science. Lean manufacturing's heritage will not prove of any help in Knowledge-Work.

Noise or Signal?

One would think that it is pretty easy to build the basic frequency analysis tables, perform root cause analysis for finding Common and Special Cause and then act from there. Many march to that beat. But those are only tools. When used without a system that can generate signals, they will miss a lot of potential for inquiries that would have been triggered with automation. A lot of the 'bad' will never be picked up.

Evidently, those tables are rightfully required to ascertain with certitude that we are dealing with Common or Special Cause variation. Many go blindly for the 'frequency' trap and WILL fix the issues that are most often arising and impacting the biggest amount of 'days lost'. This is wrong. If it does not impact the constraint, please treat it as 'Special Cause' – forget it and move on – instead of increasing in a permanent fashion your cost overhead layers for curing an ailment that causes no harm. You write those off against excess capacity, not with green money!

This habit of fixing everything and treating it as an improvement is the main cause of our financial demises. Every time you do this, you are increasing the layers of cost overheads in a permanent manner. If you want the shortest road to financial hardship, this is the best way. Indirect costs are invisible to the naked eye and impossible to remove once they become operational as they are intertwined with everything else.

Noise or signal? It did not matter up to this point.

To differentiate between the two, you need to discern between a yellow signal, which may indicate in a timely manner possible Common Cause, or a red signal for potential Special Cause. You won't get far if you do not have systems designed to discern between Common and Special. To that end, in agile, nothing.

The benefits of buffer penetration signals are that they are meant to detect Common Cause[177]. Many will point to the fact that they 'seem' to be based on average and that on average well, everything is average. Not so. Buffers can be sized to emit more or less signals. They are based on average, but they are appended to the end of the 50% average of the lead time distribution. They are thus no longer averages or are they still? They lie in the sensitive zone. Well beyond the average trap.

Back to buffer penetration signals and frequency and root cause analysis. When you get such a signal, an entry in the frequency log is warranted. It is a signal? It is noise? Too early to tell yet. Something – based on a system to cater for your system – is warning you. You can't see it, smell it or feel it but there is something for you to inquire about. This is the difference between reacting to signal or noise. For that you need systems to detect Common and Special Cause. Dr Eli Goldratt's system are all meant to deal with Common Cause. Mr. Reinertsen says this is where the low hanging fruits are.

And in this book, many of these buffers – CCPM (manage Time) and DBR (manage Load and Flow/Scope) – are linked to Little's Law arithmetic. I have made an illustration below with novel content:

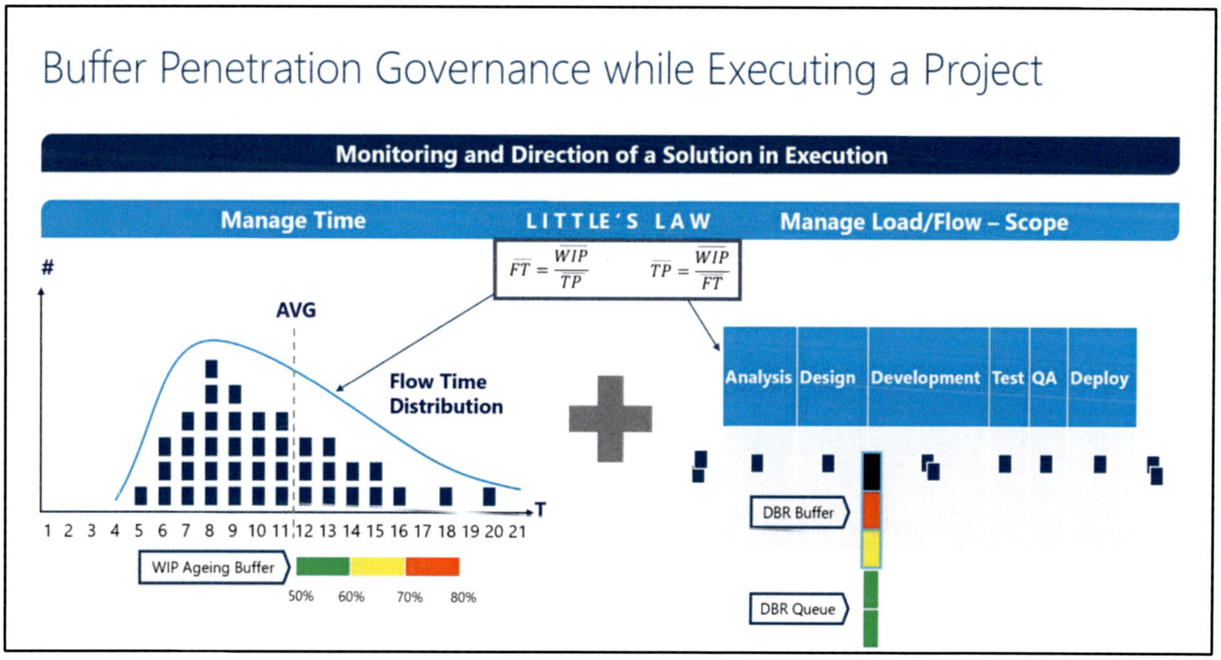

177 Special Cause always finds a way to sneak in, let it be remembered.

It is important to note in the various illustrations of the ToC buffers that little is devoted to the actual data structure of each given that they all serve different purposes with the same colors yet are treated with the same brush.

See the table below for such an observation:

Signal & Purpose	Data Structure	Color
CCPM Consumption Buffer To signal the need to finish work as we are eating the CCPM consumption buffer too fast.	Vector[178] – Displacement, Force, Speed. One dimension. Retractable and unidirectional	Green, Yellow, Red – similar wo WIP ageing but can go from one to color to the next and back repeatedly
WIP Ageing Buffer To signal the need to finish a work item	Vector – Displacement, Force, Speed. One dimension. Uni directional	Green, Yellow, Red – similar to CCPM Buffer but cannot step back from red, to yellow, or green in most cases
DBR Buffer To signal the need for replenishment.	Scalar[179] – Discrete units of work – Quantity. One dimension. Bi directional.	Yellow, Red, Black
DBR Queue To fill with work the 'Waiting for' semi column of the constraint just below the DBR Buffer	Queue – To stack work right below the DBR Buffer. One dimension. Uni directional	Green
CCPM Buffer Burn Rate Indicator of lateness to the CCPM Plan To render on a relative scale all	A Coefficient (scalar) The ratio between two time-based unit of measure. (Buffer consumption and Project Completion). Yields multiple results. Two dimension and relative scale with numerous collisions possible as we have seen in chapter 3.	Green, Red – no Yellow but blue from now on Depending of relative value to '1', which is always the relative DRUM beat.

[178] A vector is a quantity that has both a magnitude and a direction. In our case, the direction is the distinguishing factor and behaves in an analog like manner (think of a mercury filled thermometer) as the buffer goes in one direction and retract in the other. Except for the case of the WIP Ageing Buffer in most case.

[179] A scalar (or a scalar quantity) is a discrete unit of measure. Colors can be used as such units of measure of magnitude in our case. The colors describe the magnitude which is the only characteristic of a scalar.

projects irrespective of size, budget, timeline, scope etc. to facilitate decision-making among an unlimited number of projects		Color Yellow is not needed. See chapter 3 on social engineering
CCPM Rope[180] (NEW) It shows you when the optimal time to start a project comes about when the we are forging ahead faster than planned.	A Date (scalar) The revised end date of the current project to connect with the CCPM staggering functionality	Blue It is a date trigger. When shall we start a new project next?

For example, the red color on the WIP ageing means to get the **work out** asap as this same color on the DBR buffer would mean to let new **work in** asap with a rope signal.

The CCPM buffer is a vector (Green, Yellow, Red). But the DBR buffer – in reality – is made up of 2 components: a 'green' queue where work can accumulate under the DBR buffer zone and a vector (Yellow, Red, Black), which constitute the DBR buffer. When the green queue is empty, no signals have yet been emitted. This is why I made this queue visible beneath the DBR buffer as I always had he bad reflex of thinking that this signalled a yellow state.

The CCPM and WIP Ageing Buffer data structures are vectors that depict speed and velocity. The DBR Buffer is a scalar and deals with discrete units of work.

The signification of the colors – for the DBR Buffer - from green to black can be found below. They are standard colors in the Theory of Constraints playbook.

- Green: The queue has at least one work item into it
- Yellow: The buffer is two third full. We have here a plausible Common Cause
- Red: The buffer is one third full. It is a cause of concern as the constraint could starved. Immediate action is appropriate. For example, pre-emptively sending a manual rope signal could be well advised. This is a plausible Special Cause
- Black: The buffer is empty – this only applies to the DBR buffer by the way – we need an all hands-on deck alert as we are facing some drastic situation

You can take note immediately that the other buffers or coefficients only use green, yellow and red. I have introduced a new color – blue – for the Buffer Fever Chart in chapter 3 as the yellow color is moot and plainly not indicative of the state of affairs. Another novelty contained in this book is the blue CCPM Rope management by exception signal. When you are going too fast, it warrants a notice!

[180] This is a new management by exception signal and uses the color blue. It has a counter balancing effect when the CCPM indicators are doing too well. It is a sign to hurry up for what is up next in the pipeline. An illustration of this signal and its impact on staggering can be found in Appendix D

Buffers, Money, Time and Variability

I love principle V11 from Mr. Reinertsen's work.

Principle V11: " Buffers trade money for variability reduction"

I am quite certain that if I were to add the last few words as follow, I would be equidistant with the essence of Mr. Reinserten's original principle:

" Buffers trade money for variability reduction. Variability that is accumulated with the passage to time"

One of the arguments I wish to make is that Mr. Reinertsen – without finding a precise and explicit quote of his to that effect – links the passage of time with the accumulation of variability. I think it is always 'implied' but never spelled out, so I am taking the liberty to articulate it. The need for cadence and synchronisation is medicine that must be administered through time to tame variability. That much is clear in his writings and principles and it cannot be contradicted, especially upstream.

Throughout this book, we have argued that management by exception with leading indicators of risk materialisation physicalized by buffer penetrations were free. They do not trade money for variability per se, but I would say they are the next best thing as they perceive the arrival of risk and allow you to react in a timely fashion. They operate in a manner that is in sync with time but somewhat orthogonal in that signals are generated irrespective of the passage of time. When it is time, it will be time. But it cannot be predicted nor facilitated with the use of cadences or synchronisation for example nor with any of Mr. Reinertsen's 175 Flow principles.

Here, I must wear my accountant's hat. And maybe alter principle V11 <u>with my own words</u> – and to serve my purpose - as follows:

'Systems – designed to tame Common Cause - trade money (CAPEX & OPEX) for variability elimination <u>with no concern for the passage of time, cadence or synchronisation</u>'.

Let me explain:

<u>Inventory systems</u> incur both CAPEX and OPEX[181] money. But they have this intrinsic capacity to self correct through time. No need for cadences, meetings or synchronisation to achieve this. You let time pass in a passive state. Things will take care of themselves through the transactions that are entered randomly in the normal course of operations[182]. If for example, you take out 3 gallons of paint and the system has a negative quantity on hand of 5, then you will walk out with your 3 gallons and the system will create all the necessary corrections to have the new

[181] I do not remember who said this, but I still laugh today. When in doubt as to where you should charge, follow this heuristic: CAPEX, if it does not exist. OPEX, if it does not work!

[182] Obviously, a physical count may be required once in a while in non perpetual inventory systems and let it be said that no system can disarm ill intent, fraud or human turpitude.

quantity on hand self-adjust. Bad variability caused by the passage of time simply does not exist in this context. Inventory systems tame Common Cause variation by design.

Payroll applications have the same capabilities.

All, and I mean all, accounting mishaps will self correct after 2 accounting fiscal years. There are no exceptions to this rule. Time can roll, it won't change a thing. The systems just described are robust and unaffected by the passage of time. They tackle Common Cause, systemic issues by design.

The link that I wish to make is that variability will go quadratic with the passage of time especially if you manage on the scope axis – as this is the case for most agile frameworks, models, flavors. Mandatory cadences are suitable and provided for in these models out of the box for that very purpose.

The trigger mechanism for the CCPM – and DBR - buffer penetration is in no way linked to 'clocked time' in a programmed manner and have been designed with no concerns – nor needs – for cadence and synchronisation. The amazing thing is that it comes almost at no cost if you have a half decent lead time distribution for your work tickets to drill a plan with the CCPM buffer.

Orthodoxies in project execution – Time or Scope?

Here is a passage taken from Mr. Reinertsen's book. The parenthesis and bold are mine and I have put them in strike thru mode on top of that as I had difficulty understanding Mr. Reinsertsen's essence of the sentence below:

> "Today's orthodoxy **~~(PMI)~~** constrains the scope of work and drives variability into timing. The new paradigm **~~(Scrum)~~** constrains timing and drives variability into the scope of work. These two approaches are fundamentally different."

In an exchange with Mr. Reinertsen regarding the passage above, I needed some clarifications as his writing is very dense – at least for me as a French speaking native. He gave me the following answer, which in no way is an endorsement of this chapter nor of this book as he was not even aware that I was writing one at the time.

From Mr. Reinertsen:

> "There is no 'golden rule' that says "schedule is always more important than scope" but instead that we should develop a clear enough understanding of our economics to express a trade-off between scope and schedule in a common unit of measure like "life-cycle profit impact". One should not sacrifice 20 percentage points of gross margin to save a week of cycle time, and nor should you sacrifice 20 months of cycle time to save 1 percentage point of gross margin. Your trade-off between scope and schedule must be in a common unit of measure like "life-cycle profit impact"."

Reading between the lines, and knowing Mr. Reinertsen's work over the years, it is safe to say that he shows positive affective predispositions toward the time axis. I do as well. We all should.

In a Throughput weary situation, the trade off between cycle time and money is not a focus since keeping the constraint busy is a good enough financial proposition in our model which addresses both the time and money generation aspects. No model is perfect, but this is how the Theory of Constraints would position itself: keeping the constraint busy maximizes Financial Throughput and will get the work done in the fastest manner possible under all scenarios. If no time is wasted at the constraint, time is on your side!

PMI Critical Path Management vs ToC Critical Chain Management

The books by Dr John Ricketts and Bob Sproull provide all the details contrasting the PMI CPM approach to Project Management against ToC's CCPM approach. It just has every possible detail in highlighting the differences while in project execution.

For my sensibility, I must express out loud the main benefit of CCPM's chain plan and its corresponding buffer appended at the end of the plan. The PMI CPM put buffers every where: tasks, milestones etc. leading to the following nightmare:

> The 'stress' associated with any update of the CPM plan is that the critical path will change every time. A CCPM plan sticks for the journey and buffer penetration gives you all the management acuity that you could ever desire from a system designed to trap Common Cause variation.

I will stop the comparisons here. Except for one more thing that is akin to agile: CCPM favors late starts, delaying commitment and putting pressure to diminish the amount of parallelism throughout. The staggering function of CCPM will please the heart and the mind of all Product Owners, Scrum Masters, and Developers alike as it gives real time information to help optimize the orchestration of all pending work's optimal start dates. A strategic and tactical stratagem to managing capacity.

You can't get more aligned to agility than with CCPM.

Cadences and Synchronisation in Execution Mode[183]

We need to set the stage for this section. We are in the 'Jeep' and marching thru our Journey: the execution phase in one word. The planning has been done. The business requirements are encapsulated in a target scope that will be executed in an undetermined amount of time but within a reasonable time frame. Probabilistic forecasting supported by Little's Law will provide a decent plan that can track deviations, pave the way to Explicit Risk Management and Common Cause management.

Our tools, processes, teams and everything we need to execute are well understood. It is reasonable to expect that most of us work in such environments. Meetings are planned and scheduled for promoting software into production and the likes, to interact upstream etc.

---

[183] I wrote several passages pertaining to Kanban cadences in my first book.

In this chapter, we will leave the budgeting dimension out and focus on the Time and Scope axes only whilst executing a project. We will remember that the Resources developing projects are part of OE – Operating Expenses and not TVC – Totally Variable Costs. There is no point in accounting or budgeting for them in most instances - as they would be full time employees or contractors under long term contracts - and we will assume that such is the case here. As for the tools, servers, utilities we will make the assumption that plenty of capacity is untapped as our target company has just discovered Throughput Accounting and the 5 Focusing Steps and in doing so, opened the flood gates to slack Capacity by properly applying the first three steps of the 5 Focusing Steps with brown money.

To 'do' agile infers that we can execute, do things right first so as to get better at getting the right things done subsequently. Repetition is the mother of all skills. To 'be' agile is another story. I cannot think of a better article on the topic than that of DJA – dated August 2013 – which in essence says that being efficient first by doing things right and delivering, keeping your word is what builds trust[184]. Nothing else. Those in the to 'be' agile camp do not think as such and borrow a different path, intangible in my view. Trust is asymmetrical. In that sense, you need to deliver the goods in a consistent manner. It is tangible and measurable. Taking that path will also reveal your biggest strategic asset: your capacity, what you can do, and what you cannot do. Capacity needs flow. Mastery of one's capacity is not an agile forte as the constant sprint interruptions just neuter flow, which is a predicate for proper capacity measurement.

The delivery environments are provided in a to 'do' agile context and can be made both predictable (delivery date) and stable (delivery rate) very easily. Using a CFD provides visual proof of your performance, once the delivery and demand lines are parallel. Stable and predictable systems stand a better chance of being around next year! Agile – and Scrum in particular – deems that everything in our environment is in the 'Complex' domain. Not so as we have discussed at length the attributes of the 'Jeep' in an earlier chapter.

There has been plenty covered on managing on the time axis earlier on. I won't delve into the ailments of managing on the scope axis as the degrees of freedom are always on the brink of going quadratic. At this point, I simply want to fill 4 arrays that fit Mr. Reinertsen's principles regarding the passage of time, cadences, synchronisation, as remedies to dampen accumulated variability.

In the following 4 sections, my aim is to list practices, principles – or whatever we may call them – that fit in the arrays. They could refer to a ritual, a 'dogma' without necessarily naming it. But mostly sticking to the topic of to 'do' agile. WIP limits, queueing or technical things of the likes à la Reinertsen are allowed because this is what is invisible but what those who 'do' agile 'see'.

Note to the reader: Many of the ensuing 'pro-CCPM' arguments are taken directly or modified from the books 'Epiphanized' from Bob Sproull, Etienne du Plooy's 'Throughput Accounting Techniques' or 'Reaching the Goal' from Dr John Ricketts. I do add my touch here and there!

---

[184] SCRUM use of the 3 pillars of transparency, inspection and adaptation to define TRUST coupled with the 5 values. This is an example of aiming at 'being' agile. Delivering and keeping your words is more in line with the concept of 'doing' agile.

Cadences With Synchronisation

"Cadence is the use of a regular, predictable rhythm within a process. This rhythm transforms unpredictable events into predictable events. It plays an important role in preventing variability from accumulating in a sequential process. Cadences involve processing work at regular time intervals. We can use cadence with or without synchronisation.[185]"

Cadences and meetings go hand and hand to the extent that it always makes good business sense to plan and reserve the resources ahead of time according to the proper rhythm. My point being that if you are all green – especially for daily meetings – then there is no point in attending. Let people work.

At the portfolio level, the Buffer Fever Chart should tell you how many of your numerous projects should attend. I am reminded – and use this sentence of Patrick Steyaert good day or bad day – that "the cost of decision-making at the portfolio level defeats the purpose of decision-making". Just spare people the enormous burden of getting ready for attending meetings that cover the same agenda all the time and that are costly to run and prepare for.

Back to cadences, as we go along, we will fill this table to see what we can bring to our consciousness:

TOPIC	CADENCE Processing Work at regular time intervals		SYNCHRONISATION Have multiple tasks start of finish at the same time	
	With Cadence	Without Cadence	With Synchronisation	Without Synchronisation
E1: The Principle of Quantified Overall Economics: Select actions based on quantified overall economic impact.	Planning performed before every Sprint (Scope axis)		Yes	
F9: The Principle of Cadenced Meetings: Schedule frequent meetings using a predictable cadence.	All of Scrum ceremonies		Yes	
Non CCPM planning (Agile) encourages early start.	I claim that induced timeboxing stress puts pressure on starting fast to the expense of increasing WIP and the Product Backlog		Yes	

185 Mr. Donald Reinertsen. Preamble to chapter 7. The principles of product development

CCPM and target scope favor late start and early finish with the staggering function and the virtual integration point	Staggering function supports late start. Synchronisation is achieved by reacting to the signals of the CCPM consumption buffer that provides the rope signal and the alignment on the time axis to start new projects. Information is provided with cadence with scheduled meetings and without cadences when a project is officially launched with the integration points arrived at	**Yes**	**Yes**	**Yes**
Buffer Fever Chart	**Portfolio meetings are optimized**		**Yes .. But not all projects need be invited**	

Cadences Without Synchronisation

Here is a table supporting the topic above.

TOPIC	CADENCE Processing Work at regular time intervals		SYNCHRONISATION Have multiple tasks start of finish at the same time	
	With Cadence	Without Cadence	With Synchronisation	Without Synchronisation
F7 - The Cadence Reliability Principle: Use cadence to	**Staggering function of the**		Yes	Yes

make waiting times predictable	CCPM buffer consumption sends signals to start projects at optimal and revised dates with or without synchronisation			
F6: The Cadence Capacity Margin Principle: Provide sufficient capacity margin to enable cadence.	This basically refers to SLACK and for this purpose, synchronisation is required at the beginning for the integration point to minimize parallelism at the start, but not during execution. It happens at the beginning of execution of many projects when we use the virtual integration point to inhibit parallelism and kill early starts. (see chapter 3 – section Constraints in the Work Execution - At least one, maybe more!)		Yes	Yes
F8: The Cadence Batch Size Enabling Principle: Use a regular cadence to enable small batch sizes.	This is hard to fit all the time with synchronisation. Unless you are in a timeboxing environment. But would not work for FLOW systems			Yes

	See TOC remark from JR – Dr John Ricketts further down on Principle F8			

Synchronisation With Cadences

''We can treat synchronisation as a separate issue from cadences. Cadence causes events to happen at regular time intervals. Synchronisation causes multiple events to happen at the same time. Synchronisation involves making multiple tasks start or finish at the same time. We can synchronize with or without cadence.[186] ''

TOPIC	CADENCE Processing Work at regular time intervals		SYNCHRONISATION Have multiple tasks start of finish at the same time	
	With Cadence	Without Cadence	With Synchronisation	Without Synchronisation
F15: The SJF Scheduling Principle: When delay costs are homogeneous, do the shortest job first.	Yes	Yes	Self Explanatory. But see Dr John Ricketts point of view further down This can apply to both scenarios: with and without cadences	
F16: The HDCF Scheduling Principle: When job durations are homogeneous, do the high cost-of-delay job first.	**Yes**	**Yes**	Self Explanatory. But see Dr John Ricketts point of view further down This can apply to both scenarios: with and without cadences	
F17: The WSJF Scheduling Principle: When job durations	**Yes**	**Yes**	Self Explanatory.	

[186] Mr. Donald Reinertsen. Preamble to chapter 7. The principles of product development

and delay costs are not homogeneous, use WSJF.			But see Dr John Ricketts point of view further down This can apply to both scenarios: with and without cadences	

Synchronisation Without Cadences

TOPIC	CADENCE Processing Work at regular time intervals		SYNCHRONISATION Have multiple tasks start of finish at the same time	
	With Cadence	Without Cadence	With Synchronisation	Without Synchronisation
Creating the virtual integration point when setting up a portfolio of CCPM projects so that they finish at the same time. This prevents early starts and neuters the proliferation of parallelism		**Self Explanatory**	Yes	
E10: The First Perishability Principle: Many economic choices are more valuable when made quickly		Self Explanatory	**Yes**	**Yes**
F10: The Synchronization Capacity Margin Principle: To enable synchronization, provide sufficient capacity margin	**Yes**	Having everybody planning for a Train Release helps in creating SLACK	**Yes**	
F11: The Principle of Multi project Synchronization: Exploit scale economies by synchronizing work from multiple projects.		**Same as above ...**	**Yes**	
F12: The Principle of Cross-Functional Synchronization: Use synchronized events to		Same as above ...	Self Explanatory. But see Dr John Ricketts point of	

facilitate cross functional trade offs.			view further down	
F13: The Synchronization Queueing Principle: To reduce queues, synchronize the batch size and timing of adjacent processes.		A bit debatable	Self Explanatory. But see Dr John Ricketts point of view further down	
Buffer Fever Charts for Portfolio management – Transposes all dimensions of a project into 2 relative scales based on time			**Yes**	

Synchronisation and Cadences Together

"Using both Cadences and Synchronisation is best.[187]"

TOPIC	CADENCE Processing Work at regular time intervals		SYNCHRONISATION Have multiple tasks start of finish at the same time	
	With Cadence	Without Cadence	With Synchronisation	Without Synchronisation
Scrum	Sprints and matching meeting cadences. SCRUM		All sprints start and end at same date – SCRUM	
Scrum	Standardized Artefacts and ceremonies ease mastery of the learning curve – SCRUM		Ceremonies are synchronized - SCRUM	
Scrum	Promotion into production at precise intervals for all Sprints – SCRUM		Yes	
Target Scope Projects	CCPM – Health of all projects can be monitored with Buffer Fever	Yes	Yes	Yes

[187] Mr. Donald Reinertsen. Preamble to chapter 7. The principles of product development

	Chart on a relative scale			

No Synchronisation and No Cadences

This section is an ode to decoupling. To attain reliability, we are all familiar with Kanban systems that decouple input cadences from delivery cadences to replace management by planning with measurement by observation. A system of interrupts through the use of cadences – with or without synchronisation - is foundational to fight variability accumulated by the passage of time.

In the previous chapter, we covered the art of decoupling that T generators bring to the table as input, output and value – how stuff is sold and for how much - are orthogonal from one another.

Here, I enter slippery territory and claim that with TA, CCPM, DBR and TOC, we can decouple management from the time axis when executing target scope projects. Management by exception signals are blind to the passage of time, can be silent for a while or very noisy when needed. They can go from Red, to Green to Yellow without any restrictions or conditions. Under these terms, cadences are not required and one can go about almost without synchronisation[188].

I love this new twist on decoupling for Knowledge-Work to enable better flow. Don't you?[189]

TOPIC	CADENCE Processing Work at regular time intervals		SYNCHRONISATION Have multiple tasks start of finish at the same time	
	With Cadence	Without Cadence	With Synchronisation	Without Synchronisation
CCPM plan never changes. Unlike the critical path who, after each update, changes and causes a lot of operational stress. Agile plans are moving targets		Yes		Yes
The CCPM buffer is at the end of the critical chain plan. It is conceived to finish the project		Yes		Yes

[188] I did not say 'with no synchronisation' as the rope signal at the beginning of a target scope projects initiates a form of synchronisation as does the virtual end date integration when launching multiple projects.

[189] I am not advocating that coordination ceremonies and interfaces with other teams are no longer required by any stretch.

early. Non CCPM plans have buffers everywhere: tasks, milestones etc.				
The DRUM in the DBR construct		Yes		Yes
The Rope signal in the DBR construct		Yes		Yes
The Buffer mechanism		Yes		Yes
All management by exception signals covered with the Black, Red, Yellow, Green and Blue colors		Yes		Yes

Small batch size is a benefit of adopting cadences and synchronisation.[190] Cadences and synchronisation are also of great help in product development. No arguments here. While managing on the time axis, it is also mandatory to keep the scope chewable to be realized in an 'agile' time frame of a few weeks.

I like to remind every one here that we are not concerned about the execution of a plan, but rather the execution of the work that was previously planned. Now that everything we need to get us to going from the start to the finish line has been provided, we run with the baton to 'do' agile and pace ourselves to the various signals.

The heading of this section could very well have been labeled 'Management by Exception'. Generation of advanced signals of potential risk materialisation are orthogonal to time. Cadences and synchronisation are opaque to these signals generated by robust systems that have been designed to tame Common Cause Variation.

It makes it a perfect conduit to management by exception. Such signals have been given a lot of space since the beginning of this book. They will be emitted at certain points in time, but time is not the trigger, nor a factor. If it were, then buffer consumption that would be red one day could never revert back to green, then yellow and back to green. With the Buffer Fever Chart, we operate in relative scales that accommodate different scopes, budgets, teams, divisions, projects sizes, and portfolios, countries etc.

In the next section, I am pointing to Appendices and gathered many of Mr. Reinertsen's principles[191]. They are all correct and nothing is wrong with any one of them.

---

[190] This is straight from the TPS playbook. ToC uses another approach to enable small batch, limit WIP with CCPM and DBR.

[191] Starting work late vs early. I could not find a principle on that in Mr. Reinertsen's principles. But I must be

wrong.

However, when nuanced with the Exploitation or Subordination phases of the 5 Focusing Steps, we get some interesting 'YES and NO' match with Throughput Accounting.

This exercise is all meant to be fun and not stir controversy. I make it a duty to read Mr. Reinertsen's book once a year and always make new connections in my brain.

Mapping of Mr. Reinertsen Flow Principles to Throughput Accounting and Theory of Constraints Lens

This section has been done separately and there could be duplication with the sections above regarding cadences and synchronisation. But the depth of the discussion is in no way comparable as Dr. John Ricketts' contribution speaks volume.

The aim here is to see how well Flow principles and Throughput Accounting/Theory of Constraints mesh.

Dr John Ricketts has shown great generosity and contributed with his comments. Every time you see 'JR', don't ask: it is Dr John Ricketts' insight which is an ear shot away from Dr Eli Goldratt as they spent years on the IBM Consulting Services project. This undertaking is fully documented in the book 'Reaching the Goal'.

I would like to remind the reader that Mr. Reinertsen's principles are geared towards second generation Lean product development. Mr. Ricketts comes from a Theory of Constraints angle and his work experience at IBM was more concentric to software, services, and technical strategy perspective.

They are thus both right all the time!

All models are wrong. Some are useful.

In order to tame cognitive overload and to keep this outstanding work that will please specialists, the section on principles is to be found in Appendix. Dr John Ricketts traverses a good chunk of the 175 principles of Mr. Reinertsen like only he can do.

Here is the mapping:

1. ECONOMIC PRINCIPLES – Appendix E
2. QUEUING PRINCIPLES – Appendix F
3. VARIABILITY PRINCIPLES – Appendix G
4. WIP CONSTRAINTS PRINCIPLES – Appendix H
5. FLOW CONTROL PRINCIPLES – Appendix I
6. BATCH SIZE PRINCIPLES – Appendix J
7. FAST FEEBACK PRINCIPLES – Appendix K
8. DECENTRALISATION PRINCIPLES – Appendix L

Going to Gemba in Knowledge-Work – MR. Donald Reinertsen

A final word on meetings.

One day, on Twitter and a few years back, Chris Matts was really cornered by the essence of the 'Gemba' meeting in Knowledge-Work. I immediately forwarded him the article on the topic written by Mr. Reinertsen.

After a brief exchange, he was good to write his daily blog!

In essence this is what Mr. Reinertsen exposes us to:

It makes little sense to go to where the work is done for one part because it is invisible, our choices about remedies as well, and the perfect conditions for observation do not occur. In fact, what is observed is invisible.

And quoting Mr. Reinertsen: "My point is that mere observation, while tremendously powerful in manufacturing, is hopelessly inadequate in product development."

> "So, if product development is your game, don't think that going to gemba is going to solve your problems – it won't even identify them. Almost nothing that is truly important is visible in the physical environment of engineering. Critical issues like batch size, overlap of activities, sequencing of tasks, margin in the design, architectural partitioning choices, and risk management strategy are not apparent by observing the physical objects."

In my opinion, going to the Gemba is one too many importations Lean manufacturing has gotten away again with agile and Knowledge-Work. Handle with care. And let people who actually know what they are doing, do the work. No assembly required.

My personal message to you is this: be the gamba. Let people come to you. Show them your know-how to 'do' agile. Then become a leader. You won't become a leader unless you know how to 'do' agile. Don't fall for mastering procedures, roles, rituals, ceremonies and responsibilities. Learn instead how to hit the ground running.

I can see a connection with Lucas' critique in importing the manufacturing 'Gemba' practice blindly to Knowledge-Work. Can't you?

Variation on the main Theme at Execution Time

All the work and thoughts of Mr. Reinertsen have stood the test of time. This chapter changes nothing to that. To 'do' product development, it is perfect and in harmony with this book and my previous one.

When the time comes to execute, we can reap the benefit of additional tools. This is my purpose.

Here are in short form the small contribution I would like to make from both my books. I put a lot of emphasis on to 'do' agile. I am positioning myself at execution time and nowhere else, well mostly!

- What most approaches fail at is not in the planning itself, but in how the *execution* is *managed*. In both my books, we are not thinking about the *execution of the plan*, but more specifically about the *execution of the work* (work that was presumably planned) with the use of leading indicators and *Management by Exception*.
- Paraphrasing from my book 'Tame Your Work Flow': 'DBR and CCPM buffers are not mechanisms to compensate for unforeseen events nor to reduce or remove variability. Rather, they are devices to make variability detectable and manageable before it produces damages. They serve as leading indicators of risk materialisation. There are two such buffers and they have nothing to do with 'padding':
    - One buffer is for monitoring variability and detecting risk materialisation in the execution of the project (CCPM buffer)
    - The other buffer is for protecting the constraint from variation (special or common) and providing operational leading signals of oncoming risk materialization (DBR buffer) during execution

Conclusion – Let People Work

Time is a great source of concern for agile. It is a pollinator of variability according to them. Cadences and synchronisation are remedies that work no matter what and can be considered as system designed mechanisms.

I wanted to claim at the beginning of this conclusion that systems that trap Common Cause are immune to the variability induced by the passage of time. But I won't. I will instead say that all agile systems are tightly coupled with time and that the approach proposed in this book is loosely coupled with the passage of time.

Now, I want to focus on the core of this chapter.

Mr. Reinertsen gives to agile, tools and principles that every agilist needs to master. Taken individually or as a whole, they are additive: the more the better.

They are in the preventive medicine cabinet but do not emit management by exception signals of their own. But they are quick resolve solutions and by the time you enact them, the results are in the bank. Decision-making and causality. Nothing smells more of Throughput Accounting than this.

Management by exception can also be used on top and above these principles. They are system based and designed to tame Common Cause. Buffer technology from the Theory of Constraints and the support they give to Throughput Accounting for laser focus actions that will actually work according to the laws of causality have no match yet in agile.

One benefit that was not mentioned is that such systems prevent you from going on wild goose chases to find improvement opportunities. Remember, the only goose we want is the one with the golden egg! It lays where Common Cause lives: within your systems. In the Jeep.

Systems can also address variability issues without resorting to tame time and using cadences and synchronisation only. Systems that emit signals are of great benefit and play a role in dampening the overburdening of workers so that they can spend time working and skip a cadence or two when nothing out of the ordinary stands out. Oddly, time can stand still!

You must be wondering what is my point. My point is that the CCPM Buffer and DBR technologies come at basically no costs as depicted in the practical example set forth in details in chapter 3. At execution time, you can do with management by exception without regard to cadence nor synchronisation. You have a system meant to deal with Common Cause! It will send signals. Get ready for them. Other than that, let people work.

Try it. If you have a half decent Kanban Lead Time distribution, just do it.

Those advocating synchronisation and cadences for the sake of risk management, product development, strategy implementation, service delivery, development process and retrospectives have plenty of benefits to reap from these practices upstream as well. That 'stuff' upstream must be done properly and all forms of communication and socialisation must prevail.

For example, a lot of efforts are required upstream to tame the 'fuzzy front end'. At that location, having extra capacity is a must. The constraint should never be located there. Have as many coordination, transaction, setup activities on non constraint locations thru the use of cadences and synchronisation as you need and it would not matter on costs. It is on the contrary totally acceptable, warranted and within the parameters of Throughput Accounting.

While executing, you could very well be hitting the constraint in some way or another. Let's say it is the case for the sake of discussion. Capacity is scarce at the constraint. All forms of pre programmed administrative rituals are not necessarily conducive to exploiting the constraint. This is my point.

I am all for planning properly. But my proposition to you is that when the rubber meets the road at execution time, we should not be concerned anymore with the execution of the plan but rather with the execution of the work. Every thing we own and master in terms of tools, processes, interactions is built into this 'plan'. Execution should leverage this vast, predictable and stable knowledge with a modern technology that is fit for purpose and that costs close to nothing to implement for Knowledge-Work.

I am of course targeting the CCPM buffer, DBR and the BBR coefficient from your free CCPM plan. If a plan is free, it cannot be considered as waste by Lean and Agile. This is a point worth remembering again!

Taming Common Cause Variation is best served with systems that can detect variations from a normal state. It fits like a glove with a new variation of mine on Principle V11:

'CCPM plans are system based – and at execution time - tame Common Cause without requiring money for variability reduction and without any regards for the passage of time.[192]'

I would like to remind the readers that time has ONE degree of freedom whereas scope can go quadratic rapidly with an unlimited number of degrees of freedom. Want to tame complexity? Manage on the time axis with the tools provided in this book. The tools only involve brown money most of the time, especially to leverage a portfolio with Critical Chain plans with multiple projects – orthogonal to size, scope or schedule - with corresponding CCPM consumption buffers and Buffer Fever Charts.

Let people work ...

[192] We are talking agile and to that extent projects of a few days, to a few weeks and to the extreme case a month are chewable.

APPENDIX A – 1,000 COIN TOSSES AND VARIABILITY

If some of you are not familiar with the 1,000 coins toss experiment that Mr. Reinertsen often refers to, I will simply resume it in three short sentences followed with an illustration further down:

1) You set a counter to zero and you flip a coin a thousand times
2) When you hit tail, you had one to the counter
3) When you hit head, you subtract one to the counter

The pattern we want you to predict is how often will that counter cross zero. How often will this variable cross the X axis while flipping a fair coin 1,000 times?

Well, 500 such occurrences! This is what our reptilian brain would say. But in fact, the X axis – in red below - will be visited all but 28 times. This experiment is being performed on computers all day long. The findings are such that after 1,000 coins toss, it is fruitless to proceed any further as the X axis line will never be crossed again. That means that in your lifetime, it will not happen. This means that if you do not tame variability due to time, you will never catch up. Or is it an issue?

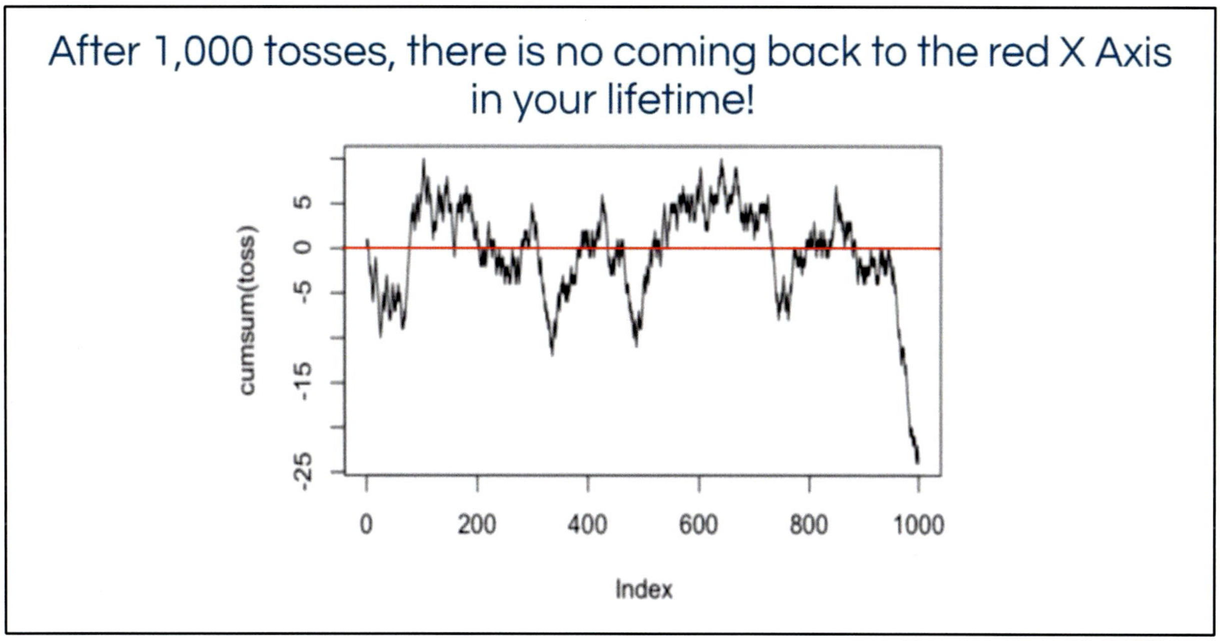

APPENDIX B – THE THEORY OF CONSTRAINTS IS NOT AN APPROACH TO MANAGING COMPLEXITY (AND WHY WE SHOULD JUST STOP OVER COMPLICATING THINGS) – BY JUSTIN ROFF-MARSH

TOC *is* an approach to the management of complex systems, but it's quite incorrect to describe it as an approach to the management of complexity. The distinction is important—and interesting.

If you look in the TOC practitioner's box of tools, you won't find differential equations or Monte Carlo simulations. What you will find is a simple, quick-n-dirty approach to the management of certain types of complex systems (business units), that proceeds from the *elimination of complexity*.

That's right. Conceptually, Step One in every TOC application is, *First, eliminate complexity*. The unwritten postscript to Step One is. *If, at any time, the process on which you're working becomes chaotic, then return to Step One.*

If a system is truly complex then, by definition, it is unmanageable. Eli did not figure out a way to do the mathematically impossible. If he had, he would have started a hedge fund! Eli's genius was such that he figured out a way of cheating.

He recognized that management typically manages systems in such a way as to cause them to become chaotic (and therefore, to exhibit complex behaviors). They then scratch their little heads and puzzle over how to manage the mess that they have created. Their conclusion (correctly) is that they can't manage the process as a whole. Their next step is to recognize (again correctly) that while the system as a whole is chaotic if they zoom in on the discrete elements of the system, those elements, viewed in isolation, are exhibiting perfectly predictable behavior. They then conclude (incorrectly) that if they optimize all those elements, then they will optimize the performance of the system as a whole.

The careless assumption in this formulation was clear as day to Eli. He understood (as a result of his background in the physical sciences) that for a system to perform optimally, its elements must operate suboptimally.

For example, in order for your organization's payroll department to make the expected contribution to the success of your greater organization, it must have sufficient slack to process payments to employees *every single* pay period—not just 90% of them. It turns out that the amount of slack required to provide 100% confidence (as opposed to 90%) that staff will get paid when expected is A LOT. If you optimize the performance of a payroll department, you can drive an organization into bankruptcy in a quarter or two!

Back to Eli's genius approach to cheating. Rather than attempting to manage a chaotic system—an endeavor that Eli would definitely have described as *idiotic*—his approach was to use brute force to eliminate the chaotic behavior and, consequently, the complexity.

This can be done by injecting a large amount of slack into the system. You could do this by adding resources, of course, but this takes too long. The quickest method is to choke the release of work into the system. As every traffic engineer knows, if you choke the input to a chaotic flow, the chaos quickly disappears.

Once chaos—and therefore, complexity—has been eliminated, the next challenge is to figure out how to optimize flow without allowing the system to descend into chaos again.

Now, Eli taught us all how to do that. Identify the one resource which, when fully loaded, will result in the optimal system output. Designate this resource as *The Constraint.* And then deliberately over-resource all non-constraint resources to the degree necessary to ensure that the Constraint does not move. Finally, couple the release of work into the system to the rate at which work is processed at The Constraint.

Simple, right? Genius, actually. But it's critical to understand that *we are not managing complexity.* We are brute-forcing systems to exhibit behavior simple enough to enable us to manage them with a quick-n-dirty heuristic.

No differential equations. No mathematical mumbo-jumbo. We'll leave the management of complexity to the cost accountants with their well-intentioned, but wrong-headed "scientific" approach.

We must all remind ourselves, periodically, that TOC is not a mathematical framework. It's not a business philosophy. It's an amazingly effective, quick-n-dirty approach to wrangling complex systems so that they can make us bucketloads of money.

That's why Eli invented it. And that's how we should be using it. (God bless his soul.)

APPENDIX C – THROUGHPUT ACCOUNTING ZERO METRICS - TRIPWIRES

The Throughput Accounting Zero metrics !!!!!

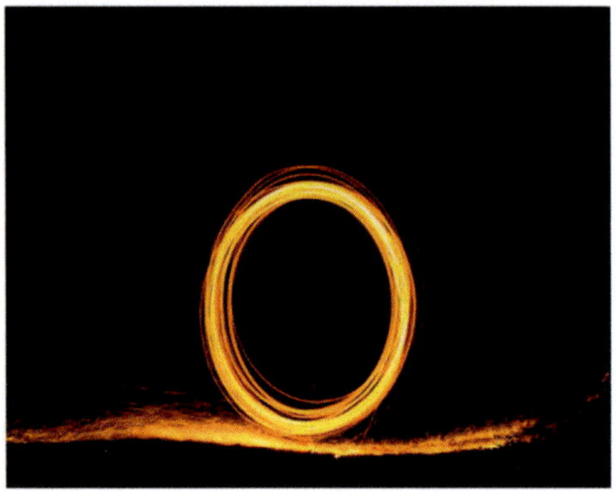

Throughput-Dollars-Day

- The cost of delivering late
- Delivery performance metric. Should equal zero!
- The bigger the Throughput of an order, the faster the growth of the metric
- It is computed by assigning to every late order a value equal to its throughput multiplied by the number of days the order is late

The Throughput Accounting Zero metrics !!!!!

Inventory-Dollars-Day

- The cost of finishing early
- Measure of excess inventories
- Indicates the degree of seriousness of excess inventories
- Represented by the amount of money invested in inventory multiplied by the number of days early the order is completed

APPENDIX D – MODERN STAGGERING with CCPM Rope Signal – Upstream of CCPM Buffer

Staggering from CCPM is a gift to all stakeholders involved in a project. A missing dimension is when fresh staggering information lies to the left of the CCPM Consumption Buffer.

The improvement submitted here is for situations where execution of a project is going much faster than anticipated. The traditional configuration will not send a signal. Sometimes, going too fast warrants such signaling.

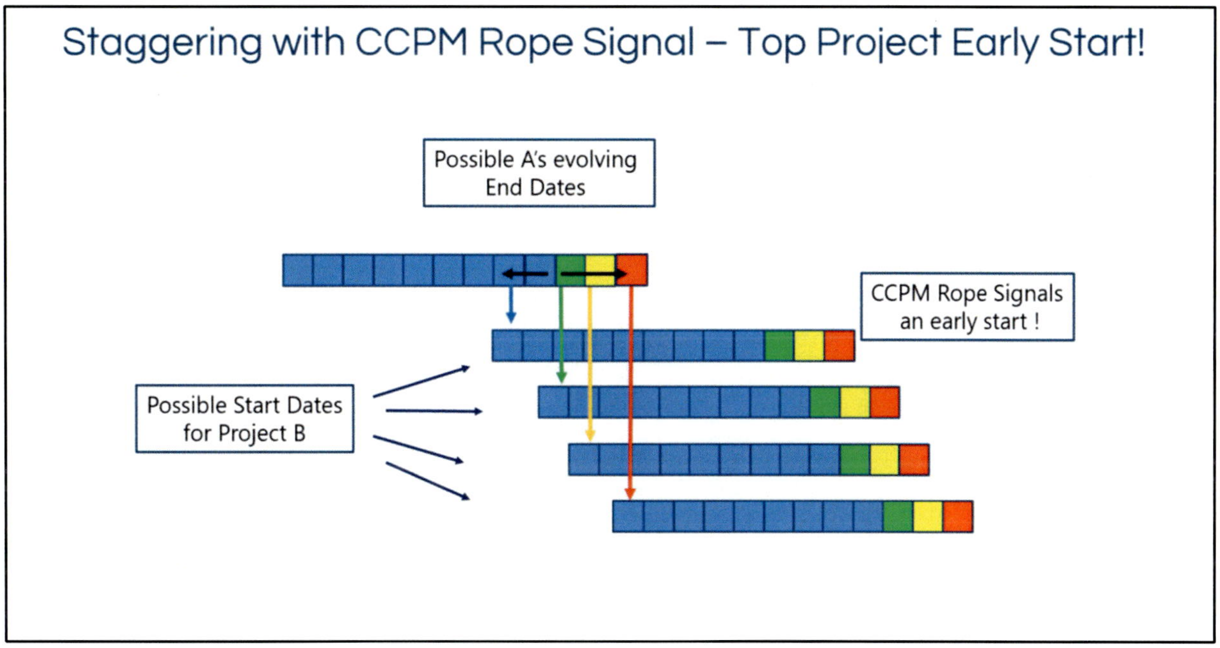

APPENDIX E - ECONOMIC PRINCIPLES[193]

Mr. Reinertsen's Economic Principles	Throughput Accounting and Theory of Constraints and 5 FS	Agreement (YES/NO)
E1: The Principle of Quantified Overall Economics: Select actions based on quantified overall economic impact.	Always evaluate in terms of Delta TH, Delta I and Delta OE – and in that order - for overall effect.	YES
E2: The Principle of Interconnected Variables: We can't just change one thing.	Impacting the Constraint: A concerted action at the right point can have quadratic results. The higher the level of interdependencies and degrees of freedom, the more impact a small action can have on the overall system. However, to 'maintain' Inherent Simplicity – as Mr. Reinertsen says – we may have to do many complicated things, notably sometimes to maintain the constraint where it lies. Note again: Inherent Simplicity is not something you manage or strive to architect or design. It is something that you understand and appreciate flying at 3,000 feet in the air.	YES and NO In Mr. Reinertsen's book, principle E2 is supported with Fig 2-1, an illustration of five key economic objectives for sensitivity analysis. You can assume that sensitivity analysis and marginal analysis are the same. ToC is of course based on that. However, the illustration would pose some interrogation from a Throughput Accounting lens.
E3: The Principle of Quantified Cost of Delay: If you only quantify one thing, quantify the cost of delay.	ToC - Rank projects by Throughput Rate (operational or financial) generated at the constraint. But there are potential problems that Cost of Delay better addresses. Especially among software projects, Throughput is not the only consideration. Some	YES and NO Sometimes different outcomes with measuring with Throughput Rate. But cost of growing queues is not to be ignored no matter the justification for starring a project.

[193] Please read the excellent and very recent LinkedIn Post on that topic. Kasaraboina, Omprakash. Dynamic batch size: A re-look at U-curve optimization.

	projects are mandatory for legal/regulatory reasons, yet they generate no Throughput. Other projects are approved because they enhance the Throughput-generating capability of the constraint even though the software itself generates no Throughput. Finally, some software projects are approved because they reduce Investment or Operating Expense of non-constraints, and these deltas flow into Net Profit without generating additional Throughput. JR[194]	
E4: The Principle of Economic Value-Added: The value added by an activity is the change in the economic value of the work product.	From Dr Kelvyn Youngman: You add value everywhere. This is best expressed as follows: **'Exploitation and Subordination Reframed as Productivity and Utility':** 1) Exploiting Constraint adds: Productivity 2) Non -Constraint adds: Utility	**YES and ... From Dr JR** **TA - Throughput Accounting - measures economic value added as NP = T – OE. However, this is calculated for finished products, not work products, for two reasons:** **1)Finished products generate T, but work products do not.** **2)TA – Throughput Accounting - stays away from activity-level measurement because Activity-Based Costing leads to mismeasurement.**
E5: The Inactivity Principle: Watch the work product, not the worker.	5 FS – Be constraint savvy. Etienne Du Plooy principle 'systems Focus': Performance measurement is focused on improving the system's performance **at** the Constraint. Workers should be kept busy there. Workers at non constraint points can go fishing, it would not make a difference.	**YES but ...** **Inactivity correlates with utilization metrics, which TOC abhors. JR**

[194] JR = Dr John Ricketts

E6: The U-Curve Principle: Important trade-offs are likely to have U-curve optimizations.	From Dr John Ricketts:[195] The TOC Buffer Principle: Buffers protect against unpredictable variation. Some buffers are explicitly bi-directional because they protect against both low and high variation. For example, when skills are buffered, the buffer zones are red (too low), yellow, green, yellow, red (too high) to indicate that too many consultants on the bench is as bad as too many projects without adequate skills. (See "Reaching the Goal.") Although the earliest buffers described by TOC are explicitly uni-directional (with just green, yellow, red zones), they are implicitly bi-directional. For example, stock/inventory buffers are typically represented this way to protect against stock-outs. Nevertheless, over-stocks are also undesirable. They can happen due to cancelled orders, returned merchandise, or clerical errors. (Source: Eli Goldratt) Thus, the optimal buffer level is always in the middle, spanning the green and yellow zones. When the buffer level strays into a red zone -- either high or low -- that's suboptimal.	NO PERFECT MATCH U Curves are a perfect example of 'all models are wrong, some are useful' Fixed costs are allocated in this model and the time dimension is not present. I will say no more on that as the following article – also listed in the References section – does a very good job: Kasaraboina, Omprakash. Dynamic batch size: A re-look at U-curve optimization.
E7: The Imperfection Principle: Even imperfect answers improve decision-making.		YES and … by Dr Ricketts "It is better to be roughly right than precisely wrong." [John Maynard Keynes]

[195] If you have not read Dr John Ricketts' book 'Reaching the Goal', do yourself a favor. Get it. One my friends was working at IBM Rochester lab developing patents in NY before 9/11. During our discussion, it so happened that we ran into John's picture. She told me that he was always there with Dr Eli Goldratt. (She of course knows Eli's face but did not know his stature). Dr Goldratt said that Dr Ricketts had run the most impressive application of ToC ever. And for Knowledge-Work of all things. And in so doing, managed the fleet of consultants, RFP, resource leveling for many, many years at IBM. Do not underestimate this book and the knowledge and joy it will bring you.

		TOC follows this principle by establishing buffers that are initially sized with rough rules of thumb rather than precise benchmarks. Experience has shown that the rules of thumb are good enough to get a quick start on TOC implementation, and a delayed start doesn't improve performance enough to matter.
E8: The Principle of Small Decisions: Influence the many small decisions.	TA – A small decision at the constraint can have order of magnitude effect on overall performance. In his book, Mr. Reinertsen makes a connection with the 80-20 Pareto rule. The reader may the interested in visiting Chapter 1 – Flawed Mental Model number 8 where we say that Pareto looks more like 99-1 than 80-20 when ToC is applied!	YES TOC refers to these as leverage points because small input produces big output. JR
E9: The Principle of Continuous Economic Trade-offs: Economic choices must be made continuously	TA - Dr John Ricketts – Decision-making principle – The effect of a proposed change can be assessed by comparing its net profit and return on investment on the baseline System Focused Principle – Etienne du Plooy - Performance measurement is focused on improving the system's performance **at** the Constraint	YES but .. Some important trade-offs are not economic – at least not directly. Strategic positioning (deciding which products and services to offer) seeks survival first, then prosperity. Furthermore, it may be impossible to create a viable economic justification for some projects undertaken during strategic horizon 3 (seeds of

		future business), yet those embryonic ventures are necessary for a business to survive by evolving. JR
E10: The First Perishability Principle: Many economic choices are more valuable when made quickly.	Time is always a factor in Throughput Accounting. It goes for decision-making as well that is facilitated by the various ToC models and applications. They are so simple that they indeed allow to short cut complex decisions into simple ones and therefore make de decision-making cycle as short as can be. The zero dollars metrics in TA are quite interesting in that regard: Throughput-dollars-day (cost of delivering late) and Inventory-dollars-day (cost of finishing early) ... In an ideal world, they must be equal to zero. I have included these 2 metrics in Appendix C. They are part of the manufacturing industry, but they are intriguing...	YES but ... I would say timing is a factor. Faster is not always better. For instance, if I deliver a truckload of inventory to a customer ahead of the due date, they may not have staff to unload it or space to store it. Delivering on time – "timing" – is more important than time – "speed." JR
E11: The Subdivision Principle: Inside every bad choice lies a good choice.		Yes and ... By Dr Ricketts ToC has its own thinking process that produces various diagrams, including the Conflict Resolution Diagram (aka "Evaporating Cloud"), Current Reality Tree, and Future Reality Tree. Rather than subdividing decisions to seek good choices, the TP models cause-and-effect relationships. Bad choices are often based on invalid

		assumptions. Injecting better assumptions and/or specific actions then eliminates conflicts and produces good choices that transform current reality into future reality.
E12: The Principle of Early Harvesting: Create systems to harvest the early cheap opportunities.		No ... by Dr Ricketts TOC does not advocate early harvesting because it's just one of many possible strategies. TOC instead advocates decisive competitive advantage but doesn't specify one strategy to achieve it. For instance, first movers may pursue early cheap opportunities, but fast followers can negate the first mover advantage. Furthermore, product/service quality and rapid/reliable delivery may trump price even if they're not part of early offerings.
E13: The Principle of Decision Rules: Use decision rules to decentralize economic control.	Throughput Accounting was built to share a decision-making process that could be leveraged in a decentralized way for anyone in the organisation. Unit, Product, Division, Team, Individual levels etc	YES and ... I agree that decision rules are helpful, but the centralization-decentralization debate has been going on for decades. Centralized decisions are notorious for missing local

		variances. But decentralized decisions are one source of conflict in organizations. For instance, the production manager wants to minimize WIP while the inventory manager wants to match finished goods inventory to demand while the finance manager wants to minimize investment in inventory while the marketing manager wants extra inventory in order to offer volume discounts. Any of those decentralized decisions can create conflict. It would be great to have a unified view, but the reality of large organizations is the decisions get spread across multiple managers because they're too big a job for one manager. JR
E14: The First Market Principle: Ensure decision makers feel both cost and benefit.	Always base decision on marginal impact on TH, I and OE. Revenue and costs are within the decision-making perimeter	YES
E15: The Principle of Optimum Decision Timing: Every decision has its optimum economic timing.	Ford competed on space, Ohno on Inventory (small batch size) and Goldratt on the time axis. ToC helps in making decisions with models and architecture that provide support and automation. We know that humans are bad at making decisions and that tools to automate are always welcome. Make all decisions based on delta TH, I and OE in that order	YES

E16: The Principle of Marginal Economics: Always compare marginal cost to marginal value.	Think like a financial analyst with marginal analysis ... However, sometimes focusing only on marginal costs may lead to overproduction. This principle is definitely inspired from micro economics. Reaching the lowest cost may mean overproduction. For maximising services in the governmental sectors, this may need to be interpreted differently as we aim to maximize service which is never in line with the equilibrium between marginal revenue and marginal cost. I am definitely, definitely cherry picking here. In a Throughput Accounting world, the line is not blurred between maximising services for a government (Operating Throughput) or maximising cash for a manufacturing company (Financial Throughput)	YES and NO
E17: The Sunk Cost Principle: Do not consider money already spent.	Throughput Accounting – Only concerned with marginal impact of decisions. Sunk costs - when used improperly - would find their way in the current and proposed solution anyway, therefore showing their irrelevance and cancelling each other out as irrelevant costs. When I have issues with someone not understanding sunk costs, this is what I have them to do. Sunk costs would show under ALL the proposed alternatives and thus, be trivial. Let me remind readers of the definition of sunk costs: 1) It happened in the past. 2) It is a fixed cost. YES EMPLOYEES WORK ARE FIXED COSTS IN A TA PARADIGM! 3) It has no salvage value.	YES and .. I agree that sunk cost is not a sound basis for deciding whether to continue a project. Instead, if decision to continue is based only on remaining investment, ROI goes exponential. For instance, suppose at project launch the expected investment is \$1 million, Throughput will be \$2 million, and ROI=2/1. When the project was 50% complete, remaining I=\$500K and ROI=2/0.5. Today, the project is 80% complete, so remaining I=\$200K and ROI=2/0.2. The

	Everybody misses the third point. If the work you have done until this point can still be leverage in some ways, then it is not a sunk cost!	closer to completion it gets, the less investment remains and the higher ROI goes. On the other hand, it rarely makes sense to complete a project where the actual benefit will be substantially lower than expected. JR
E18: The Principle of Buying Information: The value of information is its expected economic value.	Throughput Accounting – always value impact on the deltas – TH, I and OE in that order. The value of information to support management decisions is indeed its economic value. But a lot of systems generate information that cannot be quantified that way. For instance, businesses must report income tax withholding, employee retirement funding, and sales tax. While all are useful for the government and for employees, none of that information is itself a Throughput generator. JR	YES
E19: The Insurance Principle: Don't pay more for insurance than the expected loss.	I think this is equivalent to the cost of perfect information.	YES but ... Dr Ricketts Throughput Accounting does not address insurance directly, but insurance premiums would be included in Operating Expenses. TA uses Delta Analysis to compare alternatives. If self-insurance based on expected loss is less than the insurance premiums, Delta Analysis would tend to favor self-insurance. However, the purpose of insurance is often to

		protect against catastrophic loss. Suppose the annual expected loss is \$10,000 and the premium is \$12,000 but the coverage is up to \$1 million. If the business would be bankrupted by self-insuring a loss greater than \$250,000, paying a premium greater than expected loss might be a sensible decision.
E20: The Newsboy Principle: High probability of failure does not equal bad economics.	Newsboy is up early so making decision fast and early helps in creating contact with market and generate feedbacks.	
E21: The Show Me the Money Principle: To influence financial decisions, speak the language on money.	The most famous quote from Dr Goldratt: 'Help me help you make more money now and in the future' still resonates today! Ravi Gilani's words of wisdom come to mind equally: 'Make more and more rupees over time.' I would like to point here that the notion of profits is in no way related to cash in the bank. You can have stellar profits for years and not have 2 pennies to rub together.	YES and ... Late in his life, Dr Goldratt came to realize that money isn't everything. JR

APPENDIX F – QUEUING PRINCIPLES

Mr. Reinertsen's Queuing Principles	Throughput Accounting and Theory of Constraints and 5 FS	Agreement (YES/NO)
Q1: The Principle of Invisible Inventory: Product development inventory is physically and financially invisible.	In some cases, having the work and queues visible on Kanban boards can be a medicine to that ailment. In my book, you can see and manage 3 types of queues: Queues in the Work Flow, Work Process and Work Execution. Putting a financial price tag is another story altogether but knowing where to act according to the constraint makes good financial sense. Cost accumulation of projects are very visible is you look at the General Ledger under the Investments accounts and CAPEX or OPEX categories.	YES and NO Not sure anybody should care about invisible product development inventory unless its invisibility leads to over-investment. I assume Mr Reinertsen is referring to physical products. As you know, digital products may be physically invisible yet financially visible. And many services have no inventory at all. JR
Q2: The Principle of Queueing Waste: Queues are the root cause of the majority of economic waste in product development.	DBR minimizes the size of Queues by design, optimizes Flow and Throughput by acting on the constraint	YES with a twist This assumes that the constraint is internal. If the constraint is external[196], then the inability to meet market demand is the issue, not queueing. JR
Q3: The Principle of Queueing Capacity Utilization: Capacity utilization increases queues exponentially.	Throughput Accounting – All of the ToC recognizes this and all of its architecture was built with this in mind. The excess capacity can only be used to support the constraint. If you see a non constraint work 'too much' they are not subordinating to the	NOT for DBR Capacity of the constraint must be fully utilized. A minute lost on the constraint is a dollar lost forever.

[196] Internal vs External constraint is something I address in the TA classes for CPA since it is easier to grasp in the 'visible' world. Suffice it to say that the jury is out on this one as I sincerely believe – as Beau Ganas and Ravi Gilani – that you must have a dominant share of the market to experience such a constraint. (Coke, Carter Pillar etc). Your only resolve here would be to lower your prices, which is a Throughput Accounting anti pattern. Other than that, you have a sales or marketing constraint as the market cannot absorb your product. As an historical note, Eli Schragenheim first raised this point to Dr Eli Goldratt. (Start-ups may experience a market constraint assuredly)

	constraint! The only queue that should be apparent is in front of the constraint. Queues are not likely to appear even when we wish the constraint to be occupied at 100%. The 'Rope' which signals replenishment operates under a queue discipline itself: when the buffer dictates it, then replenish! Choking the release of Work is also a common cure.	DBR neuters queue proliferation Excess Capacity exists everywhere else.
Q4: The Principle of High-Queue States: Most of the damage done by a queue is caused by high-queue states.	ToC - chokes the release of work to solve this problem. DBR is meant to reduce WIP and queue states to a minimum	YES
Q5: The Principle of Queueing Variability: Variability increases queues linearly.		No .. Dr Ricketts TOC does not address queueing, which is a major subject of its own. Whether variability increases queues linearly or exponentially depends on things like queuing discipline (FIFO, LIFO, PQ, WFQ), arrival rates (not consistent over time), and balking (leaving queue before service).
Q6: The Principle of Variability Amplification: Operating at high levels of capacity utilization increases variability.	As a PHD in physics, Dr Goldratt knew that a system work at its peak when all of its components have operating at less that maximum capacity. Productive, protective and excess capacities are all part of the equation to have everyone subordinate to the constraint to avoid capacity overdrive.	YES and ... This holds at the constraint but DBR is there to optimize
Q7: The Principle of Queueing Structure: Serve pooled demand with reliable high-capacity servers.	Nothing to add	YES ... Dr Ricketts The TOC Aggregation Principle applies

		here. It observes that variation is lowest when multiple independent sources of variation are aggregated. For instance, variability of product sales is highest at retail locations and lowest at the central warehouse that replenishes those retailers. Therefore, holding most inventory at the warehouse and distributing only the minimum necessary to cover daily sales at retailers substantially reduces inventory holding and the need for discounts to clear excess inventory.
Q8: The Principle of Linked Queues: Adjacent queues see arrival or service time variability depending on loading.	One must realize that there are 3 queues in DBR: The constraint, upstream of the constraint – also called sprint capacity – and downstream of the constraint. Unlike JIT where all processes can have a domino effect – and destabilizing – one the next process. DBR absorbs that variability and ignores those signals and treats them as noise	YES
Q9: The Principle of Queue Size Optimization: Optimum queue size is an economic trade-off.	The queue is identified at the constraint with DBR mechanism. All other parts of the system have capacity above and in excess of the constraint to tame queue proliferation. You have the choice to manage the entire system or simply focus on the constraint	YES
Q10: The Principle of Queueing Discipline: Queue cost is affected by the sequence in which we handle the jobs in the queue.	The systems are designed for maximizing Throughput. No matter how jobs arrive, there is no other approach that will get	YES and ... Rather than focusing on queue cost (operating expense),

	them out of the system faster, irrelevant of queuing discipline. The speed at which a specific work item goes thru the constraint is the deciding factor. (So yes, we could decide based on revenues which item could go first.)	TOC focuses on Throughput. If every item in a queue is identical and their due dates don't matter to customers, then queueing discipline doesn't matter. However, if items are differentiated and customers specify different due dates, a queue discipline other than FIFO would maximize Throughput. For example, exiting the queue strictly by due date is one possibility. Another is exiting the queue by highest Throughput first, subject to due dates is another. JR
Q11: The Cumulative Flow Principle: Use CFDs to monitor queues.		NO .. Dr Ricketts TOC establishes buffers so that queues won't form except in specific locations: 1) work orders waiting for release, 2) work in process ahead of the constraint, and 3) complete work. If the constraint is internal, buffer depletion ahead of the constraint triggers release of work orders. If the constraint is external, depletion of finished goods inventory triggers release of work orders.

Q12: Little's Formula: Wait time = Queue Size/Processing Rate.	ToC uses Little's law in an Operations Management and deterministic context. TP = WIP/FT	**YES and more ...**
Q13: The First Queue Size Control Principle: Don't control capacity utilization, control queue size.	ToC – DBR, S-SBR and CCPM are orchestrated with this in mind. The rope sends a replenishment signal when needed.	**YES**
Q14: The Second Queue Size Control Principle: Don't control cycle time, control queue size.		**NO ...** **See Q11**
Q15: The Diffusion Principle: Over time, queues will randomly spin seriously out of control and will remain in this state for long periods.	DBR Scheduling is meant to counter that in a dynamic and systemic fashion ...	**YES and NO**
Q16: The Intervention Principle: We cannot rely on randomness to correct a random queue.	Indeed, we must have a systemic approach ... DBR is meant for that in an automated way with buffer penetration signals	**YES**

APPENDIX G – VARIABILITY PRINCIPLES

Mr. Reinertsen's Variability Principles	Throughput Accounting and Theory of Constraints and 5 FS	Agreement (YES/NO)
V1: The Principle of Beneficial Variability: Variability can create economic value.	You have the choice: you manage the entire system or you focus on that part of the system that has limited capacity.	YES
V2: The Principle of Asymmetric Payoffs: Payoff asymmetries enable variability to create economic value.		YES
V3: The Principle of Optimum Variability: Variability should neither be minimized nor maximized.	Good systems and architectures absorb variability. Behavior towards Common Cause and Special Cause is often dictated by presence or absence of systems	YES and NO .. Dr Ricketts TOC treats variation as an external influence that cannot be changed. Instead, TOC uses buffers to reduce the negative effects of variation. We need to remember that buffers are physicalized in units but are used to tame time
V5: The Principle of Variability Pooling: Overall variation decreases when uncorrelated random tasks are combined.	Negative covariance at work!	See Q7
V6: The Principle of Short-Term Forecasting: Forecasting becomes exponentially easier at short time-horizons.	TA principle by Dr John Ricketts – Demand principle – Forecasts are usually wrong, but reacting to actual demand is usually right (ROPE)	YES
V7: The Principle of Small Experiments: Many small experiments produce less variation than one big one.		NO ... Dr Ricketts TOC doesn't address experiments. But the amount of variation produced by any experiment depends on many factors, including experimental design, sample size, sampling method,

		instrumentation, and replication. It's not just a question of one big versus multiple small experiments.
V8: The Repetition Principle: Repetition reduces variation.	Correct. And having the same system serves that purpose	YES
V9: The Reuse Principle: Reuse reduces variability.	Correct.	YES
V10: The Principle of Negative Covariance: We can reduce variance by applying a counterbalancing effect.	Similar to Principle V5	YES
V11: The Buffer Principle: Buffers trade money for variability reduction.	Correct	YES
V12: The Principle of Variability Consequence: Reducing consequences is usually the best way to reduce the cost of variability.	Before starting work, make sure all the gates are open and clear! Equivalent to Full Kitting in ToC	YES
V13: The Non-linearity Principle: Operate in the linear range of system performance.	Buffer Penetrations are good indicators if you are operating within optimal range of performance. WIP Ageing, CCPM, DBR and S-DBR buffer signals. Be wary of too many or too few signals!	YES and ... Dr Ricketts Not all systems have a linear range of performance, especially when there are multiple measures of performance: speed vs. economy vs. endurance.
V14: The Principle of Variability Substitution: Substitute cheap variability for expensive variability.	Downstream resources are cheapest to come to help the constraint ... Upstream resources are more expensive as they have a purpose to always improve sprint capacity. You can make up the time lost on the constraint by acting fast downstream. But that money lost on throughput at the constraint is forever lost. Slack upstream of the constraint can help in keeping the constraint busy. Slack downstream of the constraint	YES and ... Dr Ricketts Yes, assuming equal capability, substitute cheap for expensive. However, downstream resources also need sprint capacity to make up time lost on the constraint or any task ahead of it in order to fulfill a due date commitment. And whether any particular resource is cheap or expensive

	can help in respecting delivery dates.	depends entirely on the skill set required.
V15: The Principle of Iteration Speed: It is usually better to improve iteration speed than defect rate.	ToC – Speed at the constraint (Throughput rate) determines system performance	And Vice Versa This statement is arguable in a software context. If software is defective, it doesn't matter how fast it's delivered or how it performs in production. A counterargument is lowering the defect rate accelerates delivery because there's less rework. JR
V16: The Principle of Variability Displacement: Move variability to the process stage where its cost is lowest.	ToC – Be constraint savvy and think in terms of TH, OE and I when making decisions within your processes. Being constraint savvy is also a factor. Many costs (setup, batch, coordination, transaction) have no economic impact at non constraint locations due to the permanent availability of slack in the system due to excess, protective and idle capacity	YES but ... Be concerned about what a cost is and where it matters. Average costs or cost per 'number' are always a mirage. Remember COSTS vs CO$TS ?

APPENDIX H – BATCH SIZE PRINCIPLES

Mr. Reinertsen's Batch Size Principles	**Throughput Accounting and Theory of Constraints and 5 FS**	**Agreement (YES/NO)**
B1: The Batch Size Queueing Principle:	ToC - Reducing batch size reduces cycle time	YES
B2: The Batch Size Variability Principle: Reducing batch size reduces variability in flow.	Correct	YES but ... Dr Ricketts The smaller the batches, the more balanced capacity is needed, but that means that disruption anywhere becomes disruption everywhere. Therefore, TOC advocates balanced flow, not balanced capacity. For an internal constraint, TOC establishes sprint capacity everywhere except the constraint, which has none. Although TOC favors smaller batches, it doesn't favor one-piece batches.
B3: The Batch Size Feedback Principle: Reducing batch size accelerates feedback.	Correct	YES
B4: The Batch Size Risk Principle: Reducing batch size reduces risk.	Correct	YES
B5: The Batch Size Overhead Principle: Reducing batch size reduces overhead.	TA – Overhead (coordination, setup and transaction costs) away from the constraint has no economic impact. But it does matter at the constraint. Pre-determinable cost Principle - Etienne du Plooy: Products and services are integral to a system as a whose costs and expenses are largely pre-determined irrespective of volumes the	YES and NO

	system produces or sells. A fair portion of costs and expenses will be incurred no matter what the level of production is and for **that reason TVC and OE should never be allocated to products or services**	
B6: The Batch Size Efficiency Principle: Large batches reduce efficiency.	Correct	YES
B7: The Psychology Principle of Batch Size: Large batches inherently lower motivation and urgency.	Correct	NO ... Dr Ricketts TOC says nothing about motivation. That said, this principle deserves a reference that proves it's true. In my own experience, I haven't seen any connection between batch size and motivation. On the other hand, I have seen operators throw tantrums when they were forced into interrupting batch processing to set up for a higher-priority job.
B8: The Batch Size Slippage Principle: Large batches cause exponential cost and schedule growth.	Correct	YES
B9: The Batch Size Death Spiral Principle: Large batches lead to even larger batches.	Daniel Doiron - Correct ... Data structure algorithm ... Clusters of clusters tend to cluster together (regarding data) – From Dr Knuth. But this may not apply to projects as Dr Ricketts pointed to me.	YES
B10: The Least Common Denominator Principle of Batch Size: The entire batch is limited by its worst element.	TA – Dr John Ricketts – Utilisation principle – The only utilisation that matters is at the constraint. Chain Principle - A system can only produce as much as its weakest link, the Constraint, will allow	YES

	Constrained system principle – Etienne du Plooy - Every system has **at least one** Constraint that determines the system's performance. Without a Constraint, a system is **incapable** of generating Throughput	
B11: The Principle of Batch Size Economics: Economic batch size is a U-curve optimization.	ToC – This applies at the constraint only. No impact on costs anywhere else as slack capacity is present. Dr John Ricketts Capacity Principle – Unbalanced Capacity is always more productive because the constraint can be used as a 'proxy' to manage the entire system. Ignore the constraint and then you have to manage the entire system. U curve optimization at the system level leads to high WIP	YES and NO Valid point at the constraint only. Non constraint points must adjust batch size to needs of constraint
B12: The Principle of Low Transaction Cost: Reducing transaction cost per batch lowers overall costs.	ToC – This applies at the constraint only. No impact on costs anywhere else. Plenty of SLACK and excess capacity at non constraints. Also, in one case that crosses my mind: Shipping large batches to save shipping costs is false economy. Reducing transaction costs per batch may also lead to local optima and overproduction which is bad for subordination but can be appropriate at the constraint.	YES and NO Depends if you are at a constraint point or not. Costs matter at the constraint, everywhere else has excess capacity by design to subordinate to the constraint
B13: The Principle of Batch Size Diseconomies: Batch size reduction saves much more than you think.	ToC – true at the non constraint as you produce according to the need and pace of constraint in the spirit of subordination. Constraint may need to use optimal (and maybe bigger) batch size at times for the sake of exploitation	YES and NO Depends if you are at a constraint point or not
B14: The Batch Size Packing Principle: Small batches allow finer tuning of capacity utilization	Correct	YES
B15: The Fluidity Principle: Loose coupling between product subsystems enables small batches.	Correct	YES

B16: The Principle of Transport Batches: The most important batch is the transport batch.	TA – Dr John Ricketts – Buffer Principle – Strategically placed units or time for contingencies minimizes the spread of disruption across an entire system - DBR – Drum Buffer Rope is the ultimate transport mechanism to maintain Flow and reduce WIP. Pulling can only occur at the constraint. TA – Daniel Doiron – In terms of costs, the only place where it would matter is at the constraint. Transportation costs are irrelevant at non constraint point be it will small, big or same size batches. Remember that costs are defined as either cash outflow (which setup costs never are but at the constraint) or lost opportunity for revenues (cash inflows because of a hiccup at the constraint. (Paraphrased from Debra Smith)	**YES**
B17: The Proximity Principle: Proximity enables small batch sizes.	Correct. Is there a message here for remote work due to COVID?	**YES**
B18: The Run Length Principle: Short run lengths reduce queues.	Correct	**YES**
B19: The Infrastructure Principle: Good infrastructure enables small batches.	DBR is such an infrastructure along with 5 FS and CCPM	**YES**
B20: The Principle of Batch Content: Sequence first that which adds value most cheaply.	Throughput Accounting: always rank by Throughput rate, ie the speed at which a product goes thru the constraint. **In that context, sequencing has little impact as speed at the constraint is always optimal ...**	**YES**
B21: The Batch Size First Principle: Reduce batch size before you attack bottlenecks.	The Lean Pool Flow metaphor.	**YES**
B22: The Principle of Dynamic Batch Size: Adjust batch size dynamically to respond to changing economics.	Debatable? A good system can absorb that. For example, capacity constrained Kanban systems absorb variability.	**YES and NO**

APPENDIX I – WIP CONSTRAINTS PRINCIPLES

Mr. Reinertsen's WIP Constraints Principles	Throughput Accounting and Theory of Constraints and 5 FS	Agreement (YES/NO)
W1: The Principle of WIP Constraints: Constrain WIP to control cycle time and flow.	Proper DBR sizing – a variation on WIP constraint - at the constraint once Flow Efficiency has been attained, leads to maximum Throughput	YES and ...
W2: The Principle of Rate Matching: WIP constraints force rate-matching.	ToC ... as long as the understanding between adjacent processes is limited to 2 processes. Upstream of the constraint and downstream of the constraint.	YES but ...
W3: The Principle of Global Constraints: Use global WIP constraints for predictable and permanent bottlenecks.	YES ... Permanent bottlenecks it is ... DBR uses the global WIP construct ...	YES
W4: The Principle of Local Constraints: If possible, constrain local WIP pools.		YES
W5: The Batch Size Decoupling Principle: Use WIP ranges to decouple the batch sizes of adjacent processes.	Adjacent processes are not like a JIT system. There is the constraint, upstream of the constraint (as many processes as you want) and downstream of the constraint (as many processes as you want) What matters is the time between a rope signal is sent and when it arrives at the constraint ... Be it physicalized by one, five or twenty processes	YES but ...
W6: The Principle of Demand Blocking: Block all demand when WIP reaches its upper limit.	1)ToC – Choking the release of work into the system when it becomes unstable. Take the time required until the problem is solved. 2)No rope signals sent when WIP is adequate in the system	YES
W7: The Principle of WIP Purging: When WIP is high, purge low value projects.	Similar to choking the release but with work already in the system	YES
W8: The Principle of Flexible Requirements: Control WIP by shedding requirements.	Correct	YES

W9: The Principle of Resource Pulling: Quickly apply extra resources to an emerging queue.	ToC and slack capacity allocation	**YES**
W10: The Principle of Part-Time Resources: Use part-time resources for high variability tasks.	Downstream resource of the constraint preferably.	**YES**
W11: The Big Gun Principle: Pull high-powered experts to emerging bottlenecks.	Correct	**YES and .. Dr Ricketts** **Occasional firefighting is normal.** **Constant firefighting is a symptom of big problems.**
W12: The Principle of T-Shaped Resources: Develop people who are deep in one area and broad in many.	Correct	**YES**
W13: The Principle of Skill Overlap: Cross train resources at adjacent processes.	Correct	**YES**
W14: The Mix Change Principle: Use upstream mix changes to regulate queue size.	Correct	**YES**
W15: The Aging Principle: Watch the outliers.	WIP ageing ... Management by exception signals	**YES**
W16: The Escalation Principle: Create a preplanned escalation process for outliers.	Correct	**YES**
W17: The Principle of Progressive Throttling: Increase throttling as you approach the queue limit.	Raiding an overloaded constraint is tampered with cooling signaling for additional work into the system. Buffer signaling can be adjusted. When you do not receive a signal or when you receive too many, it is time to Throttle.	**YES**
W18: The Principle of Differential Service: Differentiate quality of service by workstream.	Actually, the same process would treat all request based on Throughput rate at the constraint. Maybe no need for a different workstream	**YES**
W19: The Principle of Adaptive WIP Constraints: Adjust WIP constraints as capacity changes.	ToC – DBR scheduling self adjusts in all cases. Sometimes it is necessary to adjust DBR buffer size if you receive too many or too few signals	**YES**
W20: The Expansion Control Principle: Prevent uncontrolled expansion of work.	DBR Scheduling	**YES**

W21: The Principle of the Critical Queue: Constrain WIP in the section of the system where the queue is most expensive.	5 FS and DBR Buffer	**YES**
W22: The Cumulative Reduction Principle: Small WIP reductions accumulate.	Not sure what that means	**YES**
W23: The Principle of Visual WIP: Make WIP continuously visible.	Correct	**YES**

APPENDIX J – FLOW CONTROL PRINCIPLES

Mr. Reinertsen's Flow Control Principles	Throughput Accounting and Theory of Constraints and 5 FS	Agreement (YES/NO)
F1: The Principle of Congestion Collapse: When loading becomes too high, we will see a sudden and catastrophic drop in output.	I have not seen this in practice. What I have seen is lead times lengthen once a factory reaches its maximum output. But I have not seen the output itself collapse. JR	Interesting
F2: The Peak Throughput Principle: Control occupancy to sustain high throughput in systems prone to congestion.	DBR Buffer	YES
F3: The Principle of Visible Congestion: Use forecasts of expected flow time to make congestion visible.	Not sure how to apply to ToC as DBR aims at managing this	YES
F4: The Principle of Congestion Pricing: Use pricing to reduce demand during congested periods.	Agreed. Throughput rate through the constraint	YES
F5: The Principle of Periodic Resynchronization: Use a regular cadence to limit the accumulation of variance.	DBR signaling is meant for that. It does not come with a cadence per se however ... The DRUM is a cadence but replenishment is done with the buffer signals and the rope	YES and NO
F6: The Cadence Capacity Margin Principle: Provide sufficient capacity margin to enable cadence.	TA – TOC – Capacity is managed with the 3 types of capacity – Productive, Protective and Idle. Cadence does not apply in capacity as replenishment is done when required by an algorithm that sends a rope signal. But yes, there is a DRUM beat in DBR which is akin to a cadence without synchronization!	YES and NO
F7: The Cadence Reliability Principle: Use cadence to make waiting times predictable.	TA- TOC – Wait time is managed with DBR. The DRUM is a beat. Buffer and Rope are additional components.	YES and NO
F8: The Cadence Batch Size Enabling Principle: Use a regular cadence to enable small batch sizes.	TOC turns it around: It says release work into process when demand pulls it through, and that may or may not happen on a regular cadence. JR	YES and NO

F9: The Principle of Cadenced Meetings: Schedule frequent meetings using a predictable cadence.	Whether this is beneficial depends on the purpose of the meeting. If it's just communication about status, that can be done with email or a reporting app. If it's to make decisions, the schedule of meetings should correspond to decision points, which may not be frequent. For instance, it's pointless to schedule frequent meetings to discuss the annual budget outside the budget process, which is probably just one quarter or so. JR	YES
F10: The Synchronization Capacity Margin Principle: To enable synchronization, provide sufficient capacity margin.	Correct. ToC has 3 kinds: Productive, Protective and Excess	YES
F11: The Principle of Multiple project Synchronization: Exploit scale economies by synchronizing work from multiple projects.	Staggering functionality of CCPM and Buffer Fever Chart with multiple projects. Prevents from early start, parallelism and late completion like PMI CP. CCPM rather supports late start, limits parallelism and early completion of overall project. Buffers are to be found everywhere in PMI CPM. ToC CCM has one buffer at the end resulting in a plan that never changes. Every time an update occurs on a PMI CPM project, the critical path changes and creates chaos.	YES This assumes the projects all use the same resources and process – and synchronization reduces/eliminates conflicting demands. In software, however, projects do not scale that way. Adding more people to a late project makes it later [see Brooks' Law]. JR
F12: The Principle of Cross-Functional Synchronization: Use synchronized events to facilitate cross functional trade offs.	Correct. Nothing specific to ToC	YES
F13: The Synchronization Queueing Principle: To reduce queues, synchronize the batch size and timing of adjacent processes.	Principle F13 is a JIT system like concept as it is worded. In DBR, only the constraint is allowed to pull as opposed to a JIT system where each step can do so. The 'adjacent processes' is an acceptable construct if it is made of 1) all downstream processes taken as a whole and 2) all upstream processes taken as a whole.	YES and NO

	Read note from Dr Lisa Lang in chapter 2 regarding JIT buffers on adjacent processes: Having 'buffers' with column WIP limits at every process gate resembles JIT – Just in Time - systems where buffers are encountered at the entry point of every phase. These systems are very fragile and kill flow. When a problem occurs, the entire chain is impacted, and Special Cause Variation signals spiral out of control. DBR does not need 'speed bumps'. Problems at the constraint are reflective of Common Cause Variation. The flow from upstream of the constraint is based on *time*, not inventory. If a phase starves upstream and the constraint buffer is in a green state, there is no cause for concern. In a JIT system, that would trigger a chain reaction and be problematic in Knowledge-Work.	
F14: The Harmonic Principle: Make nested cadences harmonic multiples.	Do not know how to apply this to ToC	YES
F15: The SJF Scheduling Principle: When delay costs are homogeneous, do the shortest job first.	Correct for Flow Principles	YES
F16: The HDCF Scheduling Principle: When job durations are homogeneous, do the high cost-of-delay job first.	Correct for Flow Principles	YES
F17: The WSJF Scheduling Principle: When job durations and delay costs are not homogeneous, use WSJF.	Correct for Flow Principles	YES
F18: The Local Priority Principle: Priorities are inherently local.	Correct	YES
F19: The Round-Robin Principle: When task duration is unknown, time-share capacity.	DBR allows the system to self adjust and is passive to the 'duration' of a specific task. Capacity is always abundant, so time-sharing of it at non	YES and NO

	constraint point is a frequent habit.	
F20: The Preemption Principle: Only preempt when switching costs are low.	Nuance. Once committed respect queue discipline	**YES but**
F21: The Principle of Work Matching: Use sequence to match jobs to appropriate resources.	Correct	**YES**
F22: The Principle of Tailored Routing: Select and tailor the sequence of subprocesses to the task at hand.		**YES**
F23: The Principle of Flexible Routing: Route work based on the current most economic route.	Routing done on Throughput rate of highest value per unit of time at constraint	**YES but ...**
F24: The Principle of Alternate Routes: Develop and maintain alternate routes around points of congestion.	Do not know if can be applied to ToC , but should be feasible	**YES**
F25: The Principle of Flexible Resources: Use flexible resources to absorb variation.	Correct	**YES**
F26: The Principle of Late Binding: The later we bind demand to resources, the smoother the flow.	Correct	**YES**
F27: The Principle of Local Transparency: Make tasks and resources reciprocally visible at adjacent processes.	Correct ... Sprint capacity is all about that	**YES**
F28: The Principle of Preplanned Flexibility: For fast responses, preplan and invest in flexibility.	ToC – There are 3 kinds of capacity. All non constraint points have slack and extra capacity. Protective and Excess capacity bring flexibility. All non constraint points have excess capacity compared to the constraint	**YES**
F29: The Principle of Resource Centralization: Correctly managed, centralized resources can reduce queues.	TA – Aggregation principle by Dr John Ricketts, Etienne Du Plooy and Bob Sproull – Inventory and Resources are best held centrally because this is where consumption varies less.	**YES but ..** **Does this contradict E13? JR**
F30: The Principle of Flow Conditioning: Reduce variability before a bottleneck.	TA – 5 FS – DBR all geared towards this	**YES**

APPENDIX K – FAST FEEDBACK PRINCIPLES

Mr. Reinertsen's Fast Feedback Principles	Throughput Accounting and Theory of Constraints and 5 FS	Agreement (YES/NO)
FF1: The Principle of Maximum Economic Influence: Focus control on project and process parameters with the highest economic influence.	Focus on constraint and 5 FS	**YES**
FF2: The Principle of Efficient Control: Control parameters that are both influential and efficient.	TA – TH, OE and I ... Buffer Sizing ... Buffer penetration ... Buffer Signals	**YES**
FF3: The Principle of Leading Indicators: Select control variables that predict future system behavior.	TA & CCPM – Use all leading indicators that support management by exception	**YES**
FF4: The Principle of Balanced Set Points: Set tripwires at points of equal economic impact.	CCPM and DBR buffer penetration signals --- TH, OE and I The only point that matters – and it is mandatory - is at the constraint as it can affect the up time of the constraint.	**YES and NO** You can have as many tripwires as you wish any where else as there is sufficient capacity for such activities to take place. They would not impact costs. To that end I like the Zero metrics shown in Appendix C
FF5: The Moving Target Principle: Know when to pursue a dynamic goal.	Etienne De Plooy – Absolute Profitability (Net Profit) TH-OE - Throughput less Operating Expenses determines a system's Net Profit from operations In addition to Net Profit, it depicts the speeds of total System Throughput and total system Operating Expenses *It is also relevant to the change and progression of profits* ***through time*** *due to decisions, strategies and tactics* The GOAL may be revisited as needed. However, once it is agreed upon, the constraint location musts remain in place.	**YES and NO** **In "Exceeding the Goal" I describe receding goals as those that become harder to achieve over time. For instance, the goal to grow 7% per year may not sound like a big deal until you realize that the absolute goal doubles over 10 years. Thus, it's not always a matter of knowing when to pursue a dynamic**

		goal, sometimes they are set inadvertently. JR
FF6: The Exploitation Principle: Exploit unplanned economic opportunities.	TA – Dr John Ricketts – Time Principle - Maximize utilisation of the constraint – Time lost on the constraint is time lost forever	YES
FF7: The Queue Reduction Principle of Feedback: Fast feedback enables smaller queues.	DBR buffer penetration signals and CCPM execution signals are meant to tame Common Cause and support small queue sizes	YES
FF8: The Fast-Learning Principle: Use fast feedback to make learning faster and more efficient	Common Cause Variation is where the low hanging fruits are. ToC is fully geared to that end.	YES
FF9: The Principle of Useless Measurement: What gets measured may not get done.	TA – Measure at constraint only. Anywhere else is not impacting Financial Throughput. Keep few 'smart' metrics for subordination as this is the most difficult to do properly	YES TOC says people will behave according to how they are measured. If those personal performance metrics are misaligned with the business goal, conflict results. JR
FF10: The First Agility Principle: We don't need long planning horizons when we have a short turning radius.	Correct	YES
FF11: The Batch Size Principle of Feedback: Small batches yield fast feedback.	Correct	YES
FF12: The Signal to Noise Principle: To detect a smaller signal, reduce the noise.	How can this be applied to ToC. Buffers?	YES
FF13: The Decision Rule Principle: Control the economic logic behind the decision, not the entire decision.	Dr John Ricketts – Capacity principle - Unbalanced capacity is more productive because the Constraint can be used to manage the entire system	YES
FF14: The Locality Principal of Feedback: Whenever possible make feedback local.	Correct	YES
FF15: The Relief Valve Principle: Have a clear, predetermined relief valve.	Correct	YES
FF16: The Principle of Multiple Control Loops: Embed fast control loops inside slow loops.	Manage the entire system by managing the constraint	YES Question: Could this be OODA loops? JR

FF17: The Principle of Controlled Excursions: Keep deviations within the control range.	Management by exception – DBR- Delta TH, Delta I and Delta OE	YES
FF18: The Feedforward Principle: Provide advance notice of heavy arrival rates to minimize queues.	DBR – Queues are minimized by using a pull approach. Push is disabled and that reduces the odds of heavy arrival. When the buffer emits a signal, it is time to enter more tickets in the system.	Indirectly The only way this works is if advance notice enables acquisition/set-up of additional sprint capacity. If added capacity isn't available, advance notice won't help. That's why numerous container ships are anchored off the West Coast instead of unloading at the docks. JR
FF18: The Feedforward Principle: Provide advance notice of heavy arrival rates to minimize queues.	ToC self adjusts with DBR	YES
FF19: The Principle of Colocation: Colocation improves almost all aspects of communications.	Correct	YES
FF20: The Empowerment Principle of Feedback: Fast feedback gives a sense of control.	Correct	YES
FF21: The Hurry-Up-and-Wait Principle: Large queues make it hard to create urgency.	Correct	YES
FF22: The Amplification Principle: The human element tends to amplify large excursions.	Humans are exposed to Group Think, Anchoring, are bad at integrating data and are emotional. The ToC and TA are meant to serve as an equalizer ...	YES
FF23: The Principle of Overlapping Measurement: To align behaviors, reward people for the work of others.	TOC - POOGI – Has a bonus system design to that end. POOGI is the same as the 5 FS.	YES
FF24: The Attention Principle: Time counts more than money.	The best way to have Throughput go thru the roof is to cut the cash-to-cash cycle. But a deep discussion takes place on that topic for Knowledge-Work in the Mafia offer chapter.	YES

APPENDIX L – DECENTRALISATION PRINCIPLES

Mr. Reinertsen's Decentralisation Principles	**Throughput Accounting and Theory of Constraints and 5 FS**	**Agreement (YES/NO)**
D1: The Second Perishability Principle: Decentralize control for problems and opportunities that age poorly.	All decisions are made easier in TA	YES
D2: The Scale Principle: Centralize control for problems that are infrequent, large, or that have significant economies of scale.	TA – Dr John Ricketts – Aggregation Principle - Inventory and resources are best held centrally because that is where consumption varies least	YES
D3: The Principle of Layered Control: Adapt the control approach to emerging information about the problem.	Correct. Orthogonal to ToC	YES
D4: The Opportunistic Principle: Adjust the plan for unplanned obstacles and opportunities.	TA – Dr John Ricketts – The Buffer Principle - Strategically placed units or time for contingencies minimize the spread of disruptions across an entire system	YES
D5: The Principle of Virtual Centralization: Be able to quickly reorganize decentralized resources to create centralized power.	Excess, protective, and idle capacity also have the mission to create sprint capacity (upstream) of the constraint So, be ready to use all capacity at non constraint to support the constraint (exploit and elevate)	YES but ... De/centralization aren't easy to reverse, and whether such action improves management is debatable. Every improvement is a change, but not every change is an improvement. JR
D6: The Inefficiency Principle: The inefficiency of decentralization can cost less than the value of faster response time.	Dr John Ricketts: The TOC Profit Principle: Assuming TH represents value, and assuming OE & I represent cost of decentralization, given NP = TH - OE - I If $\Delta TH > \Delta OE + \Delta I$, then $\Delta NP > 0$ The TOC Profit principle puts the spotlight on effectiveness instead of the Inefficiency principle	YES and NO Sometimes the ease of decision-making with E8 and E10 is warranted. And finding the impact on costs can be easier in some circumstances and lead to the correct conclusion

	(D16) that is putting the focus on cost. TA is always more conscious on generating TH than it is on reducing costs, all other things being equal. JR	
D7: The Principle of Alignment: There is more value created with overall alignment than local excellence.	Once the GOAL is set and the constraint strategically placed, all adjacent resources must subordinate to the constraint	YES and ... Conglomerates rely on local excellence with only loose overall alignment. GE and HP are examples of companies that contradict this principle: They spun off / broke up because the value was in the parts rather than in overall alignment. JR
D8: The Principle of Mission: Specify the end state, its purpose, and the minimal possible constraints.	5 FS – Setting the GOAL is the premise of the 5 Focusing Steps. It is often called step 0. Step 7 being where to freeze the constraint at a strategic location Etienne du Plooy – TA Principle 9 - TH/OE - Throughput per (divided by) Operating Expenses determines the **productivity** of the system. Is a measure to ascertain if the system is moving towards the goal	YES
D9: The Principle of Boundaries: Establish clear roles and boundaries.	Daniel Doiron – I think what Mr. Reinertsen is referring here are invisible electric fences!	YES
D10: The Main Effort Principle: Designate a main effort and subordinate other activities.	TA – Exploiting the Constraint and subordinating to the constraint at non constraint points	YES
D11: The Principle of Dynamic Alignment: The main effort may shift quickly when conditions change.	ToC- One day you may be Herbie and need help!	YES
D12: The Second Agility Principle: Develop the ability to quickly shift focus.	TA- Dr John Ricketts - Utilisation principle: The only utilization that matters is on the Constraint	YES and NO

	Non constraint have plenty of slack and should not 'over react' to anything except when to feed the constraint.	
D13: The Principle of Layered Control: Adapt the control approach to emerging information about the problem.	DBR signaling and Buffer penetration are the place to look for information. To many or too few signals are a sign of problems	YES
D14: The Principle of Flexible Plans: Use simple modular plans.	Correct	YES
D15: The Principle of Tactical Reserves: Decentralize a portion of reserves.	Correct but most must remain centralized	YES
D16: The Principle of Early Contact: Make early and meaningful contact with the problem.	5FS – Prevent Inertia from becoming the constraint – Identify, Exploit, Subordinate and Elevate the constraint	YES Early contact and inertia are at opposite ends of the time scale. Furthermore, D16 doesn't say anything about inertia, and 5FS don't say anything about early contact. JR
D17: The Principle of Decentralized Information: For decentralized decisions, disseminate key information widely.	Correct	YES
D18: The Frequency Response Principle: We can't respond faster than our frequency response.	TA – Dr John Ricketts – Capacity principle - Unbalanced capacity is more productive because the Constraint can be used to manage the entire system	YES
D19: The Quality of Service Principle: When response time is important, measure response time.	TA – Sprint capacity before the constraint must always be improved. Throughput rate at the constraint is a main focus of Common Cause variation worry. DBR buffer is designed to prevent the constraint from starving, to warn of potential upstream problems, reduce WIP and optimize Throughput and Lead Time	YES
D20: The Second Market Principle: Use internal and external markets to decentralize control.	Correct	YES
D21: The Principle of Regenerative Initiative: Cultivating initiative enables us to use initiative.	Inherent Simplicity and all of the science behind ToC is meant for all to consume. So, locally all can	YES

	understand the basics behind Throughput, Investments and Operating Expenses. It is in line with decentralized decision making.	
D22: The Principle of Face-to-Face Communication: Exploit the speed and bandwidth of face-to-face communications.	Correct. Especially upstream	**YES**
D23: The Trust Principle: Trust is built through experience.	And with proven delivery	**YES**

EPILOGUE – MINTING MONEY & NEW ORTHODOXY

"He can run, but he can't hide" – Joe Louis

Global Scrum Gathering Berlin - 2014

In 2014, I was looking to doing something different for a living. Something that can bring happiness. I was literally unhappy professionally and tiptoed first into the world of agility. I started with Scrum, with which I grew tired of very quickly as it were. But it was a dominant – and still is – force in the market. I had never heard of Kanban at that time nor of the Blue Book that Mr. Reinertsen wrote the foreword to.[197] That changed in Berlin. Kanban is how my brain works.

Mr, Reinertsen and Mr. Snowden of Cynefin were both invited as Keynote speakers. They were outstanding and delivered their material effortlessly. I engaged with both of them and they were very generous with me.

The only common part of both keynotes: nuclear powered Navy submarines! There is a twist.

This section was not meant to be. I wanted an introduction and the usual progression to its finality. Now this book has a Prologue, meant as an Introduction, and an Epilogue, which you are reading now.

Back to my book. Here is what happened. It is an actual story.

As I was getting feedback from some very noteworthy connoisseurs, a very interesting twist came about with my exchanges with Mr. Reinertsen: 'The most successful business books provide reasons for changing behaviors' said he.

Changing behaviors takes time and doing so in my book would take me to a path that I could not even phantom as to what the first refactoring step could be. All sort of ideas crossed my mind.

Mr. Reinertsen served as a US Navy officer on nuclear submarines, my feedback loop had this message to convey to my stomach[198]:

'Your submarine just sank.'

I literally stopped for a month trying to decipher how to thread the needle of this new recipe as my book was basically done after one year of hard work. The format just was not proper to convey this new delivery and the new scope was similar to 'boiling the ocean' for me.

Here is what I had to do according to Mr. Reinertsen[199]:

Your book needs to show:

---

[197] In his foreword to the Blue Book, Mr. Reinertsen in adamant with Toyota Production Systems: TPS is first and foremost about small batches.

[198] I am very well versed in civil nuclear energy matters.

[199] These lines are almost ad verbatim and taken from Mr. Reinertsen

I. This is what you are doing today (operating at high utilisation) and maybe how you (incorrectly) justify it internally
II. Here is the problem it creates and mechanism by which it creates the problem. (e.g. queueing theory shows that this will create expensive queues)
III. Here's what you should do differently and what is likely to happen. (e.g. control start rate to keep load below 80% and cycle times will go down)

After my downed submarine, I remembered the now eternal one liner that Mr. Reinertsen serves in all his classes: 'You can't get there from here'.

I did not know what to do next, but the 3 points structure just above is also a great approach to craft and initiate Mafia offers. I could get there from here if I were I to get out of the book constraint and put this mantra when I offer professional services. You always have to sell your approach when making Mafia offers. The idea could survive, but outside the book.

Since the title of my book is 'Seeing Money Clearly', all I had left to do was help the reader mint money with a general recipe that is known to work for all companies. A 'show me the money' twist.

One morning, I woke up full of energy. In his keynote conclusion, Mr. Snowden told a funny story which ended like this:

'Submarines are meant to sunk.'

Live another day. This chapter is the consequence of all this.

Introduction

In the context delimited by the good advice of Mr. Reinertsen, a book about 'Seeing Money Clearly' would not be complete without showing you where it lies and how to 'mint' it. Minting money is all about the marginal impact of our decisions as it was demonstrated with Throughput Accounting: increase (T) – Throughput, decrease (I) - Investments and then decrease (OE) – Operational Expenses. The order is important as (I) being the denominator of ROI – Return on Investment – it is beneficial that it be lowered before (OE) when given a choice. Some authors say that what counts is the bottom-line result. To a point yes. But when in doubt, always favor (I) over (OE) for the lever effect.[200]

Minting money happens in real time when decisions are made in front of your boards – Flow Efficiency or DBR or Throughput board, the latter being fully detailed in my first book. Here we are no longer talking n terms of deltas but rather in terms of operational excellence: understanding how money and costs matter happen in real time in front of you!

Remember how we have found a way to engage teams emotionally in front of the board? The Flow Efficiency boards discussed in chapter 3 work to attain that goal as workers make their own arbitrage within their work process as to what waits and what gets done. Both queues (Waiting for and In Progress) are actively managed queues over which you have full control.

A big advantage compared to other designs.

With a DBR – Drum Buffer Rope[201] – board, teams can actually mint money in real time by either ensuring that the constraint remains busy and also by understanding how to monetize the notions of waste, inspection and free products to impact the bottom line and reduce operational risks. We are talking decision-making and actions at the individual, team, project or portfolio level that will 'preserve' or 'mutate' into green money assuredly.

This knowledge beats 'engaging'. This means empowerment in a decentralized fashion as per the following Economic Principles from Mr. Reinertsen's book below:

Economic Principles – DBR Boards
E1: The Principle of Quantified Overall Economics: Select actions based on quantified overall economic impact.
E4: The Principle of Economic Value-Added: The value added by an activity is the change in the economic value of the work product.
E8: The Principle of Small Decisions: Influence the many small decisions.
E9: The Principle of Continuous Economic Trade-offs: Economic choices must be made continuously.
E10: The First Perishability Principle: Many economic choices are more valuable when made quickly.
E13: The Principle of Decision Rules: Use decision rules to decentralize economic control.
E14: The First Market Principle: Ensure decision makers feel both cost and benefit.
E15: The Principle of Optimum Decision Timing: Every decision has its optimum economic timing.

[200] Many authors are favouring open source code to decrease the magnitude of (I), which makes sense. In doing so, are they increasing the operational complexity (OE) of their IT environment? This is never discussed and it should.

[201] My first book also addresses a more sophisticated DBR board – The Throughput Board which deals with both the upstream and downstream health of the system.

E16: The Principle of Marginal Economics: Always compare marginal cost to marginal value.

Mr. Reinertsen's entire array of FF – Fast Feedback Principles - also apply to the letter with minting money. Those principles were addressed at length in Chapter 6.

Minting Money - Execution of the Work

The below illustration defines a common process. It shows where the constraint is along with the capacities on the value stream. The BUILD phase has the least capacity – by design and by strategic choice – and will not change. Why? Because a constraint is under active management. Those arguing that in Knowledge-Work the bottlenecks always move are absolutely right as they are not managed. It is not the case for a constraint as it is not meant to move ideally.

If there is one lesson to be learnt by 'agile' and 'Kanban' in this book, it must be this one: constraints can be pinned when managed.[202]

Sprint capacity is defined as that sum of capacities upstream of the constraint. It is important to realize as those working upstream must always find ways – with brown money and SLACK – to get things done faster so that the reaction time to the constraint is always improving. Indirectly, it is a form of elevation of the constraint, step 4 of the 5 Focusing Steps. Usually, Elevation of the constraint requires green money and comes later in the 5 FS. Not in this case.

Elevation of the constraint can also cause it to move. Be wary of that and make sure you add adequate capacity upstream and downstream and then act to elevate the constraint. Cutting senselessly in OE – Operating Expenses can also make the constraint shift.

[202] It is not as if there is not market acceptance for this as countless consulting firms in Europe do in fact conduct business under this umbrella!

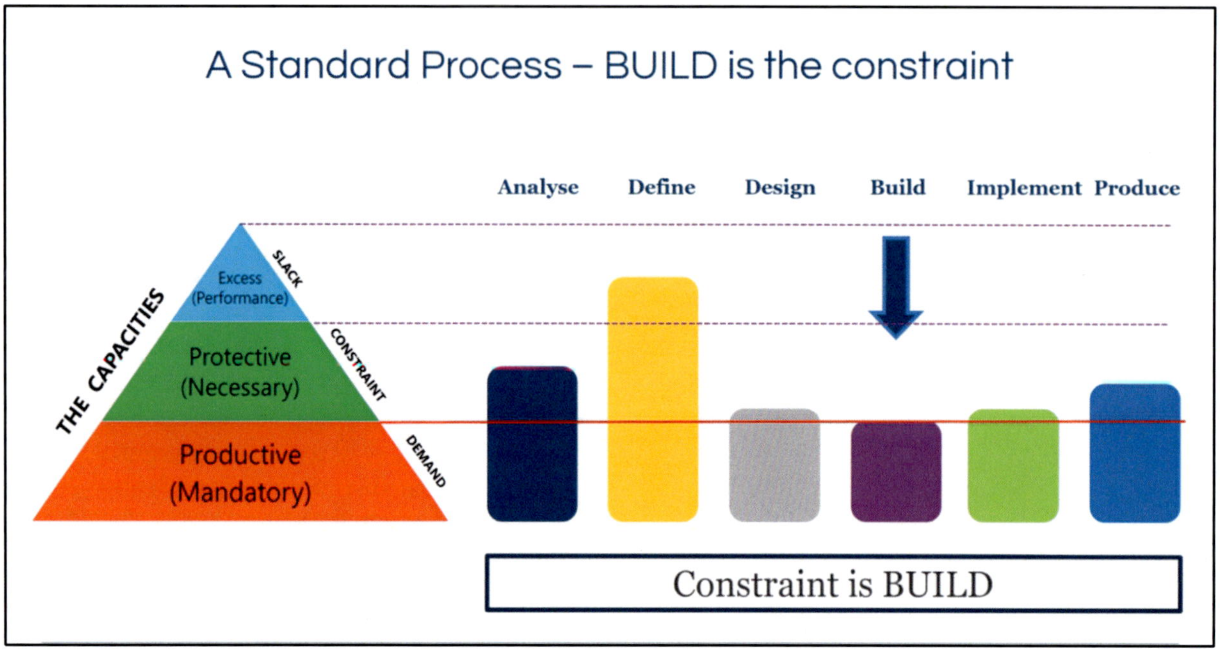

Once your CCPM plan is done and ready to be executed, it becomes a money minting press and the only valid plan. An actionable plan – managed by the team in a decentralized way - full of monetary consequences for the bottom line! Workers need no permission to print that money!

The CCPM plan will engage workers emotionally more than any other plan as you will directly impact the economics of your product on a daily basis. And the critical chain in a CCPM plan never changes as the buffer absorbs all the shocks. In a CPM plan from the PMI, every time you hit the enter key, the critical path changes and you are in for a date with entropy. Variance analysis and reports will be on the agenda. Those critical path changes are not management by exception signals. They just occur whenever you hit the enter key.

Protection of Throughput

Appearing below in point form are my preferred tips regarding Throughput preservation.

- Management by exception is sustainable only with the generation of signals. No one system can generate signals if it cannot differentiate – at the design level - between Common Cause and Special Cause. The buffers were explicitly designed by Dr Goldratt with that objective in mind.
- The TOE spread – the different between (T) - Throughput and (OE) - Operating Expenses – is the entry point for the financing of (I) Investment and assets. This cannot be overlooked in a growth mindset. This simple heuristic suggests that the decoupling of T and OE can aid to find the internal sources of funding before calling on the market for external funds.
- And lastly, applying religiously the first 3 steps of the 5FS has no equal. I cannot think of any other managerial stratagem that can be associated so rightfully with causality as the results are felt immediately. All other Improvement Initiatives model do not focus on the constraint and require green money at the get go.

Target Scope - Managing the client and the CCPM plan

There are a lot of benefits to crafting CCPM plans and monitoring the execution of the work as depicted in chapter 3. We live in a variance free world with CCPM where there are no other alternative than forging ahead and looking forward. Buffer signals aid us in adapting. Time absorbs variability.

CCPM focusses on the execution of the work that was previously planned. And in so doing effortlessly, it gives you the following weaponry already covered in chapter 3:

- CCPM Buffer Consumption – a dynamic metric that indicates how much of the CCPM buffer has been consumed, how many days more – as a percentage of the total buffer – than the original baseline that we are anticipating to finish.
- CCPM Buffer Burn Rate – the buffer burn rate tells you how fast/slow you are progressing to the schedule's original plan.
- Staggering: To appraise late or early starts of projects and share that information for the sake of coordination.
- The new CCPM Rope signal, with a blue color and will be covered later in this chapter.

Your CCPM plan captures all the variations trapped in the CCPM buffer. From there you can manage both the buffer consumption and the buffer burn rate to ascertain the pace at which you are marching toward the goal. Staggering is a nice feature of the buffer consumption to help you orchestrate pending work.

Can you think of anything more agile?

Let 's reflect on the approach that LKU – now Kanban University – had a few years ago. Kanban's forte is with probabilistic forecasting leveraging empirical data that you have collected for your environment.

What should we do now, later or never can be supported at the daily operational level with great clarity while using probabilistic forecasting. For example, during the daily meeting, the discussion as to what to do next can be nailed in the following sharp exchanges: 'A report takes 3 days, 80% of the time and an interface takes 4 days 95% of the time'. Is it time now or later? In all cases it is a tool to postpone commitment, make the right decision and transfer the risk from when we should finish to when work should start, empowering in the process the client and sharing the risk.

This works for that kind of short feedback settings and it is a great way to share the latest 'start of work' date parameters with both clients and teams.

But if you would like a two-week plan or a one-month target scope as illustrated in this book, then no flavor of Kanban stretches that far as 'time makes a mockery of all our planning and estimating efforts'. Longer horizons initiatives are not really part of the mix unless things have changed. DJA was not against plans at the time but never acted to physicalize the concept.

Target scope plans also have their own probabilistic mantra that solder the 50% CCPM buffer with a Lead Time distribution that splits the data at 50% with a Due Date Probability of 80%.

This sounds quite Kanbanesque if you ask me. I think it is a question of time before the now many Kanban communities start using CCPM plans.

You would be ill advised however were you to consider using the data that was narrated above to make a CCPM plan based on individual work item averages. It would be catastrophic.

Let's build a one-month target scope plan with the data used in the context above. I am not saying that the data or the approach are bad, but you will fall right in Lucas' critique arms in doing so. I am saying it simply does not scale as is. It needs a little splash of Little's Law.[203]

The following data about Throughput is available. It comes from different sources and is of good quality. It shows the variety of work items as well as their individual average characteristics.

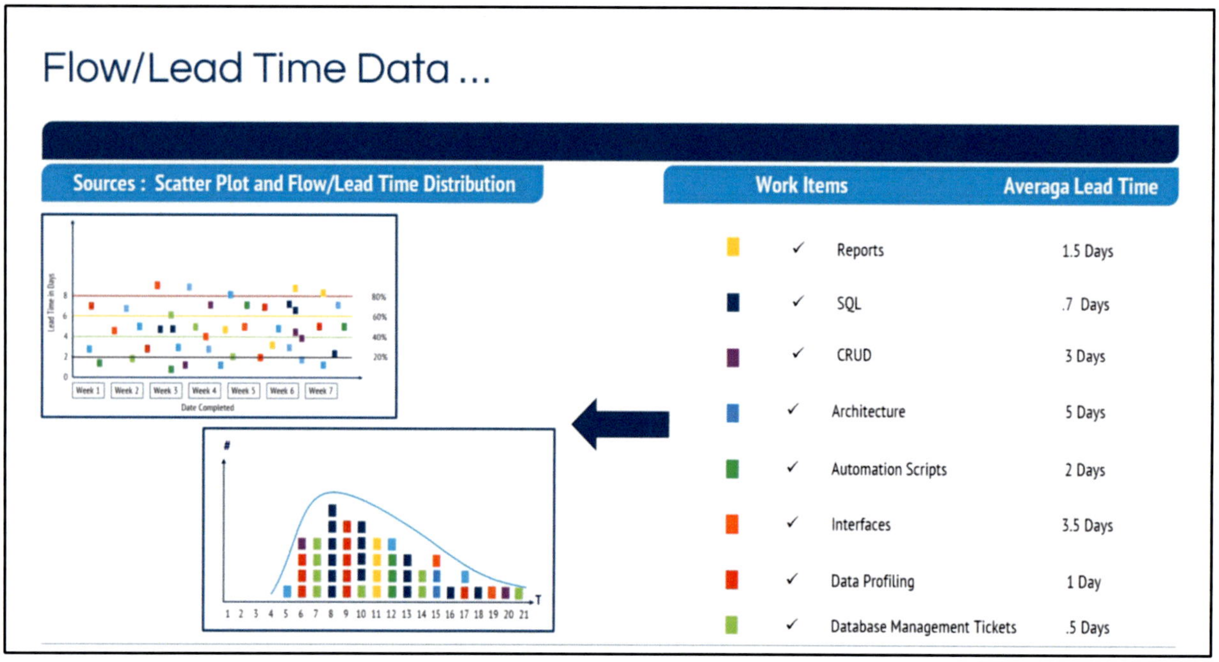

The following steps that I will do are partly wrong and mostly right, but they are intuitive. They build on what would be done on a shorter span project of 3-5 days. But in this case, I am building a target scope, aiming for a calendar of one month.

With the way you are used to work à la Kanban, I will tally my CCPM plan as follows with the specs I need to deliver:

[203] You might recall that I am not a fan of meetings. Adopting the longer horizon of target scope and leveraging the proper signals for management by exception with the buffers will reduce the actual number of meetings. To tame coordination and transaction costs, the meetings should always be planned to make cadences and synchronisation effective. I am all in favor of using cadences and synchronisation at will.

FLAWED CCPM PLAN

Work Item	Average Lead Time	Quantity	Total Time
Reports	1.5	10	15
Data Profiling	1	8	8
Architecture	2	5	10
CRUD	3	3	9
TOTAL CCPM Chain		26	42
CCPM BUFFER (50%)			21
Project Total			63

This seems actionable. But the bottom line of the forecast is wrong. First, adding averages together to further divide them to have averages again will not fare too well with those who understand statistics.

The recovery is not complicated however. We need a 'Little' help. The only thing that is right and required is the 'Quantity' tally of work items to be delivered. This sizes the target scope project.

In order to banalize all of this average data properly, we must strip off the granularity of the above table and think like you were versed with Little's Law at birth:

- Variability in work item size does not matter
- All work items are the same and not differentiable
- A work item that enters the system must exit the system. A simple count is needed (remember the Theory of Constraint does leverage the deterministic side of Little's Law, i.e. counting stuff)

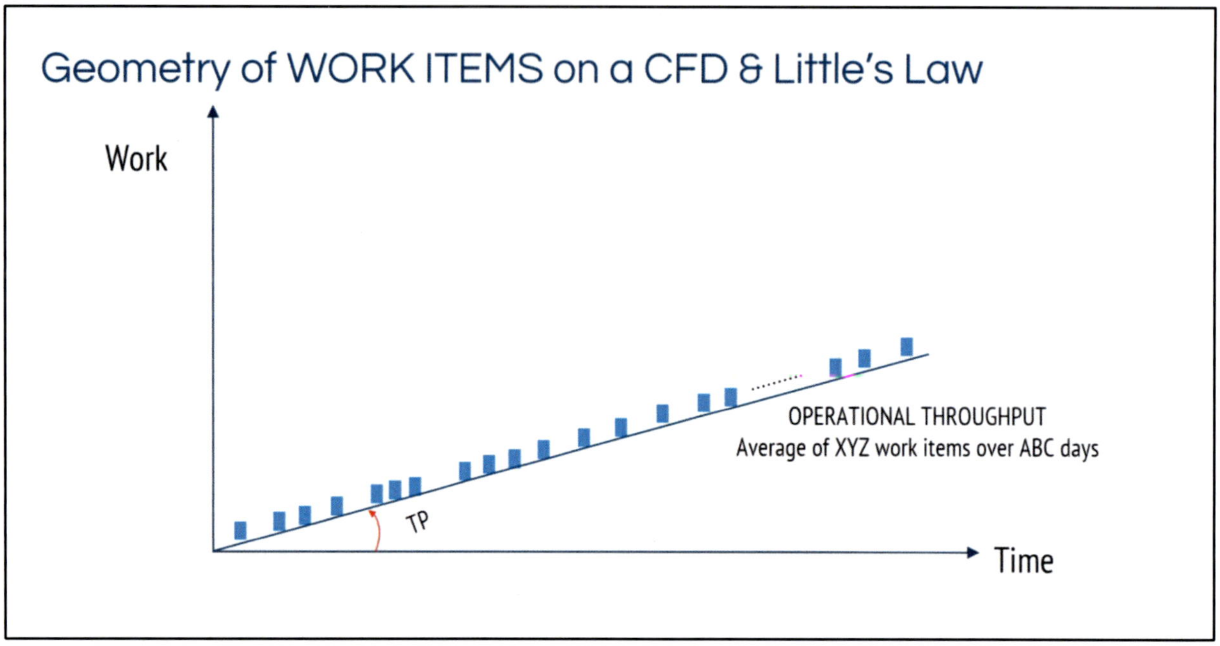

The graph above contains only one type of work item – we have banalized them all with the color blue – and the average size is the same. We count the 'stuff' that gets out over a period of days. Reports, data profiling, architecture deliverables are no more, though they do exist in reality we need to banalize them. They are just work items. Their individual size is of no concern. Little's Law is about averages, is it not? This is how the Theory of Constraints uses Little's Law.

After proper research, the following array is tallied up for target scope projects of all magnitude:

DECISION MAKING ARRAY

# Work Items	CFD Avg Time	Buffer Size	Total Time
10	7	3.5	10.5
11	8	4	12
....			
25	15	7.5	22.5
26	**17**	**8.5**	**25.5**
27	22	11	33
...			
30	25	12.5	37.5
31	26	13	39

The proper conclusion is that the original plan consisting of 26 items – no matter what they are – will take an average total time of 25.5 days. Not 63!

The instinct we had to get to a target scope duration is good. Just do without the individual work items statistics to avoid bad math and use operational throughput data instead.

You'll do fine and within a day or two, you could even get started leveraging the time dimension with a CCPM plan!

Note that the table can be used for projects of all average work item counts. It will yield the proper duration including the buffer size.

The Cash Engine

We still need to nail how we generate money. Minting deals with understanding our cost functions – that which lies upstream and downstream of the constraint mostly – in order to leverage to the fullest our capacity to generate Throughput. We will cover many such topics in the next sections. But what about making money per se?

This is where the table we just presented above for manufacturing must be nuanced. In manufacturing, each widget comes with its prize: the time spent at the constraint.

In Knowledge-Work, what matters is to understand that whatever goes thru the constraint will be pure octane for the DBR engine. This is why the various work items - with their different lead times - were 'Littlelized' with average operational throughput value yielded by Little Law's when we made the CCPM plan. If it is good for the CCPM plan, it is good for the speed at which work items go thru the constraint and generate money.

There is really no need to arbitrage what goes in based on individual work item statistics. Just prioritize as you normally would. It won't matter what scenario comes up. No other architecture will get the work done faster anyway! Little's Law just says that First in – First serve is a good proxy for attaining good results.

Here are the four steps to design your cash engine as illustrated below:

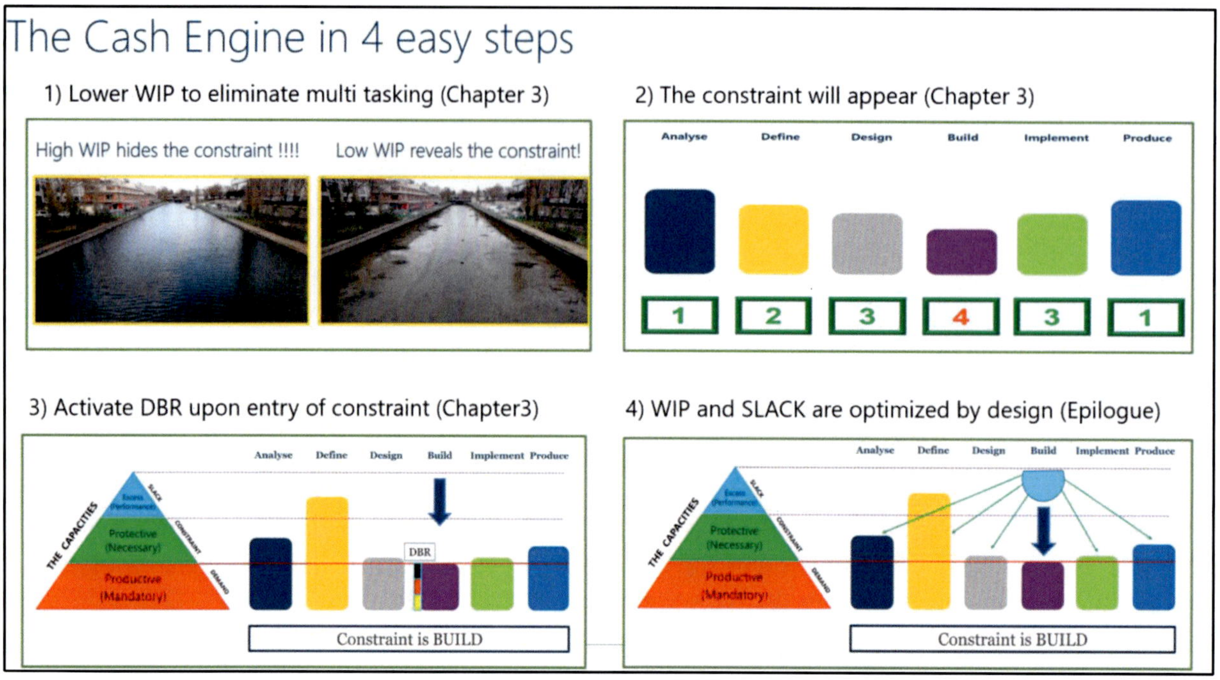

Free Products, Negative Covariance and Execution Risk

Talking about free products feels a bit odd since in Throughput Accounting, products have no costs and therefore the notion of profits per product is inconsequential.

But there is such a thing as 'free products' in Throughput Accounting and it applies to Knowledge-Work as well.

Anytime one of your products does not go thru the constraint – 'BUILD' in this case - it is deemed a free product. Design work and architecture specs never go thru the constraint and can rightfully be considered free products!

Such free products also have an impact on risk mitigation and execution. Here I will simply point to Mr. Reinertsen's Variability Principles V5 and V10:

Variability Principles – V5 and V10
V5: The Principle of Variability Pooling: Overall variation decreases when uncorrelated random tasks are combined.
V10: The Principle of Negative Covariance: We can reduce variance by applying a counterbalancing effect.

You can revisit chapter 6 to see the entire set of Variability Principles as well and their applicability while minting money. In short, not exploiting the constraint by having free products uncorrelated to the use of the constraint can still generate value at no cost.

The impact on execution risk of introducing such free products in the pipeline leads to negative covariance which decreases the overall coefficient of variation.

Inspection Points

You can have as many inspection points as you wish before and after the constraint. It is not an issue – in terms of costs - as everywhere we benefit from that free capacity on top and above of the constraint's requirements.

But you must have an inspection point upon entering the constraint and the reason is quite obvious. Before the constraint, you have not engaged the constraint and therefore it has not missed a beat. No money lost. No opportunity cost. No waste.

After the constraint, the economics change. You have had your cycle at the constraint and were you to forfeit that cycle, you would lose valuable financial Throughput, thus the mandatory inspection required upon entering the constraint.

This is a perfect match with Fast Feedback Flow Principle FF4: Set tripwires at points of equal economic impact.

Setup, Coordination & Transaction Costs

Certain activities are necessary. That is not the main concern. What matters is the economics while dealing with setup, coordination and transaction costs.

No managerial scrutiny is required but at the constraint. More than enough capacity will prevail everywhere else.

Here is an illustration of certain costs that get absorbed by excess capacity, or paid for with brown money if you prefer:

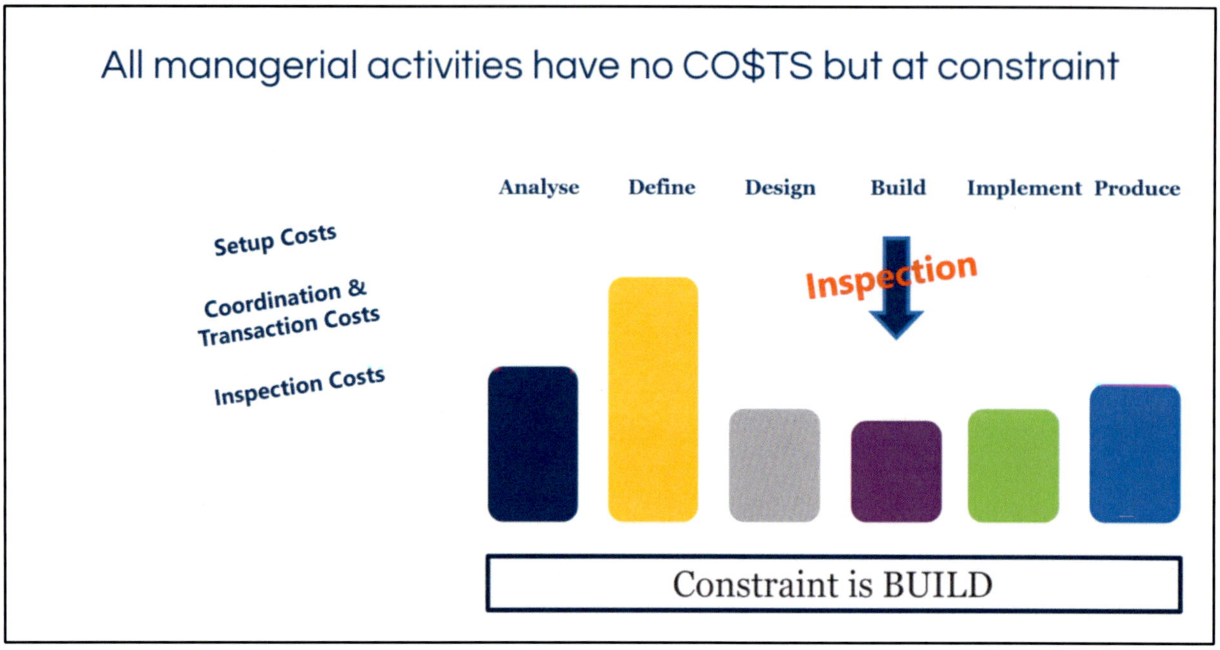

Waste – Where You Stand Matters!

Waste is observed after the constraint when we discard a product. Before the constraint, it has no economic impact and talking waste is just not sharp. The further down the ride downstream after the constraint, the higher the CO$TS as you abandon ship. Once at the Implement phase as per the illustration below, the cost will be less significant than if the product was scrapped at the Produce point.

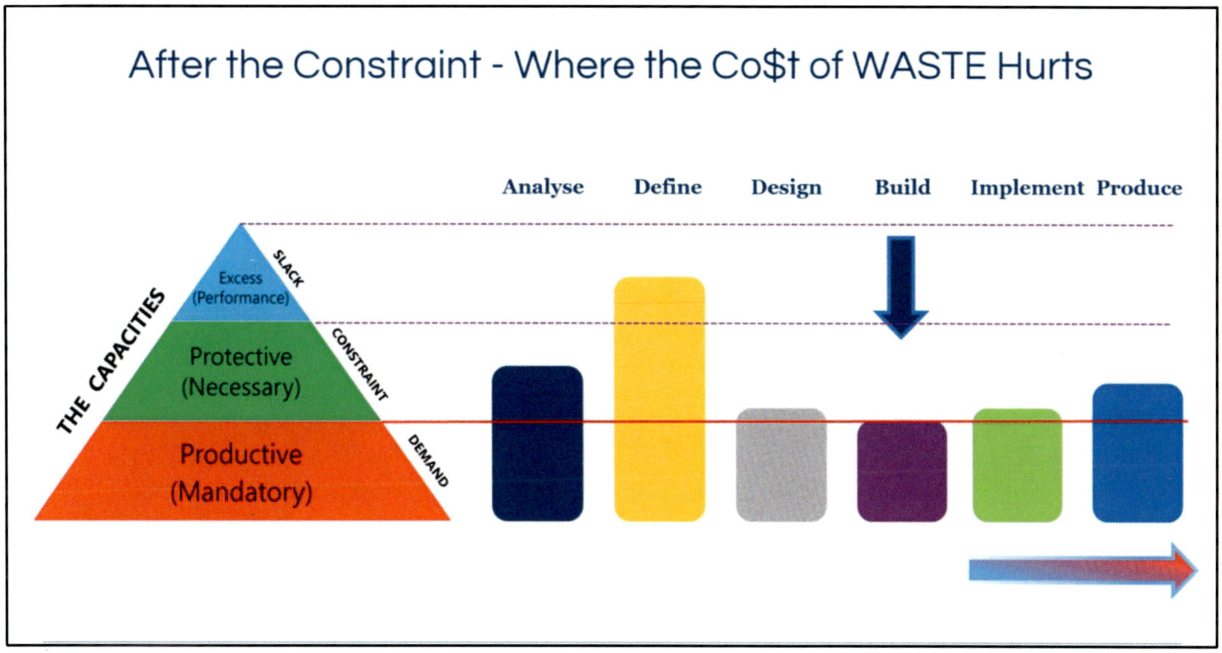

This is an important concept as one should take all the care and time required to tame the 'fuzzy font end' properly before landing at the doorstep of the constraint.

There is no point in arguing that the more 'effort' spent in properly designing or analyzing a topic is a source of waste. Quite to the contrary. Discovering that things are not acceptable after the constraint is a sin if it could have been discovered upstream of the constraint, where there are no opportunity costs to be had.

Cut me some S L A C K

We all heard the idiom: 'idle work or idle worker'. High performance organisations require slack – or idleness- to reach stellar levels of financial returns. This is why slack made the cut.

SLACK also belongs to the 'Minting Money' section as it is the propellor to create sprint capacity. Sprint capacity is the way we use brown money to increase our ability to respond to the needs to of constraint should it require better, faster response time from the upstream pipe.

Managerial scrutiny is uncalled for – well mostly - when we are away from the constraint. Lo and behold, SLACK strives where capacity is plentiful and requires zero human, system or concern as to its attribute since – to the risk of sounding repetitive – it is odorless, invisible, indivisible, not measurable and certainly intangible. Leave SLACK alone and get some rest instead.

SLACK need not be managed actively when subordinating to the constraint as taught by the Theory of Constraints. SLACK lives upstream and downstream of the constraint and there is nothing you can – or should – do about it. There are smarts - and not so smart - ways of acting with SLACK. Creating sprint capacity is an adequate use of SLACK. Using SLACK to keep busy and create excess Inventory is just pure nonsense. Go fishing or play cards. But when the constraint calls, you need to step up to the plate as they say in baseball.[204]

In chapter 2, when addressing capacity and WIP levels in the 'Corbett sanction' section, there is one thing I did not mention as I wanted to save it in the context of SLACK management. If you revisit that section, you need be reminded that reducing WIP without protective capacity at the constraint is not next to impossible. In a ToC world, it is outright impossible.[205]

Many flavors of 'agile' and 'Kanban' believe that merely reducing WIP creates SLACK. It is an example of useless tampering with the system which fosters Special Cause Variation signals. Reducing WIP when respecting the Theory of Constraints' mantras will create SLACK if the constraint is properly managed and all 3 types of capacities are well understood. Let's get this over with now in anticipation of the sheer madness of the things we do for the sake of SLACK idolisation.

I need to fetch some science from Donald Reinertsen's principles again. SLACK needs a proxy variable as it cannot be observed nor managed per se.

That proxy variable is 'capacity utilisation' and its twin brother queue size. We need to thank Mr. Reinertsen for seeing this clearly a long time ago for Knowledge-Work. It is still totally appropriate today.

So, let's take this in mind and see what we can do by understanding the illustration that follows which I collated from the work of Mr. Reinertsen – Principle Q3.

Once capacity utilisation reaches 80%, queues are likely to get out of control: a situation we want to avoid as it will destroy all hopes of having any SLACK.

[204] In sports, I think Baseball best illustrates SLACK. When the situation arises, you need to explode and execute defensively. When the pitching staff is having an excellent day, no one wastes an ounce of energy on the field. In both scenario the pitcher is the constraint and is 100% busy.

[205] There are a lot of variables involved in this discussion and it is not so obvious and can seem twisted at times. But Mr. Corbett makes a very good case of it in his book. My book goes a step further with Little's Law.

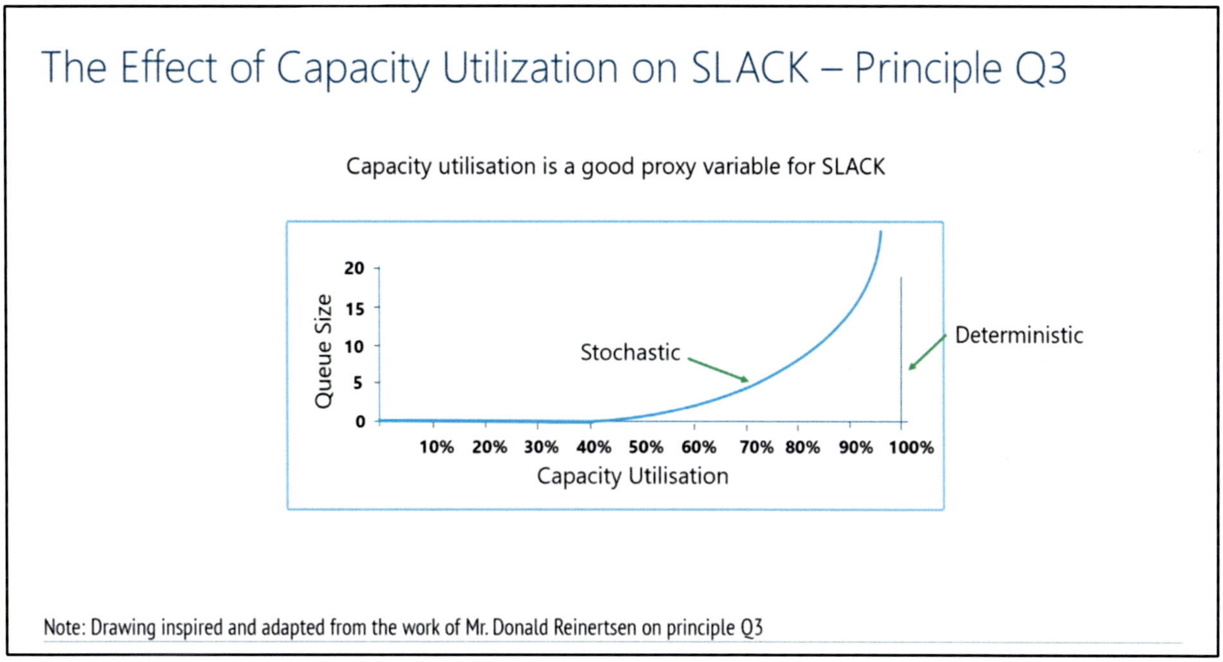

Let's now examine 3 architectures and how they fare with the management SLACK.

Stochastic – You can't get there from here

Do you remember the good old times when we 'maxed' the capacity utilisation of workers at 75% in our MS Project to bank 25% worth of SLACK? That is a stochastic way of managing capacity in the hope that we impact SLACK. It is totally useless.

Then, resource leveling came at the project level with network version of MS Project where everybody and nobody could qualify your project plans. Before you hit the ground running with your project, you have to see how realistic your MS Project plan is by using the view 'Resource Leveling'. A lot of work before day one. Speculative and needless work.

Then day one comes about. We enter the first minute. Say goodbye to your resource leveling plan. But I digress. You will probably have someone maintaining it for the duration of the project. I will stop here as I cannot imagine anything more inappropriate to do.

Never try to be righteous and control capacity utilisation by trying to control capacity utilisation with a probabilistic approach! Sometimes, virtue is its own punishment and things will get a lot worse before they get a lot worse. It is debilitating work. It is also totally useless.

Deterministic – Queuing Theory at work

The smart way to address this quagmire is to simply monitor queue size. Personal WIP limits are one sure bet. For example, a business analyst can work on 3 projects at a time and no more. A team board can only take 20 tickets at any point in time is another example of a deterministic approach to size queue and indirectly, capacity utilisation.

Column WIP limits are flawed as they emit Special Cause signals and I have covered this at length in both my books and their causality with the creation of SLACK is speculative at best;

Here are the consequences when dealing with column WIP limits reduction and impact on SLACK:[206]

1) Were you to reduce WIP limit on a non constraint emplacement, you will be lucky to have some sort of success, if at all. There is a clear and present danger in doing so as you could inadvertently move the constraint. Definitely not in the playbook.
2) Were you to reduce WIP limit on the constraint – by happenstance – you are giving an open order to overproduce as the constraint will always emit a 'rope' signal to persistently protect itself.

Reducing WIP in a CONWIP system is a better remedy and can work in creating slack as the entire system is constrained.

Queue size is a great proxy to contain capacity utilisation which then tames multi tasking and can possibly nurture SLACK indirectly. We see a path that is cumbersome in terms of degrees of freedom:

- First, diminishing queue size (WIP) decreases capacity utilisation
- Next, reduced capacity utilisation shrinks multi tasking
- Reduced multi tasking can make room for SLACK

The drawback here is that if you are in an excessive WIP environment, SLACK won't show up – if ever – as multi tasking elimination must take its toll first. It is a bit optimistic but within the sphere of the possible.

If only there was a method with near causality that existed for the creation of SLACK and optimal WIP level. Thankfully, Dr. Goldratt lived long enough to think out the DBR mechanism. Let see how this unfolds as we read what is next.

Theory of Constraint – DBR Zero Energy Solution and Inherent Simplicity

Dr Goldratt was a physicist. He understood that in nature, no one organism can survive in the long run when all of its components are operating at full throttle. In that context, SLACK is part of the system and there is no oversight as to how it should be calibrated, managed, finetuned etc. As nature will find a way, SLACK will find its way.

With this in mind, Dr Goldratt crafted systems that recognized this law of nature and made sure that SLACK was present everywhere by delivering a robust architecture. All of his applications were driven by this motivation.

Notice is given that the DBR buffer looks like a queue, as one may observe a 'pile' of work before the constraint. This mental connection with a queue analogy is a bad reflex.

The buffer's unit of measure is in fact time but need to be physicalize with 'things'. The buffer is the upstream duration of the traverse to the constraint and not a 'stack' of work although it is representing by a pile of 'stuff'!

[206] There is only one column upon which setting a 'WIP' limit – or buffer in this case – makes sense and it is at the constraint.

Elegantly simple with one degree of freedom!

Slack also absorbs variability and is a clear indicator of high performing organisations!

Heuristics to take to the bank regarding SLACK:

- If you manage the constraint instead of the entire system, SLACK will take care of itself and of the system. This is all the science you need.
- If you forfeit to find and manage the constraint - and prefer managing the entire system - you have found the perfect antidote to SLACK.

The optimal way to manage effortlessly both WIP configuration and SLACK optimisation is in a centralized fashion as per the Throughput Accounting principles covered earlier. This eliminates bad choices and variability. The DBR design fits the score.

Let there be no misunderstanding. In an excessively high WIP environment, reducing WIP will first kill multitasking before getting to – or not – SLACK.

By design, there is no doubt to be had that SLACK is right at home, all year long around the constraint as illustrated below. All other scenarios are speculative to some extent.

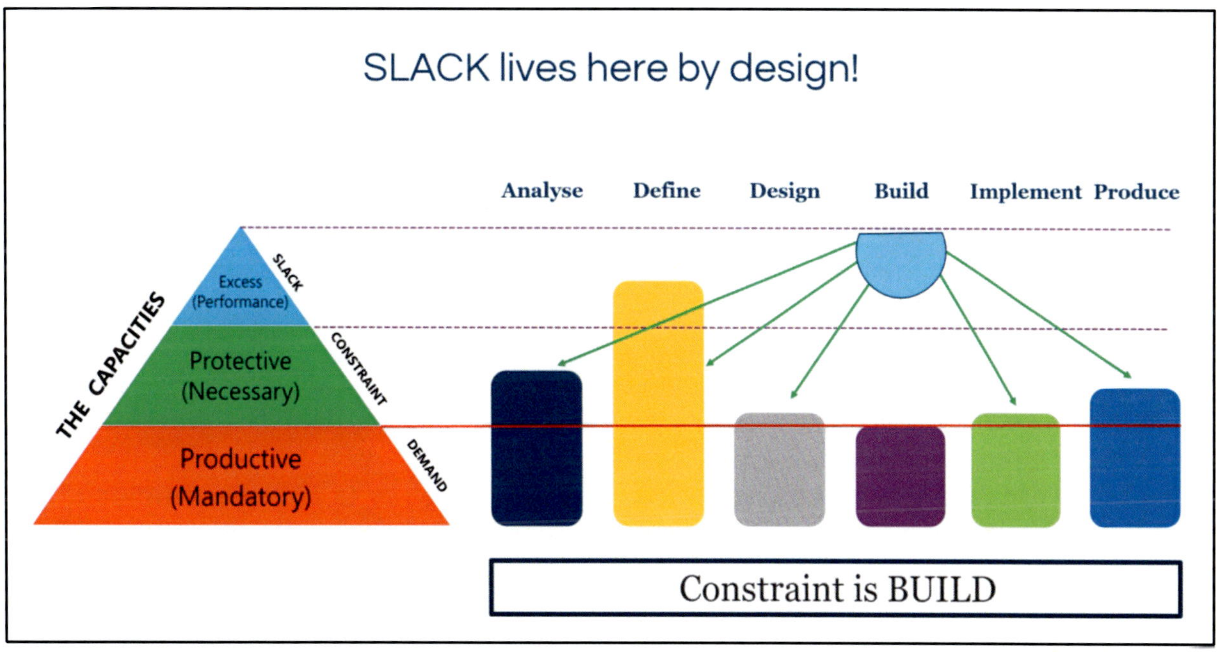

By design, there is no misunderstanding to be had that the right amount of WIP is dictated by the constraint and the DBR mechanism right before the constraint as shown below:

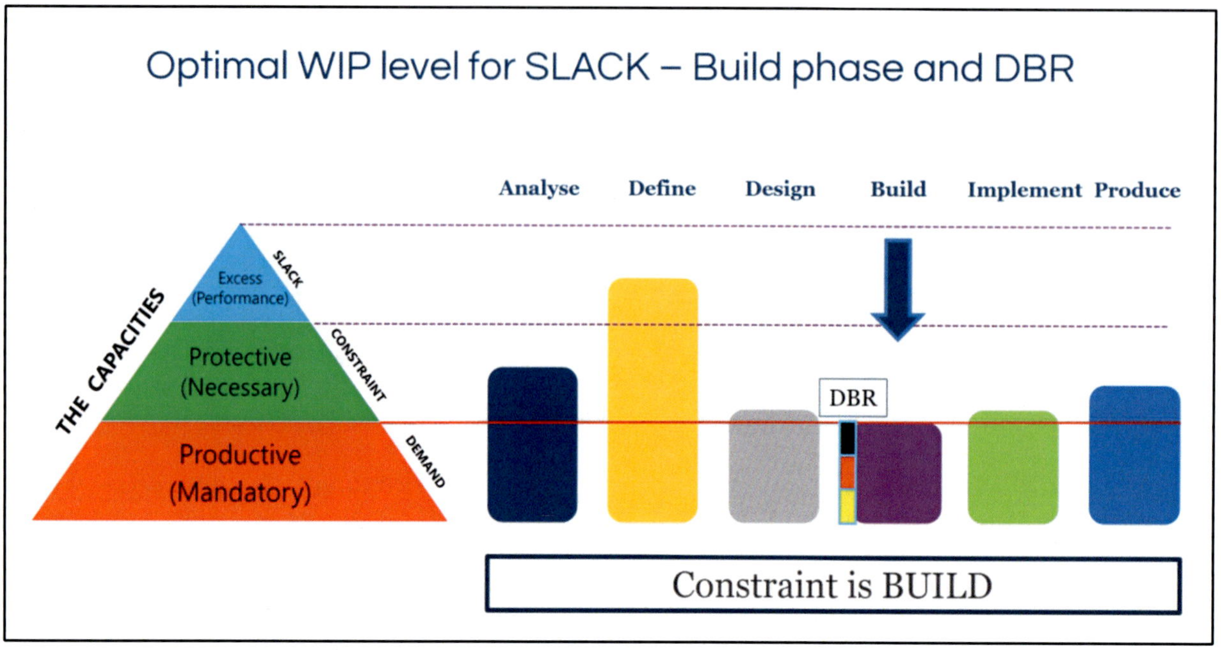

Project Review Rituals

Always know where your projects are. Upstream, at the Constraint or Downstream. And depending on the location of your project through time, bring to life the concepts of waste, inspection points, setup costs, coordination and transaction costs, buffer penetration, free products, negative covariance, staggering etc.

There is no need to discuss SLACK as it takes care of itself by design and lives effortlessly upstream and downstream of the constraint. Measuring performance where SLACK prevails will not help you generate more Throughput.

Each target scope project has a Throughput rate of its own once its CCPM agile plan is built. Just keep in mind that no matter what stratagem you way want to come up with to 'fasten' the pace, no other construct will deliver your work items faster than the one illustrated in this book. I am of course talking about 'doing' agile in an execution mind set.

What would be a proper Project Review meeting without 'variance' analysis. Variance analysis belongs to Cost Accounting. Someone always loses in a variance reporting exercise. I would just ask for one thing, stop ascertaining the labor variance of your projects – under or over budget – when you are dealing with full time employees, contractors under contract. It is brown money. It is discretionary money. If one project turns out to be Herbie, then help it out with the slack provided in the system. We have seen how the Buffer Fever Chart can be a good support for this.

As for keeping detailed timesheets per project, this is also to be questioned as no one project will ever come close to be 'somewhat' similar in the future to the one you are making now. Trying to get to a cost per project is mandated by the taxman for CAPEX or capital projects. Just clock one line per week per employee per project per budgetary code. Lose activity reporting unless there is a managerial benefit.

If you are dealing with OPEX or Operational Expenses, keep a proper tab to account for the right budget or expense accounts and again avoid over burdening data entry chores for things that are immaterial at the end.

I am saying this because I remember spending 2 days per week fixing timesheets as a Project Manager because the clients wanted 'control'. On that note there are two origins to the word control:

- The English language correctly points to mastery and understanding of what is going on. To be on top of things. Be in control.
- The French root is 'contre-role' meaning keeping multiple copies and indexes of the same historical facts. The infancy of bureaucracy.

Coming back to the topic at hand, do not forget that salaries of fulltime employees and contracts dealing with consultants are to be considered as capacity, not as a variable expense. If you account for those to discriminate between projects, you will leave money on the table. This is the most important lesson to be drawn insofar as project budgeting is concerned. And the skirmishes and 'drama' associated with projects that are running late and need more brain power must reckon that no green money is leaving the company. You are dealing with capacity and brown money. Just make the proper arbitrage decisions. It is all about want you want to get done and **not** how much it is 'costing' you as you are reassigning capacity already paid for and with which you can do as you please without thinking that using it differently than originally planned will make a difference financially.

On a more Throughput Accounting vs Cost Accounting[207] closing note and on motivation regarding project performance once a project has started[208], I have this to say:

- Throughput Accounting is more concerned with (T) and (OE), the TOE spread
- Cost Accounting makes sure that the value of the capital assets is well captured as every task is entered. At the end, good bookkeeping on (I) and the value of capital assets on the balance sheet is important to vouch for the value of the software being built
- The longer a project lasts and the more effort it consumes, the more Cost Accounting values the growth of the software asset in the books
- This creates no financial incentive for early completion – or to pull the plug on IT death marches - even though the business value to the client of undelivered software tends to go down with time

Who among us is not confronted with sempiternal and clusive frustration linked to the start date of projects? We have we all been there. You could pretty much be there right now. Damned if you start too soon and certainly damned if you start too late. Many times, projects that are a day late and a penny short can find the root cause right here: it did not start at the proper time!

It is a qualitative and judgment call for most of us. But can we bring some science?

---

[208] Project selection under CA and TA is another story that will not be addressed in this book.

DBR – Drum Buffer Rope and the CCPM plan are linked to together on that front. Joined at the hip no less. And it goes at the heart of the staggering functionality covered in appendix of chapter 3. As we have seen in chapter 3, the three components of DBR can be tied to a CCPM plan. What we have not drilled into is the following: of these components, which are exploiting and/or subordinating to the constraint. Let me illustrate:

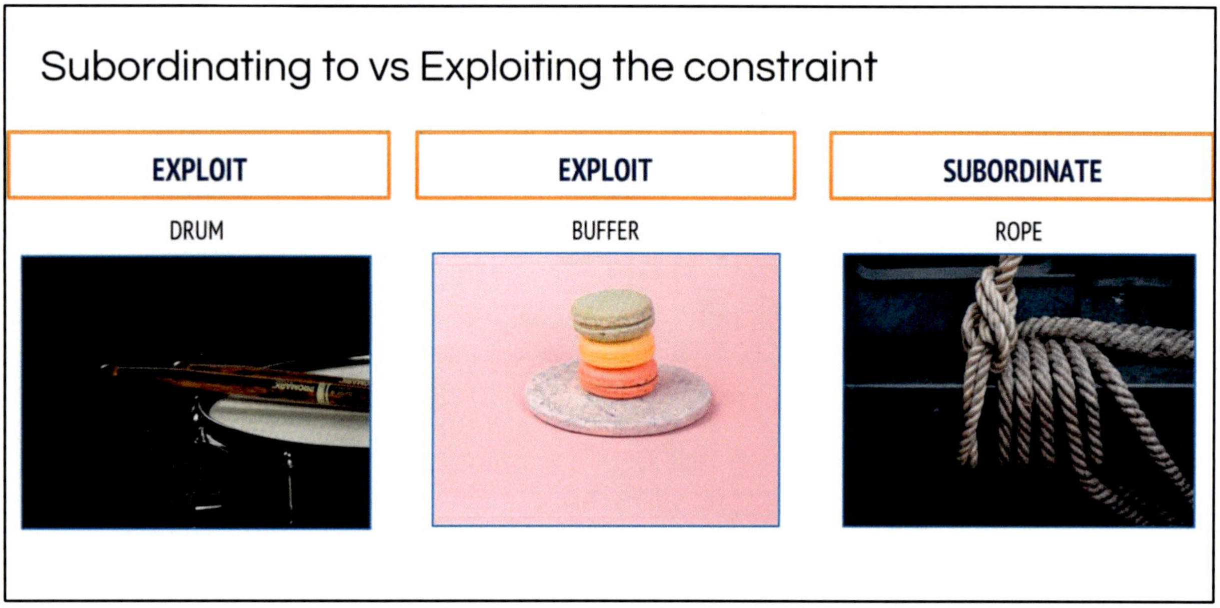

In fact, in its duty of subordinating to the constraint, the Rope fulfills the mandate to generate replenishment signals to start new projects! Remember what the rope does in our exercises in chapter 3? Before execution started, it told all involved that the project is coming to and end sometime between April 18th and April 27th .... and that we should be ready to start more work in that timespan!

But as the plan progressed, and the following status meetings were held on the following dates shown below, the Rope – as a dynamic indicator - emitted beacons as to the project's new anticipated end date. This can be connected to the staggering function. In my view, the staggering functionality is the best kept secret of how we can match DBR and the evolution of the CCPM plan to aid in orchestrating the start date of future projects.

Date of Meeting	**New CCPM Rope Signal - Staggering**
Kick off – April 1st	April 18th
April 7th	**April 24th**
April 12th	**April 16th**

While the CCPM Buffer and the Buffer Burn Rate might both be flashing green, emergent blue rope signals can create a sense of urgency as they are really acting as a counter balancing mechanism that warns you that finishing earlier than anticipated is a management by exception instance[209] as well. The reason the indicator is blue is that we are outside the traditional green, yellow and red spectrum. This new management by exception indicator is the CCPM Rope.

It is new and inspired by fiscal and monetary policy. Here is why:

> Government and central banks around the world need leading indicators of when the macro environment is either performing too good or too bad. We have plenty of leading indicators that tell us ahead of time of potential dangers. Their usual spectrum of color goes into yellow, red or even black. But we do not have a single one stating that things are going too well. This is needed too. The CCPM Rope is distinguished by the color blue and tell us that we are over performing. As usual, the entire cycle of root cause and frequency analysis might prove useful.

Therefore, the CCPM Rope is a sign that things are going extremely well and attention for orchestration of upcoming work needs to be raised, hence the reason why it belongs in the taxonomy of management by exception signals.

A discussion on Project rituals would not be complete without addressing green money and brown money. We have seen in chapter four when discussing the classical PMO in the section on resource efficiency vs flow efficiency, the nuances between brown money and green money. There is one more concern, especially at the Portfolio level reporting. If you use in these heavy human resources rituals, any player that would otherwise be busy minding the constraint, you are then using green money as the beat of the constraint might be encumbered! Flow metrics for reporting are best and come free.

New Orthodoxy - You can get there from here!

I have found a lot of inspiration in writing this book from Mr. Donald Reinertsen's definition of agility which is linked to our ability to execute, adapt and change direction at high speed!

This is where I like to be. Doing. The 'fuzzy front end' is important upstream and, in my view, should connect itself to the pipe described at a high level in this book. I will explain the economic reasons why shortly.

Once the dust settled on my first book, I also came across Dr John Ricketts' book 'Reaching the Goal'. My first reaction was that this was the book I should have read before writing the first book! It was too late. This time around, while writing this book, I made sure to re read both Dr Ricketts and Mr. Reinertsen's books over again one more time. I knew I needed to revisit them. It proved beneficial and I am sure I must have misunderstood the essence of some of his principles and erred in this book as well.

Aside from his definition of agility taken from the first line of this section, the other two major axes that always appealed to me from Mr. Reinertsen's work were 1) the need to tame Common Cause Variation in Knowledge-Work to reap low hanging fruits of financial rewards and

[209] I owe a lot to Bob Sproull who made the connection between DBR and CCPM in his book 'Epiphanized'. The idea of having the moving rope as a management by exception signal would never have crossed my mind were it not from his work.

2) Variability Principles V5, V10, V11, V12, V13 and V16, which deals more than anything else with risk management.

Variability Principles
V05: The Principle of Variability Pooling: Overall variation decreases when uncorrelated random tasks are combined.
V10: The Principle of Negative Covariance: We can reduce variance by applying a counterbalancing effect.
V11: The Buffer Principle: Buffers trade money for variability reduction.
V12: The Principle of Variability Consequence: Reducing consequences is usually the best way to reduce the cost of variability.
V13: The Non-linearity Principle: Operate in the linear range of system performance.
V16: The Principle of Variability Displacement: Move variability to the process stage where its cost is lowest.

With this practical and easy to apply knowledge, all managers, agile practitioners and especially those in charge of Agile CoE – Centers of Excellence - will find new ways to replace stale metrics with actionable ones that actually impact money. Coupled with ToC, those principles discussed above open new avenues and perspectives on risk execution and the economics of Knowledge-Work products.

CCPM – Buffers only!

CCPM – Critical Chain Project Management – is a very considerable body of knowledge. In that regard, many would question its pertinence with agility. Mary and Tom Poppendiek have openly questioned its utility based on the sheer size of the beast and its architecture!

You surely remember my questioning of Mr. Reinertsen's 'side lining' of all things ToC earlier in the book. Well, I found the source. It is in his very own book of all places!

Mr. Reinertsen brings interesting and highly technical concerns on CCPM that would merit a deep and well thought out response. But not today and not here. The focus of this book is on the connectivity of the CCPM buffer to an agile plan while respecting the gist of the CCPM construct to the letter. Remember, two prominent concerns of Dr Goldratt's focus was competing on time and taming Common Cause Variation – both topics that resonate with Mr. Reinertsen's life accomplishment.

What is taken from CCPM is only a parcel of the application: the buffers. The (BBR) - Buffer Burn Rate buffer and the consumption buffer. The BBR is simple, has a splash of Little's law, is easy to understand and leverages all of CCPM's basic construct by connecting it to a Lead Time Distribution at the 50% mark to suddenly have CCPM support agile plans.

Daily, the BBR buffer emits advanced signals of risk materialisation and supports management by exception. If you have a half decent Lead Time distribution, you can get going tomorrow with the guidance provided in chapter 3. Your daily meetings will never be the same as you may not be required to attend some of them when both CCPM indicators are green. The Buffer Consumption signal is not the most important but has great value in staggering and orchestrating your portfolio of projects and starting as late as possible. The Buffer Burn Rate is of paramount importance while executing and is the preferred buffer for managerial scrutiny.

Timelines, Queues or Buffers?

Timelines still rule for managing projects. Queues will always beat timelines. So will buffers. But the day that we quit to manage on timelines has still not risen. How can we break that bad habit first?

We need new weapons that can be used daily, in real time and that few master and can argue against. That first weapon is capacity that we have discussed at length in the first chapters. And by capacity, I mean visualisation of capacity. The next weapon is time. Timelines are always out of sync. Buffers and queues never are.

Hit the nail. Everyday. I intend to do so from now on. Repetition is the mother of all skills after all.

What about the signaling effect? This is where buffers and queues differ. And again, I had to find material in both Mr. Reinertsen's work as well as Dr Lisa Lang. Both are based on science.

The analogies are not perfect but Mr. Reinertsen would be of the opinion that WIP constraints generate 'more' timely signals and that the DBR buffer, well just not enough and too little too late for a proper reaction to take place. The reaction time is a big issue to refill the pipeline in his view. The remedy for this is of course sprint capacity upstream and excess capacity downstream that allows for 'extra speed' when the constraint or the system is under duress.

Dr Lisa Lang argues that the signaling mechanism is sufficient at the constraint only as beacons emanating anywhere else would be tainted by Special Cause Variation. When a local problem arises, the entire value stream spins out of control as in a JIT system. This is not what we want.

We are caught here between two experts with sound science and I will say that having either too many or too few signals are an issue. Mr. Reinertsen has 24 principles in chapter six dealing with Fast Feedback. They are all appropriate. They are nuanced with the reflexes of the Theory of Constraints when appropriate in the later parts of chapter 6 of this book.

Concluding Remarks

I could not help to notice that Mr Donald Reinertsen often makes references to proxy variables in his book. Yet, this concept – or precise word - is not leveraged in any one of his 175 principles. But proxy variables have extraordinary value: in TOC, they allow you to see the whole system by simply looking at a part: the constraint! Having unbalanced systems is always the case in life and the laws of physics clearly demonstrate this: all living systems cannot operate all of their parts at 100% capacity. It cannot be otherwise. Those who try to even flow by leveling capacity do so at great costs.

If there was an addition to those principles, I would say that the constraint is a proxy of the performance of the entire system and that focusing on that part is the key to prosperity!

If you have enjoyed this book, I invite you to read the first one. There is a lot of good in there as well, but I have kept the best for this book. The next book will be even better. I have a few more topics I wish to address and novelties that I want surface, namely the concept of market constraints in Knowledge-Work which runs counter clock wise to how they are dealt with in a traditional brick and mortar context.

For now, and to conclude, I would encourage you to act and use the knowledge encapsulated in this book both as a sword to forge ahead and as a shield to deflect the arguments that are always used to stick to what does not work at execution time: timeboxing and managing on the scope axis - as Sprints do - are the antidotes to 'do' agility.

Teams are great. But there is no team in a masterpiece[210].

Agilists of all allegiances, Knowledge-Workers of all breeds and CPAs: you can run, but you can't hide. There are no reasons now why you should not know how to budget, account properly with green and brown money, master the cost functions of agility and its 3 levels of capacity, understand the metrics of a modern PMO, execute a target scope plan, know how to mint money, use the leverage of the TOE spread ... and the 5 Focusing Steps!

[210] This liaison between teams and masterpieces was brought to my attention by Jurgen Appelo. I wholeheartedly concur.

QUIZ ANSWERS – SUBORDINATION VS EXPLOITATION TO THE CONSTRAINT

Exploit ≠ **Subordinate**

Thinking Fast

Thinking Slow

Exploit ≠ **Subordinate**

Overtime Allowed

No Overtime

Subordinate ≠ **Exploit**

SLACK

BUSY

Exploit ≠ **Subordinate**

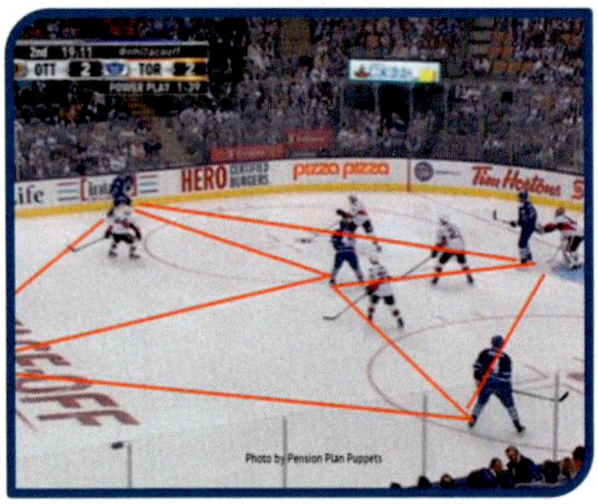

Working in parallel

Working Sequentially

Exploit ≠ **Subordinate**

Don't Stop & Measure

Start/Stop & No Measure

Subordinate ≠ **Exploit**

Higher Logical Level

Lower Logical Level

Subordinate ≠ **Exploit**

Downhill

Uphill

Exploit ≠ **Subordinate**

Schedule

No schedule

Exploit ≠ **Subordinate**

Setup Costs

No Setup Costs

Subordinate ≠ **Exploit**

Happy Customers - Utility

Making Money – Productivity

Subordinate ≠ **Exploit**

Creating Capacity

Using Capacity

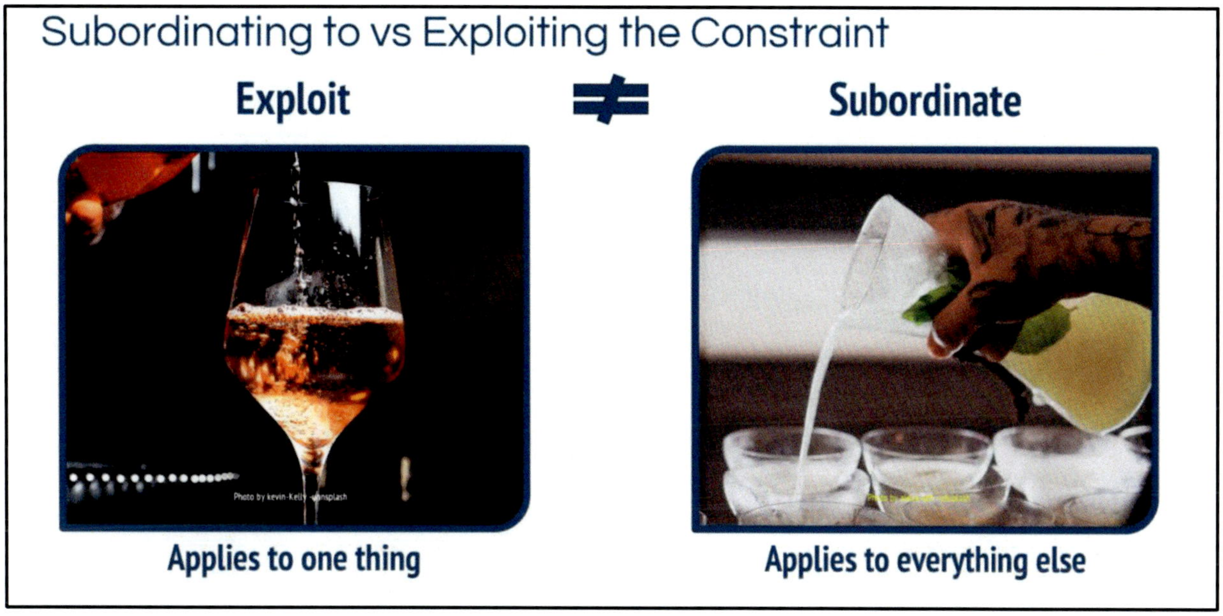
Subordinating to vs Exploiting the Constraint
Exploit
≠
Subordinate
Applies to one thing
Applies to everything else

GAME - THE HERBIE WALK BY STUART BURCHILL

Herbie – Theory of Constraints and the 5 Focusing Steps !

**Herbie is the YELLOW scout! He has BIG FEET, impeding his walking pace.
He needs to carry special shoe supplies and fill his pack sack with special feet care products:**

**15 pair of extra socks
20 tubes of cream
3 spare boots
12 Big Shoe Magazines
Powder, Etc.**

Goal: Go on a hike and get everyone safely back to camp before nightfall!

You are all scouts carrying backpacks. One of you is Herbie who has a big feet that prevents him from walking as fast as the others. He brings an overfilled backpack with feet care products.

One beat of the metronome equals one forward step with one leg.

IMPORTANT: The path is narrow, forcing everyone to walk à la queue leu leu. When you need to pass someone, tap them on the shoulder. The person you pass must then walk in place for four beats before continuing forward.

Theory of Constraints (ToC)

Goal of Session:

- Learn about the Theory of Constraints (ToC) and the 5 Focusing Steps (5FS)
- Have some fun!
- Experience team-based flow
- Learn about available training (including more ToC, Advanced Kanban, DBR scheduling, flow efficiency, throughput accounting, and much more)

What's Needed:

- Download the iOS mobile app "Simply Metronome"
- Or download the android mobile app "Simple Metronome"
  - If you cannot download either, then partner with someone who was able to download

Theory of Constraints & 5 Focusing Steps

The Theory of Constraints states that every system must have at least one constraint limiting its output - which must be managed to:

- Reduce **WIP** (the amount of work in the system)
- Speed up **Flowtime** (how quickly a unit of work gets completed)
- Increase **Throughput** (the amount of work completed per unit time)

ToC focuses improvement efforts where they will have the greatest immediate impact on the bottom line – at the constraint.

Improvement effort applied elsewhere is wasted!

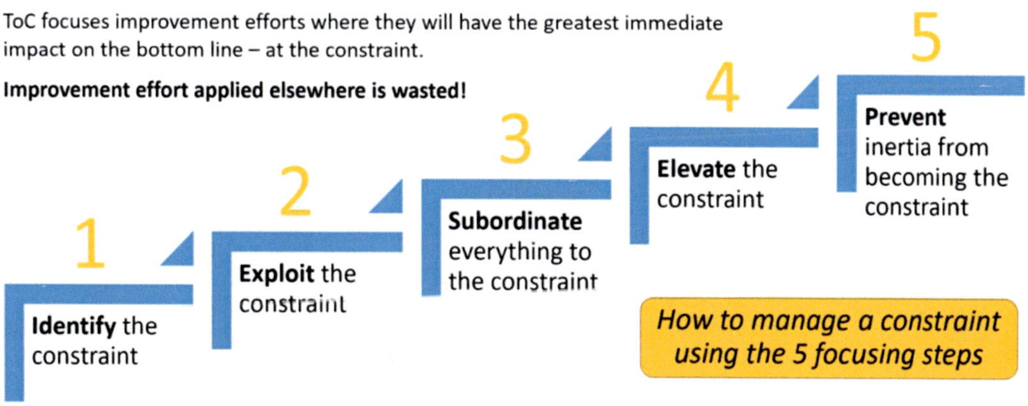

How to manage a constraint using the 5 focusing steps

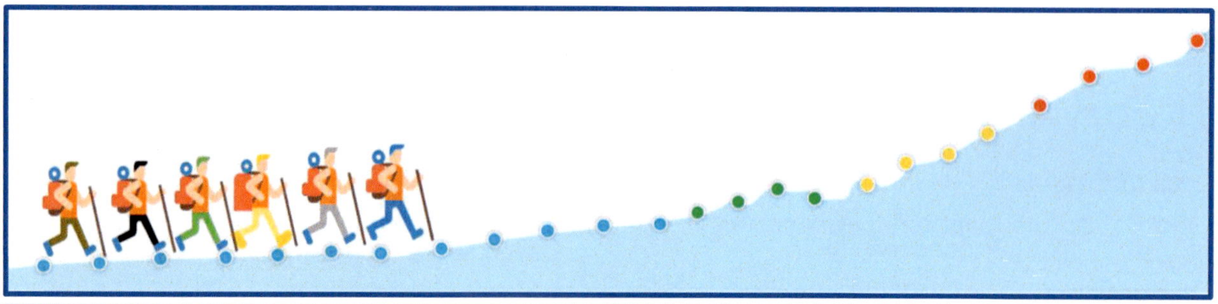

Theory of Constraints & 5 Focusing Steps

Round #1:

How long will it take for everyone to make it back to camp?

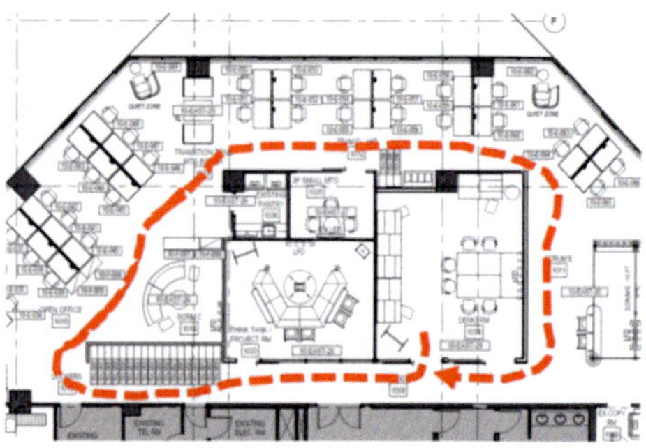

REMINDER: Everyone walks in a single line. When you need to pass someone, <u>the person you pass must walk in place for four beats before continuing</u>.

Blue Scouts walk at **100** Beats per Minute (BPM)

Orange Scouts walk at **90** Beats per Minute (BPM)

Herbie walks at **60** Beats per Minute (BPM)

Theory of Constraints & 5 Focusing Steps

1

Identify the Constraint

Identify the Weakest Link!

It's Herbie!!

Blue Scouts walk at **100** Beats per Minute (BPM)

Orange Scouts walk at **90** Beats per Minute (BPM)

Herbie walks at **60** Beats per Minute (BPM)

Theory of Constraints & 5 Focusing Steps

Questions:

What might the Scout Troop be comparable to?
A system that produces a product or service. Each scout represents an operation or a step in a production or service delivery process

What does the Scout Troop deliver?
Walked trail – the distance that the whole team has covered together

What does the trail represent?
The work to be done

What does each Scout's individual steps represent?
Processed work, handed to the next Scout behind

What do the steps between the first and last Scout represent?
Inventory or Work in Process

What is Herbie's rate determining?
The Throughput – in terms of how much path is actually being covered per unit time

Some of you arrived at camp much earlier than others. Is this useful towards the overall goal? *No. Why?*

Theory of Constraints & 5 Focusing Steps

2

Exploit the Constraint

Round #2:
How long to reach the goal?

REMINDER: Everyone walks in a single line. When you need to pass someone, the person you pass must walk in place for four beats before continuing.

Blue Scouts walk at **100** Beats per Minute (BPM)

Come on Herbie!!

Orange Scouts walk at **90** Beats per Minute (BPM)

Do your sustainable best!

Herbie walks at **70** Beats per Minute (BPM)

NOTE: Essentially, we are confirming that the constraint remains the constraint when that process is optimized.

Theory of Constrai   5 Focusing Steps

3

Subordinate everything to the Constraint

Round #3:
How long to reach the goal?

REMINDER: Everyone walks in a single line now. NO PASSING.

Herbie walks at **70** Beats per Minute (BPM)

Blue and Orange Scouts follow behind Herbie

EVERYBODY STAY BEHIND HERBIE!

Make decisions based on the constraint

PHEW !

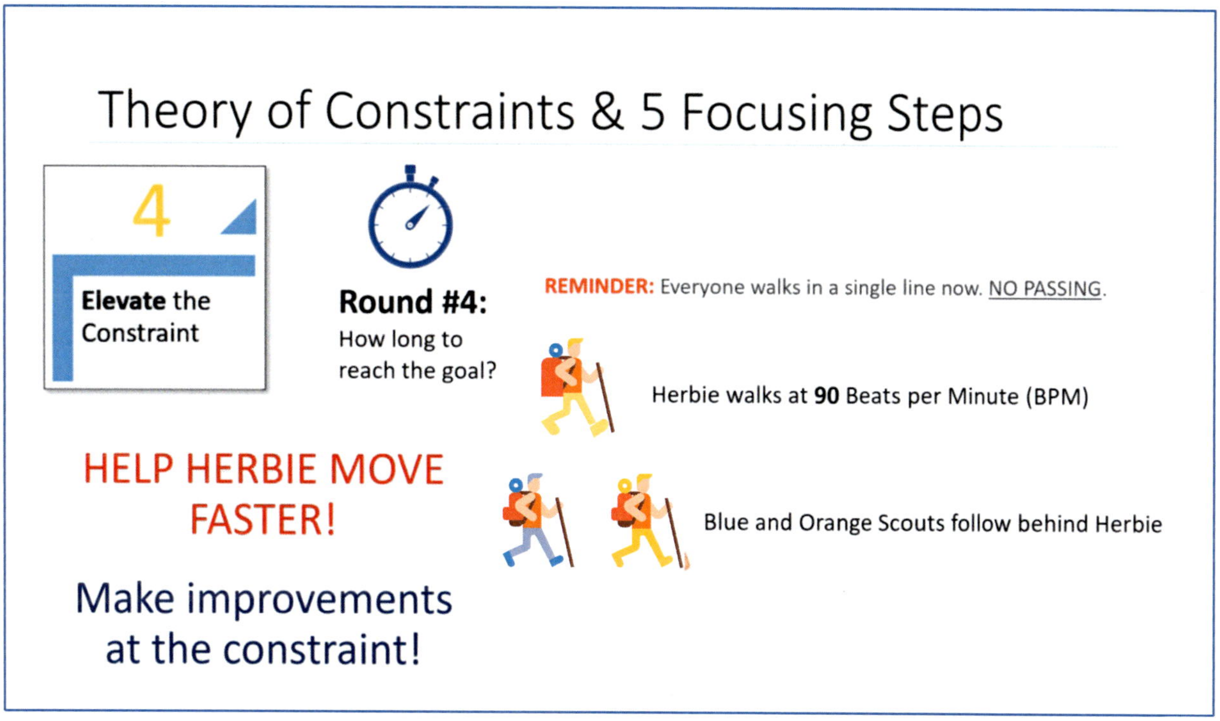
Theory of Constraints & 5 Focusing Steps
4
Elevate the Constraint
Round #4:
How long to reach the goal?
REMINDER: Everyone walks in a single line now. NO PASSING.
Herbie walks at 90 Beats per Minute (BPM)
HELP HERBIE MOVE FASTER!
Blue and Orange Scouts follow behind Herbie
Make improvements at the constraint!

Theory of Constraints & 5 Focusing Steps

5

Prevent Inertia from becoming the Constraint

KEEP AN EYE ON THE OTHER SCOUTS

Someone else may become the new constraint

Scout Troop March - 5 Focusing Steps Results

The 5 Focusing Steps resulted in a **194%** flowtime (speed) improvement!!

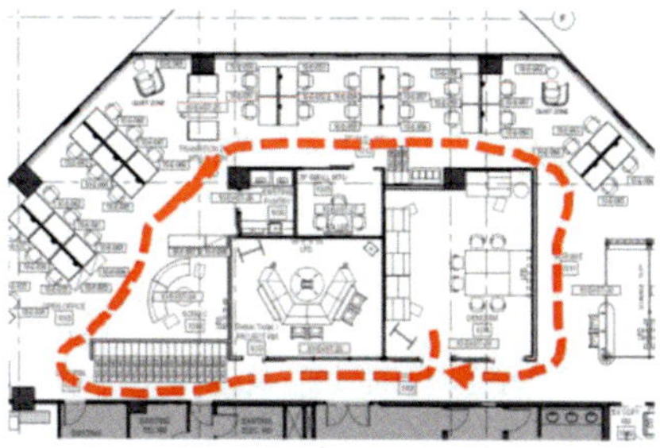

A **151%** improvement was achieved without having to change how most of the team worked.

Round	Focusing Steps	Action	Marching Time	Improvement
1	Identify the Constraint	"It's HERBIE!"	103 sec	Baseline
2	Exploit the Constraint	"C'mon Herbie! Speed up!"	81 sec	127%
3	Subordinate to the Constraint	Everybody stays behind Herbie!"	68 sec	151%
4	Elevate the Constraint	"Everybody carries a piece of Herbie's gear"	53 sec	194%
5	Repeat, and prevent inertia from becoming the constraint	N/A	N/A	

How Can We Apply What We've Learned?

- Seek out and identify the constraint in systems around you
- Focus effort only on improving the constraint – this is the only place where you can improve the overall system – effort elsewhere is wasted
- By subordinating to the constraint, interruptions and context-switching inefficiencies are reduced, while touch-time vs. wait time improves
- Increasing cross-functionality within a team, or across teams, helps to elevate the constraint, thereby reducing WIP
- Favoring flow over efficiency introduces slack, allowing team members to be immediately ready to move the work along when it is their turn to contribute
- Reducing WIP increases a teams' ability to be nimble and pivot without loss of sunk cost (i.e. inventory of work already completed while overall goal has not been completed)
- Anything else?

SHOULD THE PACK SACK CONTENT HAD BEEN SHARED EQUALLY BETWEEN SCOUTS?

SIMULATION - LITTLE's RESTAURANT BY MICHAEL KÜSTERS

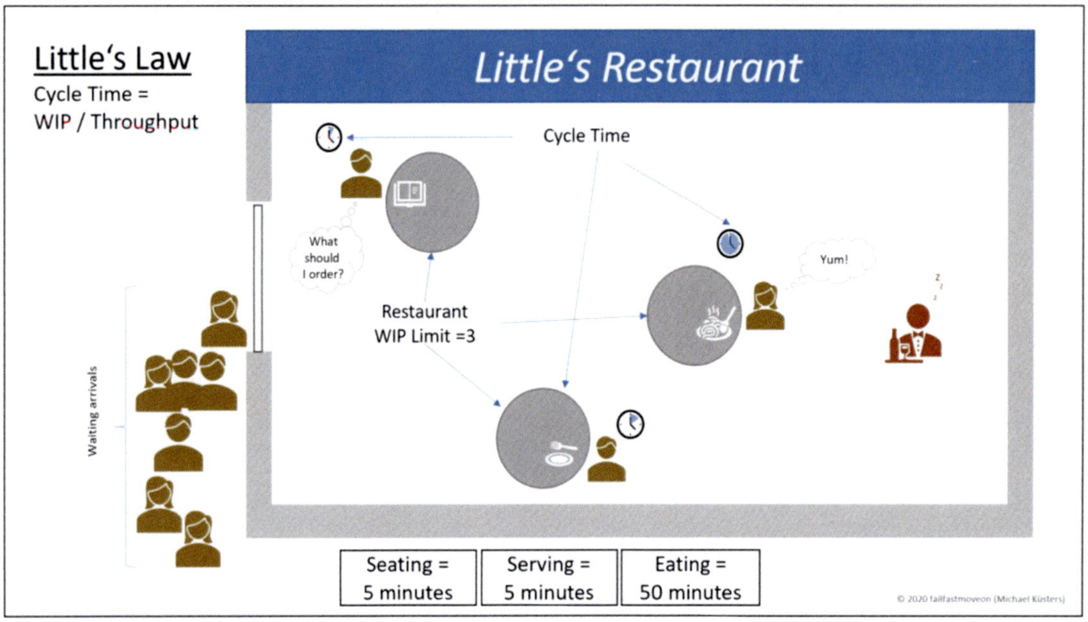

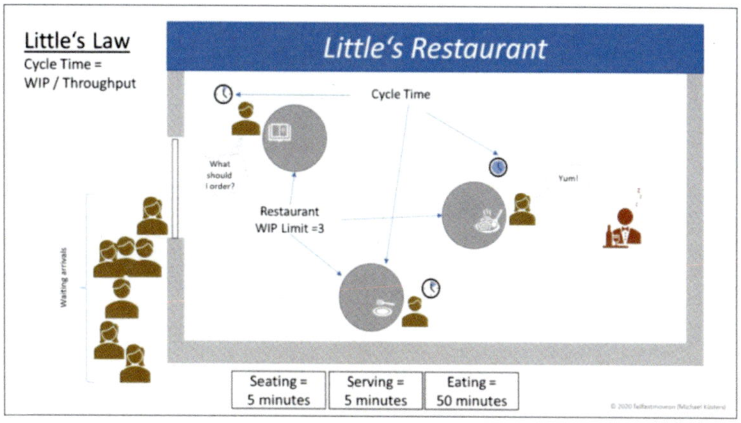

Because Little's Law works on averages, everything is averaged:

1. Customers take **5 minutes** for **seating** and placing their order.
2. **Serving** takes **5 minutes** per customer
3. A customer is **eating** for **50 minutes**.
4. A **meal costs 10€**.
5. Staff costs **20€ per hour**.
6. A **meal costs 5€** apiece to produce.

Restaurant Management:

1. „Staff" is a bucket term including waiters, cooks, cleaning etc.
2. There are 3 tables.
3. There are enough customers waiting outside.
4. There is no shortage of food.

Little's Restaurant is in trouble!

The manager is calling for help: „*We're doing terrible – if we don't improve, we will be bankrupt soon!*"

They do the math.

Little's Law Flow Metrics

1. WIP = 3
2. Lead Time = 5 + 5 + 50 = 60min
3. Throughput / h = 3

Financial Account (1h)			
Sales: 3* 10€ =	30€	Dish Cost: 3 * 5€ =	15€
		Staff Cost:	20€
Total Balance:			**-5€**

Little‘s Restaurant needs help!

The manager is calling for help: „*We‘re doing terrible – if we don‘t improve, we will be bankrupt soon!*“

The manager realizes: „*We‘re losing 5€ per hour!*“

The manager hires a Lean Consultant to optimize according to Little‘s Law.

The consultant makes their suggestions.

Optimization with Little's Law

1. Reduce system WIP

- Reduce the amount of tables to 2.

2. Set Column WIP Limits

- Set a Column WIP limit on „Seating, Serving, Eating" = 2 each.

3. Try Single Piece Flow

- Reduce the amount of tables to 1.

4. Improve throughput

- Get people seated in 2 minutes! (60% faster!)

Original Little's Law Flow Metrics

1. WIP = 3
2. Lead Time = 5 + 5 + 50 = 60min
3. Throughput / h = 3

Original Financial Account (1h)	
Sales: 3* 10€ = 30€	Dish Cost: 3 * 5€ = 15€ Staff Cost: 20€
Total Balance:	**-5€**

Calculate the new business case for Little's Restaurant!

---

1. Reduce system WIP

- Reduce the amount of tables to 2.

Original Little's Law Flow Metrics

1. WIP = 3
2. Lead Time = 5 + 5 + 50 = 60min
3. Throughput / h = 3

Original Financial Account (1h)	
Sales: 3* 10€ = 30€	Dish Cost: 3 * 5€ = 15€ Staff Cost: 20€
Total Balance:	**-5€**

Optimized Little's Law metrics

Optimized Financial Account (1h)

2. Set Column WIP Limits

- Set a Column WIP limit on „Seating, Serving, Eating" = 2 each.

Only 2 customers will be in the same stage at the same time.

What sounds simple is a logistic nightmare.

There's no longer an easy rule for cycle time – wait time wildly differs and needs to be averaged!

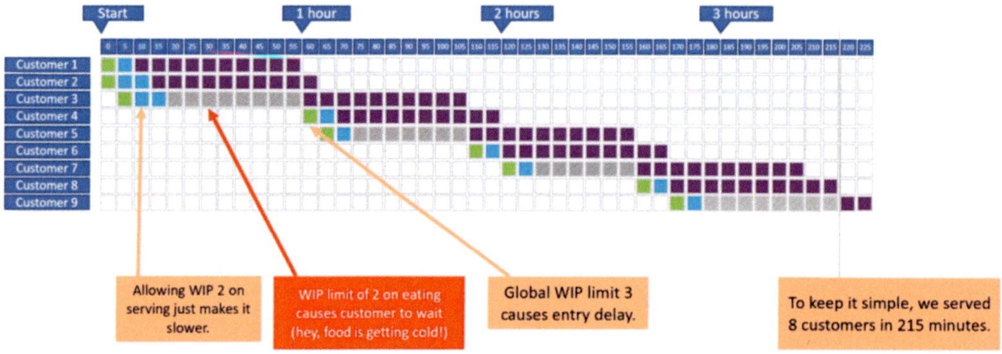

---

2. Set Column WIP Limits

- Set a Column WIP limit on „Seating, Serving, Eating" = 2 each.

Only 2 customers will get seated and receive their food initially, the third has to WAIT because of the WIP limit.

Column WIP limits permit higher throughput than a reduced global WIP limit.

But: Lead time increases dramatically due to „waiting in process"! *(as a customer, how would you like that?)*

Original Little's Law Flow Metrics

1. WIP = 3
2. Lead Time = 5 + 5 + 50 = 60min
3. Throughput / h = 3

Original Financial Account (1h)	
Sales: 3* 10€ = 30€	Dish Cost: 3 * 5€ = 15€ Staff Cost: 20€
Total Balance:	**-5€**

Optimized Little's Law metrics

1. WIP = 3
2. Throughput = 8/215 min = **2.2**
3. Lead Time ~ **80 min**

Optimized Financial Account (1h)	
Sales: 2.2* 10€ = 22€	Dish Cost: 2.2 * 5€ = 11€ Staff Cost: 20€
Total Balance:	**-9€**

---

3. Try Single Piece Flow

- Reduce the amount of tables to 1.

Only 1 customers will get admitted.

We're really killing it now – *the restaurant, that is.*

Original Little's Law Flow Metrics

1. WIP = 3
2. Lead Time = 5 + 5 + 50 = 60min
3. Throughput / h = 3

Original Financial Account (1h)	
Sales: 3* 10€ = 30€	Dish Cost: 3 * 5€ = 15€ Staff Cost: 20€
Total Balance:	**-5€**

Optimized Little's Law metrics

1. WIP = 1
2. Lead Time = 5 + 5 + 50 = 60min
3. Throughput / h = 1

Optimized Financial Account (1h)	
Sales: 1* 10€ = 10€	Dish Cost: 1 * 5€ = 5€ Staff Cost: 20€
Total Balance:	**-15€**

---

4. Improve throughput

- Get people seated in 2 minutes! (60% faster!)

We rearranged the restaurant and reduced the menu size. Customers are now ordering earlier.

We have reduced the **ordering** step time *from 5 minutes* to **2 minutes** now – a 60% improvement on seating time!

Original Little's Law Flow Metrics

1. WIP = 3
2. Lead Time = 5 + 5 + 50 = 60min
3. Throughput / h = 3

Original Financial Account (1h)	
Sales: 3* 10€ = 30€	Dish Cost: 3 * 5€ = 15€ Staff Cost: 20€
Total Balance:	**-5€**

Optimized Little's Law metrics

1. WIP = 3
2. Lead Time = 2 + 5 + 50 = 57min
3. Throughput / h = 3.15

Optimized Financial Account (1h)	
Sales: 3.15* 10€ = 31.50€	Dish Cost: 3.15 * 5€ = 15.75€ Staff Cost: 20€
Total Balance:	**-4.25€**

Little's Restaurant is bankrupt!

The manager is hopeless.

No single, and not even a combination of all suggestions made by the Lean Consultant can save Little's Restaurant.

The manager files for bankruptcy.

Acting upon Little's Law alone doesn't mean our business is successful!

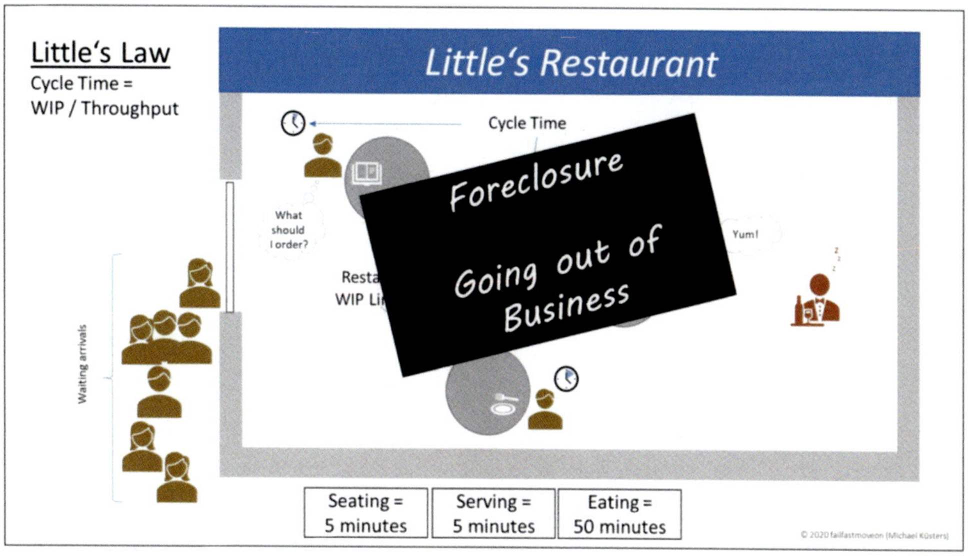

The crazy investor

An investor named Mitch shows up.

Mitch wants to buy the place and make it successful.

The manager tells Mitch how even Little's Law was no help.

Mitch is in good spirits - He must be crazy!

Mitch's Proposals

1. Increase WIP

- Add more tables: Try 4,5 – maybe even 10 tables!

Increase Lead Time

- Premium service is 100% slower, and costs +100%.

3. Increase Production Cost

- Organic food costs +100%, but people pay +100%.

4. All of the Above!

- Because forget Little's Law and Lean, that's why!

Original Little's Law Flow Metrics

1. WIP = 3
2. Lead Time = 5 + 5 + 50 = 60min
3. Throughput / h = 3

Original Financial Account (1h)	
Sales: 3* 10€ = 30€	Dish Cost: 3 * 5€ = 15€ Staff Cost: 20€
Total Balance:	**-5€**

Calculate the new business case for Mitch's Restaurant!

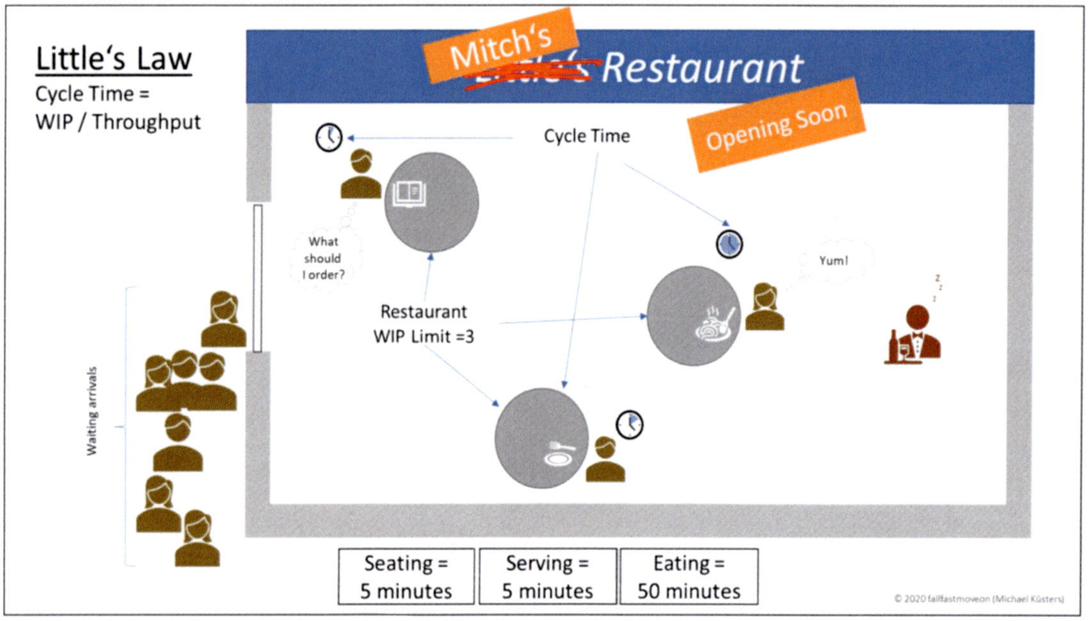

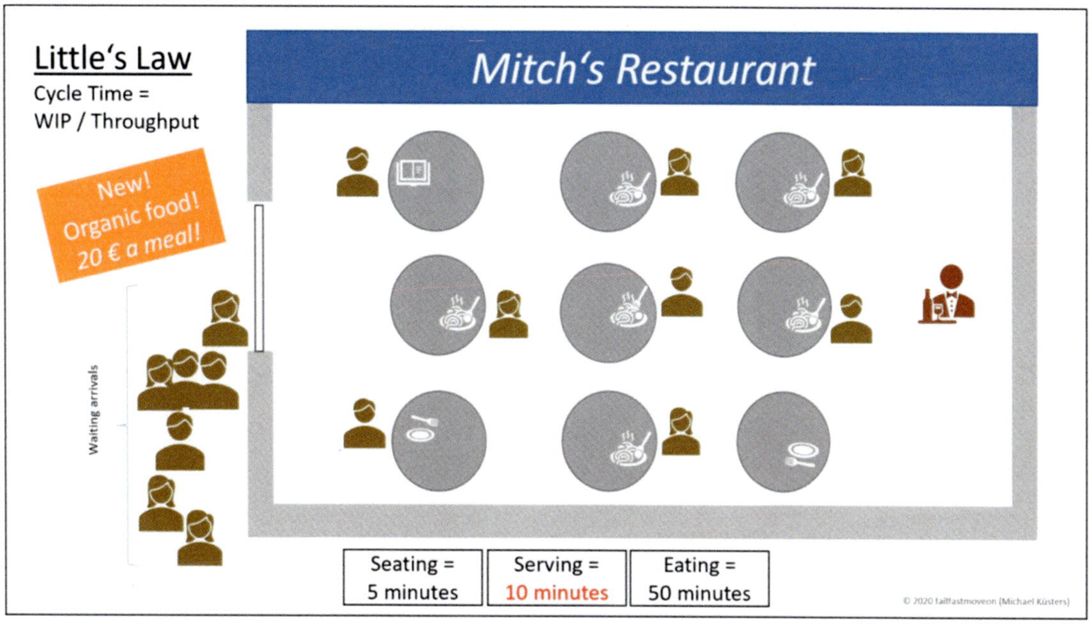

1. Increase WIP

- Add more tables: Try 4,5 – maybe even 10 tables!

Adding a fourth table doesn‘t cause any delay for customers.

Even the fifth, not even the tenth table results in an average delay – staff is still only busy 50 out of 60 minutes!

Original Little's Law Flow Metrics	
1. WIP = 3 2. Lead Time = 5 + 5 + 50 = 60min 3. Throughput / h = 3	
Original Financial Account (1h)	
Sales: 3 * 10€ = 30€	Dish Cost: 3 * 5€ = 15€ Staff Cost: 20€
Total Balance:	**-5€**

Optimized Little's Law metrics	
1. WIP = 10 2. Lead Time = 5 + 5 + 50 = 60min 3. Throughput / h = 10	
Optimized Financial Account (1h)	
Sales: 10 * 10€ = 100€	Dish Cost: 10 * 5€ = 50€ Staff Cost: 20€
Total Balance:	**30€**

Increase Lead Time

- Premium service is 100% slower, and costs +100%.

We keep the three tables.

Offering Premium service means **Serving Time** increases to **10 minutes**.

Cost **goes up** to **20€** for this service!

Original Little's Law Flow Metrics
1. WIP = 3
2. Lead Time = 5 + 5 + 50 = 60min
3. Throughput / h = 3

Original Financial Account (1h)	
Sales: 3 * 10€ = 30€	Dish Cost: 3 * 5€ = 15€ Staff Cost: 20€
Total Balance:	**-5€**

Optimized Little's Law metrics
1. WIP = 3
2. Lead Time = 5 + **10** + 50 = 65min
3. Throughput / h = 2.8

Optimized Financial Account (1h)	
Sales: 2.8 * 20€ = 56€	Dish Cost: 2.8 * 5€ = 14€ Staff Cost: 20€
Total Balance:	**22€**

---

3. Increase Production Cost

- Organic food costs +100%, but people pay +100%.

Higher quality ingredients are welcome and people pay **20€** for such a dish!

Since there is no shortage of customers, an increase in **production cost** has no effect on throughput!

Original Little's Law Flow Metrics
1. WIP = 3
2. Lead Time = 5 + 5 + 50 = 60min
3. Throughput / h = 3

Original Financial Account (1h)	
Sales: 3 * 10€ = 30€	Dish Cost: 3 * 5€ = 15€ Staff Cost: 20€
Total Balance:	**-5€**

Optimized Little's Law metrics
1. WIP = 3
2. Lead Time = 5 + 5 + 50 = 60min
3. Throughput / h = 3

Optimized Financial Account (1h)	
Sales: 3 * 20€ = 60€	Dish Cost: 3 * 10€ = 30€ Staff Cost: 20€
Total Balance:	**10€**

Mitch approves of all options.

But why not go all-in, and combine the options?

Combine all options

- Increase service time, increase tables - and increase production cost!

The **10€** quality **ingredients** are welcome and people pay an additional **10€** for such a dish!
The improved service at **10 minutes** is welcome and people pay an additional **10€** for such extraordinary service!

There's a small issue – the service time means we can only serve **5 customers** – 5/10 tables stay empty!

Original Little's Law Flow Metrics

1. WIP = 3
2. Lead Time = 5 + 5 + 50 = 60min
3. Throughput / h = 3

Original Financial Account (1h)	
Sales: 3 * 10€ = 30€	Dish Cost: 3 * 5€ = 15€ Staff Cost: 20€
Total Balance:	**-5€**

Optimized Little's Law metrics

1. WIP = **5**
2. Lead Time = 5 + **10** + 50 = **65**min
3. Throughput / h = 4.6

Optimized Financial Account (1h)	
Sales: **4.6 * 30€ = 138€**	Dish Cost: **4.6*10€ = 46€** Staff Cost: 20€
Total Balance:	**72€**

The restaurant is very profitable.

Now would be the perfect time to **hire more staff**!

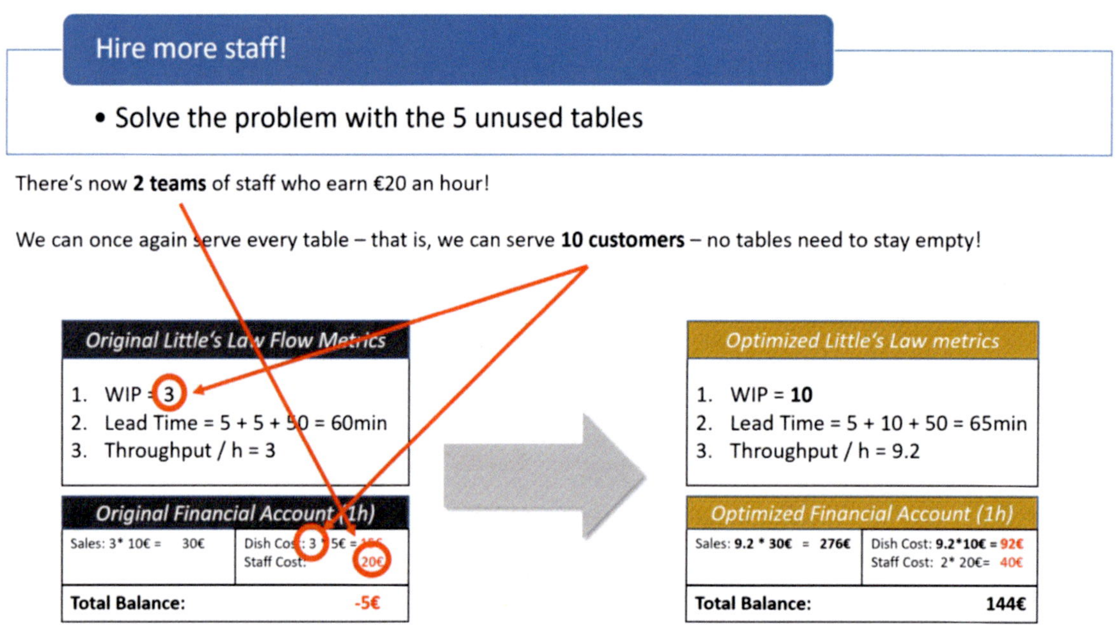

Discuss

1. Why did activity WIP limits make the process worse?
2. Why did a global WIP reduction not help, either?
3. Why did an increase in WIP improve the system?
4. Under which circumstances is increasing lead time a good idea?
5. How do you determine when you need more people?

NOTES FOR PLAYING THE SIMULATION

This simulation shows you that putting WIP limits is flawed. Especially if you put it at the wrong place.

Question:

I like the restaurant example, the assumption is that there is more demand than capacity with more tables (there is 10/hr), would be interesting to show how there is additional costs for marketing if the demand is not there :)

Answer: from Michael

If the demand isn't there, Lean Production always fails.
As a general idea, if you're producing more than is demanded, you have the waste of overproduction, and would reduce production output to the required level of demand. That's a killer as fixed costs become prohibitive.

Instead of talking about the costs of marketing, we would need to see marketing as a demand generating activity, which needs to flow into financial throughput.

In the system of Little's Restaurant, marketing would factor into staff (fixed) cost, or discount offers would factor into meal price (revenue).
In either case, the numbers are easy to calculate.

In example 1 (Limit WIP to 1), the restaurant would die even faster from marketing expenses.
In example 2 (Mitch's Restaurant), you can use the provided formulae and calculate the marginal rates at which marketing to fill the demand intake stops being valuable.

As a general note, though - there's no model that couldn't be made more complex by adding additional variables:
How about adding a probability that customers post positive/negative Google reviews, or that staff become sick? 😂

Comment from Michael on his simulation

My thought experiment, "Little's Restaurant", shows you where you can see how limiting WIP in the wrong place can be fatal for the business and how an increase of WIP can actually be the solution.

Without realizing what and where the Constraint is, limiting team-level WIP achieves -at best- nothing.

A general, sweeping statement that "limiting WIP is the solution" is flawed. This is not the case.

REFERENCES

Anderson, David A. 'Agile Management for Software Engineering: Applying the Theory of Constraints for Business Results'. The Coad Series. 2003

Anderson, David A. ''Why "doing things right" should lead "doing the right thing". David J Anderson School of Management. August 2013 https://djaa.com/why-doing-things-right-should-lead-doing-the-right-thing/

Anderson, Jeff. 'Organising toward Agility, design, grow and sustain seof-organizing structure at scale'. Agile by Design Publication. 2022

Benson, Jim and Toniane De Maria Barry. 'Personal Kanban: Mapping Work & Navigating Life'. Feb 6 2011

Benson, Jim. Death to Dependencies. Modus Operandi. https://www.youtube.com/watch?v=rrdu26fpl64

Bragg, Steven M. 'Constraint Management – A Financial and Operational Guide'. Accounting Tools Series. 2020

Caspari, John and Caspari, Pamela. 'Management Dynamics: Merging Constraints Accounting to Drive Improvement. John Wiley and Sons. 2004

Corbett, Thomas. 'Throughput Accounting'. The North River Press Corporation. 1998

Dumitriu, Dragos. 'From worst to best in 9 months'. A Brief History of Kanban for Knowledge Work (djaa.com)

Dunbar, Gordon. '80/20 vs 99.9/0.1 (Pareto vs Theory of Constraints)'. Feb 16 2017 - 80/20 vs 99.9/0.1 (Pareto vs Theory of Constraints) (linkedin.com)

Du Plooy, Etienne. 'Throughput Accounting Techniques'. General Media Press. 2016

Gilani, Ravi and Camp, Henry. 'The right metrics and when'. http://bit.ly/2AH9KZs

Gilani, Ravi and Schragenheim, Eli. 'Evaporating an active cash constraint'. Evaporating an Active Cash Constraint – Eli Schragenheim

Goldratt, Eli. Standing on the shoulders of Giants.

Hoefle, William and Marris, Philip. 'Throughput Accounting'. https://www.youtube.com/watch?v=QumnBvwf4Pk

Holt, Steve and Marris, Philip. Steve Holt about ToC and Cynefin. https://www.youtube.com/watch?v=P7U_zbosllg

Kasaraboina, Omprakash. Dynamic batch size: A re-look at U-curve optimization.

Küsters. Michael. Dependencies are not created equal. https://failfastmoveon.blogspot.com/2020/10/dependencies-arent-created-equal.html

Lang, Dr Lisa. 'Theory of Constraints Handbook – Chapter 22 Mafia Offers'.

Lee, Reginald Thomas. 'Lies, Damned Lies, and Cost Accounting: How Capacity Management Enables Improved Cost and Cash Flow Management'. Business Expert Press. 2016

Mackay, Charles. 'Extraordinary popular delusions and the madness of crowds.' December 2020

Reinertsen, Donald. 'The Principles of Product Development Flow Second Generation Lean Product Development'. Celeritas Publishing. 2009

Reinertsen, Donald. 'Going to the Gemba and its limits'. http://reinertsenassociates.com/going-to-gemba-and-its-limits/

Reinertsen, Donald. '175 Principles of Flow'. http://lpd2.com/sample-page/the-principles-of-flow/

Ricketts, John A. 'Reaching The Goal: How Managers Improve a Services Business Using Goldratt's Theory of Constraints'. IBM Press. 2007

Ricketts, John A. 'Exceeding the Goal: Adventures in Strategy, Information Technology, Computer Software, Technical Services, and Goldratt's Theory of Constraints' by John Ricketts | Apr 1, 2020

Rothman, Johanna. Resource Efficiency vs. Flow Efficiency, Part 1: Seeing Your System Resource Efficiency vs. Flow Efficiency, Part 1: Seeing Your System - Johanna Rothman, Management Consultant (jrothman.com)

Rothman, Johanna. Resource Efficiency vs. Flow Efficiency, Part 2: Effect on People. Resource Efficiency vs. Flow Efficiency, Part 2: Effect on People - Johanna Rothman, Management Consultant (jrothman.com)

Rothman, Johanna. Resource Efficiency vs. Flow Efficiency, Part 3: Managing Performance. Resource Efficiency vs. Flow Efficiency, Part 3: Managing Performance - Johanna Rothman, Management Consultant (jrothman.com)

Rothman, Johanna. Resource Efficiency vs. Flow Efficiency, Part 4: Defining Accountability. Resource Efficiency vs. Flow Efficiency, Part 4: Defining Accountability - Johanna Rothman, Management Consultant (jrothman.com)

Rothman, Johanna. Resource Efficiency vs. Flow Efficiency, Part 5: How Flow Changes Everything. Resource Efficiency vs. Flow Efficiency, Part 5: How Flow Changes Everything - Johanna Rothman, Management Consultant (jrothman.com)

Schragenheim, Eli and Camp, Henry and Surace, Rocco. 'Throughput Economics: Making Good Management Decisions'. Routledge, A Productivity Press Book. 2019

Schragenheim, Eli and Camp, Henry and Surace, Rocco. 'Throughput Economics: Making Good Management Decisions'. Routledge, A Productivity Press Book. 2019

Smith, Debra. 'The Measurement Nightmare: How the Theory of Constraints can resolve Conflicting Strategies, Policies, and Measures'. The St. Lucie Press/APICS Series on Constraints Management. 2000

Sproull, Bob and Nelson, Bruce. 'Epiphanized'. North River Press. 2012

Tendon, Steve and Doiron, Daniel. 'Tame Your Work Flow: How Dr Goldratt of 'The Goal' would apply the Theory of Constraints to rethink Knowledge Work Management'. Tameflow Press. 2020

Dr Yougman, Kelvyn. 'Exploitation and Subordination Reframed as Productivity and Utility'. https://www.linkedin.com/pulse/exploitation-subordination-reframed-productivity-utility-youngman/

Dr Yougman, Kelvyn. 'The Unrecognised Positive Impact of Operations Upon Finance'. https://www.linkedin.com/pulse/unrecognised-positive-impact-operations-upon-finance-youngman/

NFL Section from Prologue

Statistical reasoning:

https://harvardsportsanalysis.wordpress.com/2012/02/06/the-super-bowl-bill-belichick-and-letting-your-opponent-score/

Videos:
https://www.youtube.com/watch?v=y3fVn8TE2XM&feature=endscreen&NR=1
https://www.youtube.com/watch?v=y9A3oF904sw
https://www.youtube.com/watch?v=baCeMpAZIgI
https://www.youtube.com/watch?v=ZkrRTYbVmpU

THROUGHPUT ACCOUNTING RESOURCES

LinkedIn Group: TA4U – Throughput Accounting for You:
https://www.linkedin.com/groups/1907934/

https://www.tpacc.com/

MESSAGE FROM THE AUTHOR

I love systems, enjoy measuring improvement while embracing teamwork that actually works and find its way on the bottom line! Throughput Accounting helps me get alignment within and across teams and, organisations. This is a continuation from my first book 'Tame Your Work Flow' and paves the way to quite a few new avenues unexplored up until now in the field of Throughput Accounting and Knowledge Work. 'Seeing Money Clearly' is a title. This book is the conveyor.

In today's economy, the competition is fierce. Agile is all over the place: values, behaviors, beliefs, frameworks etc. Some say it is a team sports, like those who want to 'be' agile. I claim that each one of us has a personal duty to excel at attaining tangible results consistently aspiring to 'do' agile.

It is incumbent to the individual player to hone these skills if he wants to be part of any successful team.

I am bringing Throughput Accounting to CPAs, CxOs and Agile Center of Excellence with 2 classes.

- Throughput Accounting for CPAs
- Throughput Accounting for Agile Center of Excellence

If you are task oriented as I am, this book is for you.

Daniel Doiron, CPA

For more on Throughput Accounting for Knowledge-Work, visit https://www.agileagonist.com/

« Sans technique, le talent n'est rien qu'une sale manie » - Georges Brassens

« Without great solitude, no serious work is possible » – Picasso

NOVELTIES

As I forged ahead writing this book, a few things did not balance in my head. As I progressed, I found some flaws in the different models that we are accustomed to use or mistakenly take for granted when we transpose them to Knowledge Work.

The Theory of Constraints – and Throughput Accounting – are fairly new and have evolved over the years just to take into account the notion of (I) – Inventory and its metamorphosis over the years:

- Inventory (Dr Eli Goldratt)
- Inventory and Assets
- Inventory and Assets and Investments
- All the money in the system – (Things purchased by the system with cash – Dr Eli Goldratt)
- All the money trapped in the system that belongs to the firm but has not yet been converted into cash
- All the money in the system except cash (Ravi Gilani)
- All the modern based Knowledge Work soft tools required to support T Generators and Mafia Offers in the Knowledge Work where the notion of turning I into T using OE does not apply - (Daniel Doiron)

Late in his life, Brahms – the composer - was asked by his editor which one music piece he would like to revisit. He did not hesitate and aimed for opus 8. What we hear today is that of a mature Brahms.

If there is one analogy to be drawn here, it is with the 'Pools and Flows of Money' diagram. It has been accumulating layers of information and novelties by the greatest thinkers over the decades, each driving in their own directions with their specific points to make. All the work remains as good as when it was first printed, but I took it upon myself to 'dust' it off and take nothing but the best that each version had to offer. I included a few twists but no distinguishing factor for the material and physical world.

But I brought water to the mill with the Knowledge Work, where 'invisible' work thrives. I did make the first 'Pools and Flows of Money' diagram for the Knowledge Work industry inserting 'en passant' the notion of T Generators introduced by Eli Schragenheim, Henry Camp and Rocco Surace. The common notion that TVC – Totally Variable Costs – seldom applies to Knowledge Work was a challenge that I took and made one such example in Chapter 6.

The rest of the novelties can fit nicely in point form. Here they are:

- The notion of brown money (operating expenses as a source of funds) for the first 3 steps of the 5FS. (The benefits reaped from the first 3 steps of the 5 Focusing Steps often do not require new money as opposed to all other improvement initiatives that start the green money meter on day one)
- The notion of green money (operating expenses as a use of funds) to elevate the constraint at step 4
- A new and otherwise invisible diagonal DRUM line – with a Buffer Burn Rate of 1 - in the Fever Chart showing that all that is YELLOW is not that yellow in reality
- More appropriately, the YELLOW zone should be relabelled the 'BLUE' flow zone

- How downside risk is not yet represented in the Buffer Fever Chart - subject to further research (downside risk still eludes the finance community who have nothing better to show that the ill-suited semi variance)
- The totally new blue CCPM Rope signal. Meant to support staggering arbitrage. It is the only management by exception signal that is generated to warn you that ... you are going too fast and for that it has been assigned a blue color
- The starting marker for the cash-to-cash cycle becomes fuzzy as we can use plenty of brown money to sustain our march to improvements in Knowledge Work
- Putting an end to the cash-to-cash cycle as foundational for cash velocity in Throughput Accounting for Knowledge Work as the starting and end markers are now fungible (getting paid before getting the work done in a Mafia offer context just obliterates the notion of cash-to-cash cycle)
- The TOE spread. To create new vocabulary to 'slang' the importance of continuously watching that T – Throughput and OE – Operating Expenses - are diverging as a sign of healthy operations
- Operating Expenses as a source of funds. Although technically it is not valid since only changes in assets and liability accounts can be legitimately labelled as 'sources' and 'uses' of funds. But brown money comes from OE!!!
- The green DBR queue, where as many items as you wish may accumulate before the Yellow signal.
- Observing that target scope projects as described in this book make use of TOC, TA and CCPM. This supports the decoupling of management from the time axis with the use of leading signals of risk materialisation.

I also deemed a new illustration to depict the 3 levels of capacity was necessary. Thus far Dr Lisa Lang's has stood the test of time and her illustration is still very sharp and her metrics stand! I just thought that the color blue should sit atop, and red at the bottom. Totally the opposite of her design. Here is the comparison side by side:

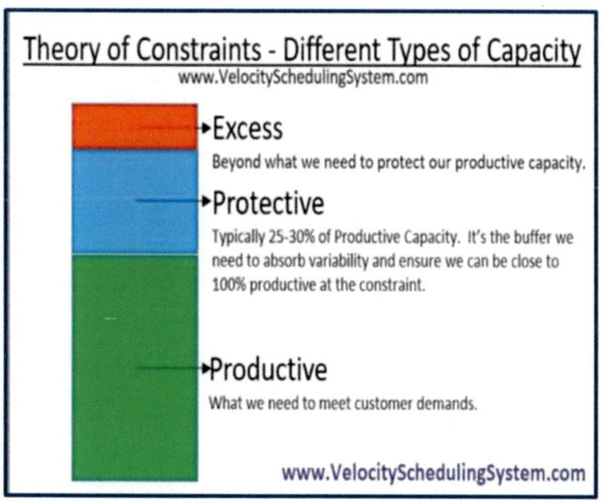

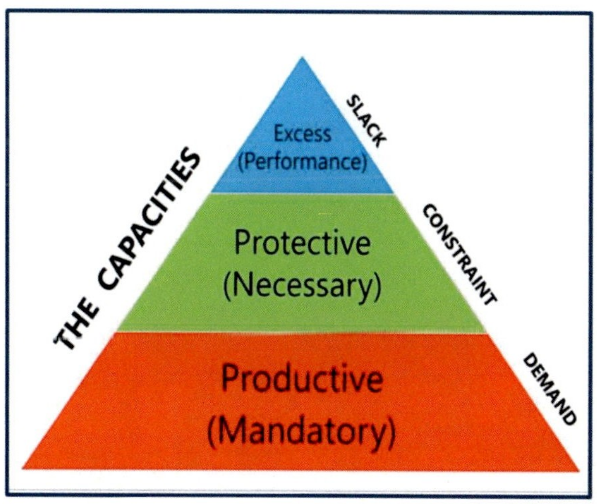

ACCOLADES

"Your achievement is commendable. I hope your book will be one of many."
Etienne Du Plooy, TPACC founder and author of the Throughput Accounting Techniques book.

"Things are never perfect. Yet they are useful and helpful. This is both."
Marcelo Lopez, AKT, CST

"... You've gathered and developed interesting ideas ..."
Donald Reinertsen, Author of "The Principles of Product Development Flow Second Generation Lean Product Development'

"Daniel, I'm enjoying your manuscript."
Dr John Ricketts, Author of 'Reaching the Goal' and 'Exceeding the Goal'

"Daniel, this is a fantastic book!"
Bob Sproull, Author of numerous books on ToC, Lean & Six Sigma

"Dan, thank you for contributing to this important body of knowledge."
Rocco Surace – Author of 'Throughput Economics: Making Good Management Decisions'. – Eli Schragenheim, Henri Camp authors

ISBN 978-1-7781232-1-4

9 781778 123214

Made in United States
Orlando, FL
17 September 2026

87759404R00186